Story and Art by
Rumiko Takahashi

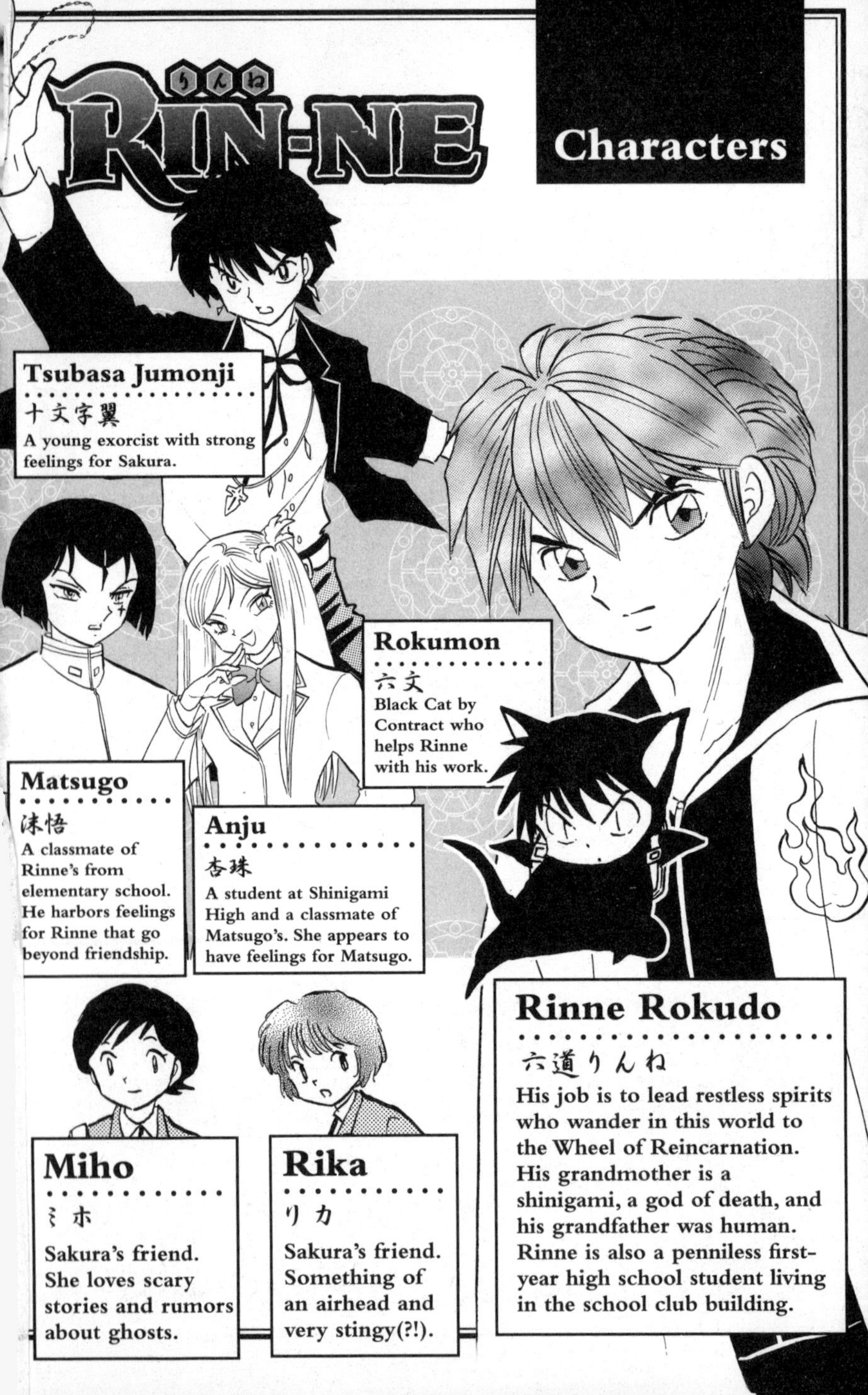

RIN-NE

りんね

Characters

Tsubasa Jumonji

十文字翼

A young exorcist with strong feelings for Sakura.

Rokumon

六文

Black Cat by Contract who helps Rinne with his work.

Matsugo

沫悟

A classmate of Rinne's from elementary school. He harbors feelings for Rinne that go beyond friendship.

Anju

杏珠

A student at Shinigami High and a classmate of Matsugo's. She appears to have feelings for Matsugo.

Rinne Rokudo

六道りんね

His job is to lead restless spirits who wander in this world to the Wheel of Reincarnation. His grandmother is a shinigami, a god of death, and his grandfather was human. Rinne is also a penniless first-year high school student living in the school club building.

Miho

ミホ

Sakura's friend. She loves scary stories and rumors about ghosts.

Rika

リカ

Sakura's friend. Something of an airhead and very stingy(?!).

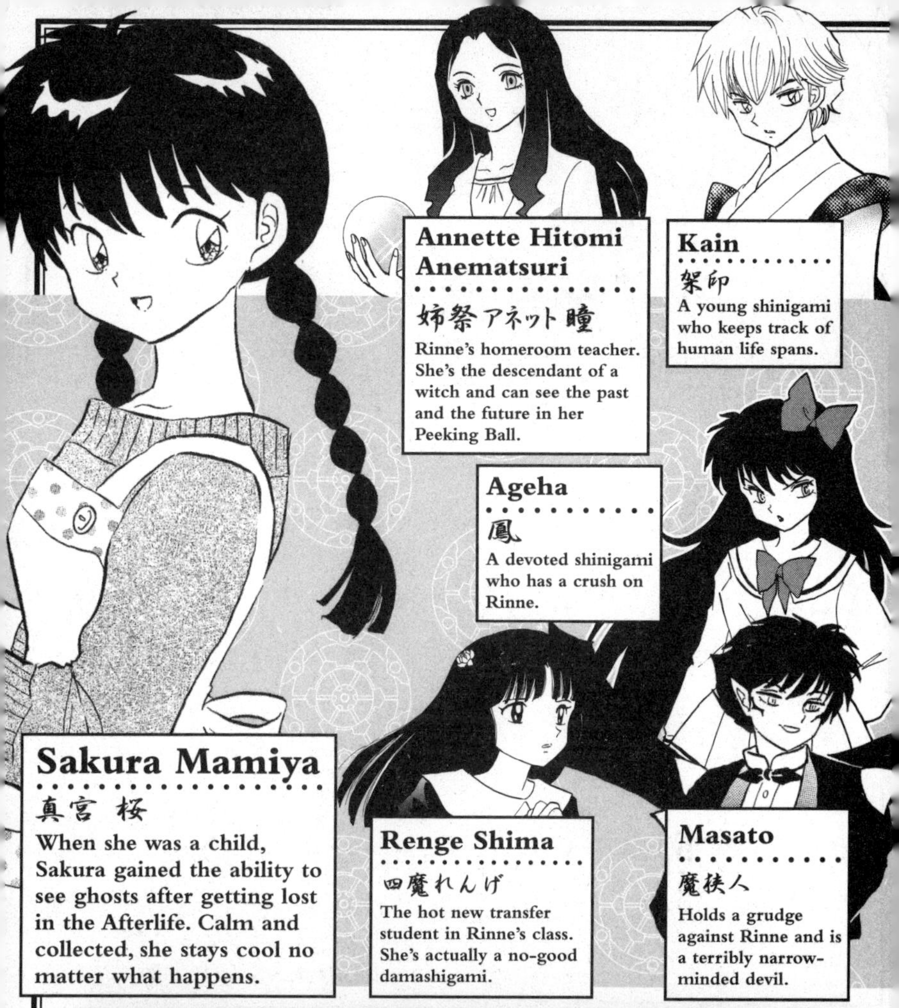

Sakura Mamiya

真宮 桜

When she was a child, Sakura gained the ability to see ghosts after getting lost in the Afterlife. Calm and collected, she stays cool no matter what happens.

Annette Hitomi Anematsuri

姉祭アネット瞳

Rinne's homeroom teacher. She's the descendant of a witch and can see the past and the future in her Peeking Ball.

Kain

架印

A young shinigami who keeps track of human life spans.

Ageha

鳳

A devoted shinigami who has a crush on Rinne.

Renge Shima

四魔れんげ

The hot new transfer student in Rinne's class. She's actually a no-good damashigami.

Masato

魔狭人

Holds a grudge against Rinne and is a terribly narrow-minded devil.

The Story So Far

Sakura, the girl who can see ghosts, and Rinne the shinigami (sort of) spend their days together, helping spirits that can't pass on reach the Afterlife, and dealing with all kinds of strange phenomena at their school.

A campsite, a traditional ghost story session, fishing at a summer festival in the Afterlife… With spirits abuzz during the summer season, it's supposed to be the time of year when Rinne can finally make some cash. Yet as the summer winds down and he still doesn't get the compensation he's expecting, Rinne's stuck being poor and hungry.

But is there hope in store for him now that the weather's colder?! Join the haunted holiday hijinks as the season shifts from autumn to winter!

RIN-NE

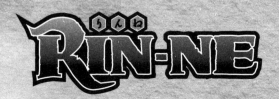

Contents

CHAPTER 259: PROMISE OF THE UNDERWORLD

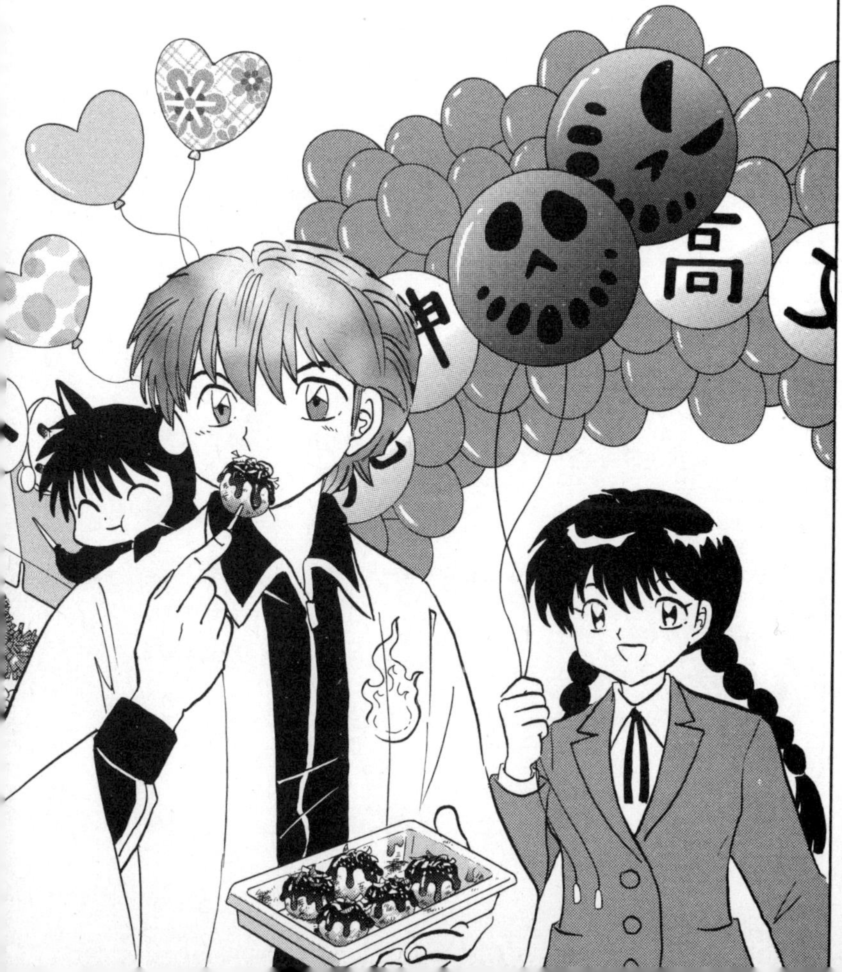

THE ELITE SHINIGAMI HIGH CULTURAL FESTIVAL?
YES. MATSUGO-SAMA SAYS HE WOULD LOVE FOR YOU TO COME.
Matsugo's Black Cat by Contract
Kuromitsu
I CAN'T.
死神一高
HE'S PROBABLY HOPING TO DEEPEN THE FRIENDSHIP BETWEEN YOU TWO.
ACTUALLY, MATSUGO-SAMA WILL BE BUSY WITH FESTIVAL DUTIES...
...SO HE SAYS TO PLEASE INVITE A FRIEND TO JOIN YOU.

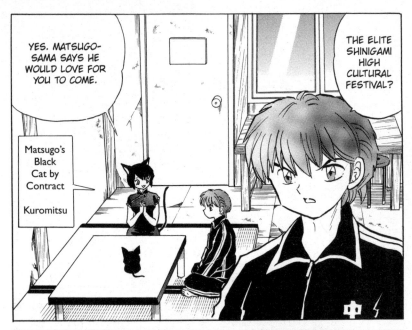

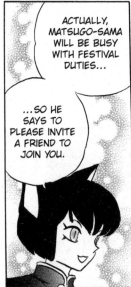

Sign: Elite Shinigami High

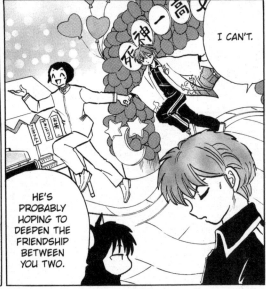

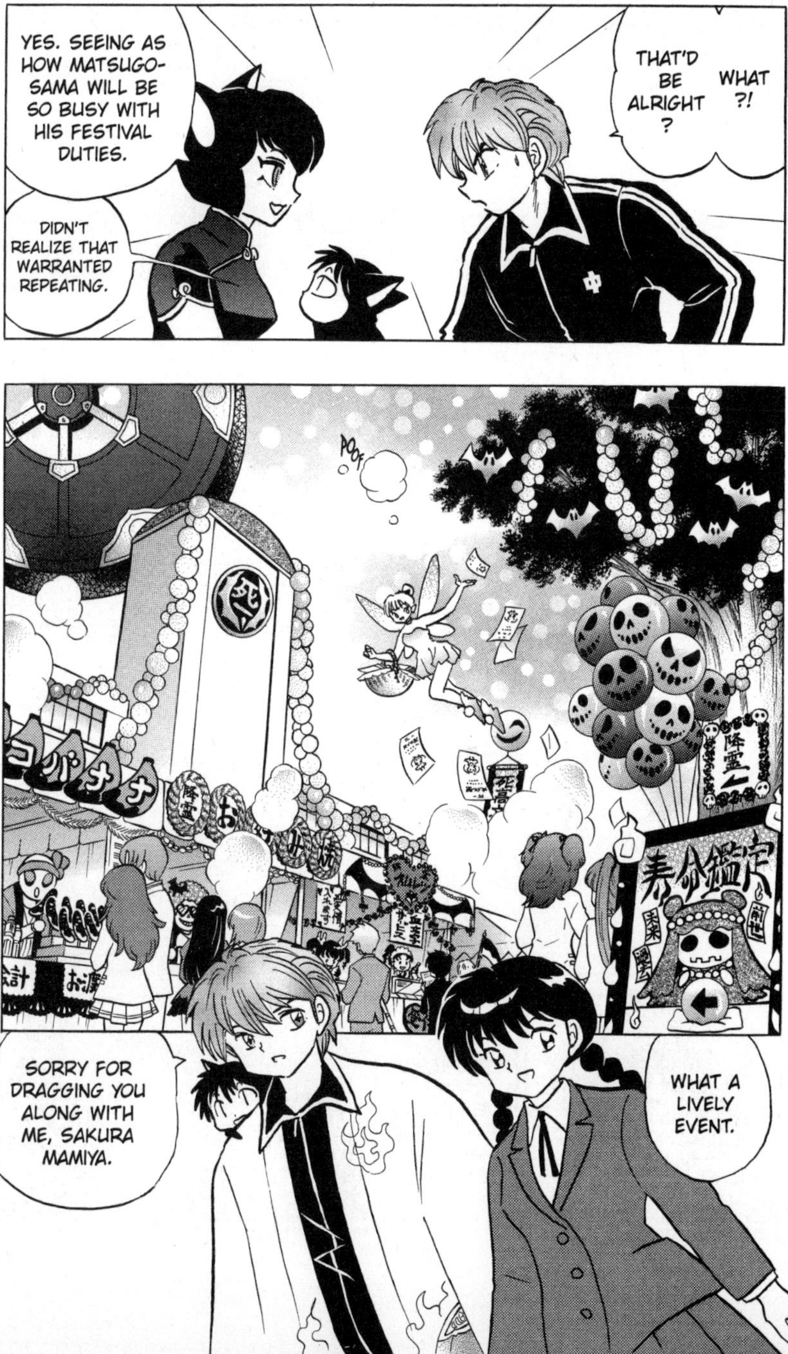
THAT'D BE ALRIGHT? WHAT?!
YES. SEEING AS HOW MATSUGO-SAMA WILL BE SO BUSY WITH HIS FESTIVAL DUTIES.
DIDN'T REALIZE THAT WARRANTED REPEATING.
POOF
WHAT A LIVELY EVENT.
SORRY FOR DRAGGING YOU ALONG WITH ME, SAKURA MAMIYA.

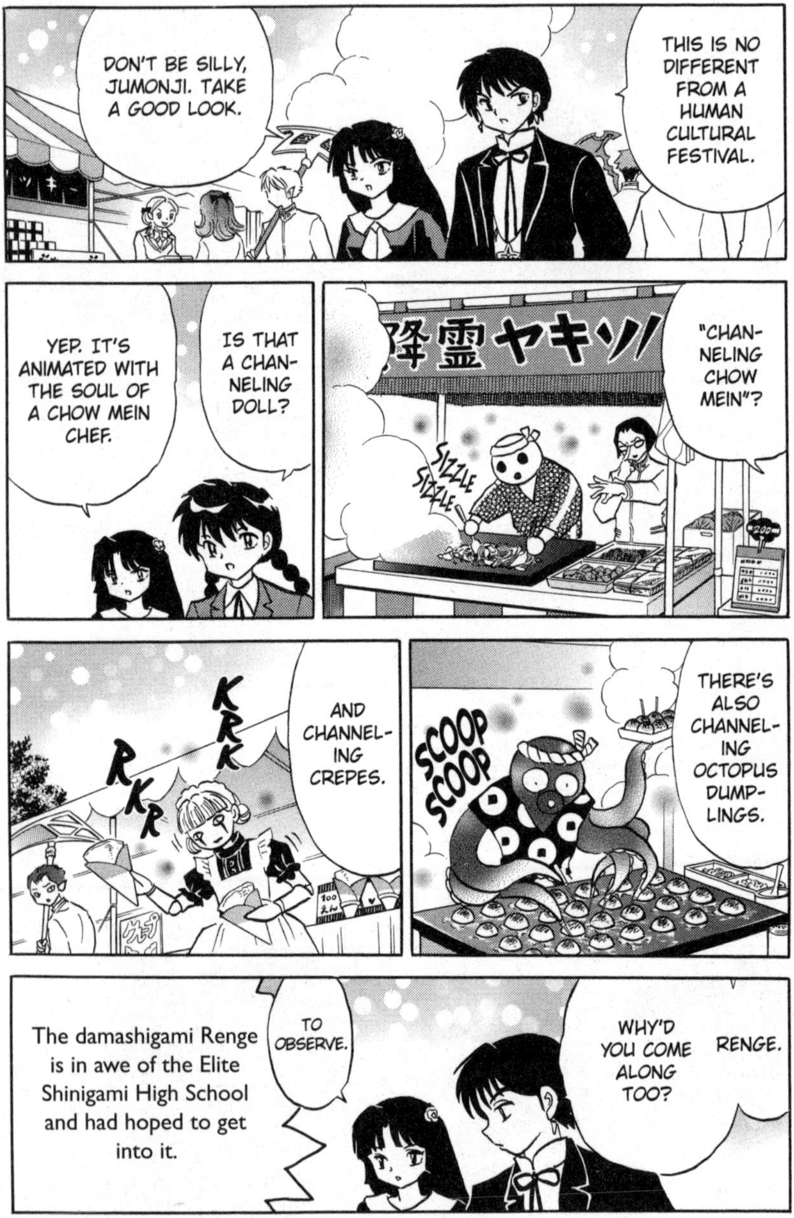
THIS IS NO DIFFERENT FROM A HUMAN CULTURAL FESTIVAL.
DON'T BE SILLY, JUMONJI. TAKE A GOOD LOOK.
降霊ヤキソ
"CHANNELING CHOW MEIN"?
SIZZLE SIZZLE
IS THAT A CHANNELING DOLL?
YEP. IT'S ANIMATED WITH THE SOUL OF A CHOW MEIN CHEF.
THERE'S ALSO CHANNELING OCTOPUS DUMPLINGS.
SCOOP SCOOP
AND CHANNELING CREPES.
KRK
RKR
100えん
RENGE.
WHY'D YOU COME ALONG TOO?
TO OBSERVE.
The damashigami Renge is in awe of the Elite Shinigami High School and had hoped to get into it.

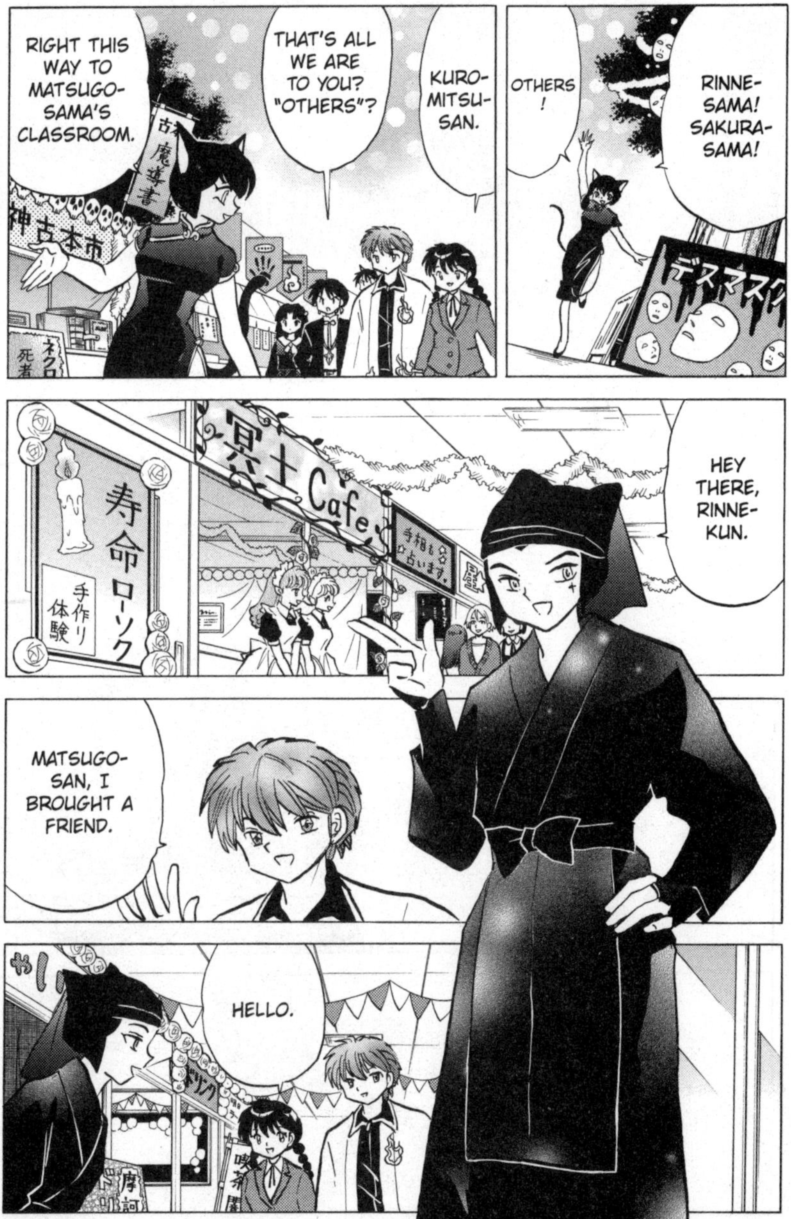
RINNE-SAMA! SAKURA-SAMA!
OTHERS!
デスマスク
KURO-MITSU-SAN.
THAT'S ALL WE ARE TO YOU? "OTHERS"?
RIGHT THIS WAY TO MATSUGO-SAMA'S CLASSROOM.
HEY THERE, RINNE-KUN.
冥土Cafe
手相も占います。
寿命ローソク
手作り体験
MATSUGO-SAN, I BROUGHT A FRIEND.
HELLO.

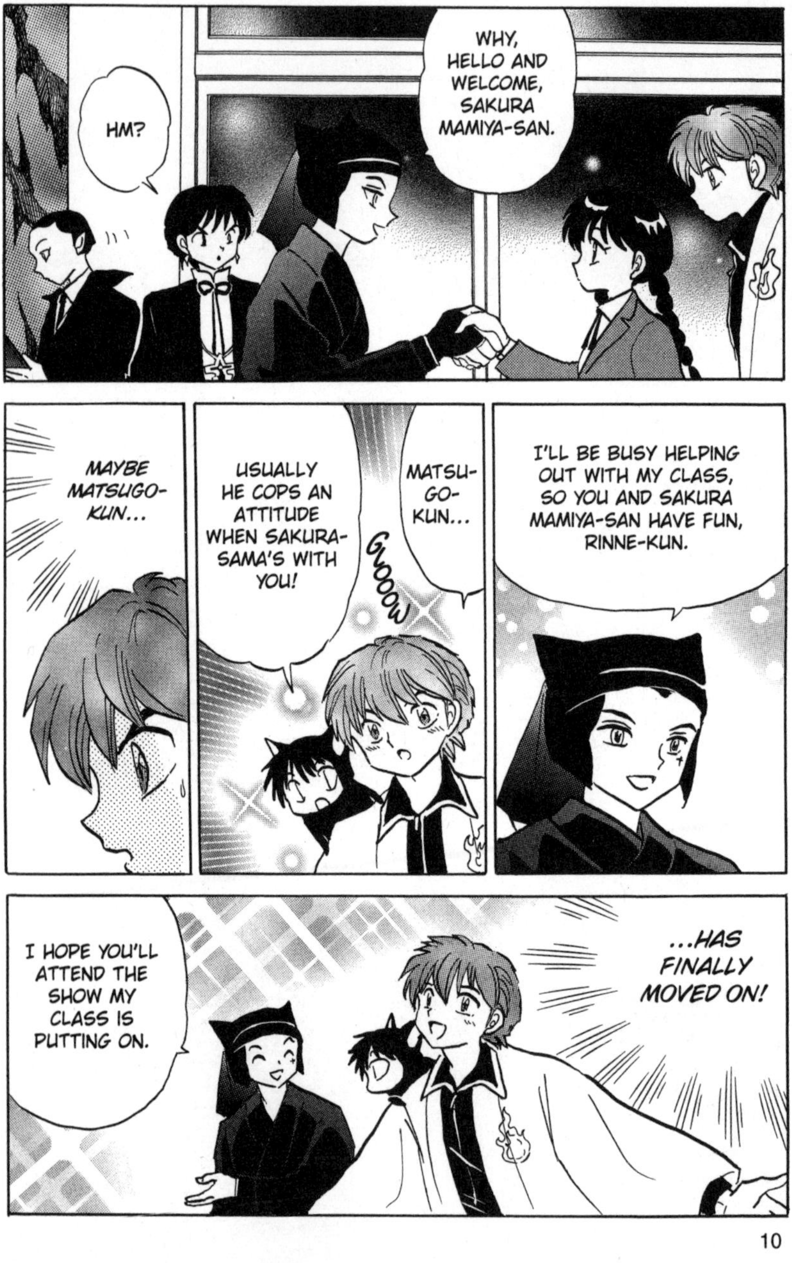
WHY, HELLO AND WELCOME, SAKURA MAMIYA-SAN.
HM?
I'LL BE BUSY HELPING OUT WITH MY CLASS, SO YOU AND SAKURA MAMIYA-SAN HAVE FUN, RINNE-KUN.
MATSU-GO-KUN...
GLOOOW
USUALLY HE COPS AN ATTITUDE WHEN SAKURA-SAMA'S WITH YOU!
MAYBE MATSUGO-KUN...
...HAS FINALLY MOVED ON!
I HOPE YOU'LL ATTEND THE SHOW MY CLASS IS PUTTING ON.

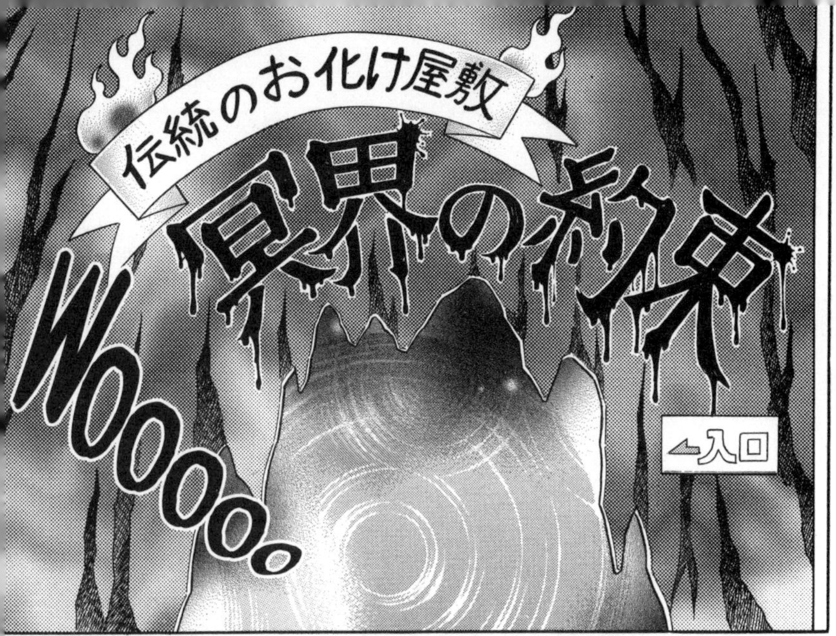
伝統のお化け屋敷
冥界の約束
入口
WOOOOOO

Banner: Legendary Haunted House Bloody sign: Promise of the Underworld Arrow: Entrance

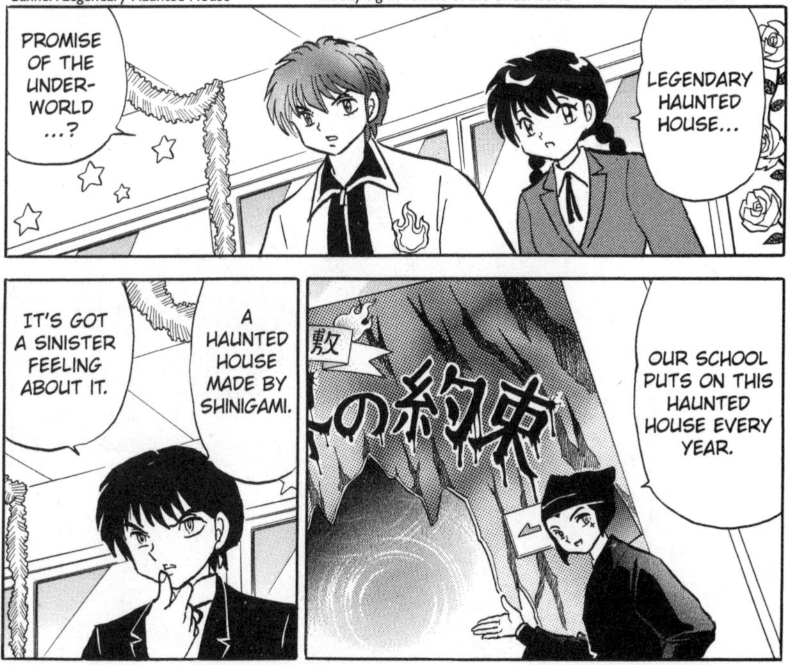
LEGENDARY HAUNTED HOUSE...
PROMISE OF THE UNDER-WORLD ...?
敷
の約束
OUR SCHOOL PUTS ON THIS HAUNTED HOUSE EVERY YEAR.
A HAUNTED HOUSE MADE BY SHINIGAMI.
IT'S GOT A SINISTER FEELING ABOUT IT.

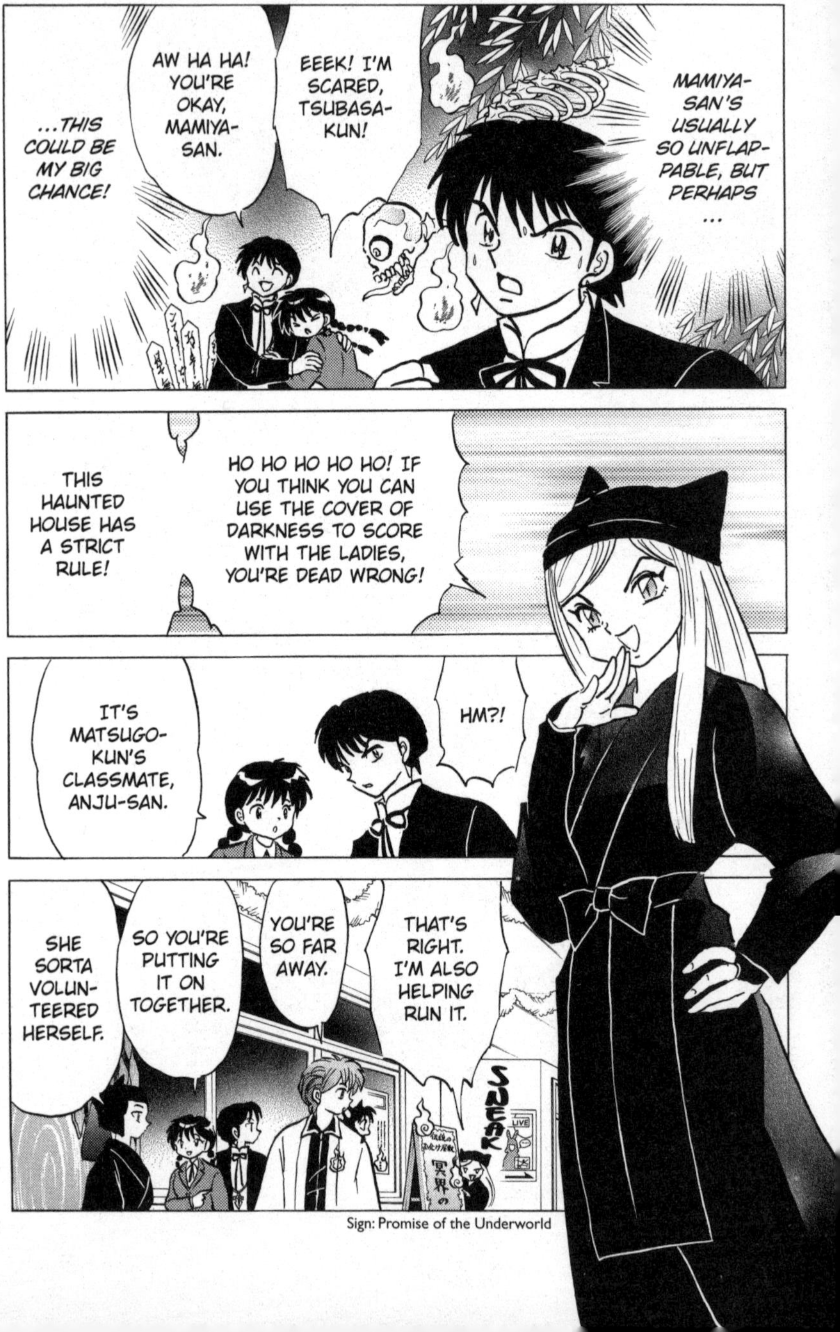
MAMIYA-SAN'S USUALLY SO UNFLAP-PABLE, BUT PERHAPS ...
EEEK! I'M SCARED, TSUBASA-KUN!
AW HA HA! YOU'RE OKAY, MAMIYA-SAN.
...THIS COULD BE MY BIG CHANCE!
HO HO HO HO HO! IF YOU THINK YOU CAN USE THE COVER OF DARKNESS TO SCORE WITH THE LADIES, YOU'RE DEAD WRONG!
THIS HAUNTED HOUSE HAS A STRICT RULE!
HM?!
IT'S MATSUGO-KUN'S CLASSMATE, ANJU-SAN.
THAT'S RIGHT. I'M ALSO HELPING RUN IT.
YOU'RE SO FAR AWAY.
SO YOU'RE PUTTING IT ON TOGETHER.
SHE SORTA VOLUN-TEERED HERSELF.
SNEAK
LIVE
Sign: Promise of the Underworld

WHAT'S THE RULE?
THE ORPHEUS RULE.
ORPHEUS?
YOU MEAN ORPHEUS FROM THE GREEK LEGEND?
Trivia regarding the Greek legend of Orpheus
WHEN ORPHEUS DIED, HE MISSED HIS WIFE EURYDICE SO TERRIBLY...
His sorrowful song
...THAT HE WENT INTO THE UNDERWORLD TO GET HER BACK.
HE MANAGED TO CONVINCE THE KING OF THE UNDERWORLD, HADES, TO LET HIM TAKE HER BACK TO THE LAND OF THE LIVING.
How-ever!
YOU MUST WALK AHEAD OF YOUR WIFE ON YOUR WAY TO THE SURFACE...
...AND NEVER ONCE TURN AROUND.
WHEN HE WAS CLOSE ENOUGH THAT HE COULD SEE THE LIGHT FROM THE SURFACE...

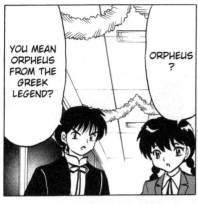

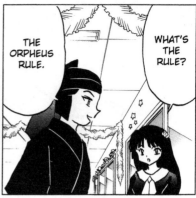

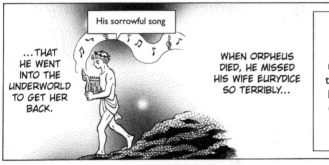

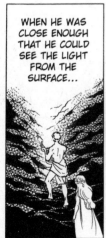

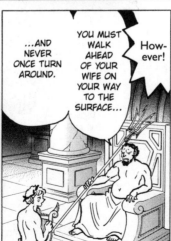

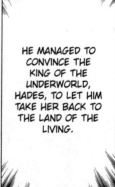

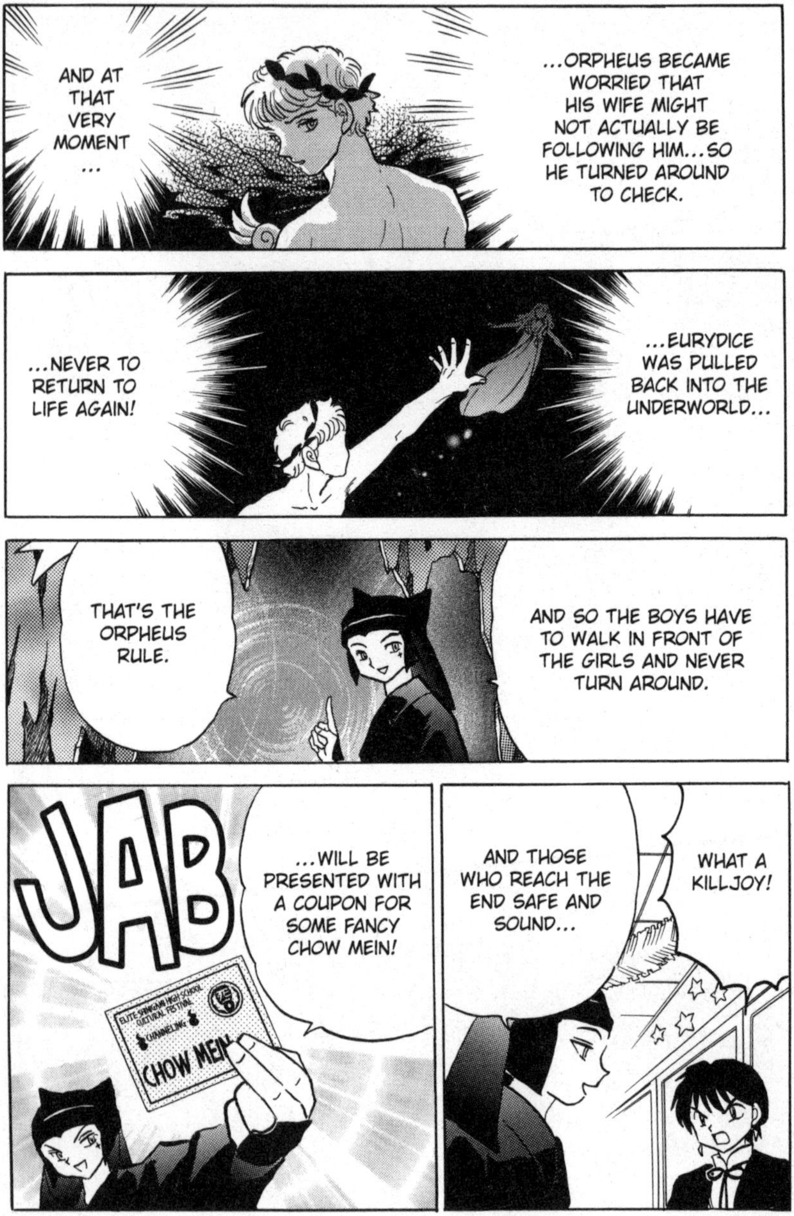
AND AT THAT VERY MOMENT ...
...ORPHEUS BECAME WORRIED THAT HIS WIFE MIGHT NOT ACTUALLY BE FOLLOWING HIM...SO HE TURNED AROUND TO CHECK.
...EURYDICE WAS PULLED BACK INTO THE UNDERWORLD...
...NEVER TO RETURN TO LIFE AGAIN!
AND SO THE BOYS HAVE TO WALK IN FRONT OF THE GIRLS AND NEVER TURN AROUND.
THAT'S THE ORPHEUS RULE.
WHAT A KILLJOY!
AND THOSE WHO REACH THE END SAFE AND SOUND...
...WILL BE PRESENTED WITH A COUPON FOR SOME FANCY CHOW MEIN!
JAB
ELITE SHINIGAMI HIGH SCHOOL CULTURAL FESTIVAL
CHANNELING
CHOW MEIN

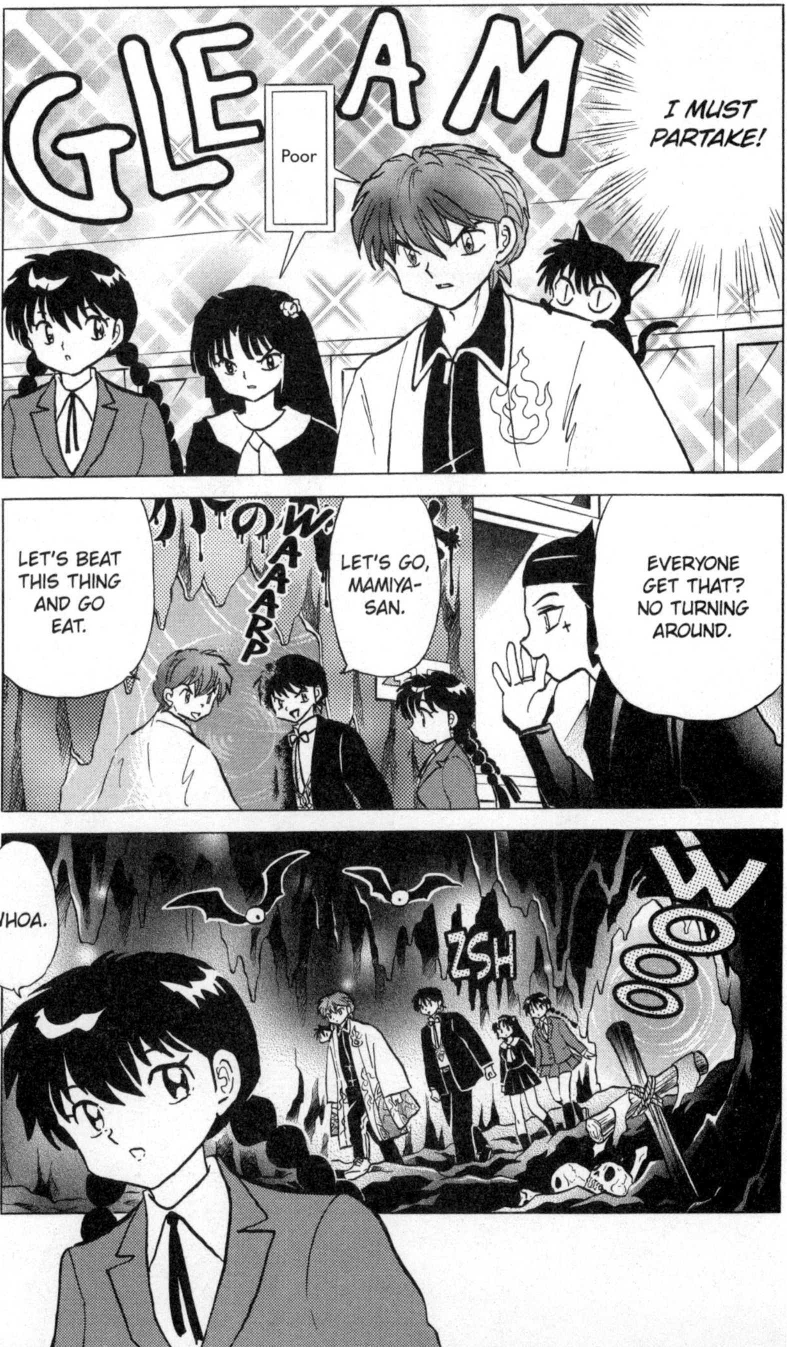

I MUST PARTAKE!
GLEAM
Poor
EVERYONE GET THAT? NO TURNING AROUND.
LET'S GO, MAMIYA-SAN.
WAAARP
LET'S BEAT THIS THING AND GO EAT.
WOOOO
ZSH
WHOA.

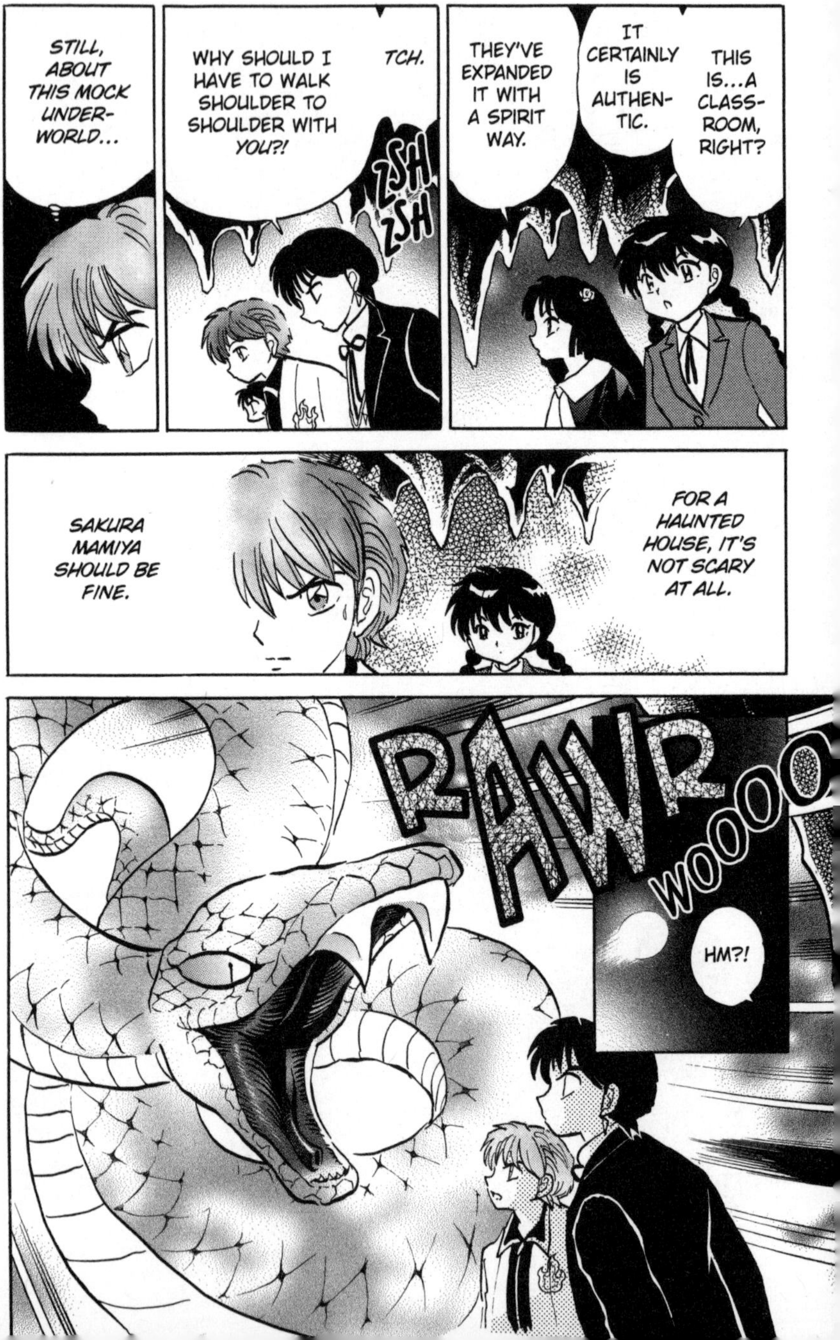
THIS IS...A CLASSROOM, RIGHT?
IT CERTAINLY IS AUTHENTIC.
THEY'VE EXPANDED IT WITH A SPIRIT WAY.
TCH.
ZSH ZSH
WHY SHOULD I HAVE TO WALK SHOULDER TO SHOULDER WITH YOU?!
STILL, ABOUT THIS MOCK UNDERWORLD...
FOR A HAUNTED HOUSE, IT'S NOT SCARY AT ALL.
SAKURA MAMIYA SHOULD BE FINE.
RAWR WOOOO
HM?!

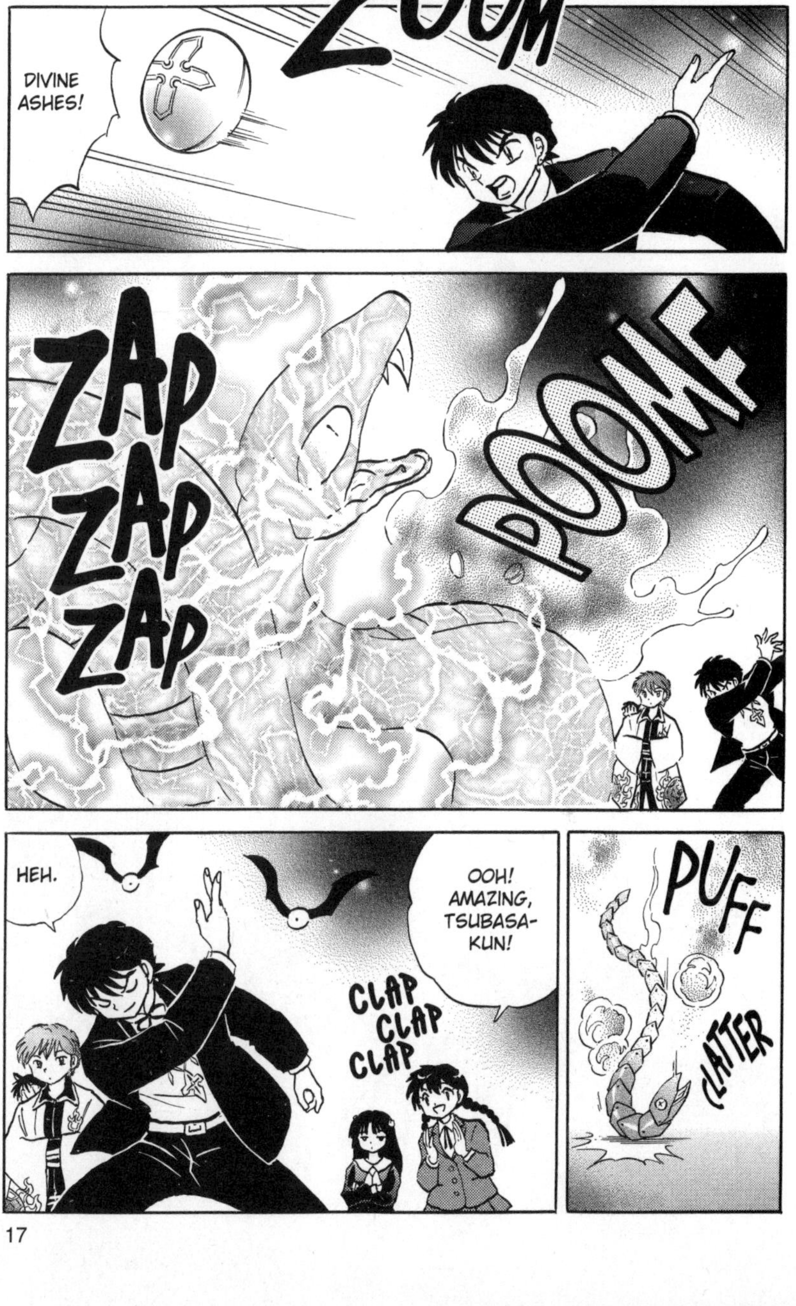
ZOOM
DIVINE ASHES!
POOMF
ZAP ZAP ZAP ZAP
PUFF
CLATTER
OOH! AMAZING, TSUBASA-KUN!
CLAP CLAP CLAP
HEH.

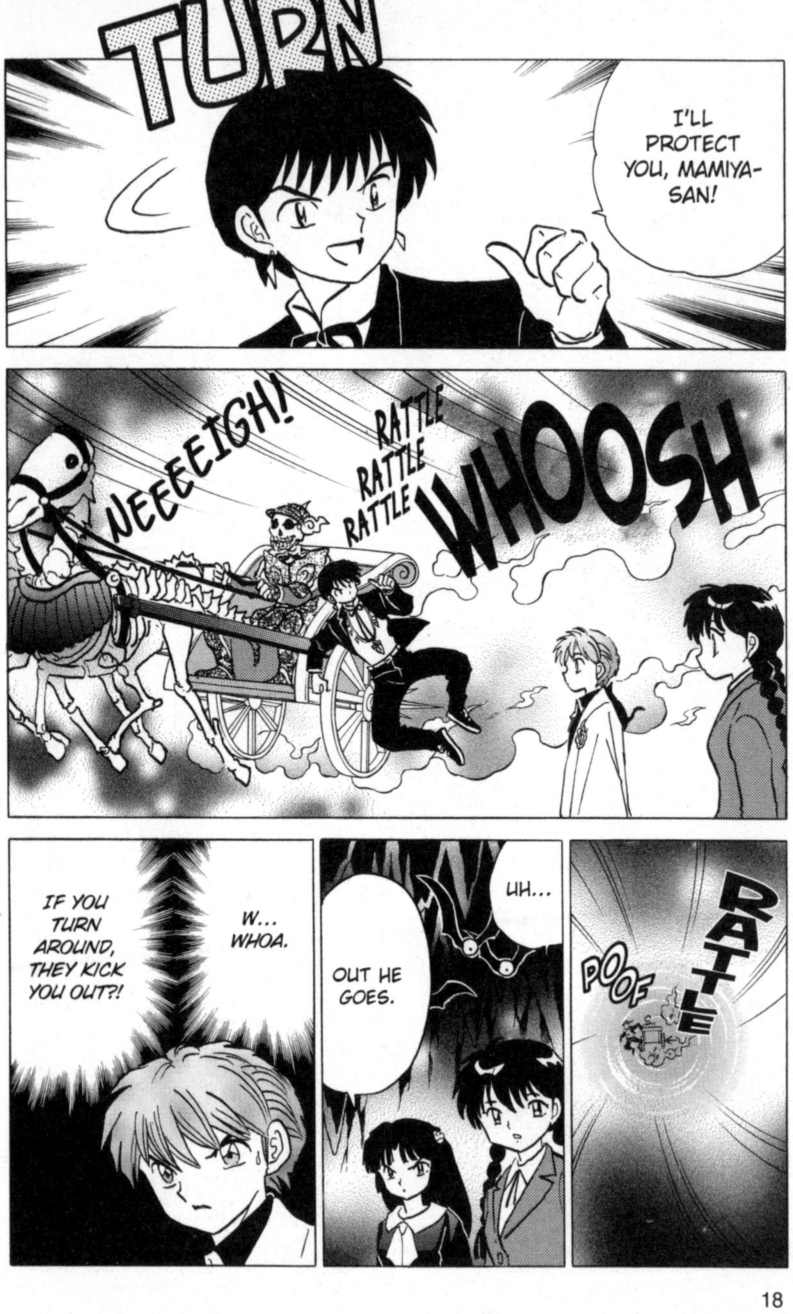
TURN
I'LL PROTECT YOU, MAMIYA-SAN!
WHOOSH
RATTLE RATTLE RATTLE
NEEEEIGH!
RATTLE
POOF
UH...
OUT HE GOES.
W... WHOA.
IF YOU TURN AROUND, THEY KICK YOU OUT?!

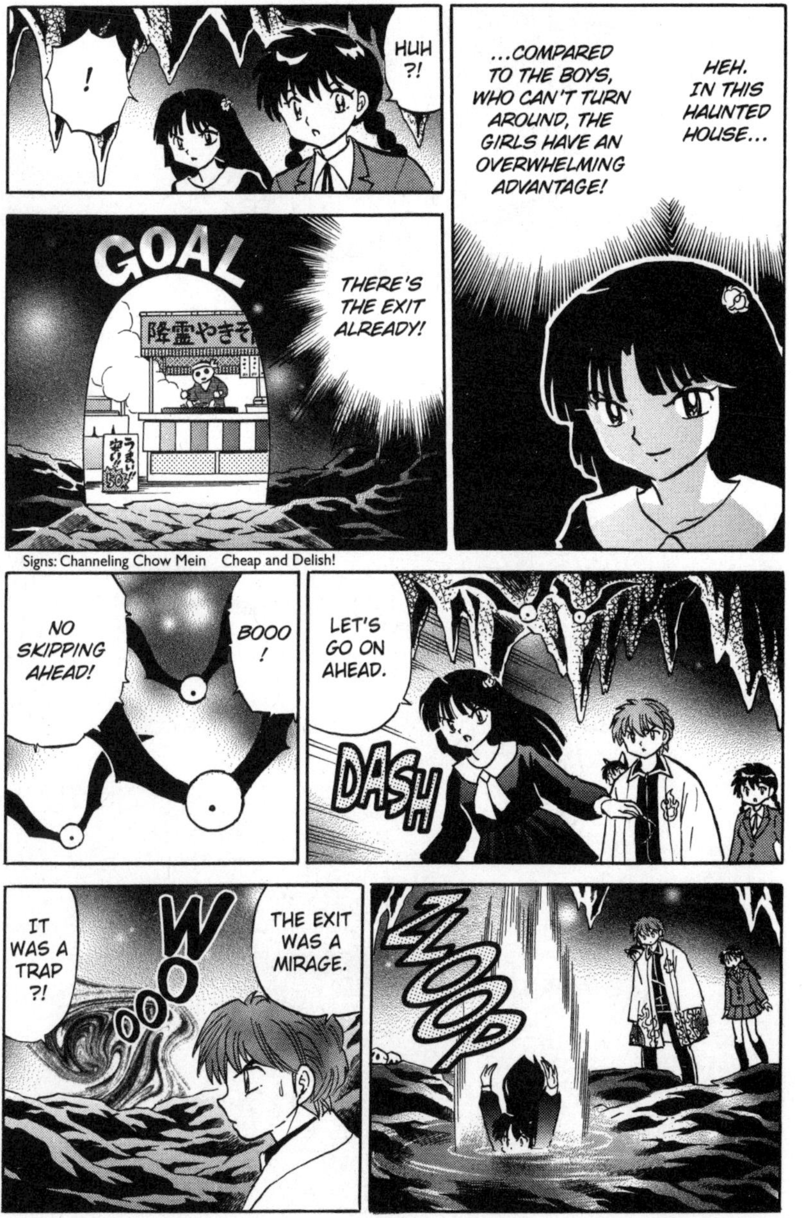
HEH. IN THIS HAUNTED HOUSE...
...COMPARED TO THE BOYS, WHO CAN'T TURN AROUND, THE GIRLS HAVE AN OVERWHELMING ADVANTAGE!
HUH ?!
!
GOAL
THERE'S THE EXIT ALREADY!
降霊やきそ
LET'S GO ON AHEAD.
DASH
BOOO !
NO SKIPPING AHEAD!
ZWOOP
THE EXIT WAS A MIRAGE.
WOOOO
IT WAS A TRAP ?!

Signs: Channeling Chow Mein Cheap and Delish!

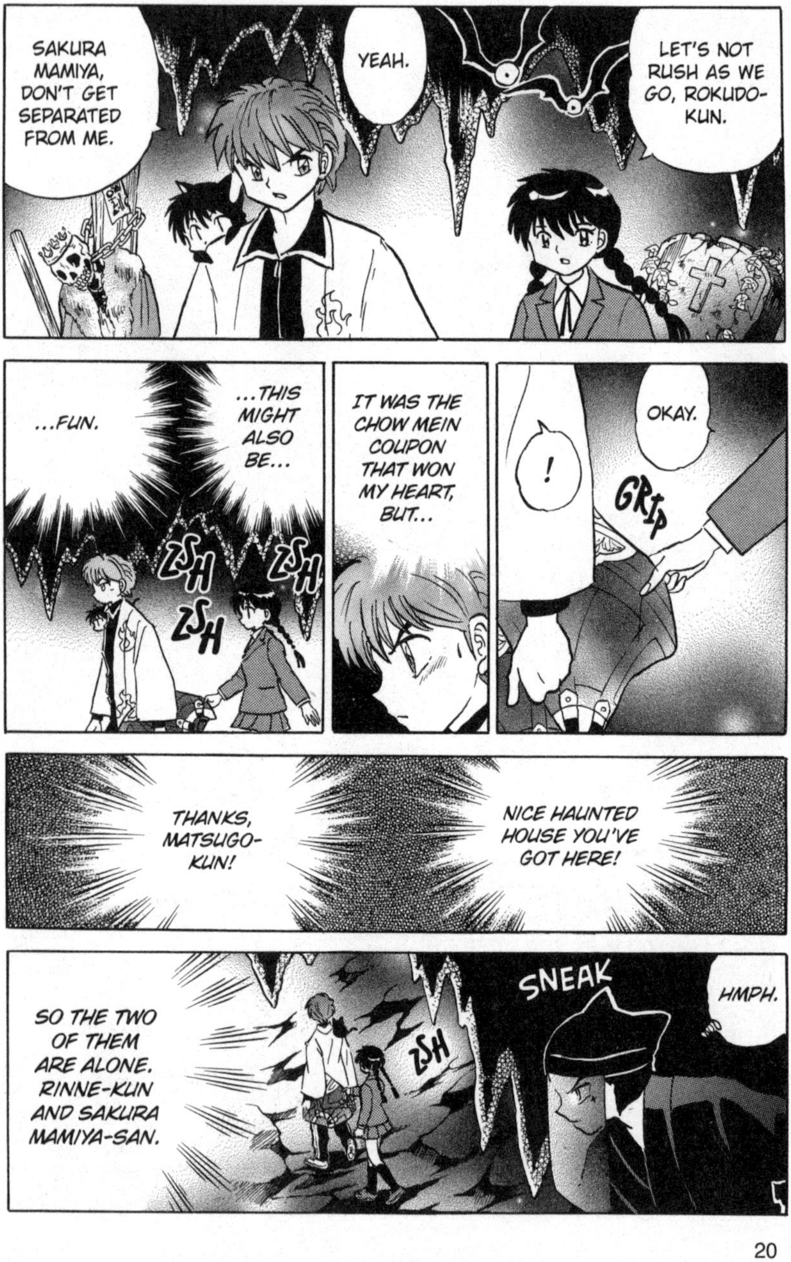
LET'S NOT RUSH AS WE GO, ROKUDO-KUN.
YEAH.
SAKURA MAMIYA, DON'T GET SEPARATED FROM ME.
OKAY.
!
GRIP
IT WAS THE CHOW MEIN COUPON THAT WON MY HEART, BUT...
...THIS MIGHT ALSO BE...
...FUN.
ZSH
ZSH
ZSH
NICE HAUNTED HOUSE YOU'VE GOT HERE!
THANKS, MATSUGO-KUN!
HMPH.
SNEAK
SO THE TWO OF THEM ARE ALONE. RINNE-KUN AND SAKURA MAMIYA-SAN.
ZSH

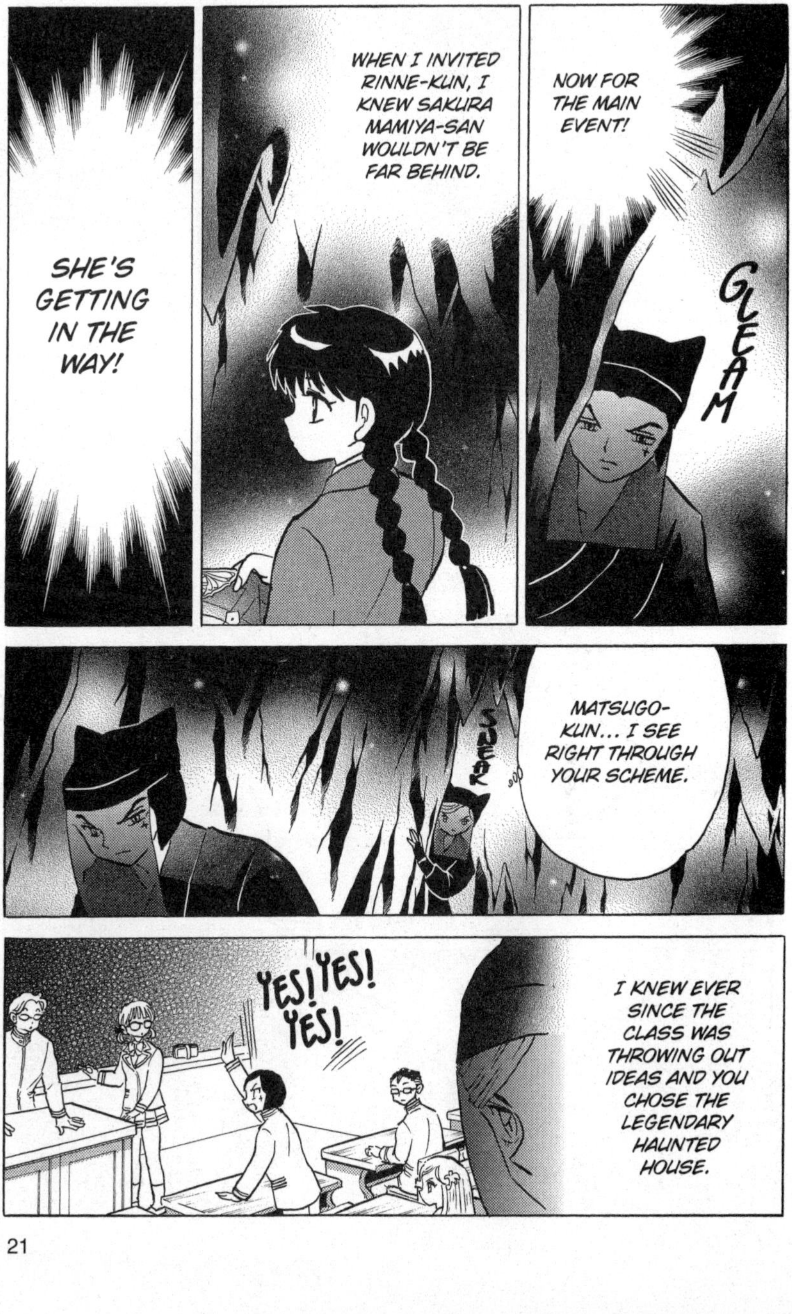
NOW FOR THE MAIN EVENT!
GLEAM
WHEN I INVITED RINNE-KUN, I KNEW SAKURA MAMIYA-SAN WOULDN'T BE FAR BEHIND.
SHE'S GETTING IN THE WAY!
MATSUGO-KUN... I SEE RIGHT THROUGH YOUR SCHEME.
SWEAT
I KNEW EVER SINCE THE CLASS WAS THROWING OUT IDEAS AND YOU CHOSE THE LEGENDARY HAUNTED HOUSE.
YES! YES! YES!

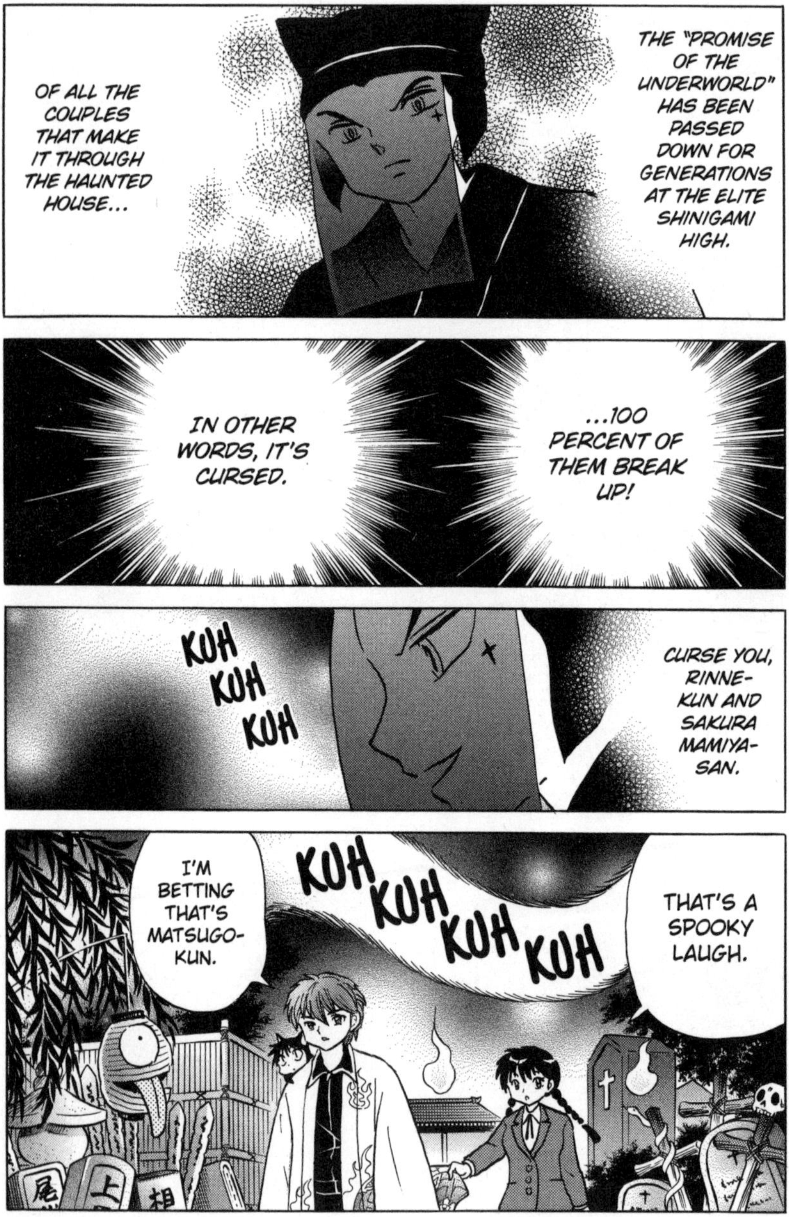
THE "PROMISE OF THE UNDERWORLD" HAS BEEN PASSED DOWN FOR GENERATIONS AT THE ELITE SHINIGAMI HIGH.
OF ALL THE COUPLES THAT MAKE IT THROUGH THE HAUNTED HOUSE...
...100 PERCENT OF THEM BREAK UP!
IN OTHER WORDS, IT'S CURSED.
CURSE YOU, RINNE-KUN AND SAKURA MAMIYA-SAN.
KUH KUH KUH
THAT'S A SPOOKY LAUGH.
KUH KUH KUH KUH
I'M BETTING THAT'S MATSUGO-KUN.

CHAPTER 260: NO TURNING AROUND

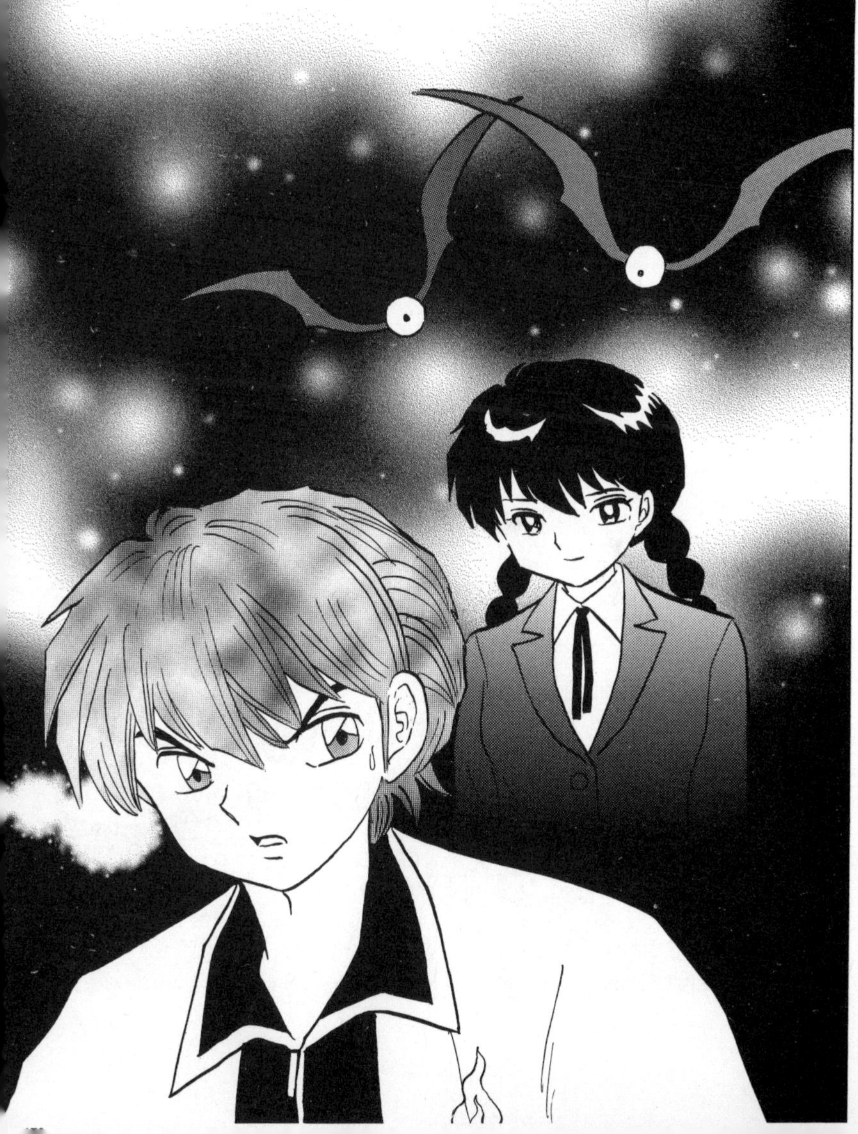

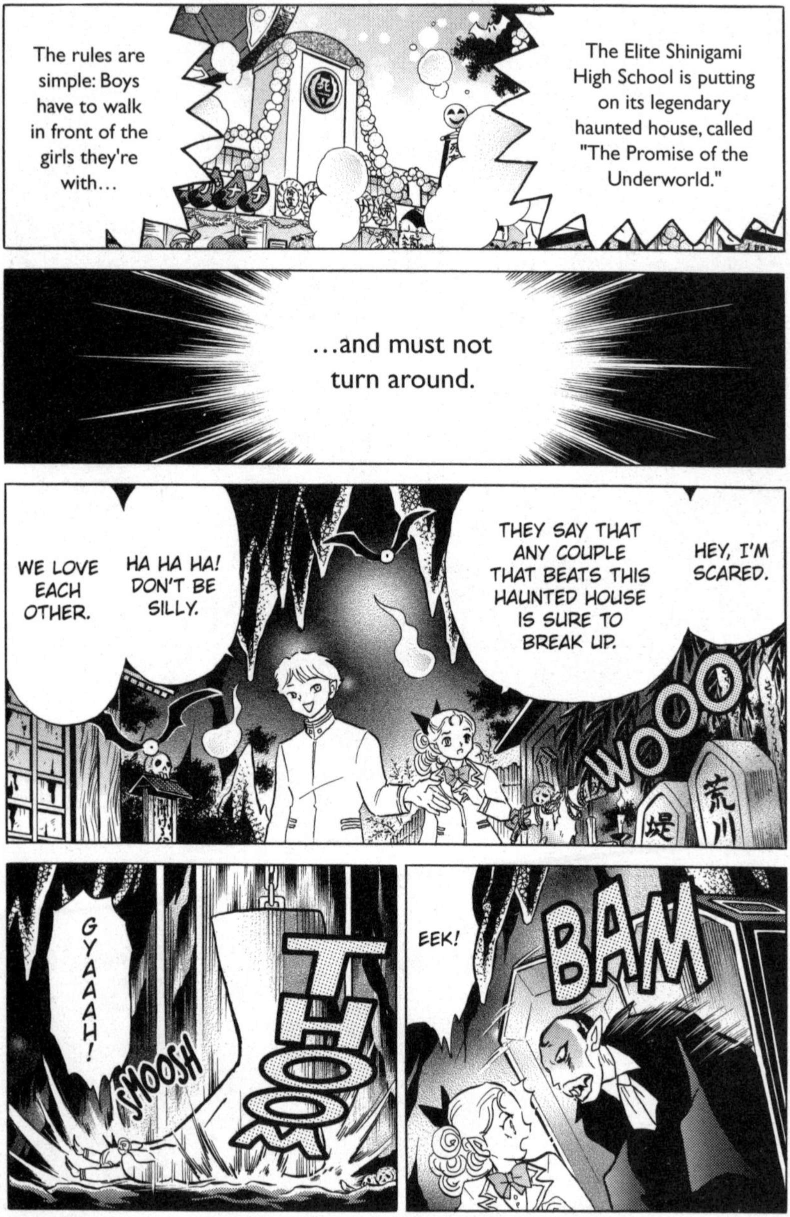
The Elite Shinigami High School is putting on its legendary haunted house, called "The Promise of the Underworld."
The rules are simple: Boys have to walk in front of the girls they're with…
…and must not turn around.
HEY, I'M SCARED.
THEY SAY THAT ANY COUPLE THAT BEATS THIS HAUNTED HOUSE IS SURE TO BREAK UP.
HA HA HA! DON'T BE SILLY.
WE LOVE EACH OTHER.
WOOOO
BAM
EEK!
THOOM
GYAAAAH!
SMOOSH

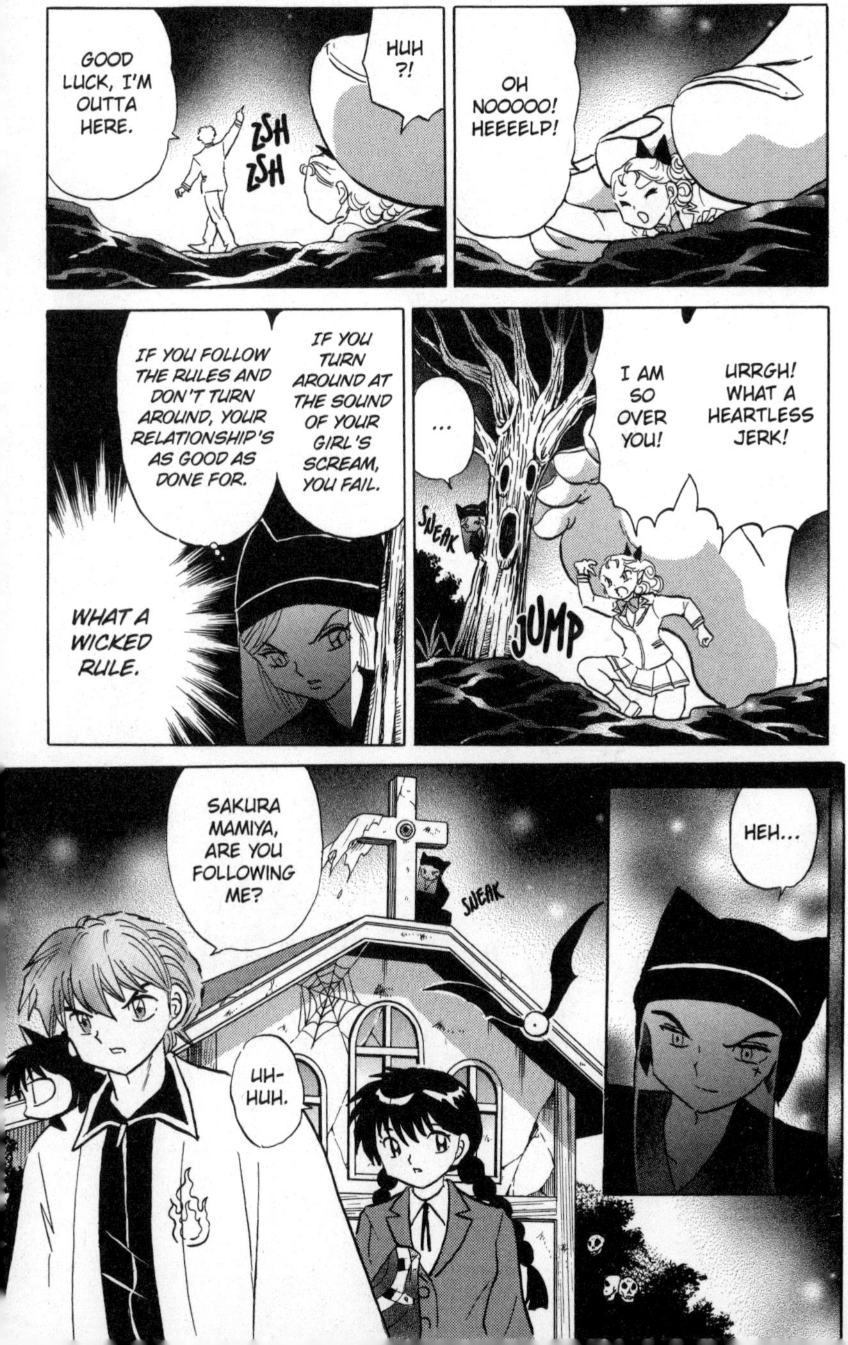
OH NOOOOO! HEEEELP!
HUH ?!
GOOD LUCK, I'M OUTTA HERE.
ZSH ZSH
URRGH! WHAT A HEARTLESS JERK!
I AM SO OVER YOU!
...
SNEAK
JUMP
IF YOU TURN AROUND AT THE SOUND OF YOUR GIRL'S SCREAM, YOU FAIL.
IF YOU FOLLOW THE RULES AND DON'T TURN AROUND, YOUR RELATIONSHIP'S AS GOOD AS DONE FOR.
WHAT A WICKED RULE.
HEH...
SAKURA MAMIYA, ARE YOU FOLLOWING ME?
SNEAK
UH-HUH.

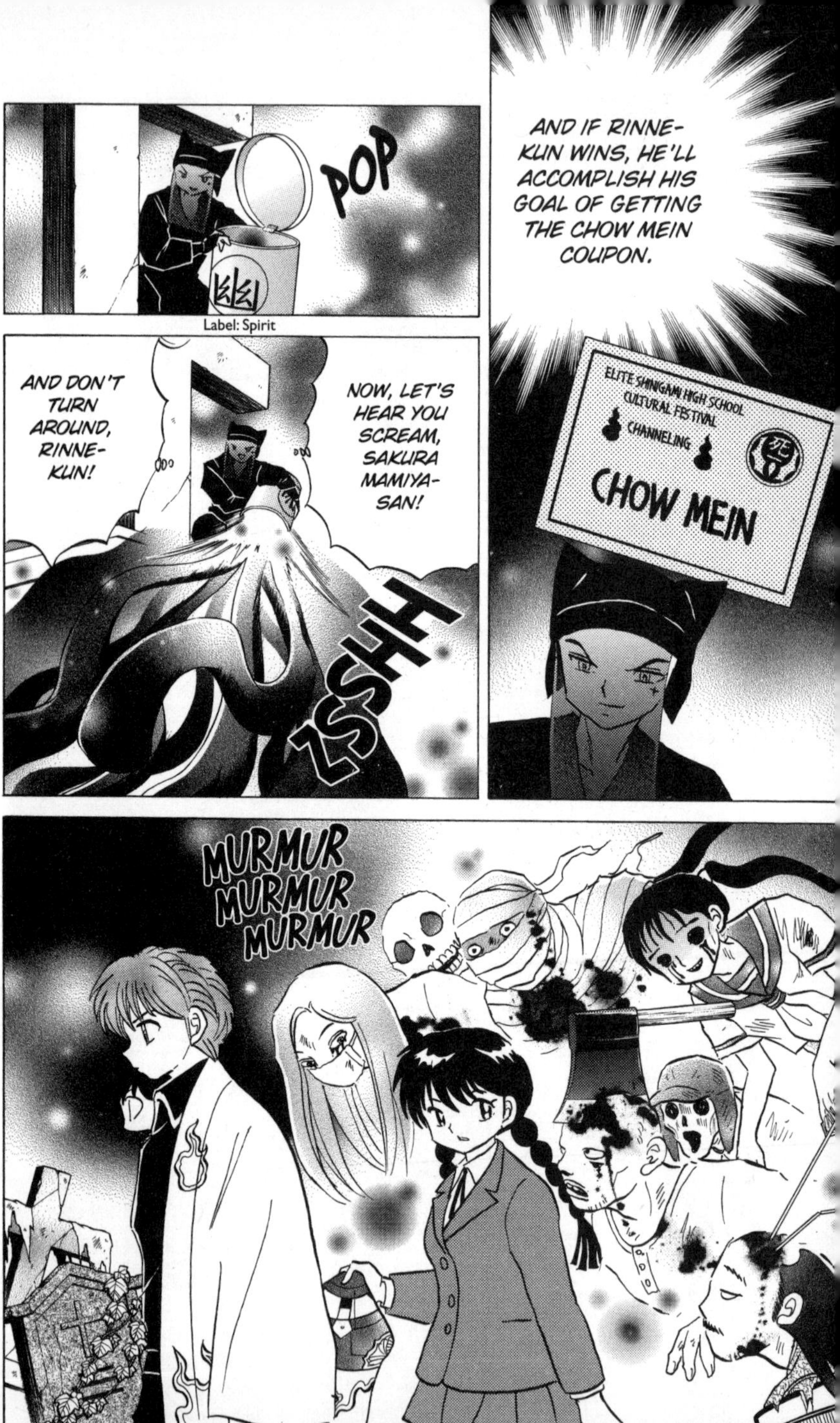
AND IF RINNE-KUN WINS, HE'LL ACCOMPLISH HIS GOAL OF GETTING THE CHOW MEIN COUPON.
ELITE SHINIGAMI HIGH SCHOOL CULTURAL FESTIVAL
CHANNELING
CHOW MEIN
POP
Label: Spirit
NOW, LET'S HEAR YOU SCREAM, SAKURA MAMIYA-SAN!
AND DON'T TURN AROUND, RINNE-KUN!
ZSSHH
MURMUR MURMUR MURMUR

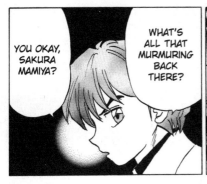

MURMUR MURMUR
I WONDER IF THESE ARE REAL.
WHAT'S ALL THAT MURMURING BACK THERE?
YOU OKAY, SAKURA MAMIYA?
YEAH, I'M FINE.
MURMUR MURMUR
GOOD.
HUH ?!
WHAT'S WITH THIS GIRL?
EVEN SHINIGAMI GIRLS WILL SCREAM JUST TO SEEM CUTER.
SWF
ANJU-KUN.
SAKURA MAMIYA-SAN DOESN'T HAVE MUCH IN THE WAY OF FEMININE APPEAL.
TCH! HOW CAN THIS BE?!
I HAD A NORMAL CONVERSATION WITH MATSUGO-KUN.
IF THOSE GHOSTS DIDN'T SPOOK HER...
SWOON

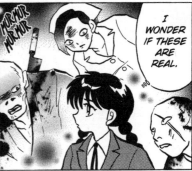

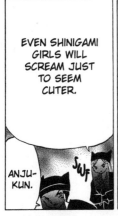

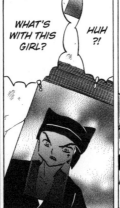

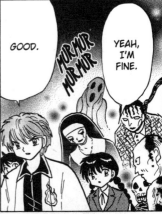

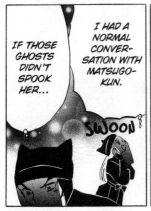

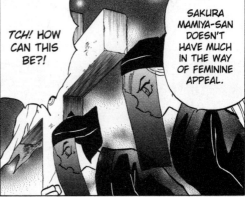

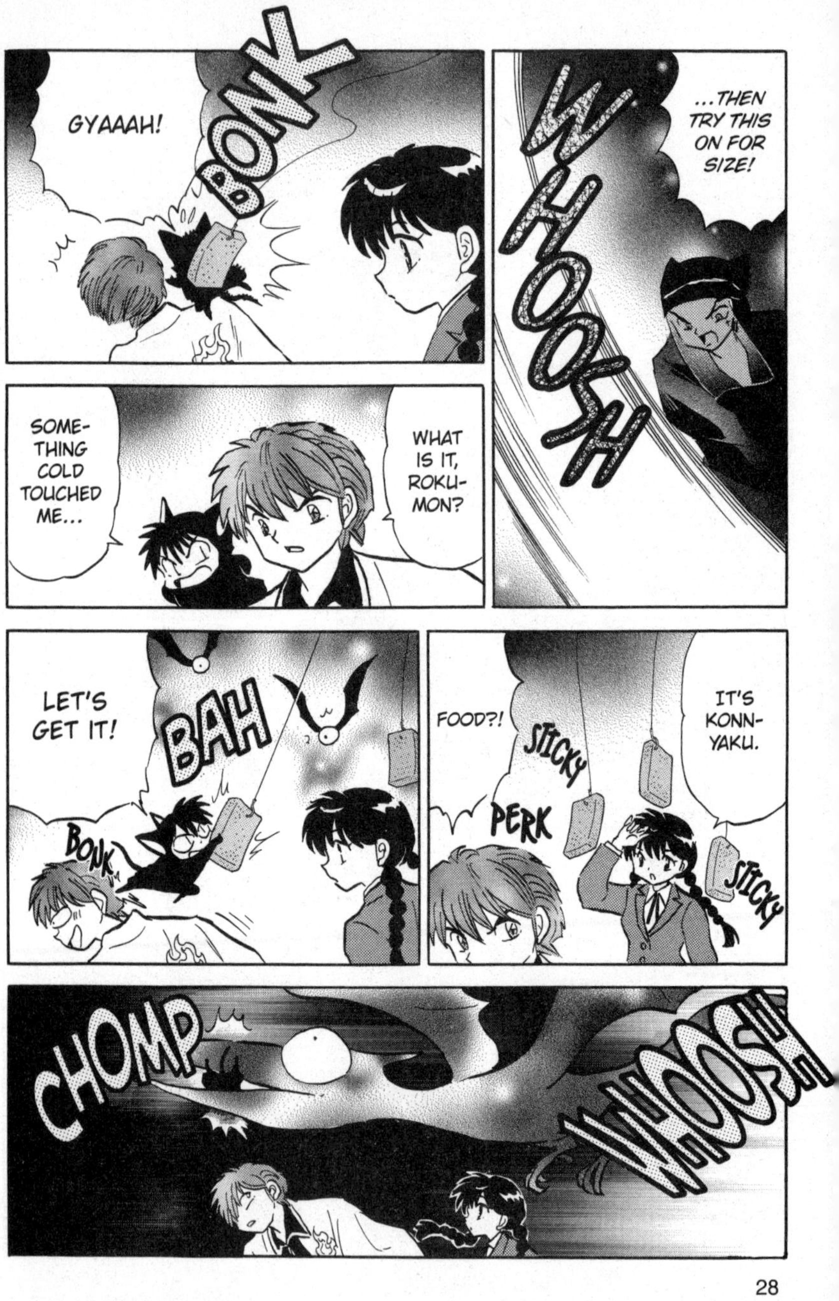
...THEN TRY THIS ON FOR SIZE!
WHOOSH
BONK
GYAAAH!
WHAT IS IT, ROKU-MON?
SOME-THING COLD TOUCHED ME...
IT'S KONN-YAKU.
STICKY
FOOD?!
STICKY
PERK
BAH
LET'S GET IT!
BONK
WHOOSH
CHOMP

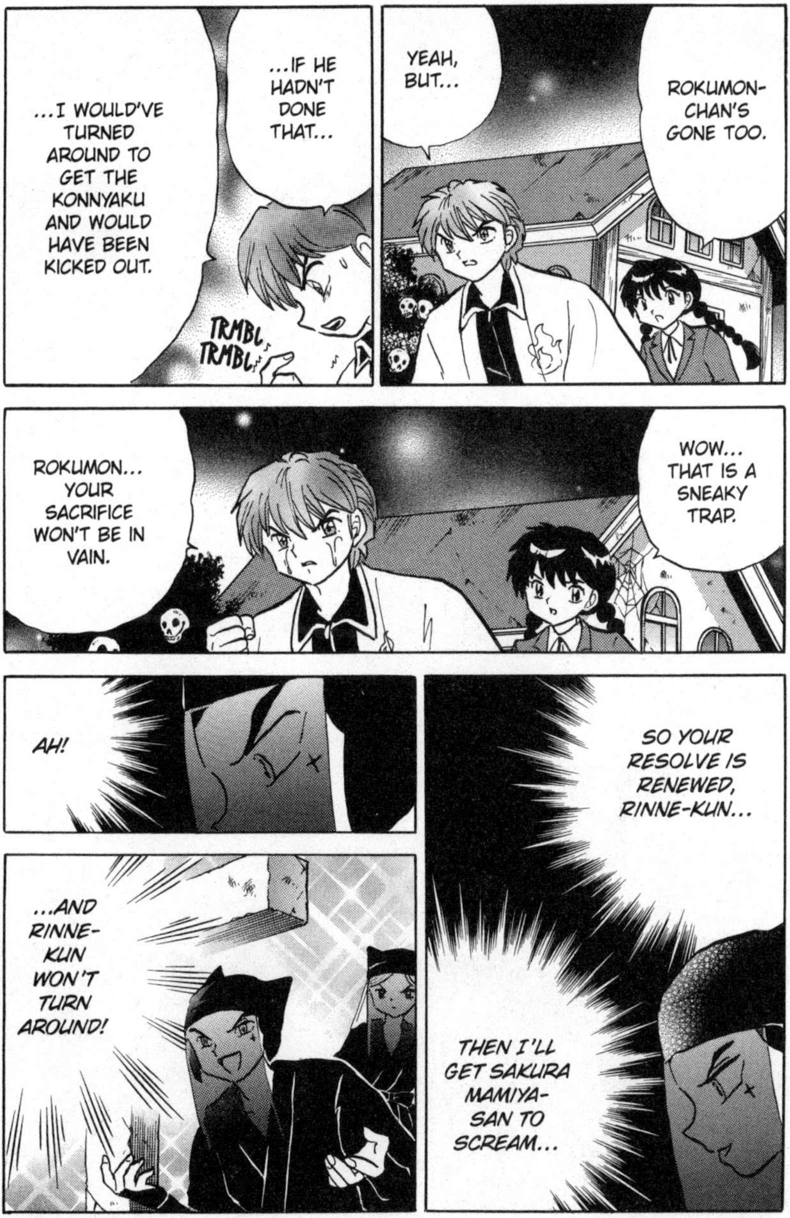
ROKUMON-CHAN'S GONE TOO.
YEAH, BUT...
...IF HE HADN'T DONE THAT...
...I WOULD'VE TURNED AROUND TO GET THE KONNYAKU AND WOULD HAVE BEEN KICKED OUT.
TRMBL TRMBL
WOW... THAT IS A SNEAKY TRAP.
ROKUMON... YOUR SACRIFICE WON'T BE IN VAIN.
SO YOUR RESOLVE IS RENEWED, RINNE-KUN...
THEN I'LL GET SAKURA MAMIYA-SAN TO SCREAM...
AH!
...AND RINNE-KUN WON'T TURN AROUND!

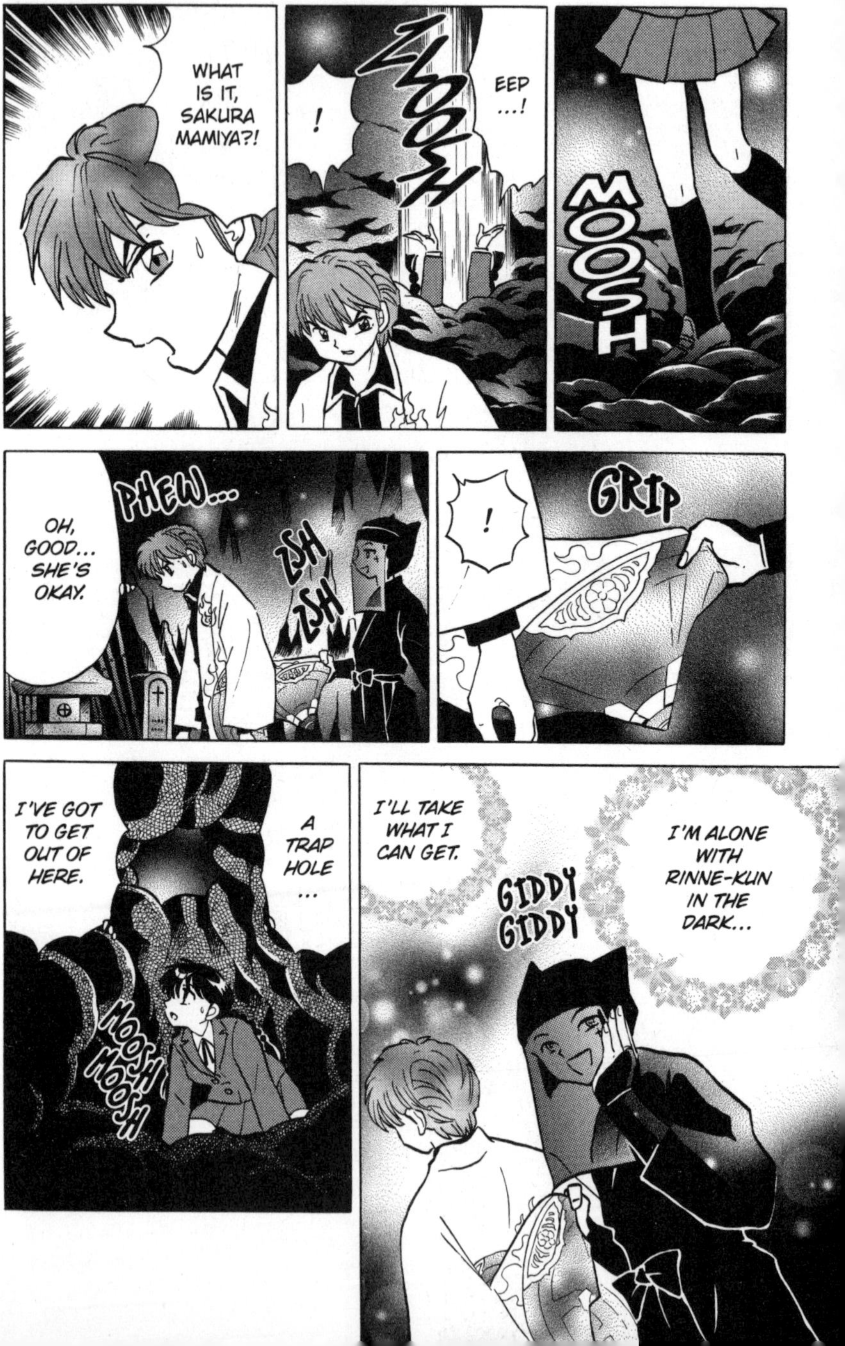
MOOSH
EEP ...!
ZLOOSH
!
WHAT IS IT, SAKURA MAMIYA?!
GRIP
!
PHEW...
ZSH ZSH
OH, GOOD... SHE'S OKAY.
I'M ALONE WITH RINNE-KUN IN THE DARK...
I'LL TAKE WHAT I CAN GET.
GIDDY GIDDY
A TRAP HOLE ...
I'VE GOT TO GET OUT OF HERE.
MOOSH MOOSH

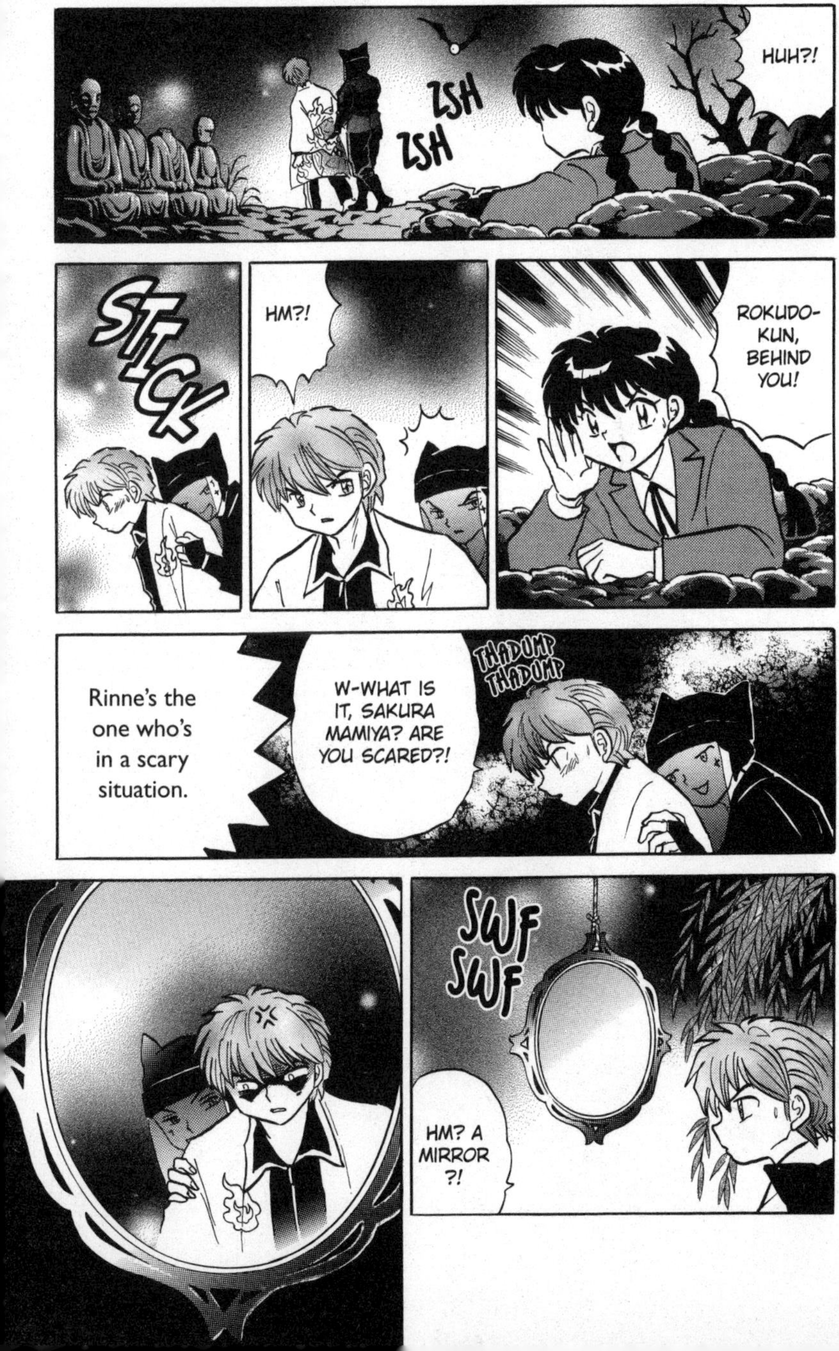
HUH?!
ZSH
ZSH
ROKUDO-KUN, BEHIND YOU!
HM?!
STICK
THADOMP THADOMP
W-WHAT IS IT, SAKURA MAMIYA? ARE YOU SCARED?!
Rinne's the one who's in a scary situation.
SWF SWF
HM? A MIRROR ?!

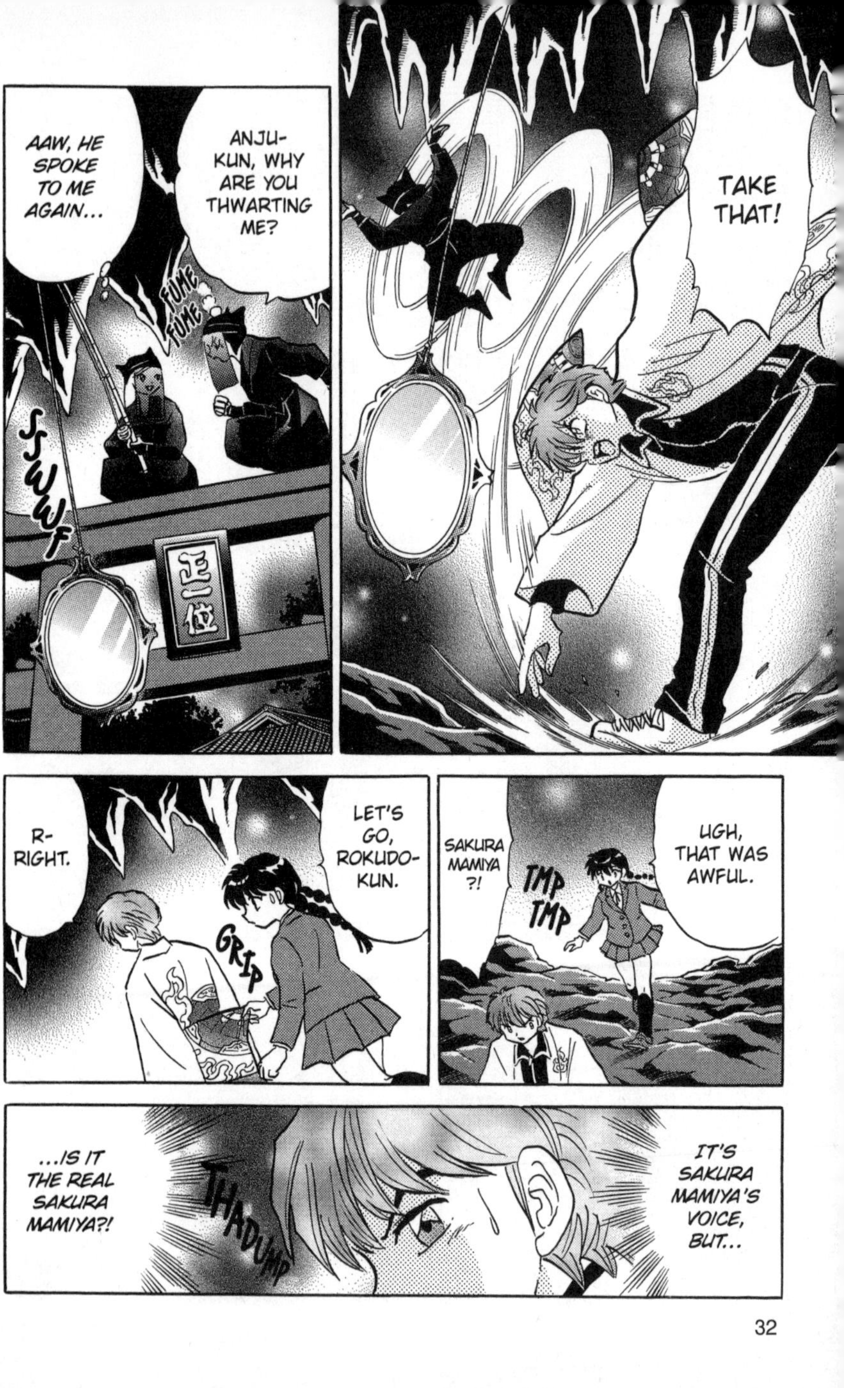
TAKE THAT!
ANJU-KUN, WHY ARE YOU THWARTING ME?
FUME FUME
AAW, HE SPOKE TO ME AGAIN...
SSWWF
正一位
UGH, THAT WAS AWFUL.
TMP TMP
SAKURA MAMIYA ?!
LET'S GO, ROKUDO-KUN.
GRIP
R-RIGHT.
IT'S SAKURA MAMIYA'S VOICE, BUT...
THADUMP
...IS IT THE REAL SAKURA MAMIYA?!

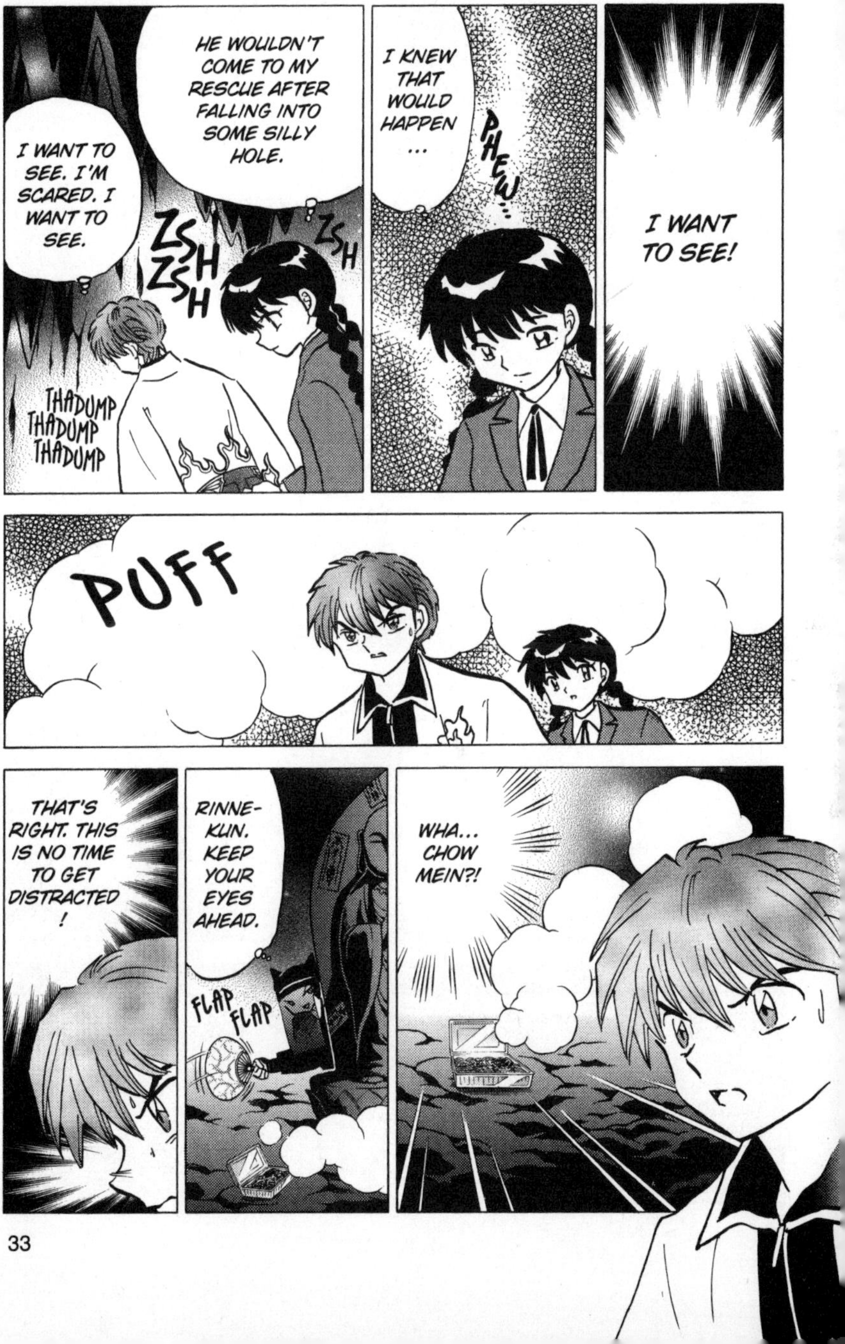
I WANT TO SEE!
I KNEW THAT WOULD HAPPEN ...
PHEW...
HE WOULDN'T COME TO MY RESCUE AFTER FALLING INTO SOME SILLY HOLE.
ZSH
I WANT TO SEE. I'M SCARED. I WANT TO SEE.
ZSH ZSH
THADUMP THADUMP THADUMP
PUFF
WHA... CHOW MEIN?!
RINNE-KUN. KEEP YOUR EYES AHEAD.
FLAP FLAP
THAT'S RIGHT. THIS IS NO TIME TO GET DISTRACTED!

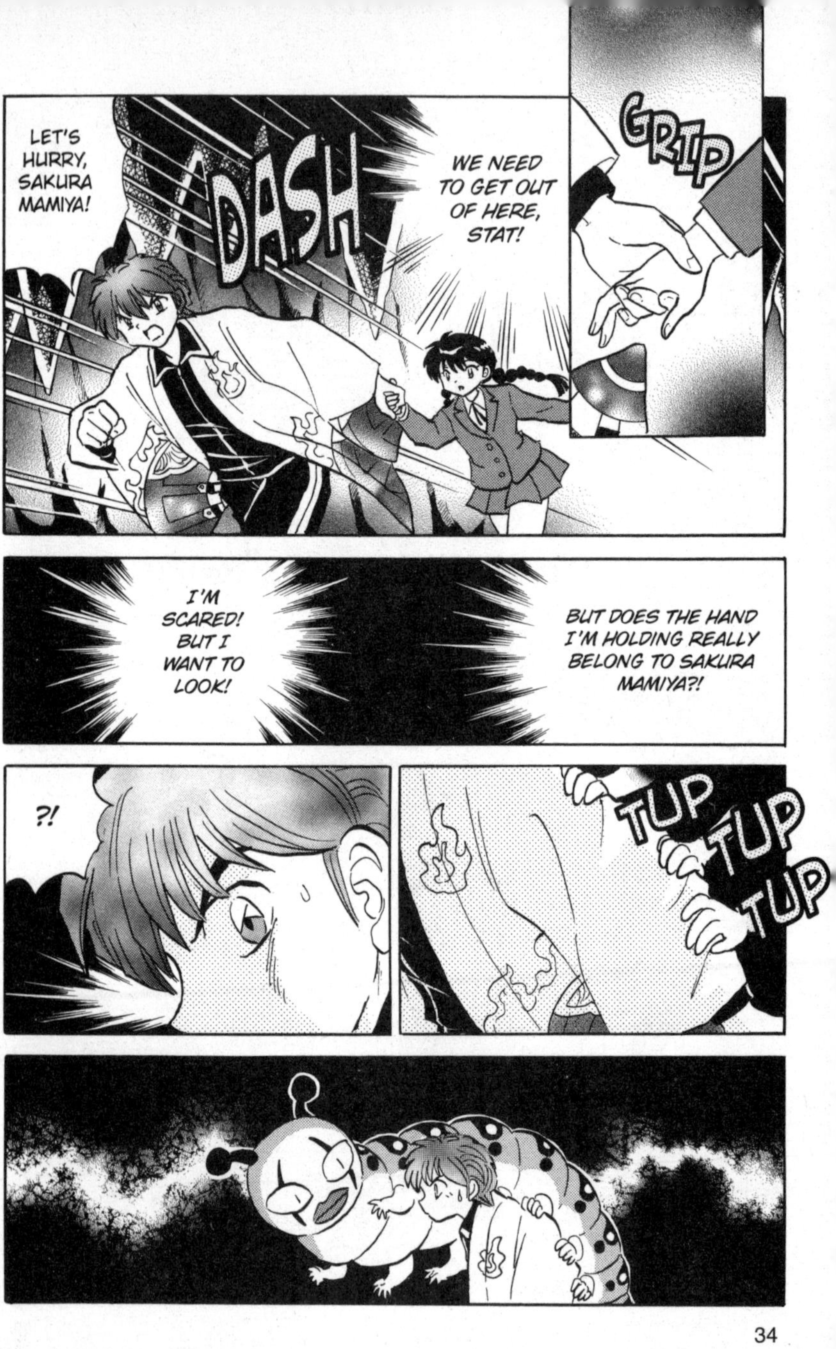
GRIP
WE NEED TO GET OUT OF HERE, STAT!
DASH
LET'S HURRY, SAKURA MAMIYA!
BUT DOES THE HAND I'M HOLDING REALLY BELONG TO SAKURA MAMIYA?!
I'M SCARED! BUT I WANT TO LOOK!
TUP TUP TUP
?!

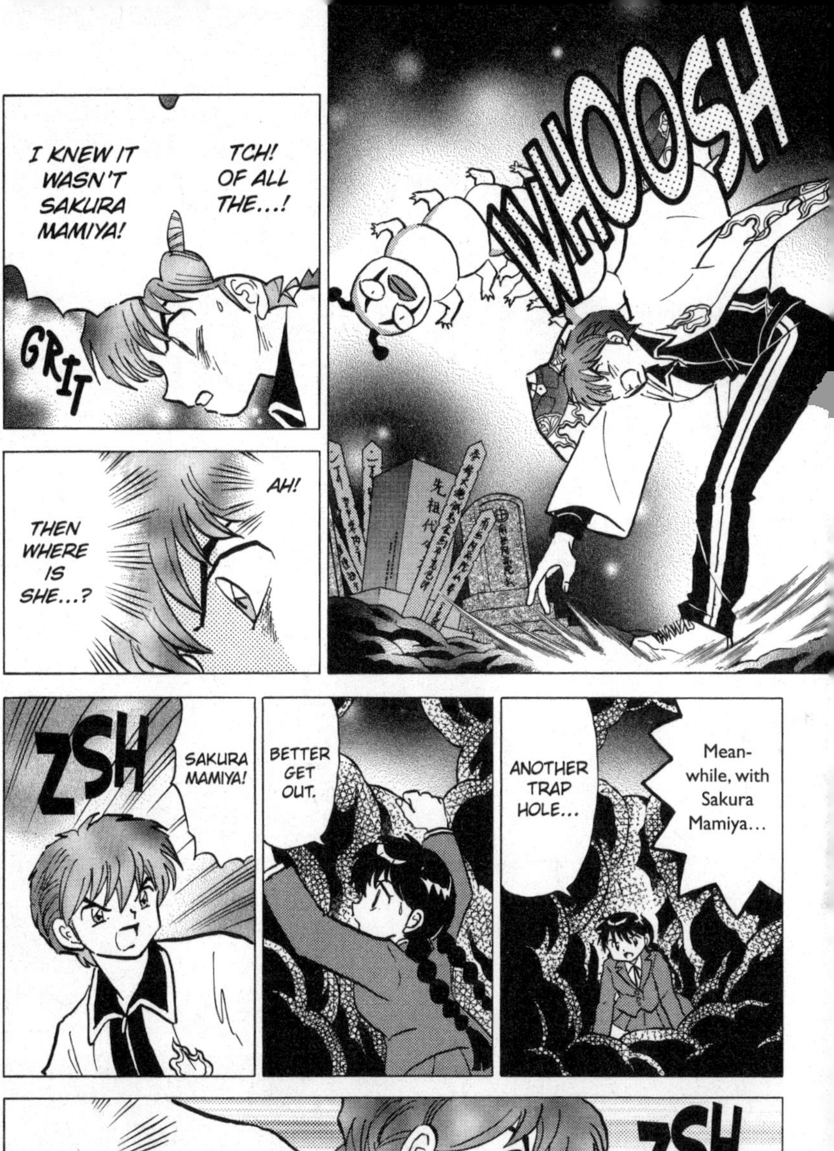
WHOOSH
TCH! OF ALL THE...!
I KNEW IT WASN'T SAKURA MAMIYA!
GRIT
AH!
THEN WHERE IS SHE...?
Mean-while, with Sakura Mamiya...
ANOTHER TRAP HOLE...
BETTER GET OUT.
SAKURA MAMIYA!
ZSH
ZSH ZSH
WHERE IS SHE?!

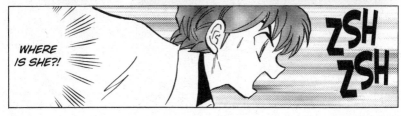

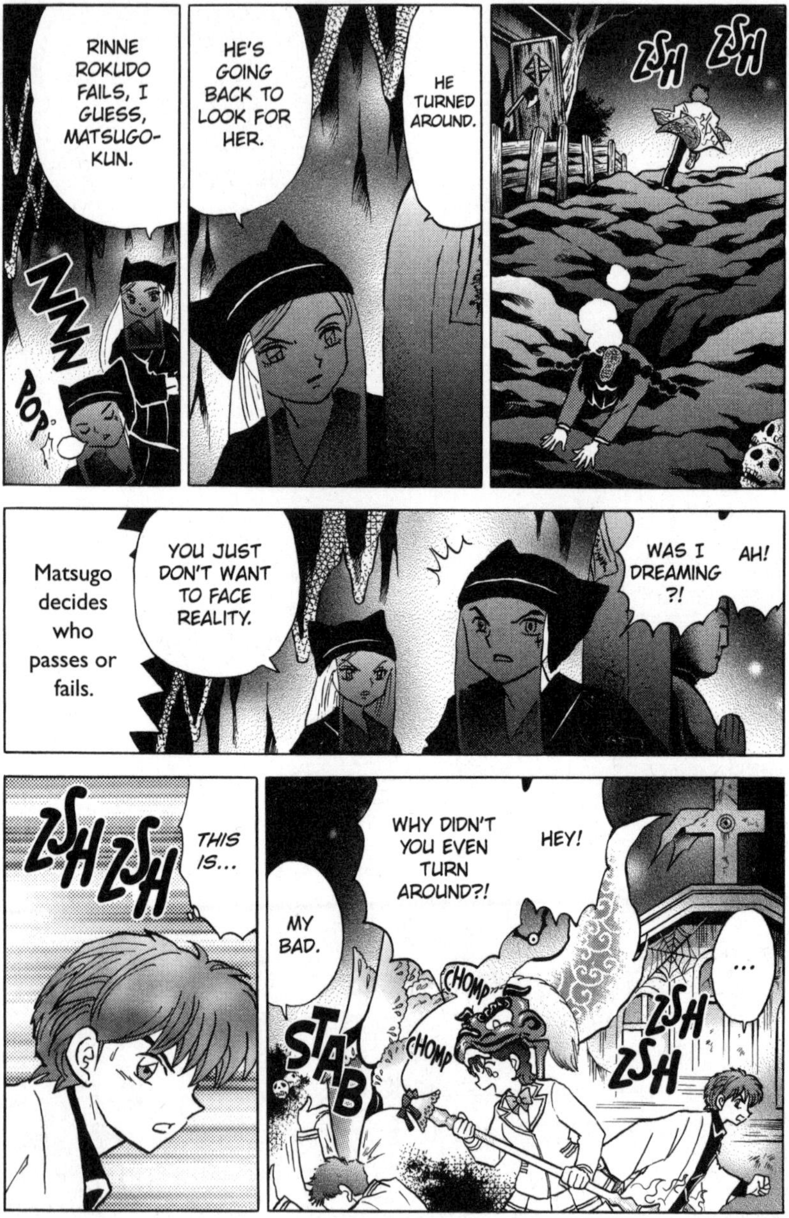
ZSH ZSH
HE TURNED AROUND.
HE'S GOING BACK TO LOOK FOR HER.
RINNE ROKUDO FAILS, I GUESS, MATSUGO-KUN.
ZZZ
POP
AH!
WAS I DREAMING?!
YOU JUST DON'T WANT TO FACE REALITY.
Matsugo decides who passes or fails.
...
ZSH ZSH
HEY!
WHY DIDN'T YOU EVEN TURN AROUND?!
CHOMP
CHOMP
MY BAD.
STAB
THIS IS...
ZSH ZSH

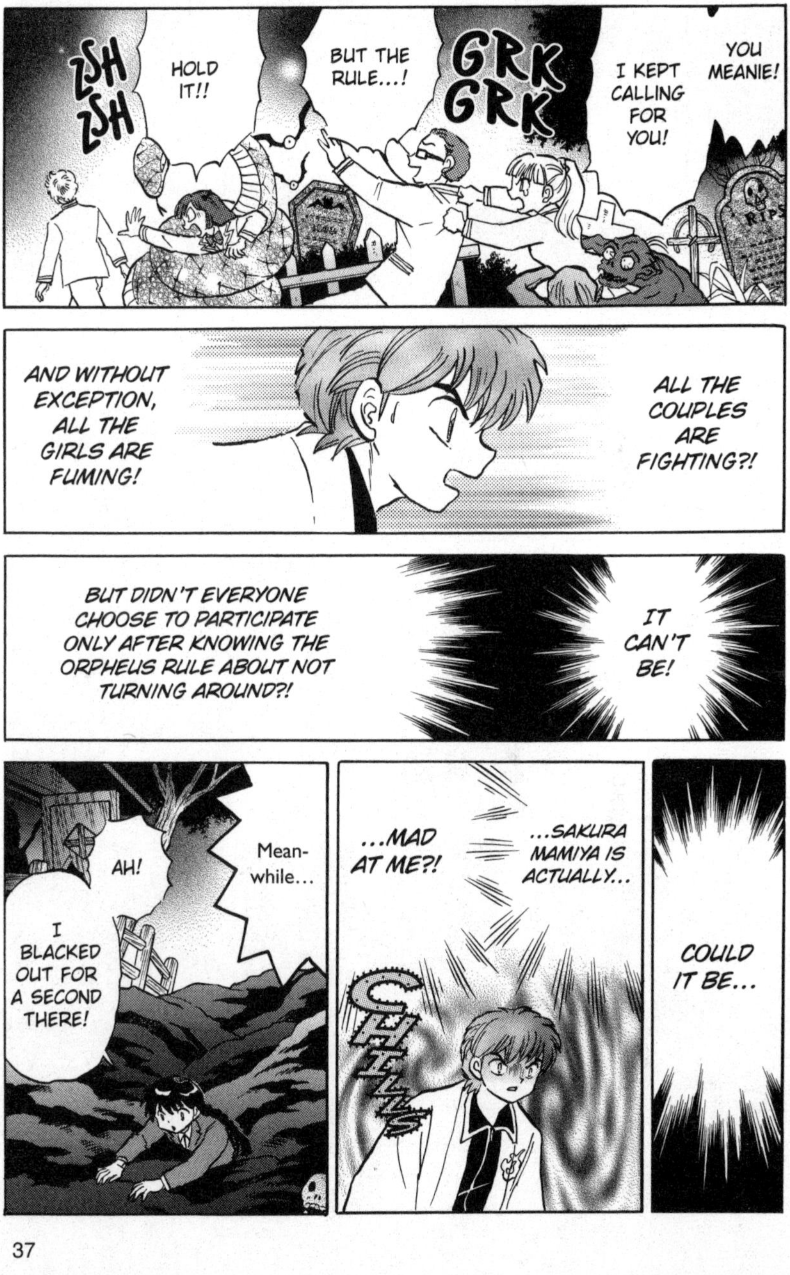
YOU MEANIE!
I KEPT CALLING FOR YOU!
GRK GRK
BUT THE RULE...!
HOLD IT!!
ZSH ZSH
ALL THE COUPLES ARE FIGHTING?!
AND WITHOUT EXCEPTION, ALL THE GIRLS ARE FUMING!
IT CAN'T BE!
BUT DIDN'T EVERYONE CHOOSE TO PARTICIPATE ONLY AFTER KNOWING THE ORPHEUS RULE ABOUT NOT TURNING AROUND?!
COULD IT BE...
...SAKURA MAMIYA IS ACTUALLY...
...MAD AT ME?!
Mean-while...
AH!
I BLACKED OUT FOR A SECOND THERE!

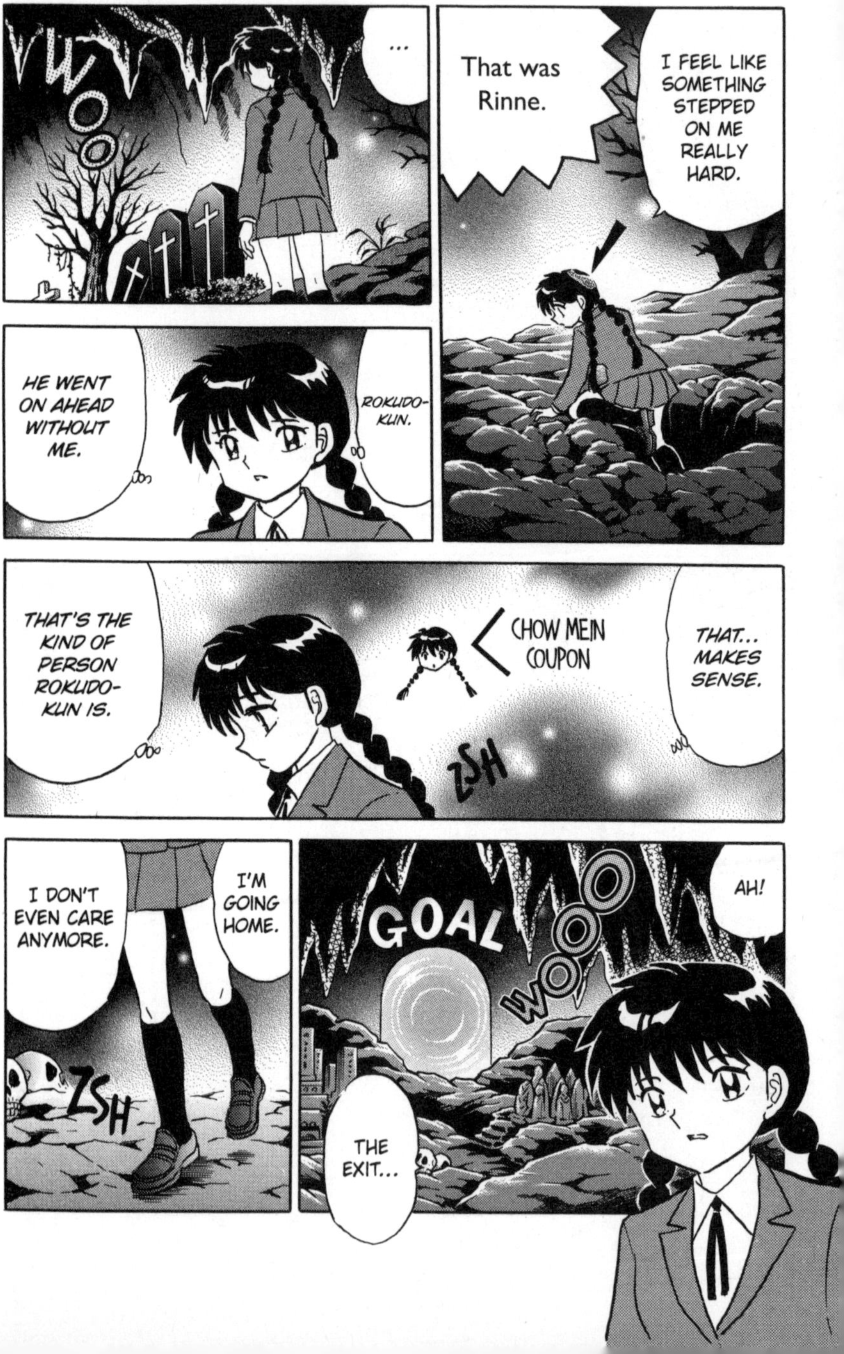

I FEEL LIKE SOMETHING STEPPED ON ME REALLY HARD.
That was Rinne.
...
VWOOO
ROKUDO-KUN.
HE WENT ON AHEAD WITHOUT ME.
THAT... MAKES SENSE.
ZSH
CHOW MEIN COUPON
THAT'S THE KIND OF PERSON ROKUDO-KUN IS.
AH!
WOOO
GOAL
THE EXIT...
I'M GOING HOME.
I DON'T EVEN CARE ANYMORE.
ZSH

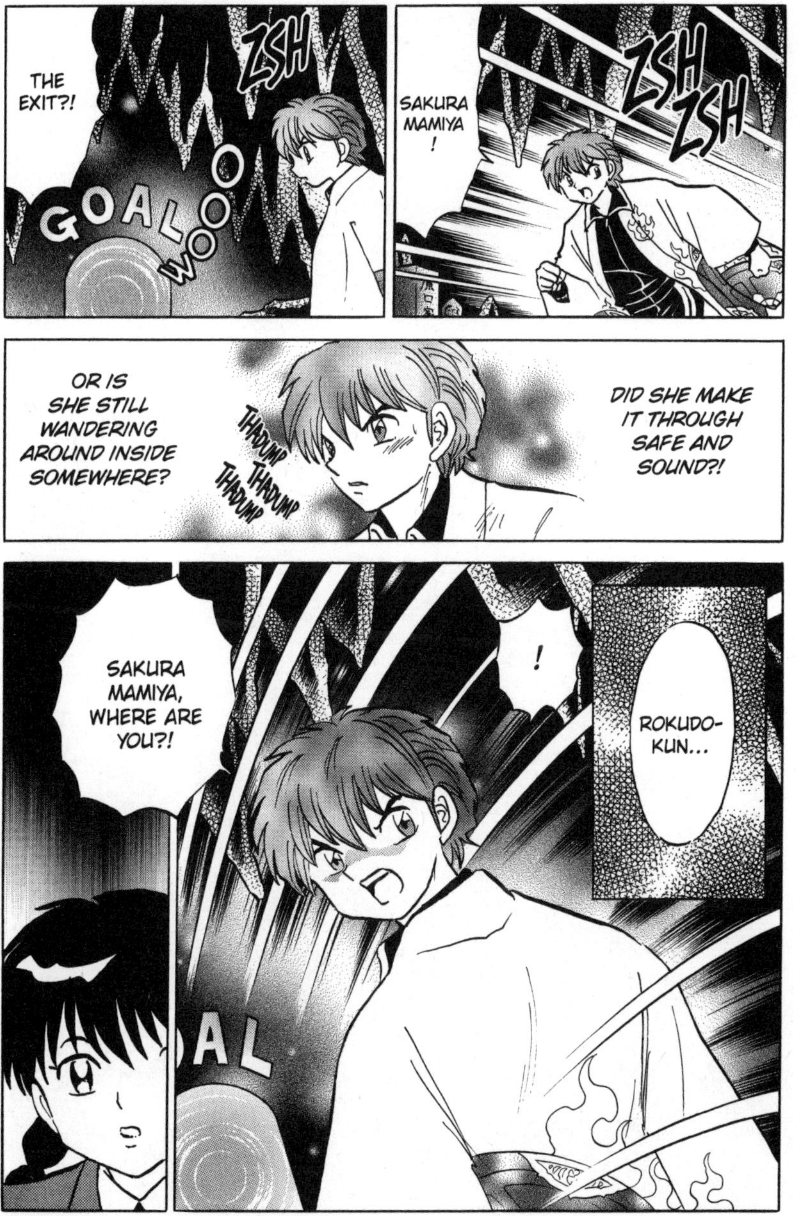
SAKURA MAMIYA!
ZSH ZSH
ZSH
THE EXIT?!
GOAL
WOOOO
DID SHE MAKE IT THROUGH SAFE AND SOUND?!
THADUMP THADUMP THADUMP
OR IS SHE STILL WANDERING AROUND INSIDE SOMEWHERE?
ROKUDO-KUN...
!
SAKURA MAMIYA, WHERE ARE YOU?!
AL

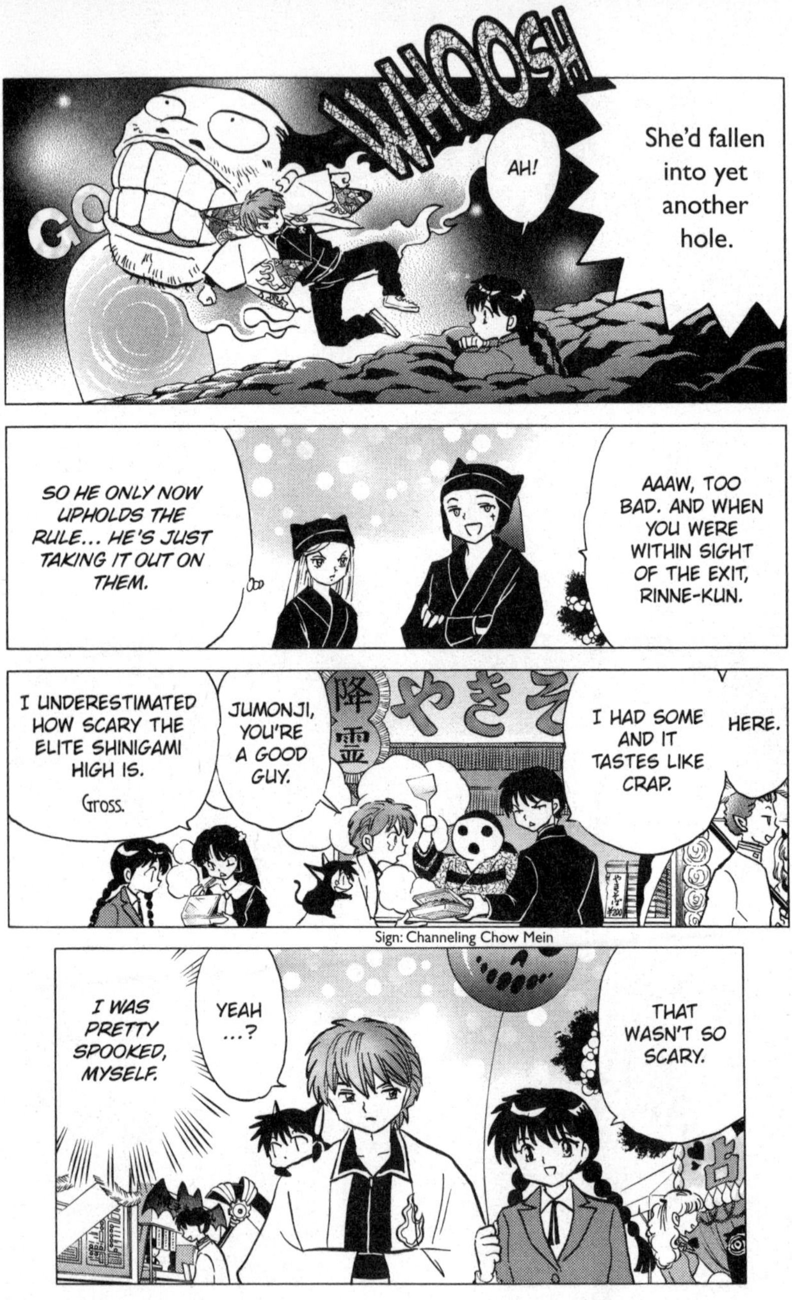
She'd fallen into yet another hole.
WHOOSH
AH!
GO
AAAW, TOO BAD. AND WHEN YOU WERE WITHIN SIGHT OF THE EXIT, RINNE-KUN.
SO HE ONLY NOW UPHOLDS THE RULE... HE'S JUST TAKING IT OUT ON THEM.
HERE.
I HAD SOME AND IT TASTES LIKE CRAP.
JUMONJI, YOU'RE A GOOD GUY.
I UNDERESTIMATED HOW SCARY THE ELITE SHINIGAMI HIGH IS.
Gross.
Sign: Channeling Chow Mein
THAT WASN'T SO SCARY.
YEAH ...?
I WAS PRETTY SPOOKED, MYSELF.

CHAPTER 261: SCREAMS ON A CASSETTE TAPE

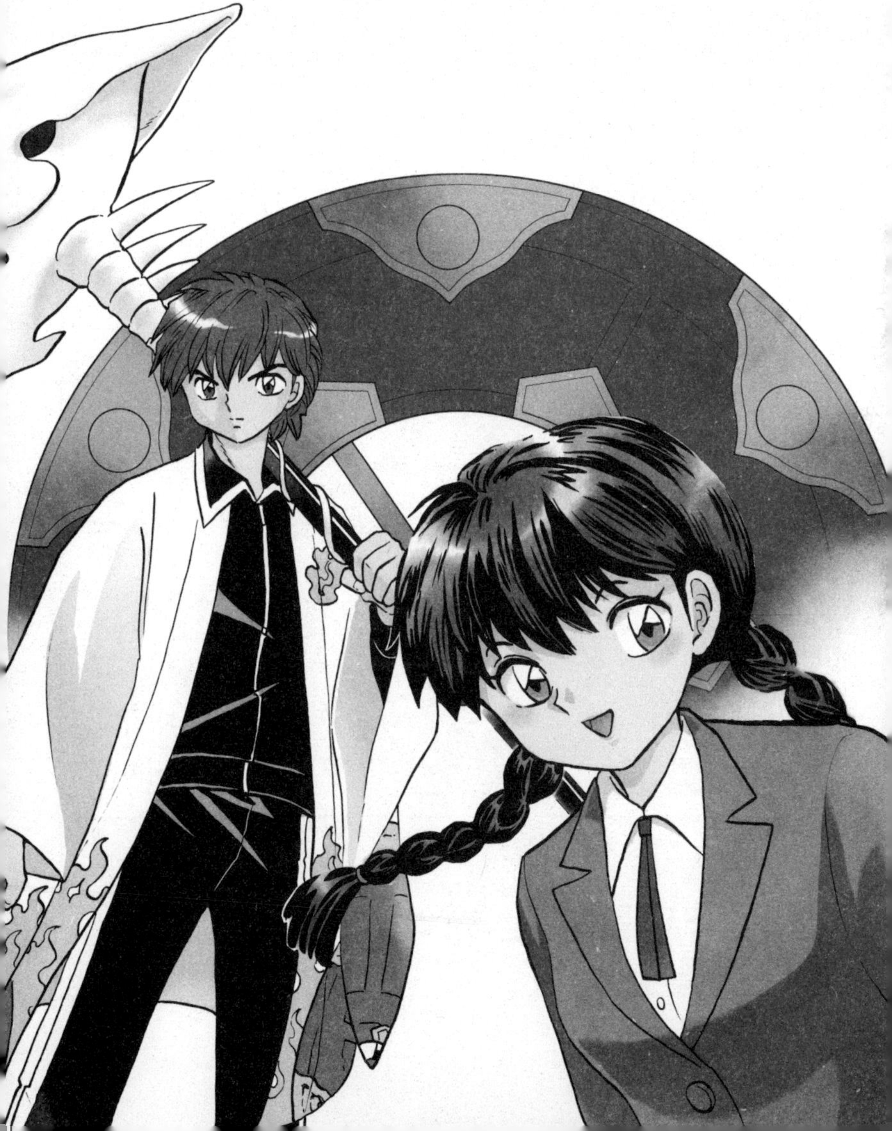

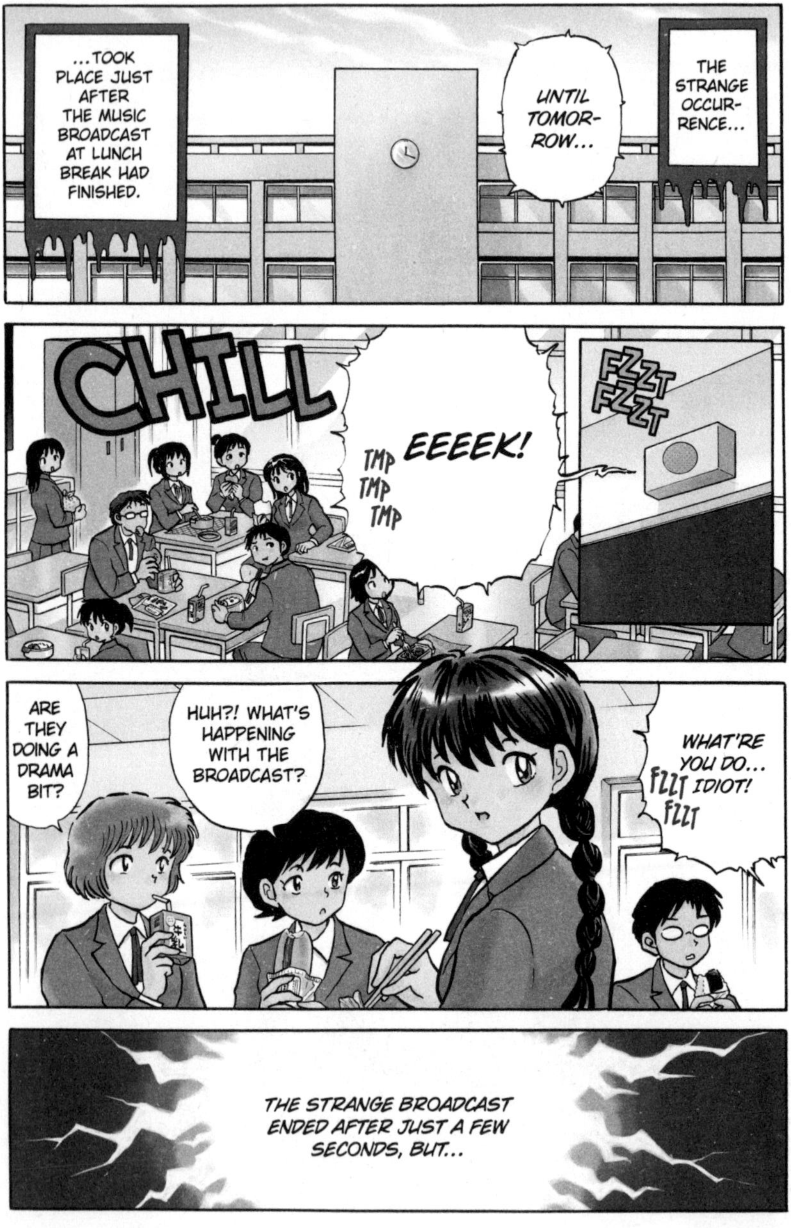
THE STRANGE OCCURRENCE...
UNTIL TOMORROW...
...TOOK PLACE JUST AFTER THE MUSIC BROADCAST AT LUNCH BREAK HAD FINISHED.
FZZT FZZT
EEEEK!
TMP TMP TMP
CHILL
WHAT'RE YOU DO... FZZT IDIOT! FZZT
HUH?! WHAT'S HAPPENING WITH THE BROADCAST?
ARE THEY DOING A DRAMA BIT?
THE STRANGE BROADCAST ENDED AFTER JUST A FEW SECONDS, BUT...

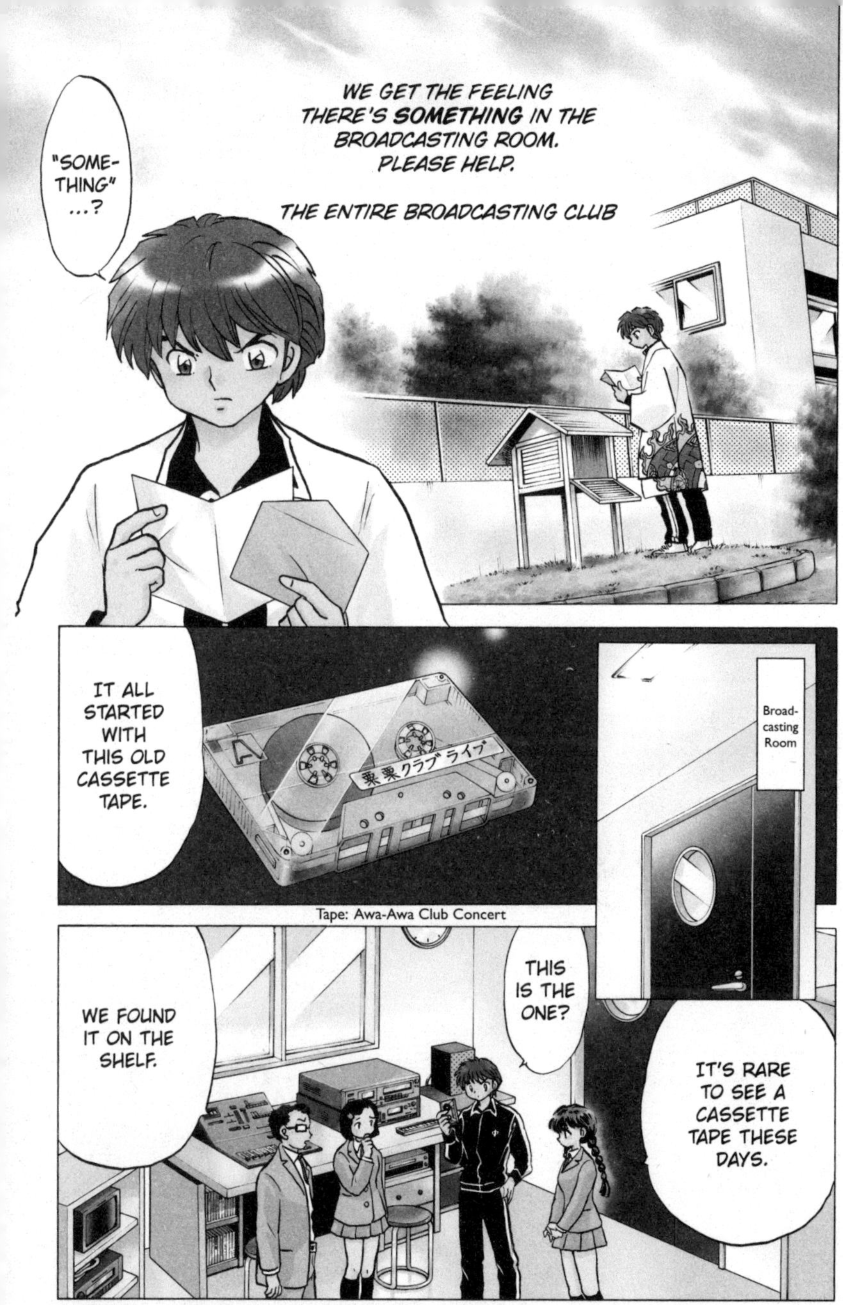
WE GET THE FEELING THERE'S **SOMETHING** IN THE BROADCASTING ROOM. PLEASE HELP.
THE ENTIRE BROADCASTING CLUB
"SOME-THING" ...?
Broad-casting Room
IT ALL STARTED WITH THIS OLD CASSETTE TAPE.
粟粟クラブ ライブ
Tape: Awa-Awa Club Concert
IT'S RARE TO SEE A CASSETTE TAPE THESE DAYS.
THIS IS THE ONE?
WE FOUND IT ON THE SHELF.

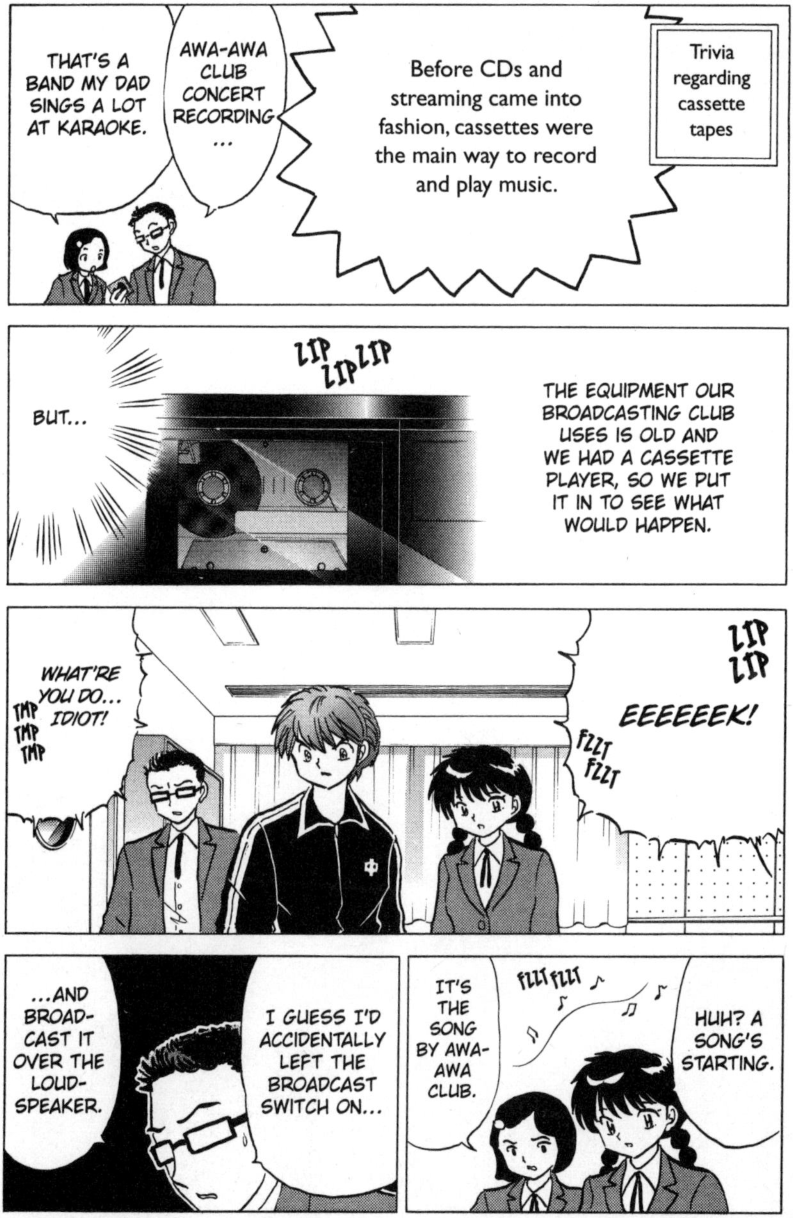
Trivia regarding cassette tapes
Before CDs and streaming came into fashion, cassettes were the main way to record and play music.
AWA-AWA CLUB CONCERT RECORDING...
THAT'S A BAND MY DAD SINGS A LOT AT KARAOKE.
THE EQUIPMENT OUR BROADCASTING CLUB USES IS OLD AND WE HAD A CASSETTE PLAYER, SO WE PUT IT IN TO SEE WHAT WOULD HAPPEN.
ZIP ZIP ZIP
BUT...
ZIP ZIP
EEEEEEK!
FZZT FZZT
WHAT'RE YOU DO... IDIOT!
TMP TMP TMP
HUH? A SONG'S STARTING.
FZZT FZZT
IT'S THE SONG BY AWA-AWA CLUB.
I GUESS I'D ACCIDENTALLY LEFT THE BROADCAST SWITCH ON...
...AND BROADCAST IT OVER THE LOUDSPEAKER.

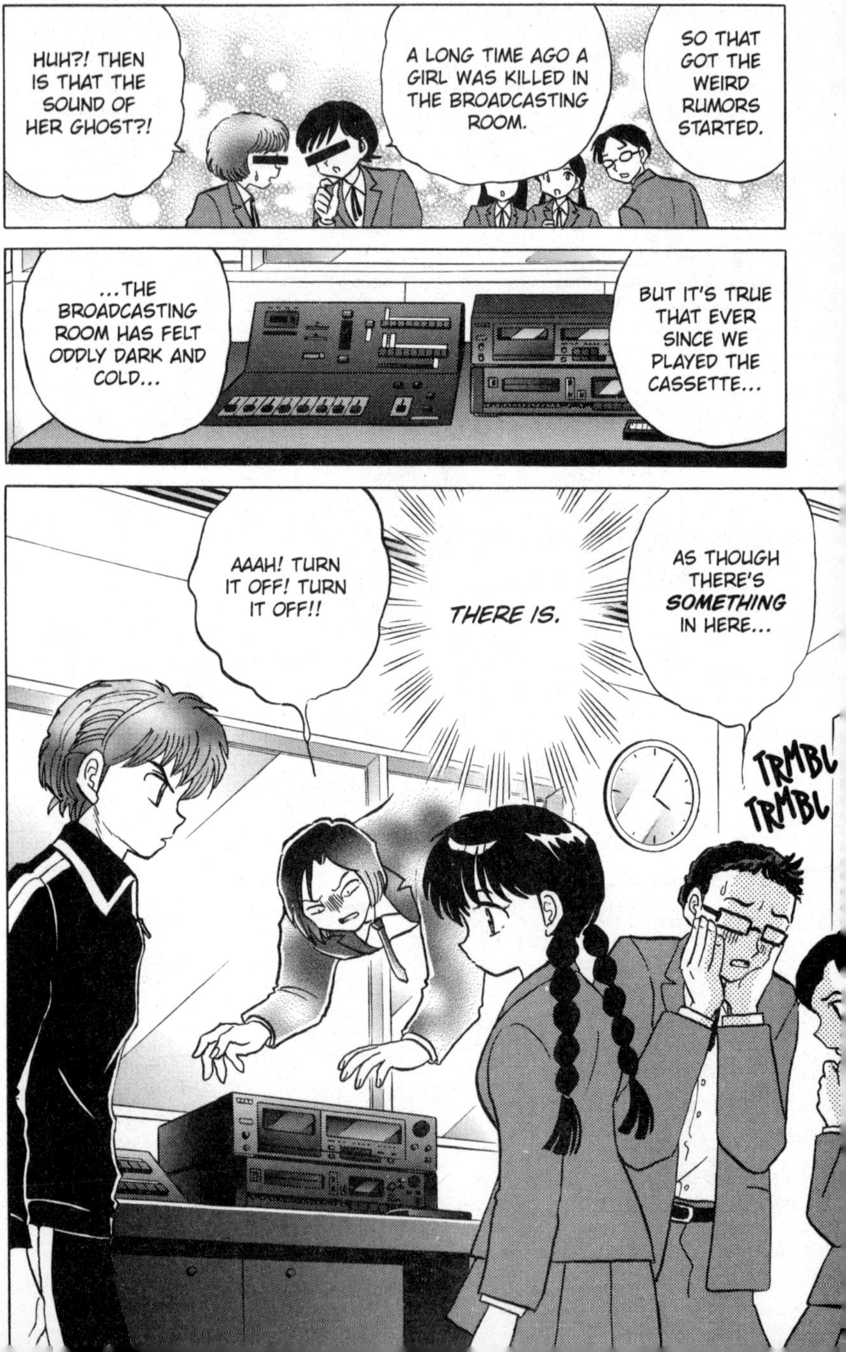
SO THAT GOT THE WEIRD RUMORS STARTED.
A LONG TIME AGO A GIRL WAS KILLED IN THE BROADCASTING ROOM.
HUH?! THEN IS THAT THE SOUND OF HER GHOST?!
BUT IT'S TRUE THAT EVER SINCE WE PLAYED THE CASSETTE...
...THE BROADCASTING ROOM HAS FELT ODDLY DARK AND COLD...
AS THOUGH THERE'S *SOMETHING* IN HERE...
TRMBL TRMBL
THERE IS.
AAAH! TURN IT OFF! TURN IT OFF!!

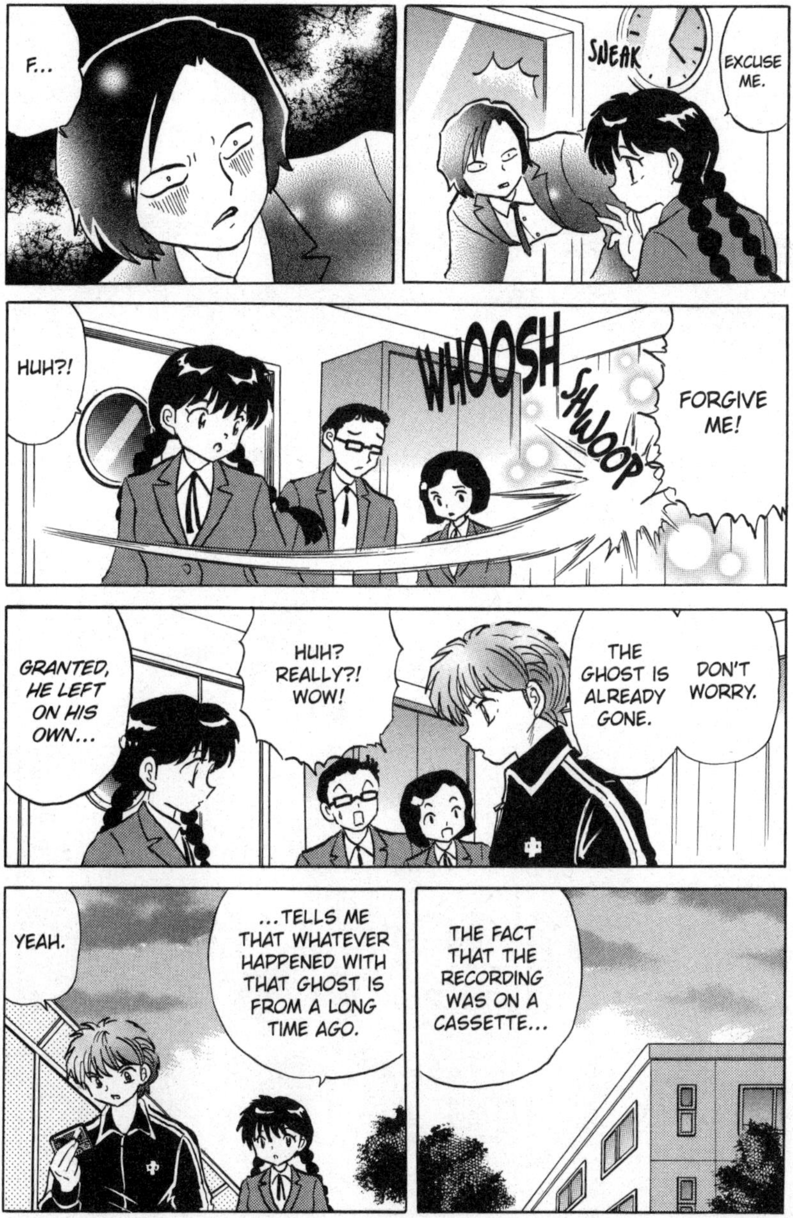
SNEAK
EXCUSE ME.
F...
FORGIVE ME!
SHWOOP
WHOOSH
HUH?!
DON'T WORRY.
THE GHOST IS ALREADY GONE.
HUH? REALLY?! WOW!
GRANTED, HE LEFT ON HIS OWN...
THE FACT THAT THE RECORDING WAS ON A CASSETTE...
...TELLS ME THAT WHATEVER HAPPENED WITH THAT GHOST IS FROM A LONG TIME AGO.
YEAH.

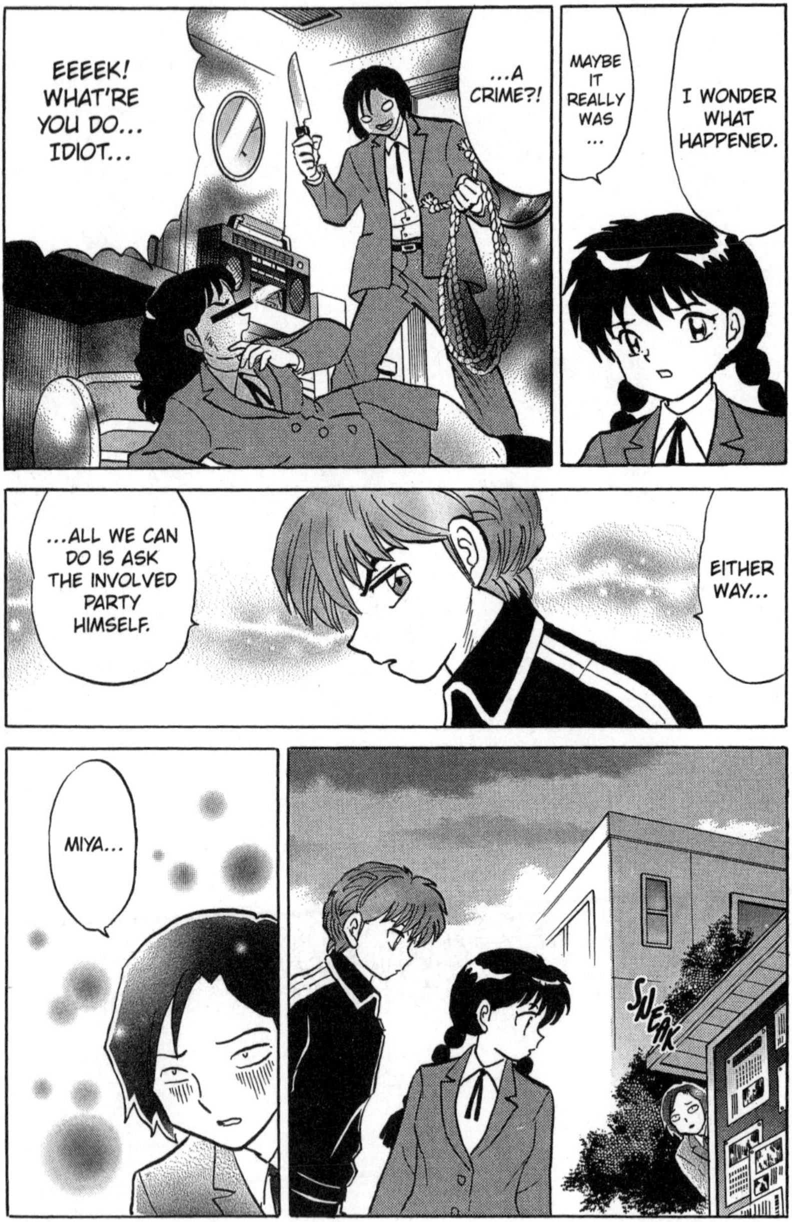
I WONDER WHAT HAPPENED.
MAYBE IT REALLY WAS ...
...A CRIME?!
EEEEK! WHAT'RE YOU DO... IDIOT...
EITHER WAY...
...ALL WE CAN DO IS ASK THE INVOLVED PARTY HIMSELF.
SNEAK
MIYA...

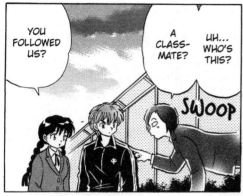

HUH?!
MIYA?
UH... WHO'S THIS?
A CLASS-MATE?
SWOOP
YOU FOLLOWED US?
ARE YOU TWO GOING OUT?
SQUIRM SQUIRM
I KNOW THIS FEELING...
I WONDER IF MIYA IS A GIRL HE LIKED.
AND HE THINKS I'M MIYA...?
UM... ABOUT THIS CAS-SETTE...
AAAAAH! I'M SO SORRY.
I'VE DONE SOMETHING IRREPARABLE.
UH, YOU DON'T HAVE TO APOLO-GIZE TO ME.
HUH?

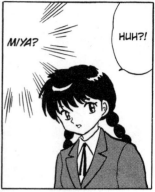

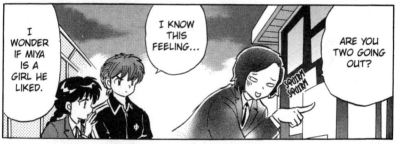

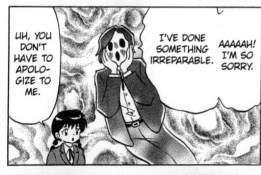

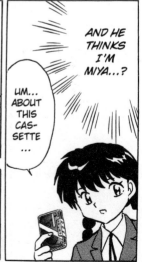

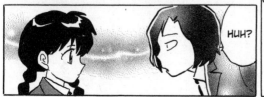

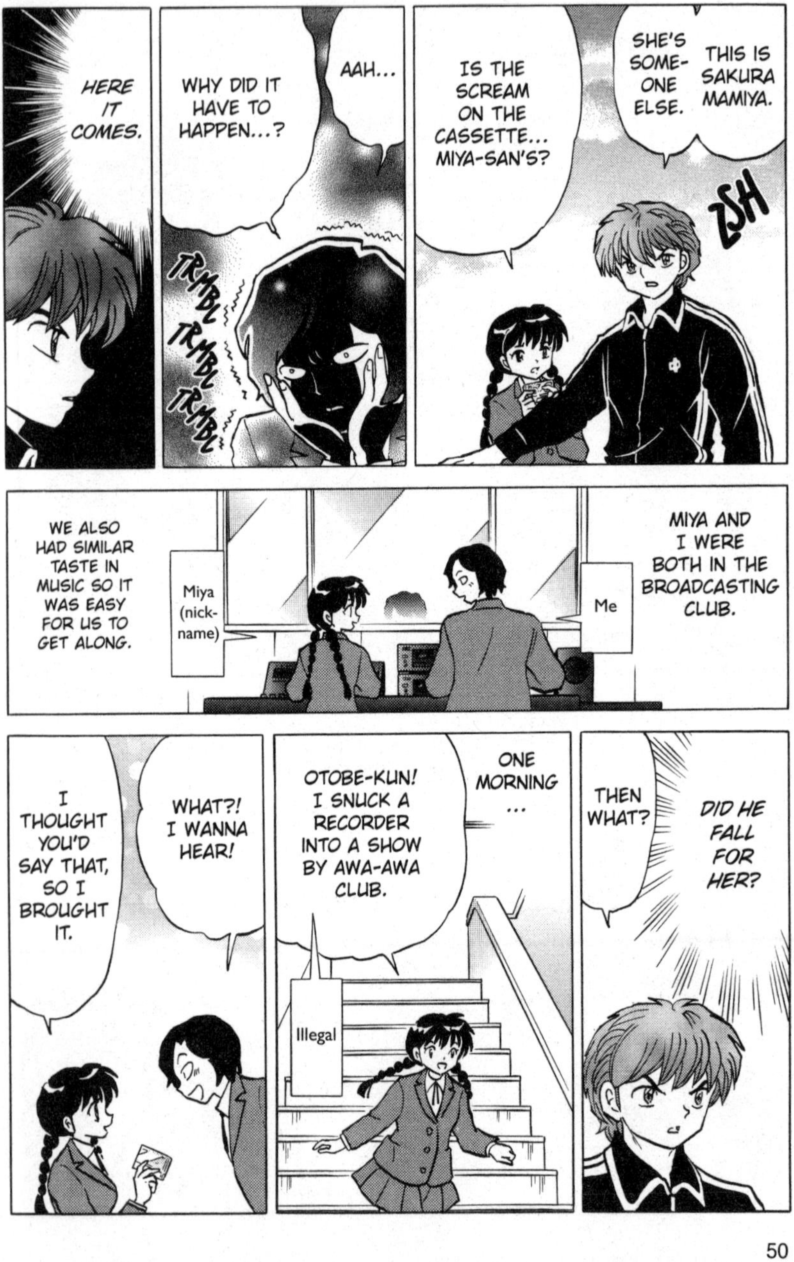
THIS IS SAKURA MAMIYA.
SHE'S SOME-ONE ELSE.
IS THE SCREAM ON THE CASSETTE... MIYA-SAN'S?
ZSH
AAH...
WHY DID IT HAVE TO HAPPEN...?
TRMBL TRMBL TRMBL
HERE IT COMES.
MIYA AND I WERE BOTH IN THE BROADCASTING CLUB.
Me
Miya (nick-name)
WE ALSO HAD SIMILAR TASTE IN MUSIC SO IT WAS EASY FOR US TO GET ALONG.
DID HE FALL FOR HER?
THEN WHAT?
ONE MORNING ...
OTOBE-KUN! I SNUCK A RECORDER INTO A SHOW BY AWA-AWA CLUB.
Illegal
WHAT?! I WANNA HEAR!
I THOUGHT YOU'D SAY THAT, SO I BROUGHT IT.

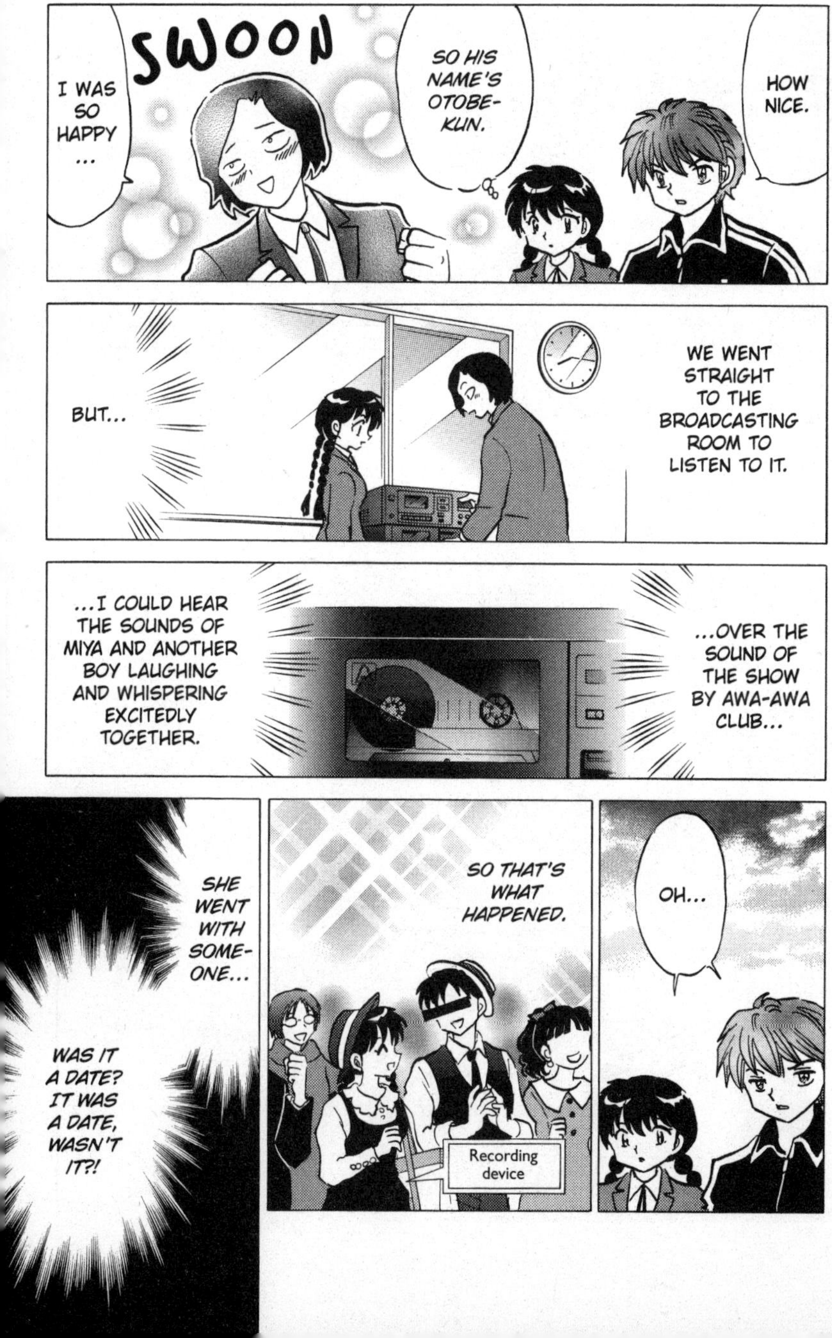
HOW NICE.
SO HIS NAME'S OTOBE-KUN.
SWOON
I WAS SO HAPPY...
WE WENT STRAIGHT TO THE BROADCASTING ROOM TO LISTEN TO IT.
BUT...
...OVER THE SOUND OF THE SHOW BY AWA-AWA CLUB...
...I COULD HEAR THE SOUNDS OF MIYA AND ANOTHER BOY LAUGHING AND WHISPERING EXCITEDLY TOGETHER.
OH...
SO THAT'S WHAT HAPPENED.
Recording device
SHE WENT WITH SOME-ONE...
WAS IT A DATE? IT WAS A DATE, WASN'T IT?!

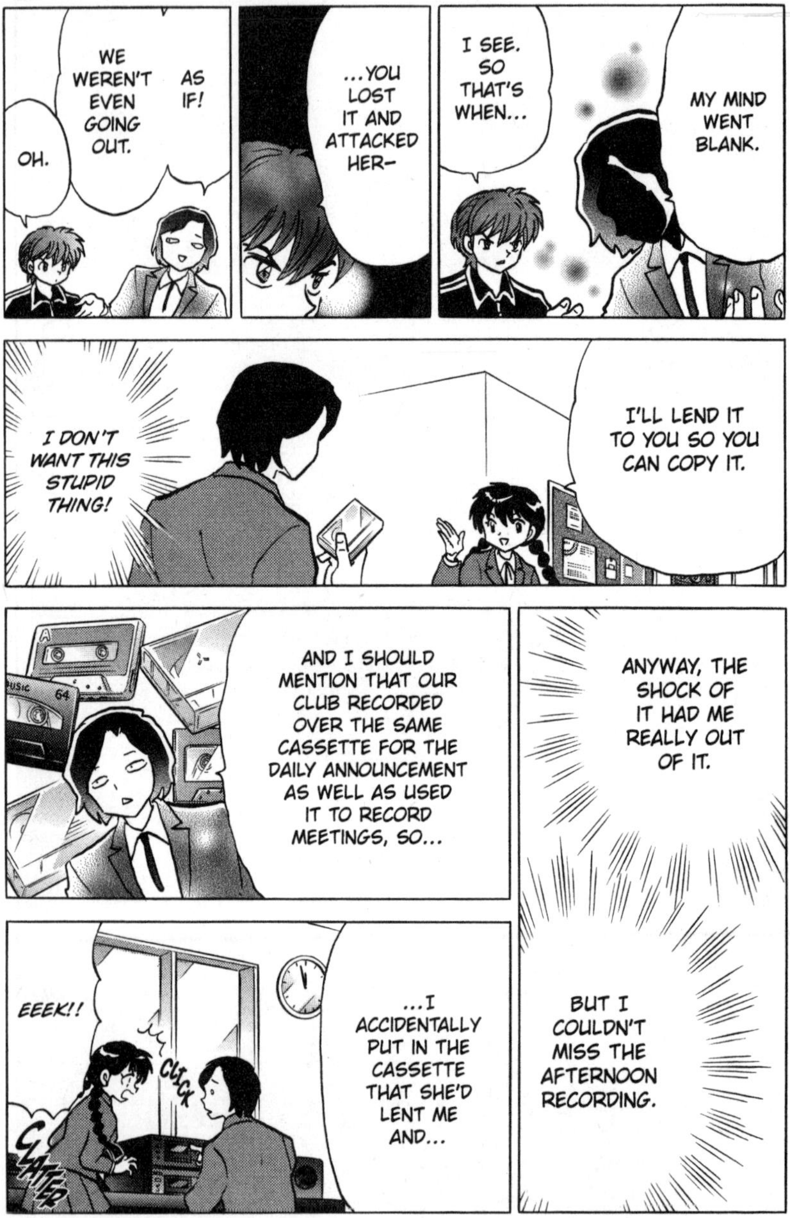
MY MIND WENT BLANK.
I SEE. SO THAT'S WHEN...
...YOU LOST IT AND ATTACKED HER–
AS IF!
WE WEREN'T EVEN GOING OUT.
OH.
I'LL LEND IT TO YOU SO YOU CAN COPY IT.
I DON'T WANT THIS STUPID THING!
ANYWAY, THE SHOCK OF IT HAD ME REALLY OUT OF IT.
BUT I COULDN'T MISS THE AFTERNOON RECORDING.
AND I SHOULD MENTION THAT OUR CLUB RECORDED OVER THE SAME CASSETTE FOR THE DAILY ANNOUNCEMENT AS WELL AS USED IT TO RECORD MEETINGS, SO...
...I ACCIDENTALLY PUT IN THE CASSETTE THAT SHE'D LENT ME AND...
EEEK!!
CLICK
CLATTER

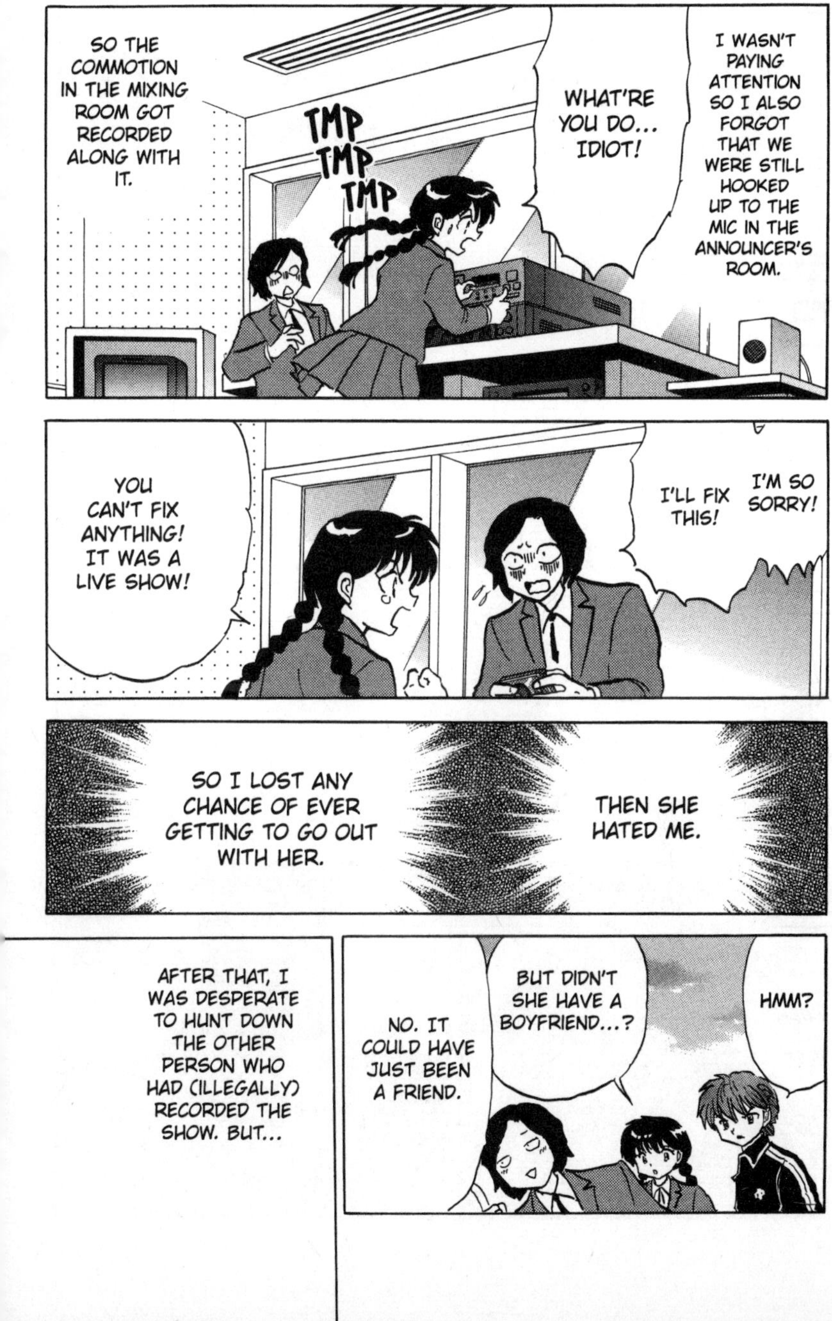

I WASN'T PAYING ATTENTION SO I ALSO FORGOT THAT WE WERE STILL HOOKED UP TO THE MIC IN THE ANNOUNCER'S ROOM.
WHAT'RE YOU DO... IDIOT!
TMP TMP TMP
SO THE COMMOTION IN THE MIXING ROOM GOT RECORDED ALONG WITH IT.
I'M SO SORRY!
I'LL FIX THIS!
YOU CAN'T FIX ANYTHING! IT WAS A LIVE SHOW!
THEN SHE HATED ME.
SO I LOST ANY CHANCE OF EVER GETTING TO GO OUT WITH HER.
HMM?
BUT DIDN'T SHE HAVE A BOYFRIEND...?
NO. IT COULD HAVE JUST BEEN A FRIEND.
AFTER THAT, I WAS DESPERATE TO HUNT DOWN THE OTHER PERSON WHO HAD (ILLEGALLY) RECORDED THE SHOW. BUT...

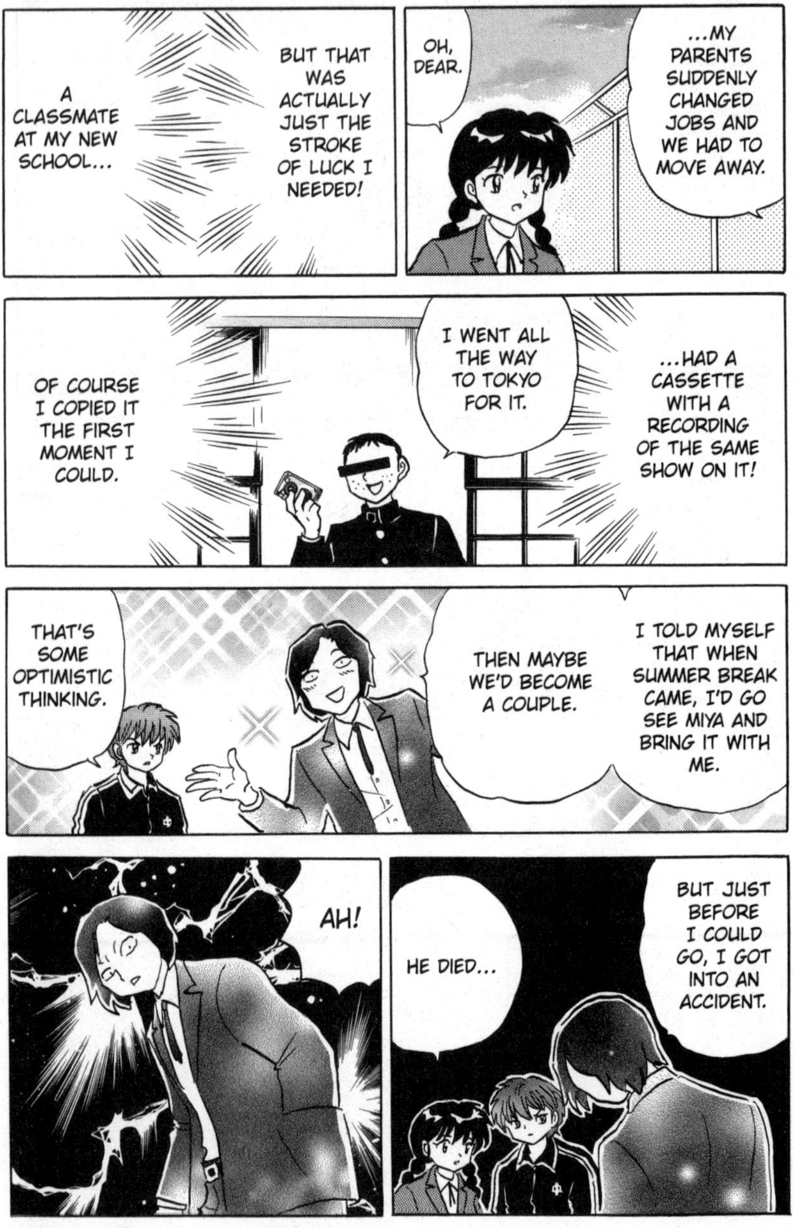
...MY PARENTS SUDDENLY CHANGED JOBS AND WE HAD TO MOVE AWAY.
OH, DEAR.
BUT THAT WAS ACTUALLY JUST THE STROKE OF LUCK I NEEDED!
A CLASSMATE AT MY NEW SCHOOL...
...HAD A CASSETTE WITH A RECORDING OF THE SAME SHOW ON IT!
I WENT ALL THE WAY TO TOKYO FOR IT.
OF COURSE I COPIED IT THE FIRST MOMENT I COULD.
I TOLD MYSELF THAT WHEN SUMMER BREAK CAME, I'D GO SEE MIYA AND BRING IT WITH ME.
THEN MAYBE WE'D BECOME A COUPLE.
THAT'S SOME OPTIMISTIC THINKING.
BUT JUST BEFORE I COULD GO, I GOT INTO AN ACCIDENT.
HE DIED...
AH!

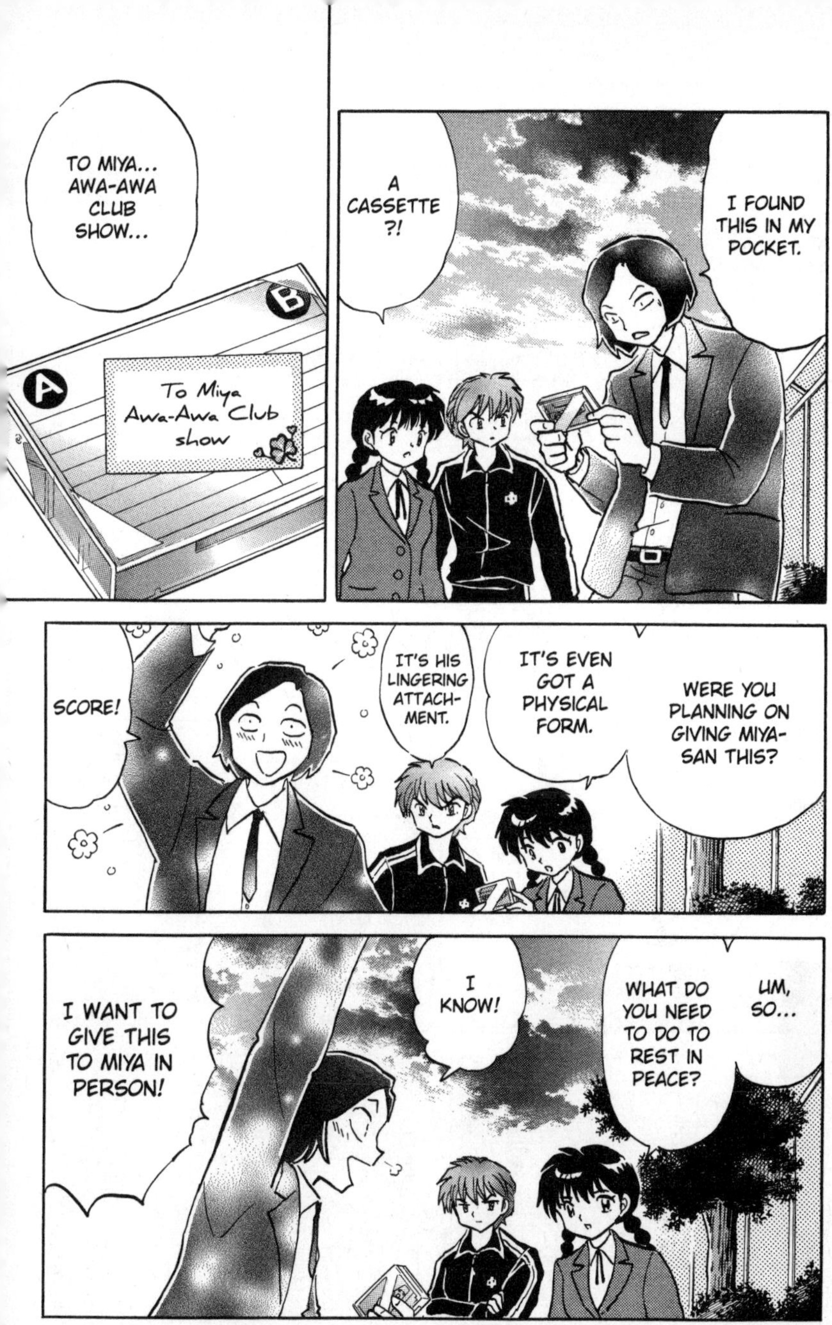
I FOUND THIS IN MY POCKET.
A CASSETTE?!
TO MIYA... AWA-AWA CLUB SHOW...
A
B
To Miya Awa-Awa Club show
WERE YOU PLANNING ON GIVING MIYA-SAN THIS?
IT'S EVEN GOT A PHYSICAL FORM.
IT'S HIS LINGERING ATTACHMENT.
SCORE!
UM, SO...
WHAT DO YOU NEED TO DO TO REST IN PEACE?
I KNOW!
I WANT TO GIVE THIS TO MIYA IN PERSON!

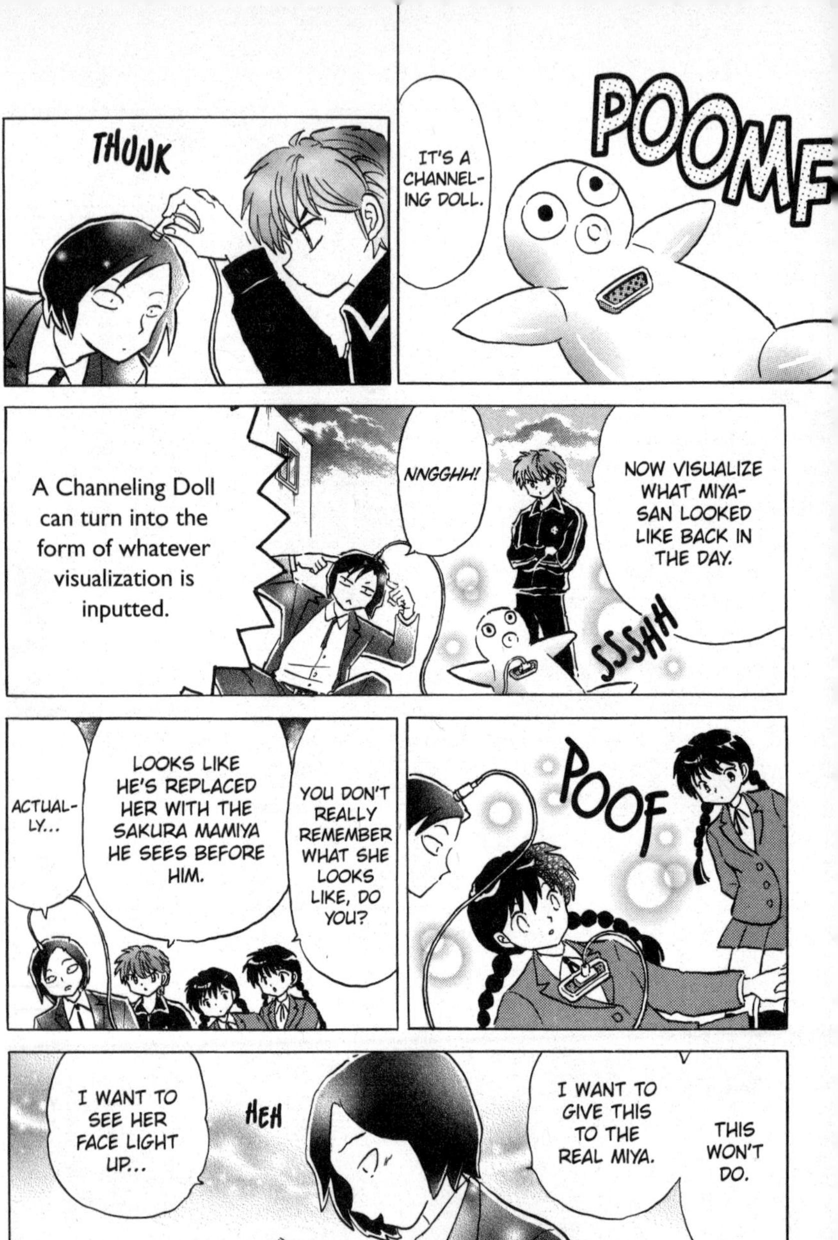
POOMF
IT'S A CHANNELING DOLL.
THUNK
NOW VISUALIZE WHAT MIYA-SAN LOOKED LIKE BACK IN THE DAY.
SSSHH
NNGGHH!
A Channeling Doll can turn into the form of whatever visualization is inputted.
POOF
YOU DON'T REALLY REMEMBER WHAT SHE LOOKS LIKE, DO YOU?
LOOKS LIKE HE'S REPLACED HER WITH THE SAKURA MAMIYA HE SEES BEFORE HIM.
ACTUALLY...
THIS WON'T DO.
I WANT TO GIVE THIS TO THE REAL MIYA.
HEH
I WANT TO SEE HER FACE LIGHT UP...

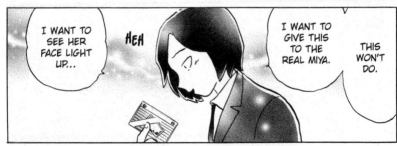

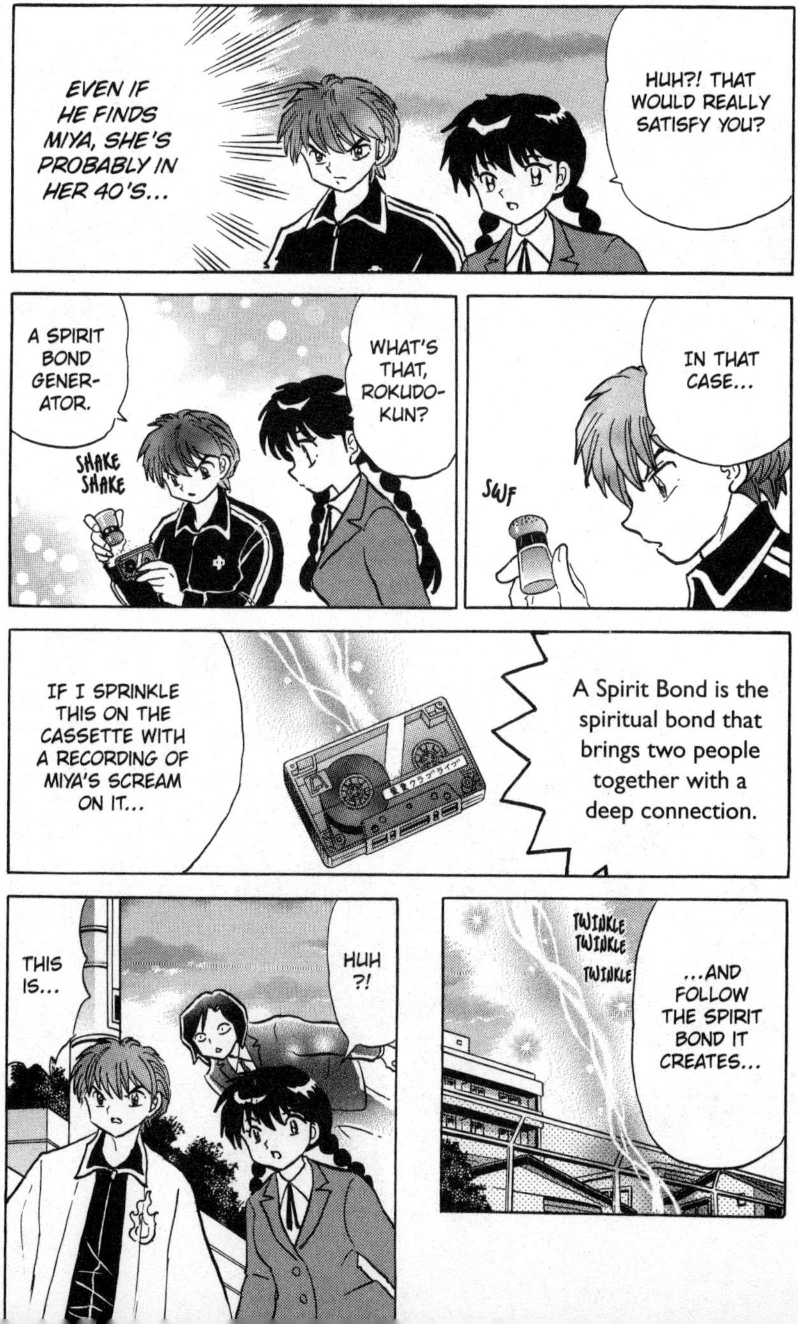
HUH?! THAT WOULD REALLY SATISFY YOU?
EVEN IF HE FINDS MIYA, SHE'S PROBABLY IN HER 40'S...
IN THAT CASE...
SWF
WHAT'S THAT, ROKUDO-KUN?
A SPIRIT BOND GENERATOR.
SHAKE SHAKE
A Spirit Bond is the spiritual bond that brings two people together with a deep connection.
IF I SPRINKLE THIS ON THE CASSETTE WITH A RECORDING OF MIYA'S SCREAM ON IT...
TWINKLE TWINKLE
TWINKLE
...AND FOLLOW THE SPIRIT BOND IT CREATES...
HUH ?!
THIS IS...

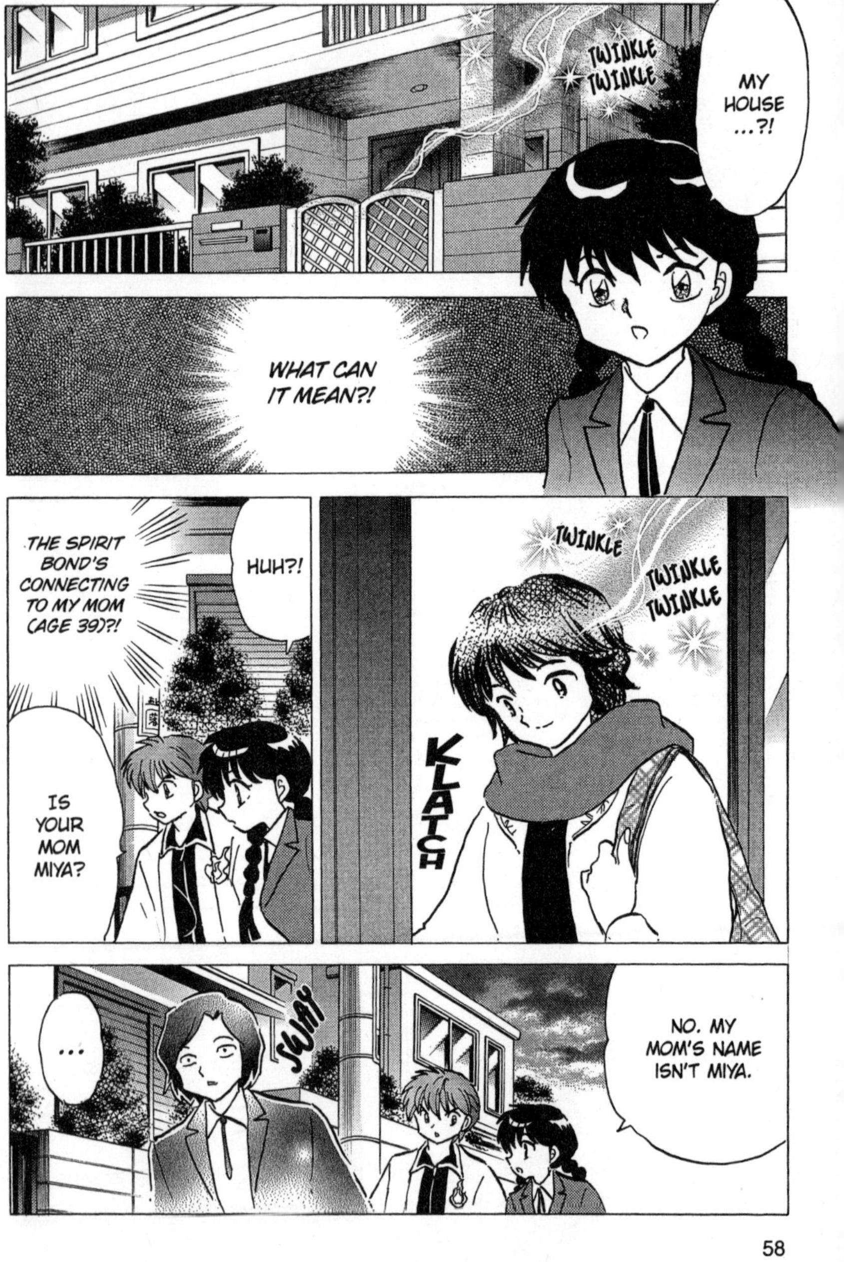
MY HOUSE ...?!
TWINKLE TWINKLE
WHAT CAN IT MEAN?!
TWINKLE
TWINKLE TWINKLE
KLATCH
HUH?!
THE SPIRIT BOND'S CONNECTING TO MY MOM (AGE 39)?!
IS YOUR MOM MIYA?
NO. MY MOM'S NAME ISN'T MIYA.
SWAY
...

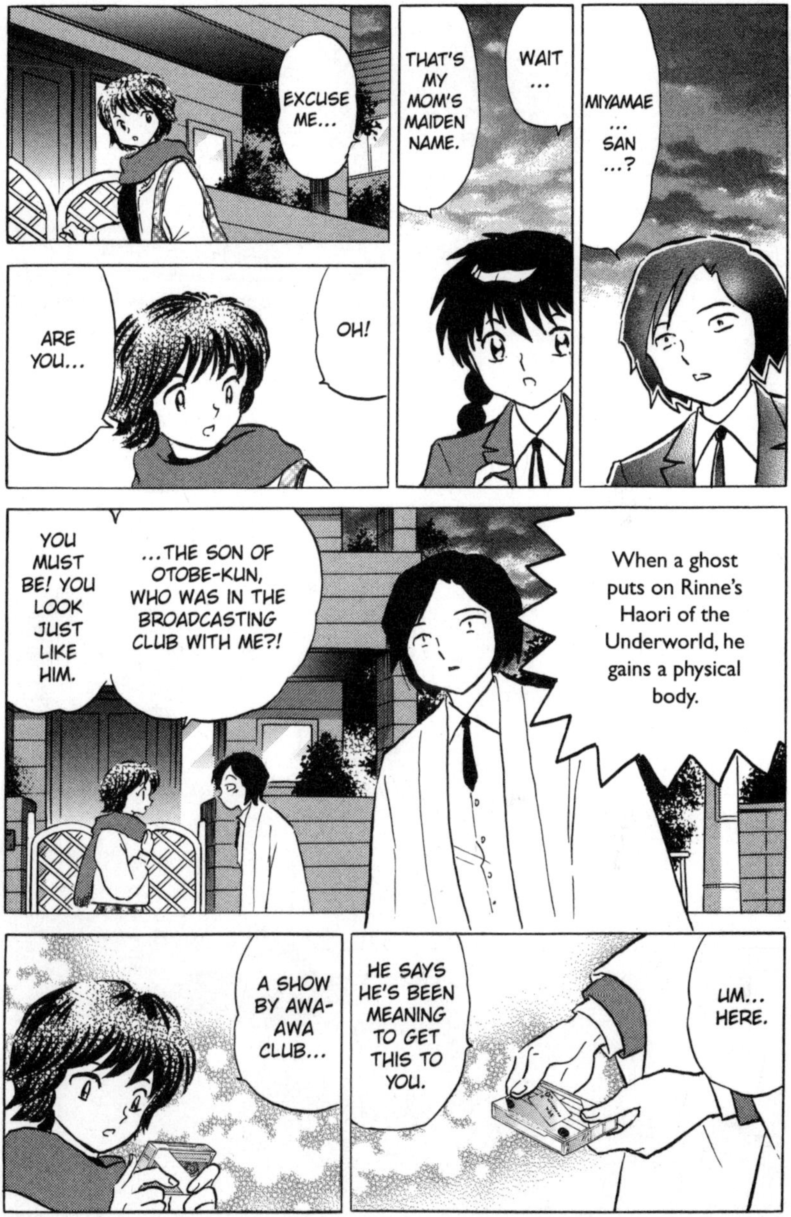
MIYAMAE ... SAN ...?
WAIT ...
THAT'S MY MOM'S MAIDEN NAME.
EXCUSE ME...
OH!
ARE YOU...
When a ghost puts on Rinne's Haori of the Underworld, he gains a physical body.
...THE SON OF OTOBE-KUN, WHO WAS IN THE BROADCASTING CLUB WITH ME?!
YOU MUST BE! YOU LOOK JUST LIKE HIM.
UM... HERE.
HE SAYS HE'S BEEN MEANING TO GET THIS TO YOU.
A SHOW BY AWA-AWA CLUB...

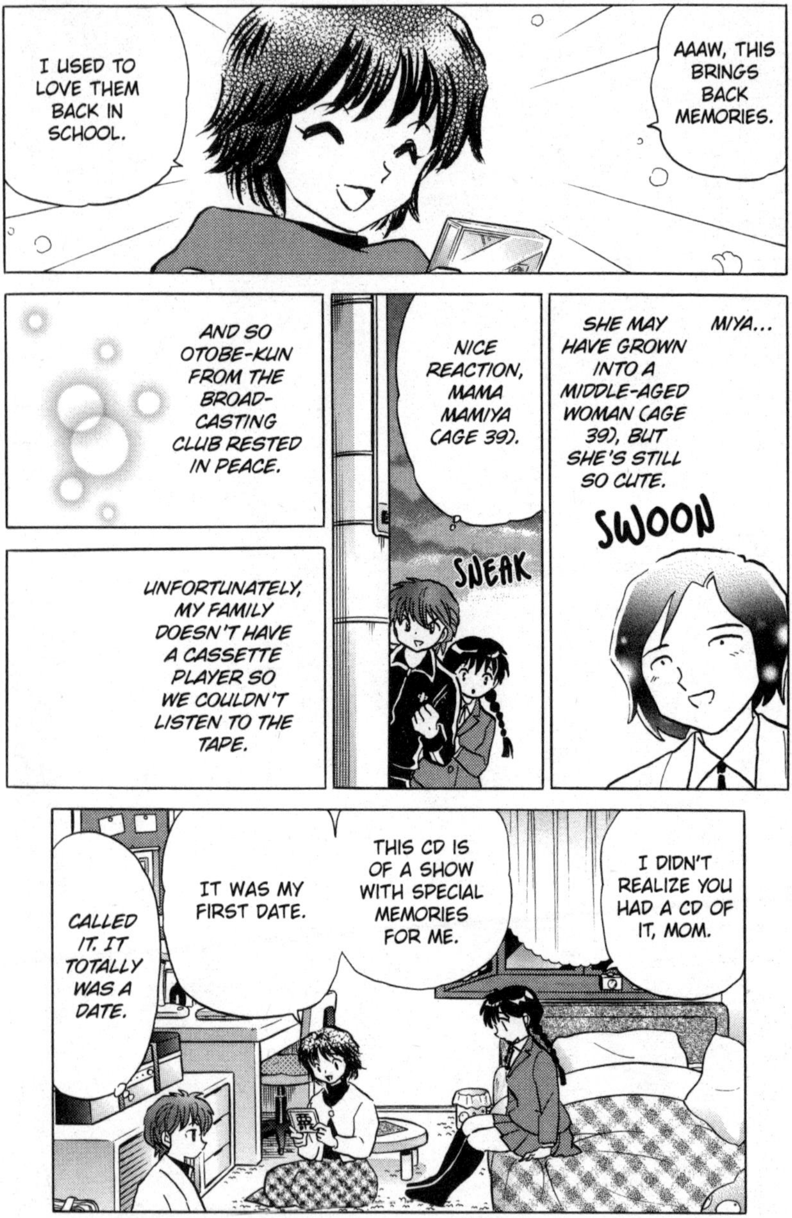
AAAW, THIS BRINGS BACK MEMORIES.
I USED TO LOVE THEM BACK IN SCHOOL.
MIYA...
SHE MAY HAVE GROWN INTO A MIDDLE-AGED WOMAN (AGE 39), BUT SHE'S STILL SO CUTE.
SWOON
NICE REACTION, MAMA MAMIYA (AGE 39).
SNEAK
AND SO OTOBE-KUN FROM THE BROAD-CASTING CLUB RESTED IN PEACE.
UNFORTUNATELY, MY FAMILY DOESN'T HAVE A CASSETTE PLAYER SO WE COULDN'T LISTEN TO THE TAPE.
I DIDN'T REALIZE YOU HAD A CD OF IT, MOM.
THIS CD IS OF A SHOW WITH SPECIAL MEMORIES FOR ME.
IT WAS MY FIRST DATE.
CALLED IT. IT TOTALLY WAS A DATE.

CHAPTER 262: COLD ROOM

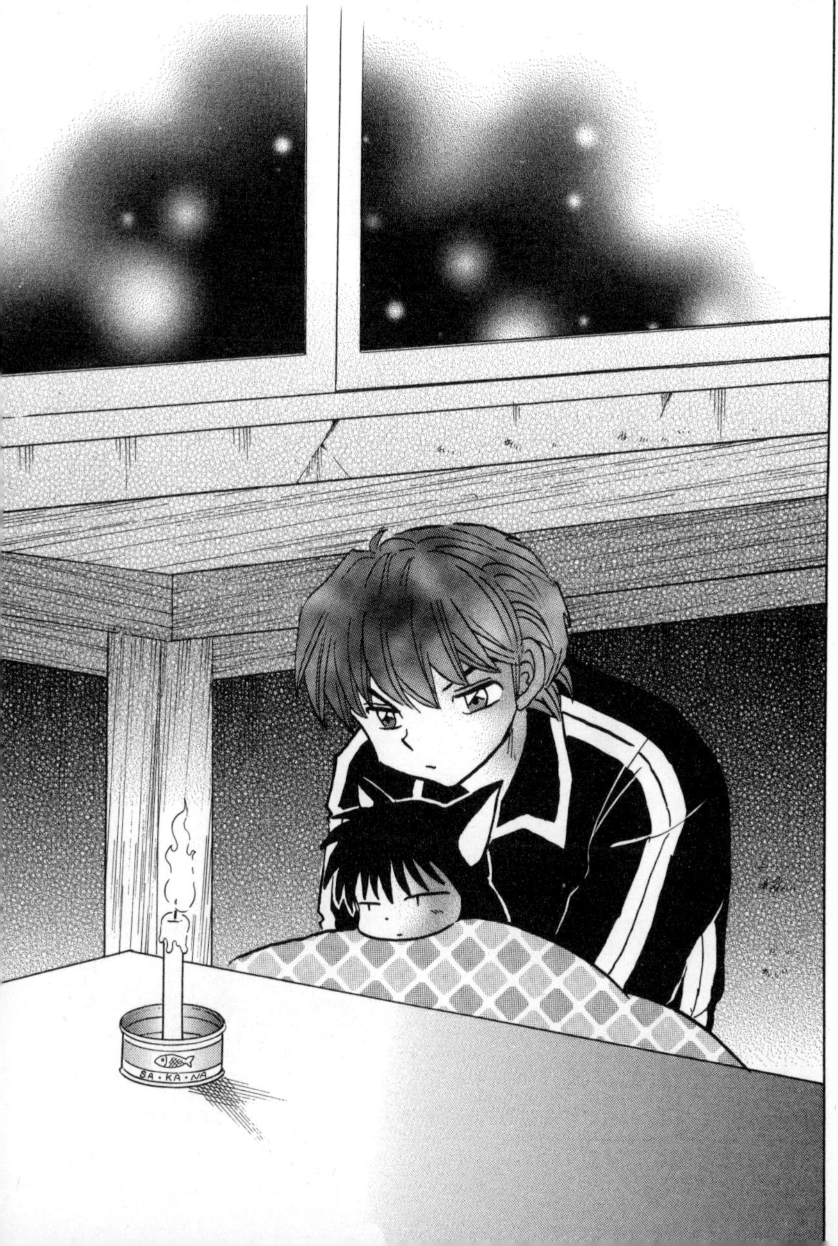
SA · KA · NA

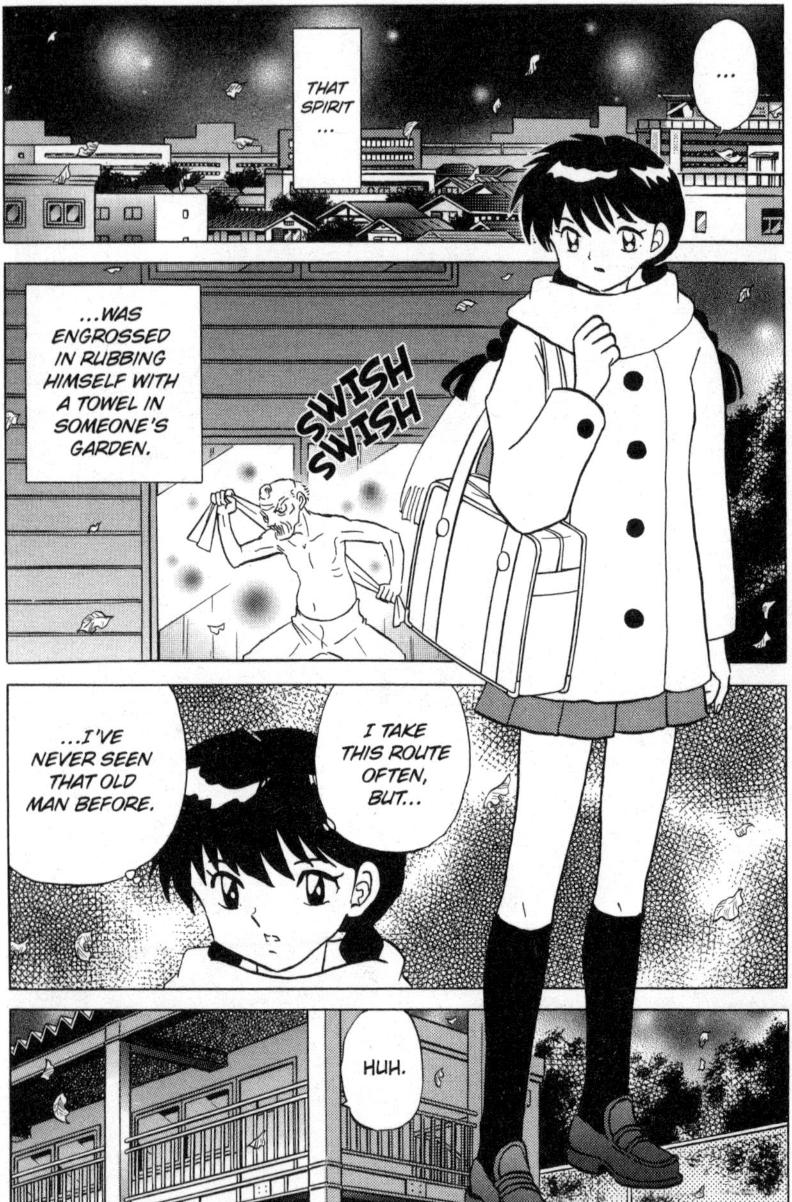
...
THAT SPIRIT ...
...WAS ENGROSSED IN RUBBING HIMSELF WITH A TOWEL IN SOMEONE'S GARDEN.
SWISH SWISH
I TAKE THIS ROUTE OFTEN, BUT...
...I'VE NEVER SEEN THAT OLD MAN BEFORE.
HUH.

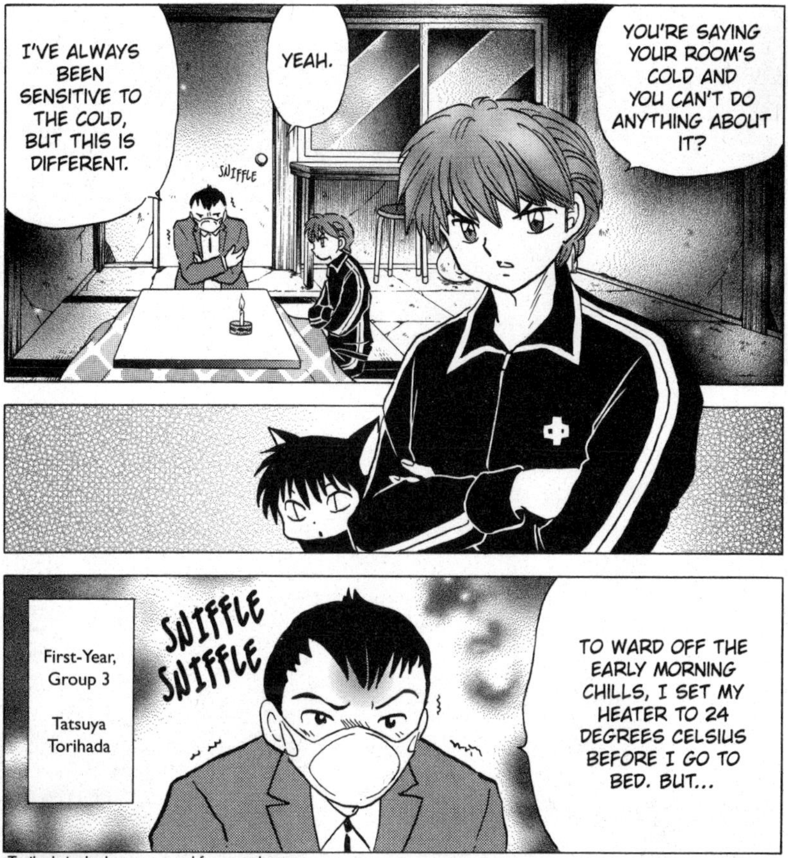
YOU'RE SAYING YOUR ROOM'S COLD AND YOU CAN'T DO ANYTHING ABOUT IT?
YEAH.
I'VE ALWAYS BEEN SENSITIVE TO THE COLD, BUT THIS IS DIFFERENT.
SNIFFLE
TO WARD OFF THE EARLY MORNING CHILLS, I SET MY HEATER TO 24 DEGREES CELSIUS BEFORE I GO TO BED. BUT...
First-Year, Group 3
Tatsuya Torihada
SNIFFLE SNIFFLE

Torihada is the Japanese word for goosebumps.

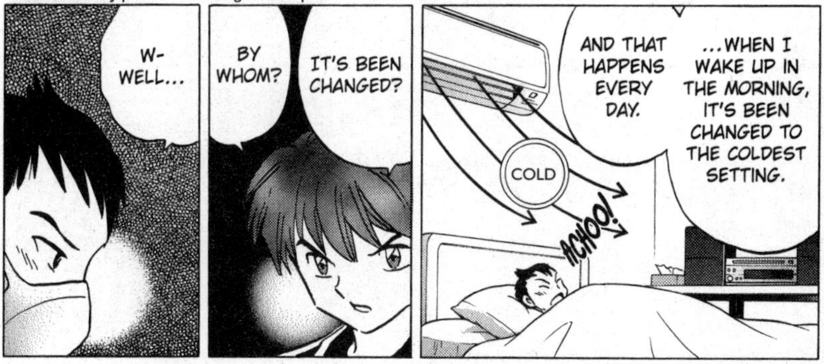
...WHEN I WAKE UP IN THE MORNING, IT'S BEEN CHANGED TO THE COLDEST SETTING.
AND THAT HAPPENS EVERY DAY.
COLD
ACHOO!
IT'S BEEN CHANGED?
BY WHOM?
W-WELL...

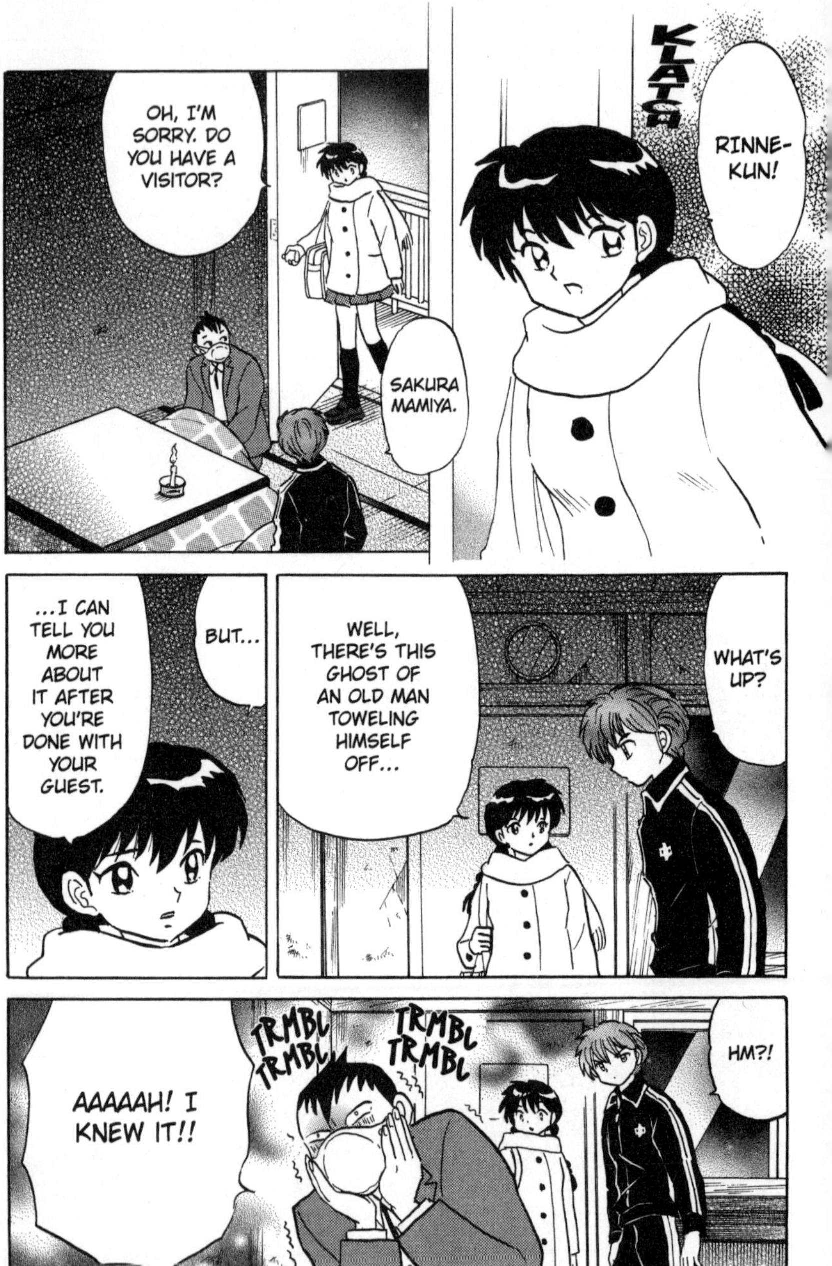
KLATCH
RINNE-KUN!
OH, I'M SORRY. DO YOU HAVE A VISITOR?
SAKURA MAMIYA.
WHAT'S UP?
WELL, THERE'S THIS GHOST OF AN OLD MAN TOWELING HIMSELF OFF...
BUT...
...I CAN TELL YOU MORE ABOUT IT AFTER YOU'RE DONE WITH YOUR GUEST.
HM?!
TRMBL TRMBL
TRMBL TRMBL
AAAAAH! I KNEW IT!!

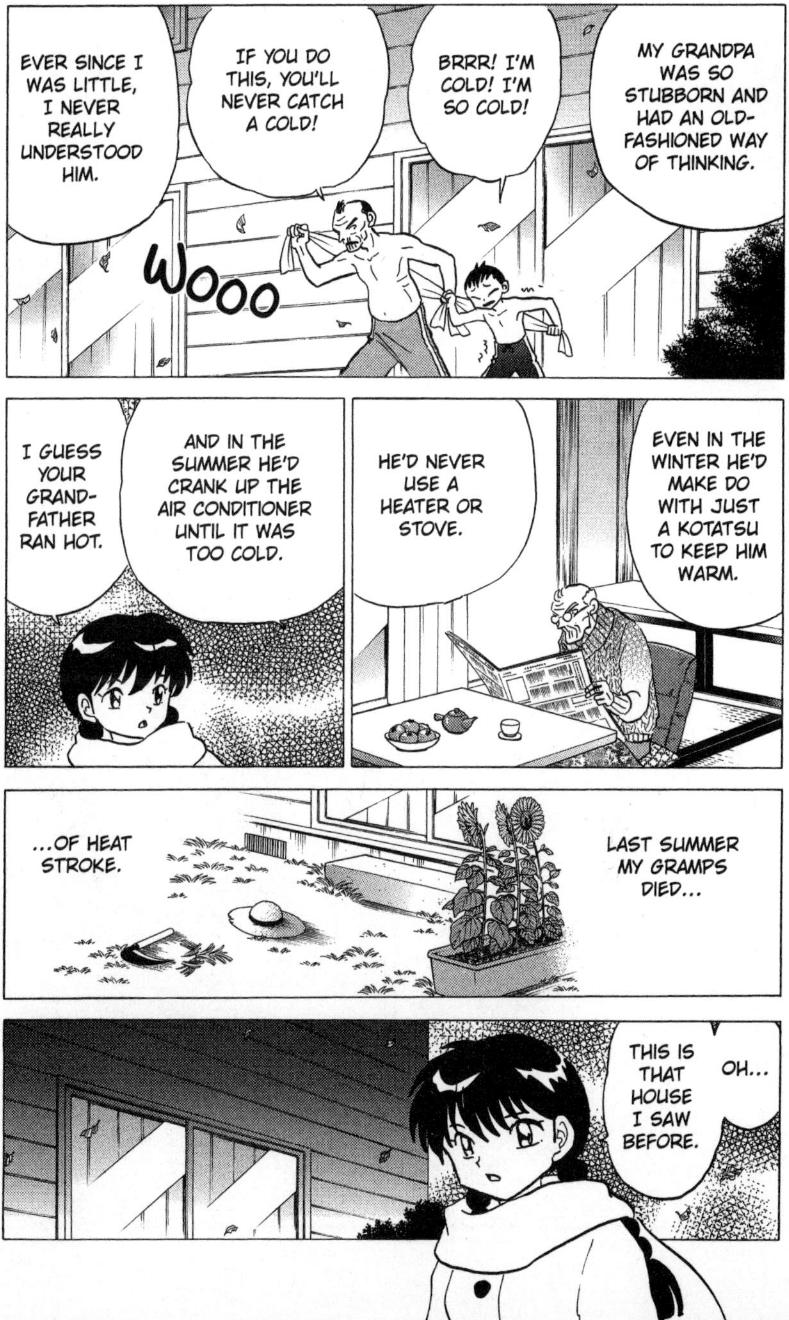
MY GRANDPA WAS SO STUBBORN AND HAD AN OLD-FASHIONED WAY OF THINKING.
BRRR! I'M COLD! I'M SO COLD!
IF YOU DO THIS, YOU'LL NEVER CATCH A COLD!
EVER SINCE I WAS LITTLE, I NEVER REALLY UNDERSTOOD HIM.
WOOO
EVEN IN THE WINTER HE'D MAKE DO WITH JUST A KOTATSU TO KEEP HIM WARM.
HE'D NEVER USE A HEATER OR STOVE.
AND IN THE SUMMER HE'D CRANK UP THE AIR CONDITIONER UNTIL IT WAS TOO COLD.
I GUESS YOUR GRANDFATHER RAN HOT.
LAST SUMMER MY GRAMPS DIED...
...OF HEAT STROKE.
OH...
THIS IS THAT HOUSE I SAW BEFORE.

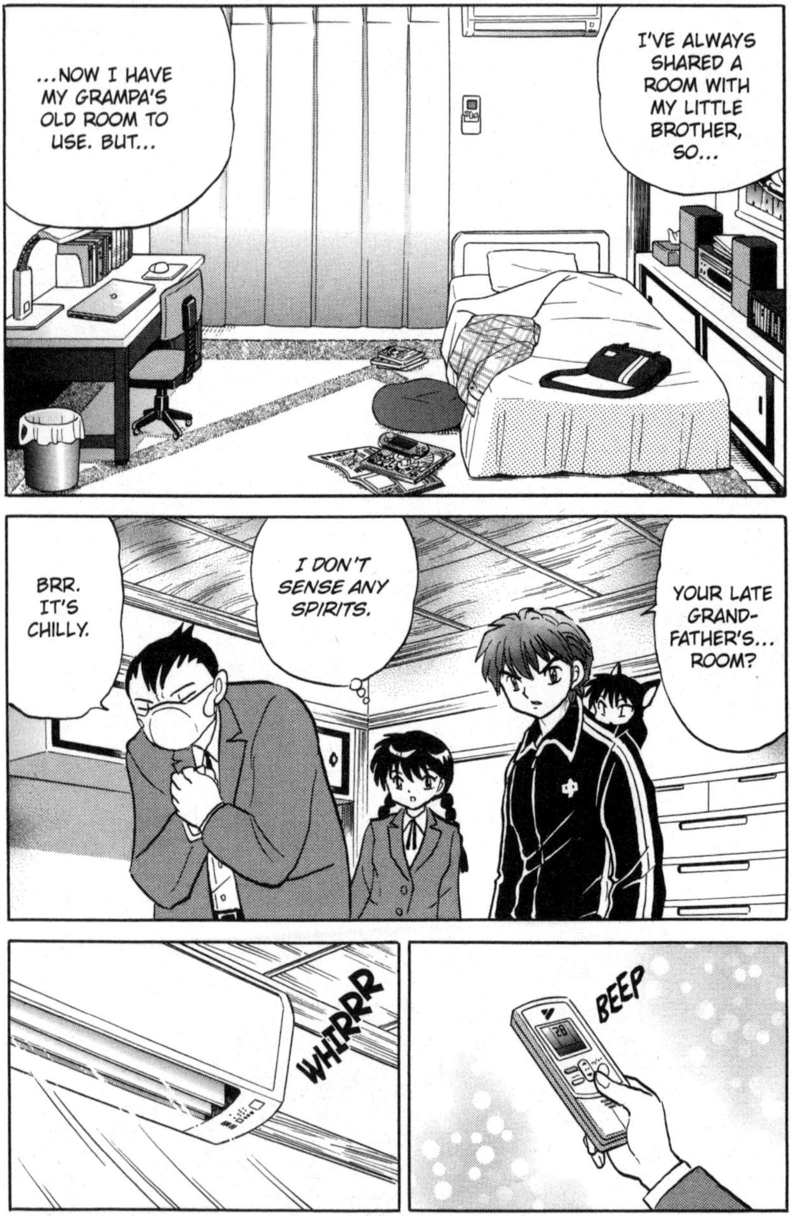
I'VE ALWAYS SHARED A ROOM WITH MY LITTLE BROTHER, SO...
...NOW I HAVE MY GRAMPA'S OLD ROOM TO USE. BUT...
YOUR LATE GRAND-FATHER'S... ROOM?
I DON'T SENSE ANY SPIRITS.
BRR. IT'S CHILLY.
BEEP
WHIRRR

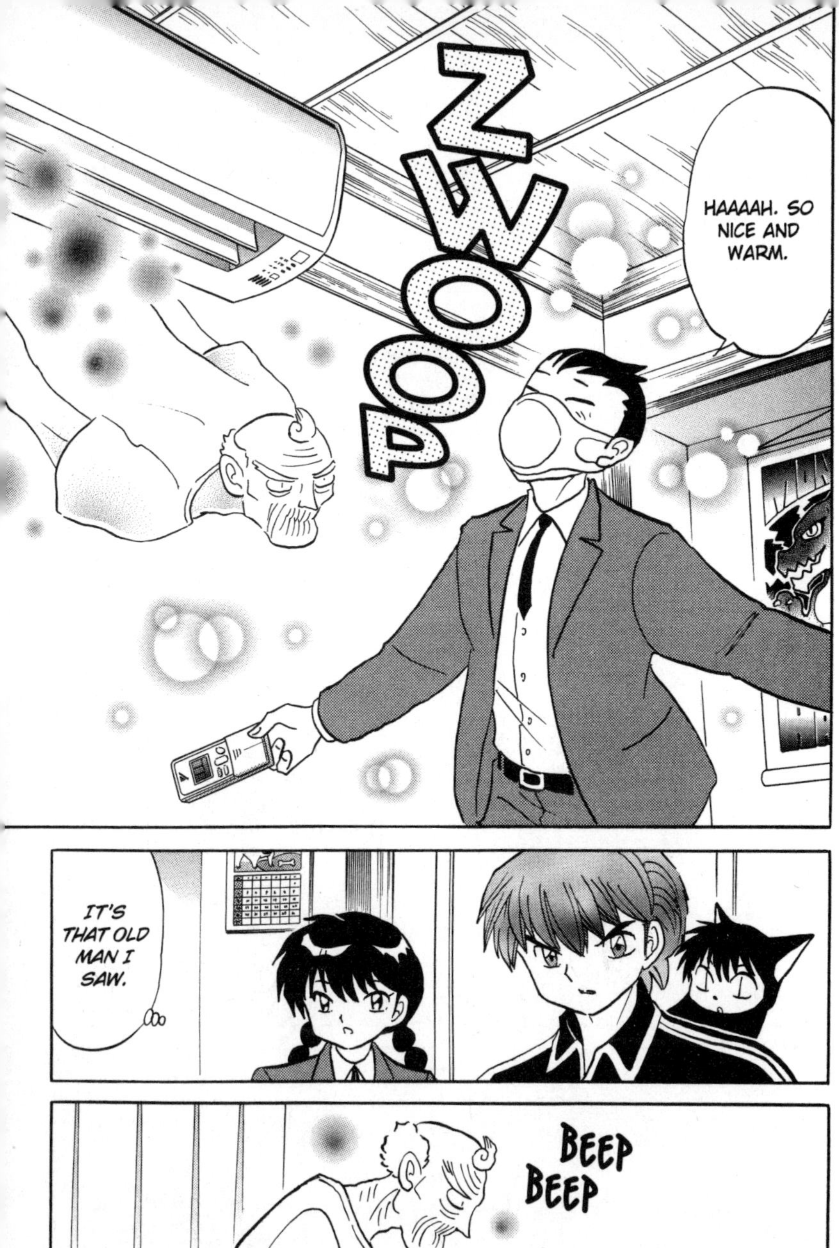
HAAAAH. SO NICE AND WARM.
PWOOZ
IT'S THAT OLD MAN I SAW.
BEEP BEEP

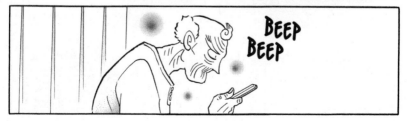

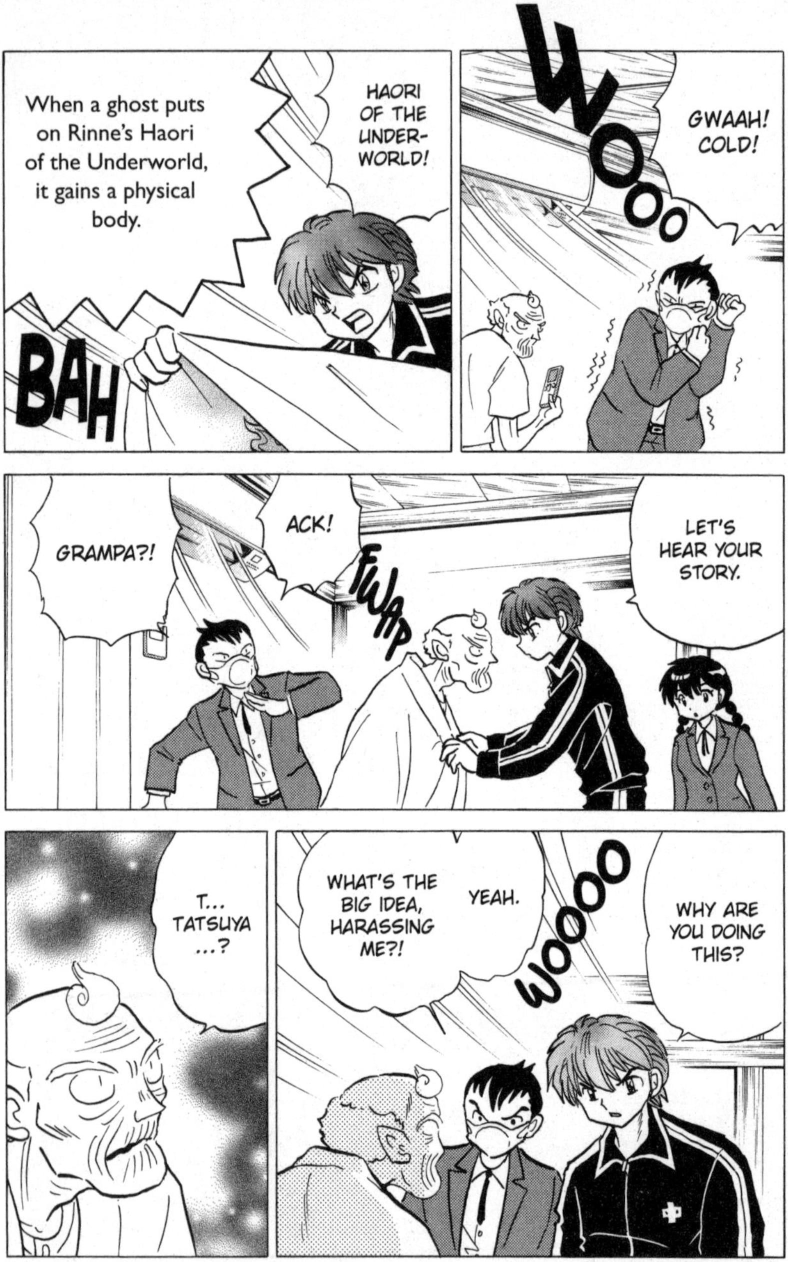
WOOO
GWAAH! COLD!
HAORI OF THE UNDER-WORLD!
When a ghost puts on Rinne's Haori of the Underworld, it gains a physical body.
BAH
LET'S HEAR YOUR STORY.
FWAP
ACK!
GRAMPA?!
WHY ARE YOU DOING THIS?
WOOOO
YEAH.
WHAT'S THE BIG IDEA, HARASSING ME?!
T... TATSUYA ...?

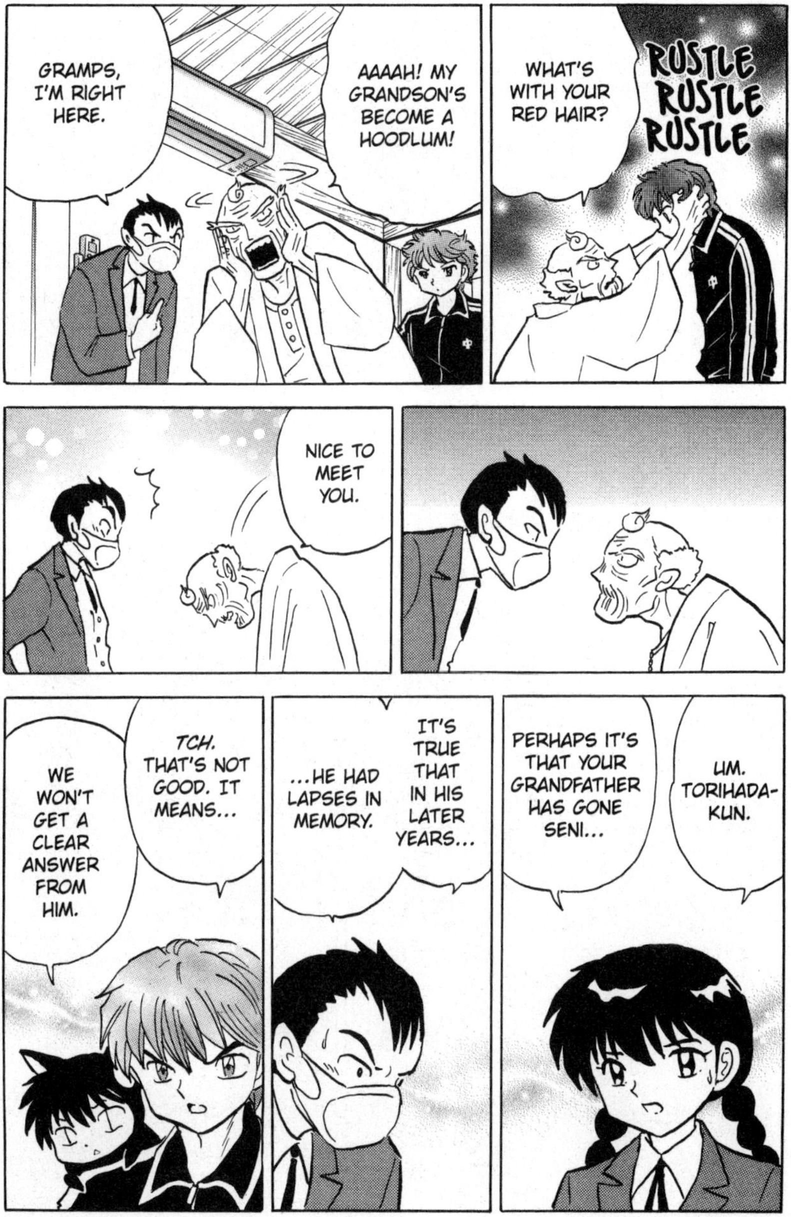
RUSTLE RUSTLE RUSTLE
WHAT'S WITH YOUR RED HAIR?
AAAAH! MY GRANDSON'S BECOME A HOODLUM!
GRAMPS, I'M RIGHT HERE.
NICE TO MEET YOU.
UM. TORIHADA-KUN.
PERHAPS IT'S THAT YOUR GRANDFATHER HAS GONE SENI...
IT'S TRUE THAT IN HIS LATER YEARS...
...HE HAD LAPSES IN MEMORY.
TCH. THAT'S NOT GOOD. IT MEANS...
WE WON'T GET A CLEAR ANSWER FROM HIM.

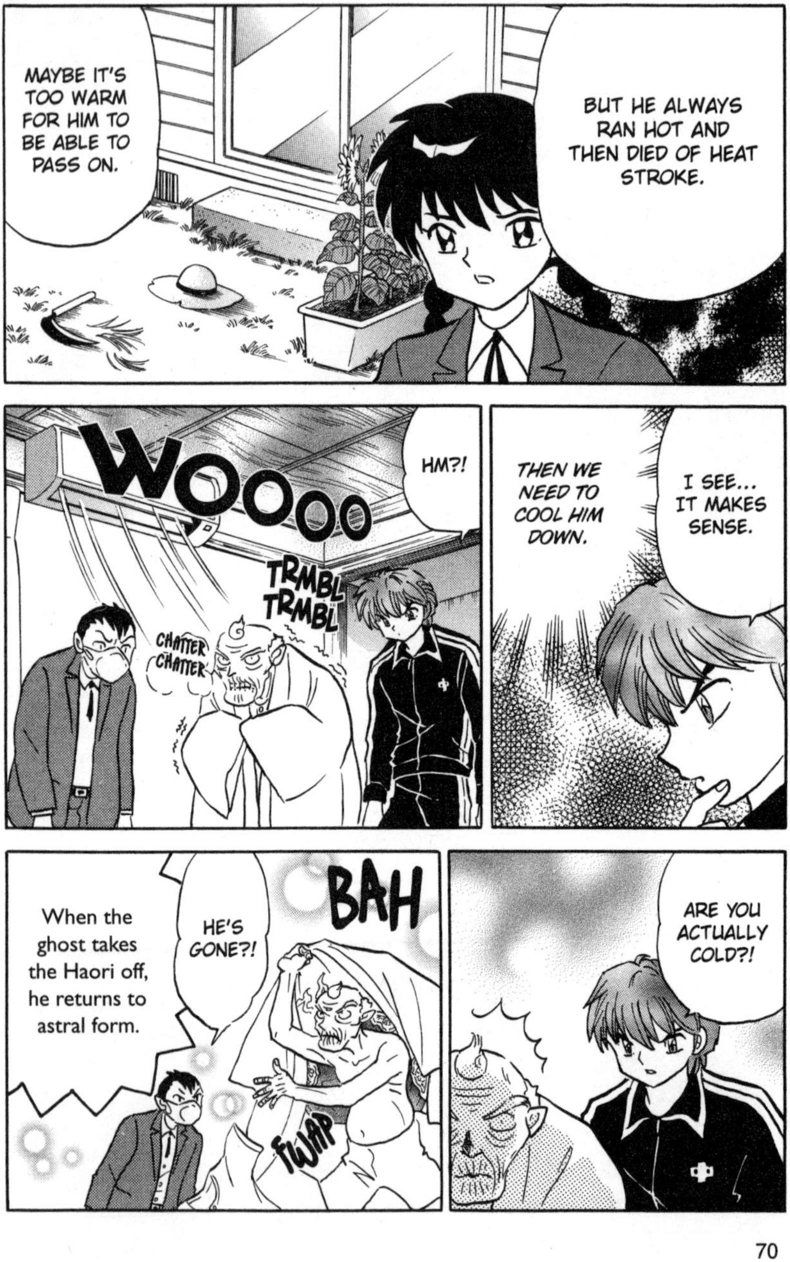
BUT HE ALWAYS RAN HOT AND THEN DIED OF HEAT STROKE.
MAYBE IT'S TOO WARM FOR HIM TO BE ABLE TO PASS ON.
I SEE... IT MAKES SENSE.
THEN WE NEED TO COOL HIM DOWN.
HM?!
WOOOO
TRMBL TRMBL
CHATTER CHATTER
ARE YOU ACTUALLY COLD?!
BAH
HE'S GONE?!
When the ghost takes the Haori off, he returns to astral form.
FWAP

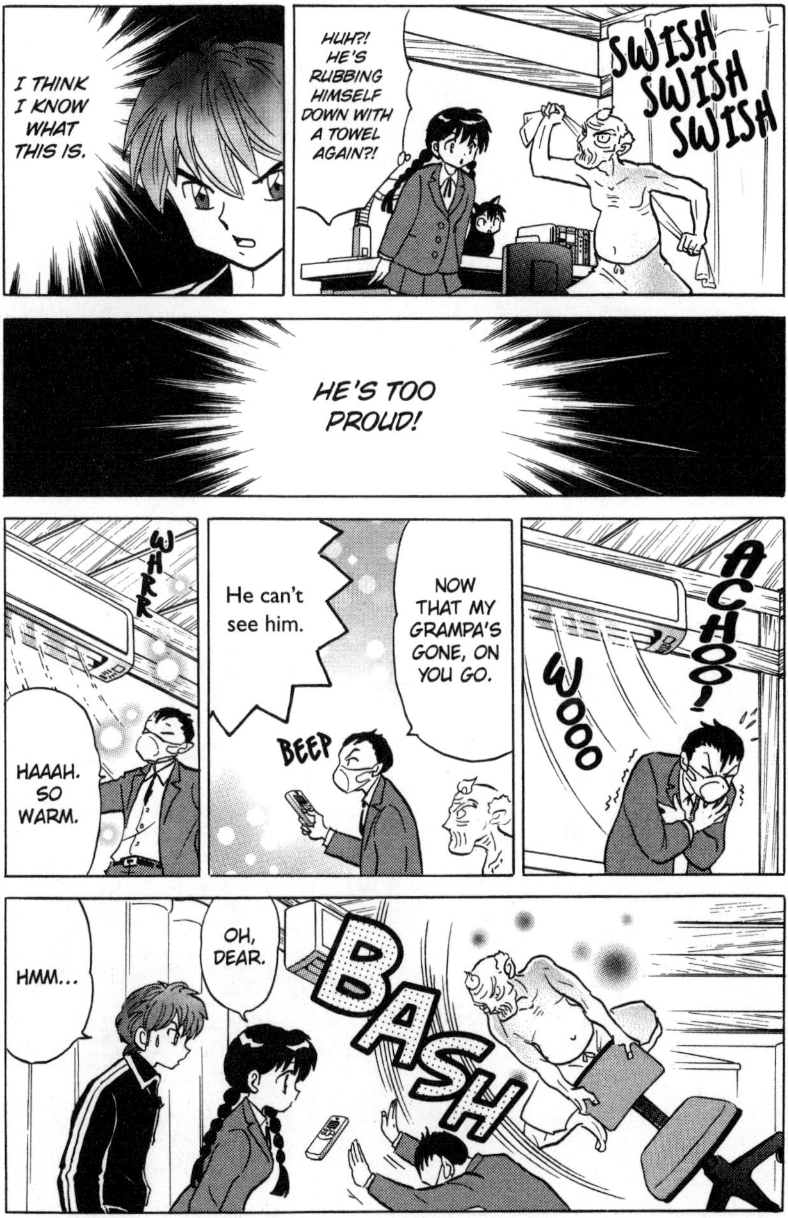
SWISH SWISH SWISH
HUH?! HE'S RUBBING HIMSELF DOWN WITH A TOWEL AGAIN?!
I THINK I KNOW WHAT THIS IS.
HE'S TOO PROUD!
ACHOO!
WOOO
NOW THAT MY GRAMPA'S GONE, ON YOU GO.
He can't see him.
BEEP
WHRR
HAAAH. SO WARM.
BASH
OH, DEAR.
HMM...

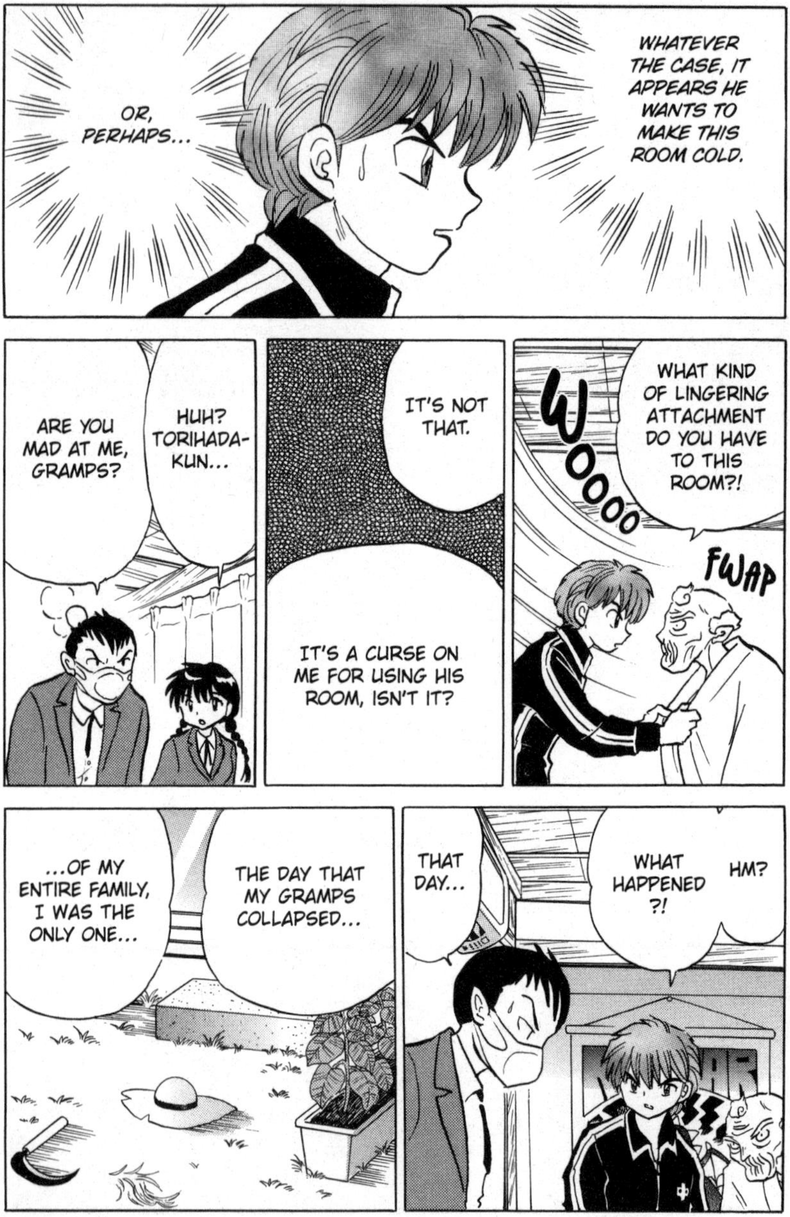
WHATEVER THE CASE, IT APPEARS HE WANTS TO MAKE THIS ROOM COLD.
OR, PERHAPS...
WHAT KIND OF LINGERING ATTACHMENT DO YOU HAVE TO THIS ROOM?!
WOOOOO
FWAP
IT'S NOT THAT.
IT'S A CURSE ON ME FOR USING HIS ROOM, ISN'T IT?
HUH? TORIHADA-KUN...
ARE YOU MAD AT ME, GRAMPS?
HM?
WHAT HAPPENED ?!
THAT DAY...
THE DAY THAT MY GRAMPS COLLAPSED...
...OF MY ENTIRE FAMILY, I WAS THE ONLY ONE...

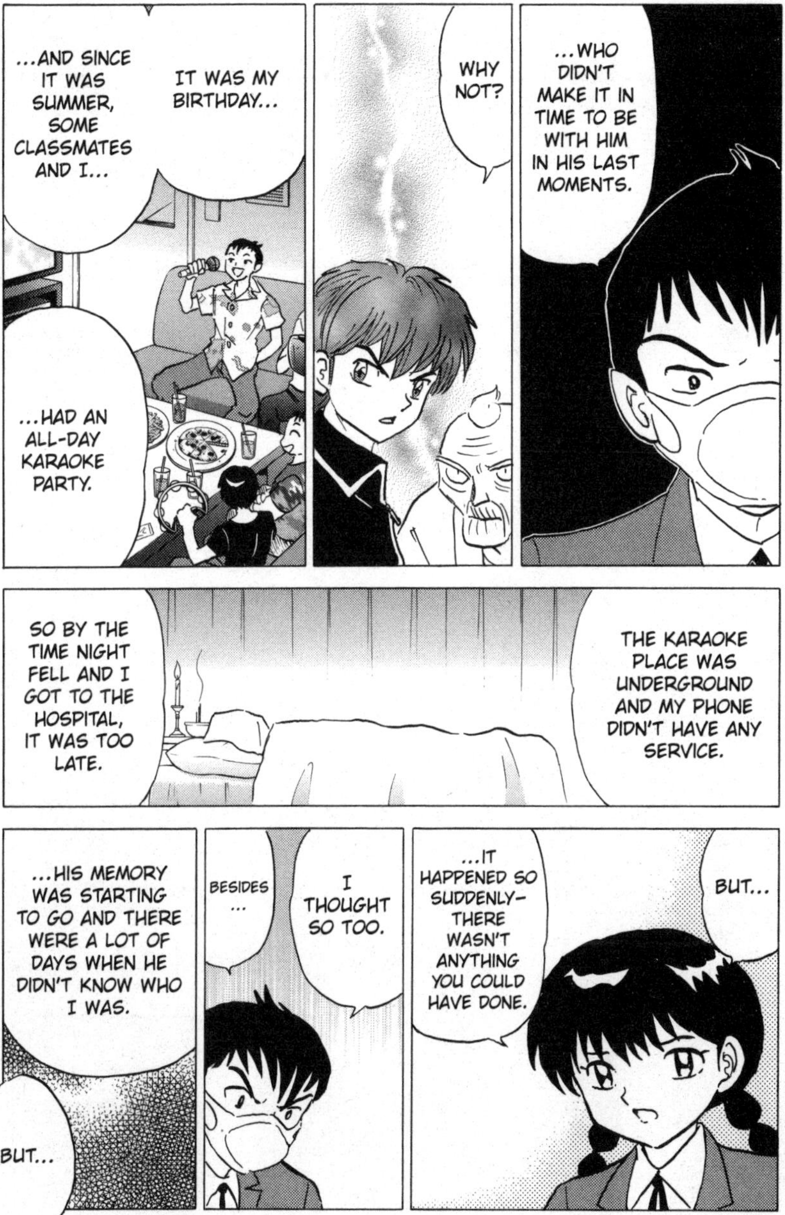
...WHO DIDN'T MAKE IT IN TIME TO BE WITH HIM IN HIS LAST MOMENTS.
WHY NOT?
IT WAS MY BIRTHDAY...
...AND SINCE IT WAS SUMMER, SOME CLASSMATES AND I...
...HAD AN ALL-DAY KARAOKE PARTY.
THE KARAOKE PLACE WAS UNDERGROUND AND MY PHONE DIDN'T HAVE ANY SERVICE.
SO BY THE TIME NIGHT FELL AND I GOT TO THE HOSPITAL, IT WAS TOO LATE.
BUT...
...IT HAPPENED SO SUDDENLY—THERE WASN'T ANYTHING YOU COULD HAVE DONE.
I THOUGHT SO TOO.
BESIDES...
...HIS MEMORY WAS STARTING TO GO AND THERE WERE A LOT OF DAYS WHEN HE DIDN'T KNOW WHO I WAS.
BUT...

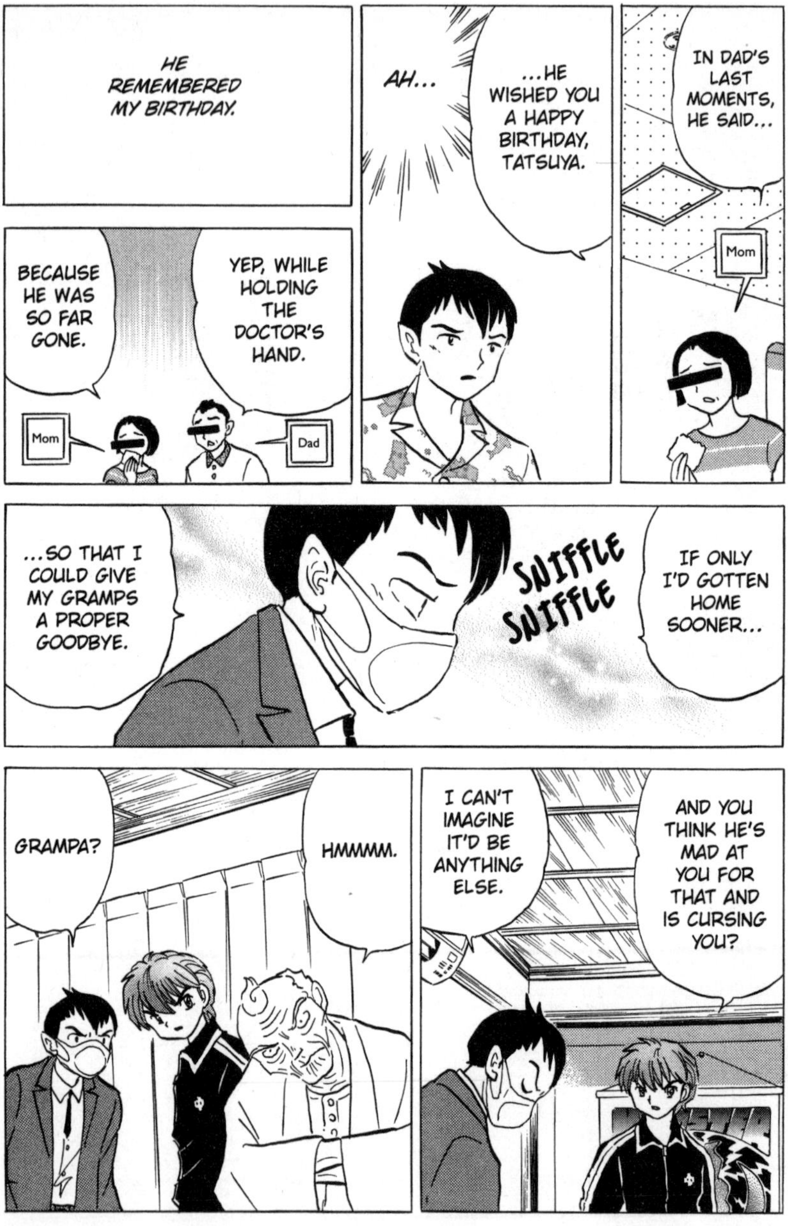
IN DAD'S LAST MOMENTS, HE SAID...
Mom
...HE WISHED YOU A HAPPY BIRTHDAY, TATSUYA.
AH...
HE REMEMBERED MY BIRTHDAY.
YEP, WHILE HOLDING THE DOCTOR'S HAND.
Dad
BECAUSE HE WAS SO FAR GONE.
Mom
IF ONLY I'D GOTTEN HOME SOONER...
SNIFFLE SNIFFLE
...SO THAT I COULD GIVE MY GRAMPS A PROPER GOODBYE.
AND YOU THINK HE'S MAD AT YOU FOR THAT AND IS CURSING YOU?
I CAN'T IMAGINE IT'D BE ANYTHING ELSE.
HMMMM.
GRAMPA?

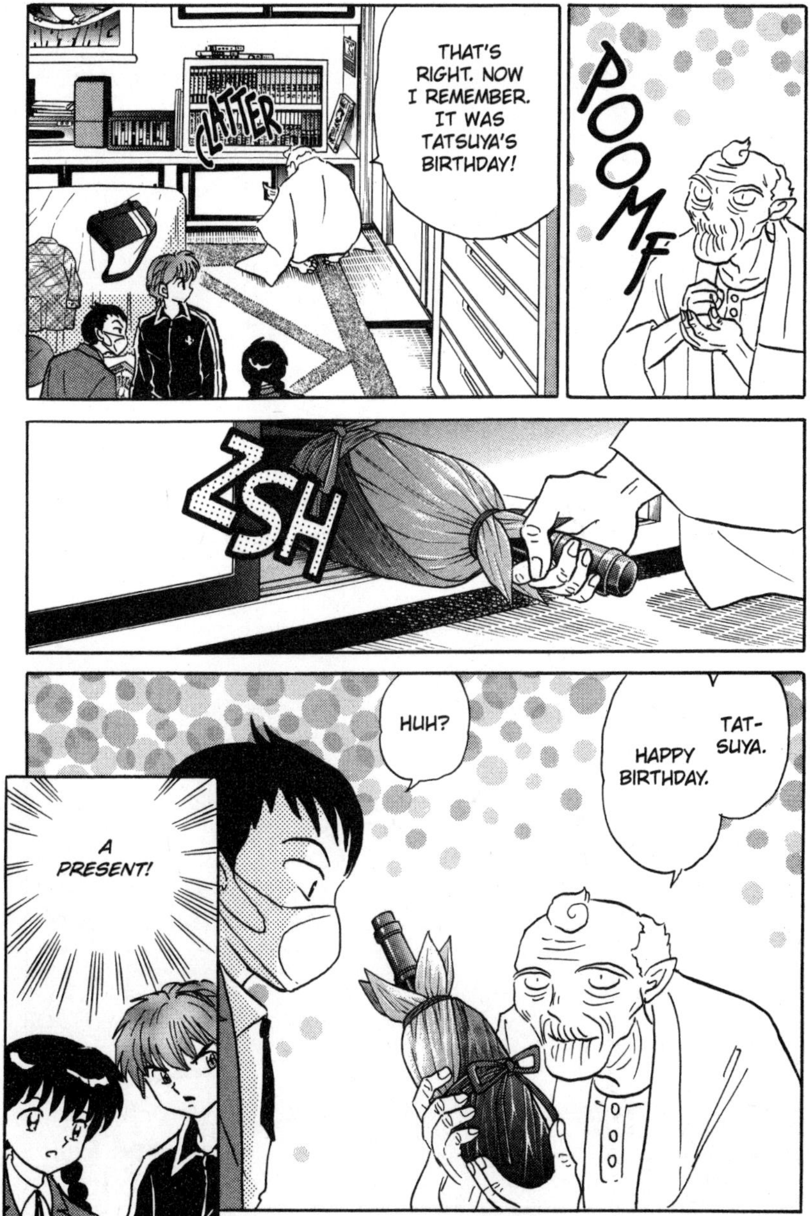
POOMF
THAT'S RIGHT. NOW I REMEMBER. IT WAS TATSUYA'S BIRTHDAY!
CLATTER
ZSH
TAT-SUYA.
HAPPY BIRTHDAY.
HUH?
A PRESENT!

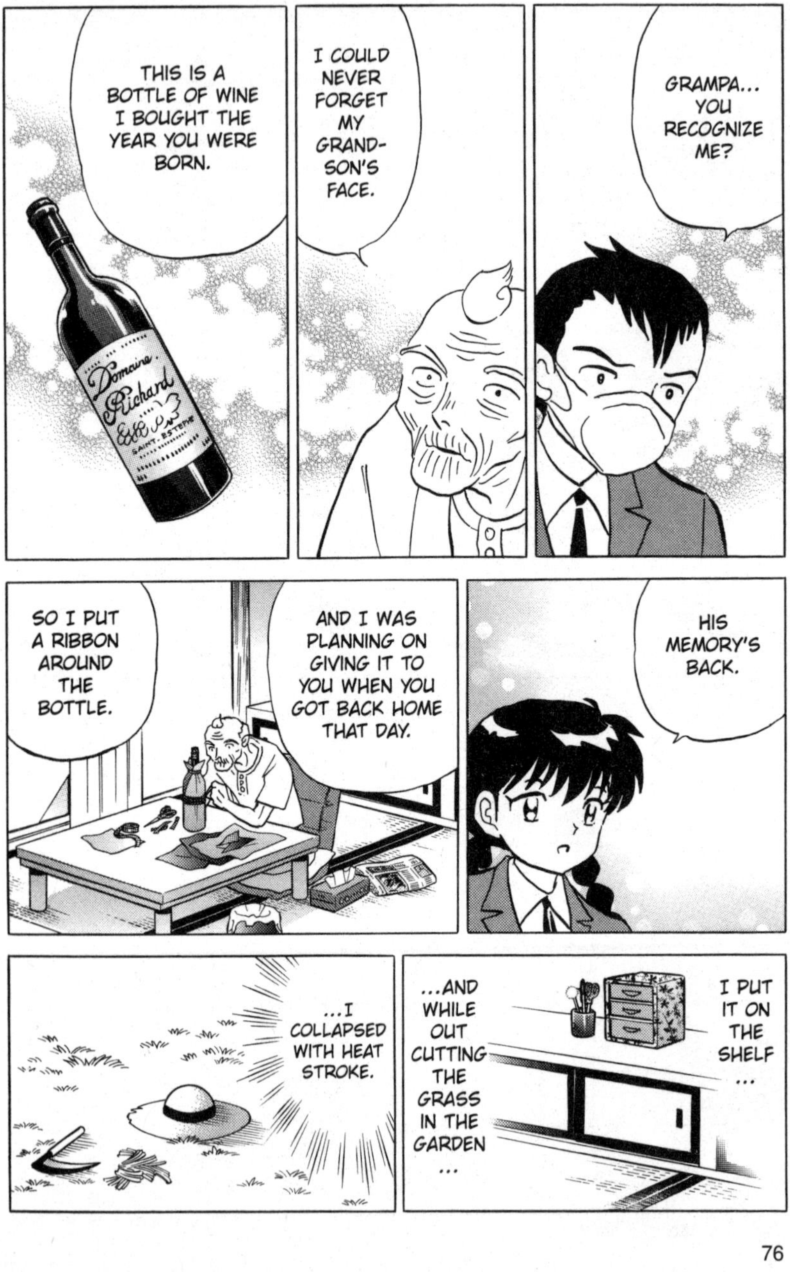
GRAMPA... YOU RECOGNIZE ME?
I COULD NEVER FORGET MY GRANDSON'S FACE.
THIS IS A BOTTLE OF WINE I BOUGHT THE YEAR YOU WERE BORN.
Domaine Richard
HIS MEMORY'S BACK.
AND I WAS PLANNING ON GIVING IT TO YOU WHEN YOU GOT BACK HOME THAT DAY.
SO I PUT A RIBBON AROUND THE BOTTLE.
I PUT IT ON THE SHELF...
...AND WHILE OUT CUTTING THE GRASS IN THE GARDEN...
...I COLLAPSED WITH HEAT STROKE.

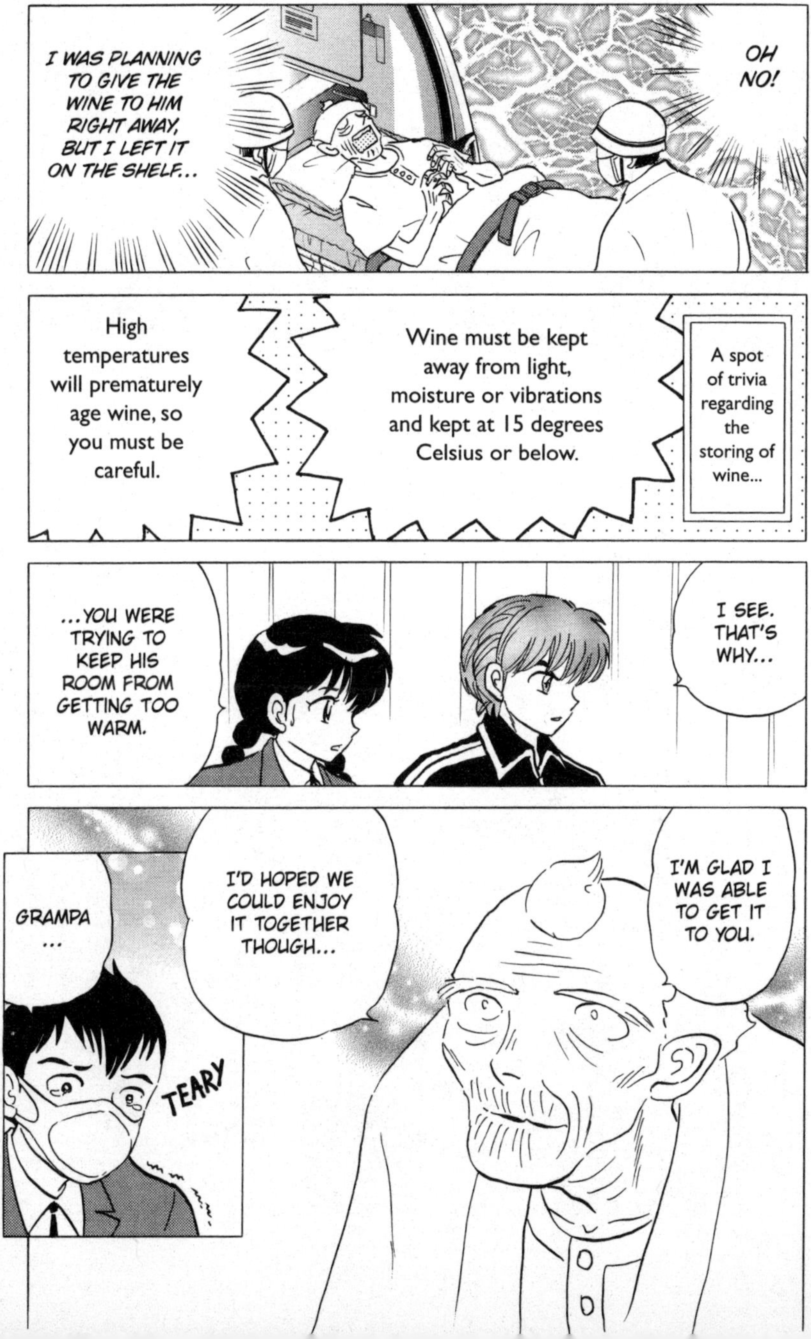
OH NO!
I WAS PLANNING TO GIVE THE WINE TO HIM RIGHT AWAY, BUT I LEFT IT ON THE SHELF...
A spot of trivia regarding the storing of wine...
Wine must be kept away from light, moisture or vibrations and kept at 15 degrees Celsius or below.
High temperatures will prematurely age wine, so you must be careful.
I SEE. THAT'S WHY...
...YOU WERE TRYING TO KEEP HIS ROOM FROM GETTING TOO WARM.
I'M GLAD I WAS ABLE TO GET IT TO YOU.
I'D HOPED WE COULD ENJOY IT TOGETHER THOUGH...
GRAMPA ...
TEARY

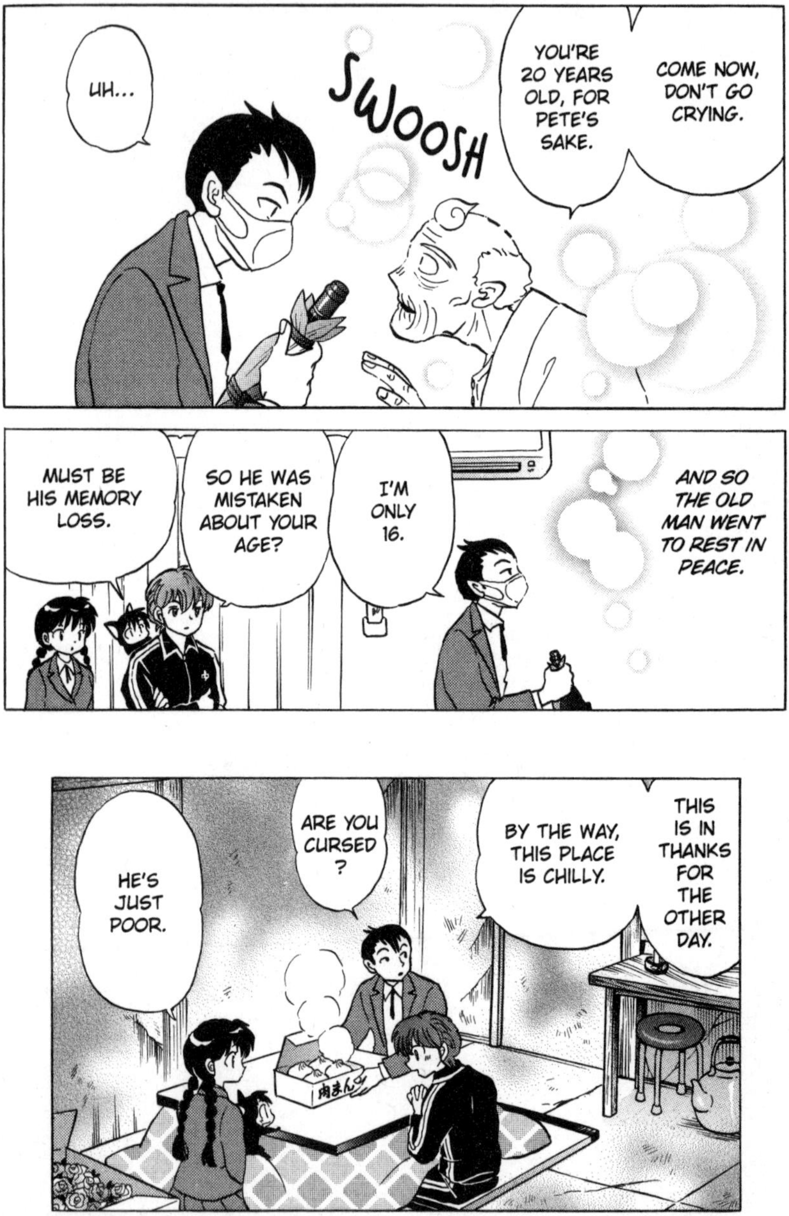
COME NOW, DON'T GO CRYING.
YOU'RE 20 YEARS OLD, FOR PETE'S SAKE.
SWOOSH
UH...
AND SO THE OLD MAN WENT TO REST IN PEACE.
I'M ONLY 16.
SO HE WAS MISTAKEN ABOUT YOUR AGE?
MUST BE HIS MEMORY LOSS.
THIS IS IN THANKS FOR THE OTHER DAY.
BY THE WAY, THIS PLACE IS CHILLY.
ARE YOU CURSED?
HE'S JUST POOR.
肉まん

CHAPTER 263: CRUNCHING

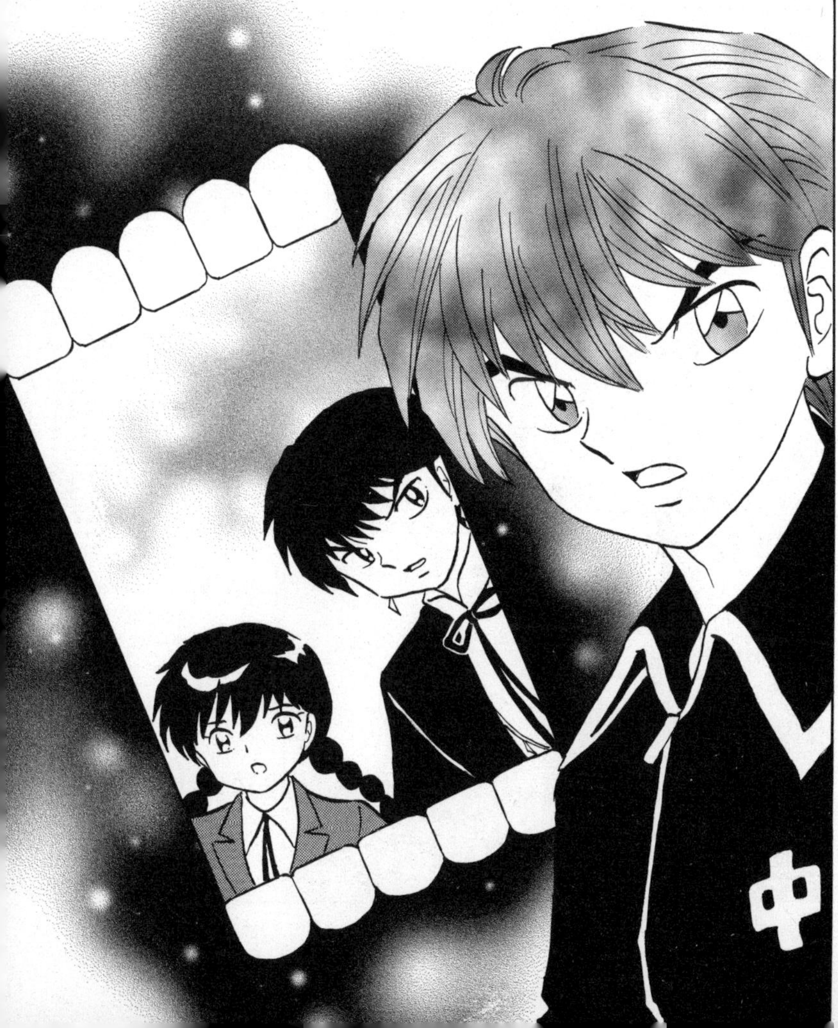
中

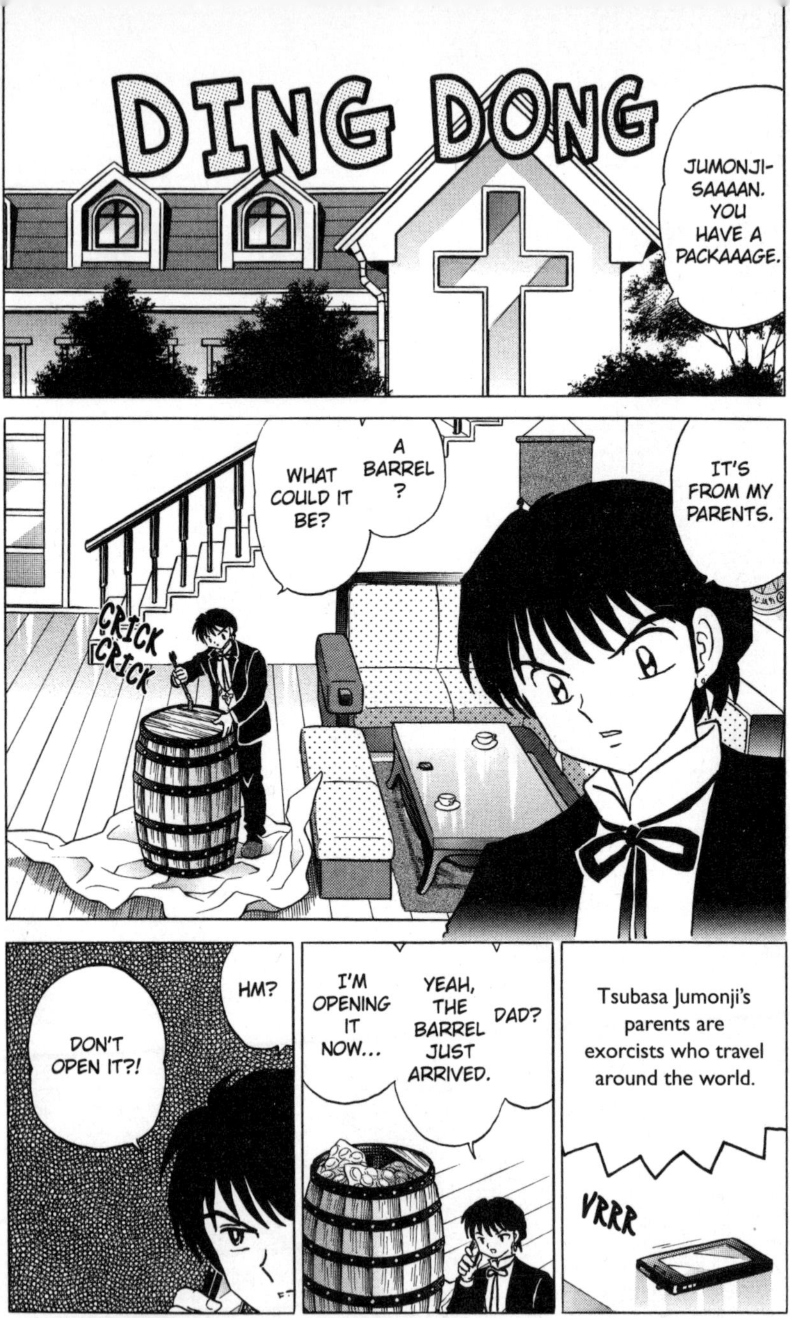
DING DONG
JUMONJI-SAAAAN. YOU HAVE A PACKAAAGE.
IT'S FROM MY PARENTS.
A BARREL?
WHAT COULD IT BE?
CRICK CRICK
Tsubasa Jumonji's parents are exorcists who travel around the world.
VRRR
DAD?
YEAH, THE BARREL JUST ARRIVED.
I'M OPENING IT NOW...
HM?
DON'T OPEN IT?!

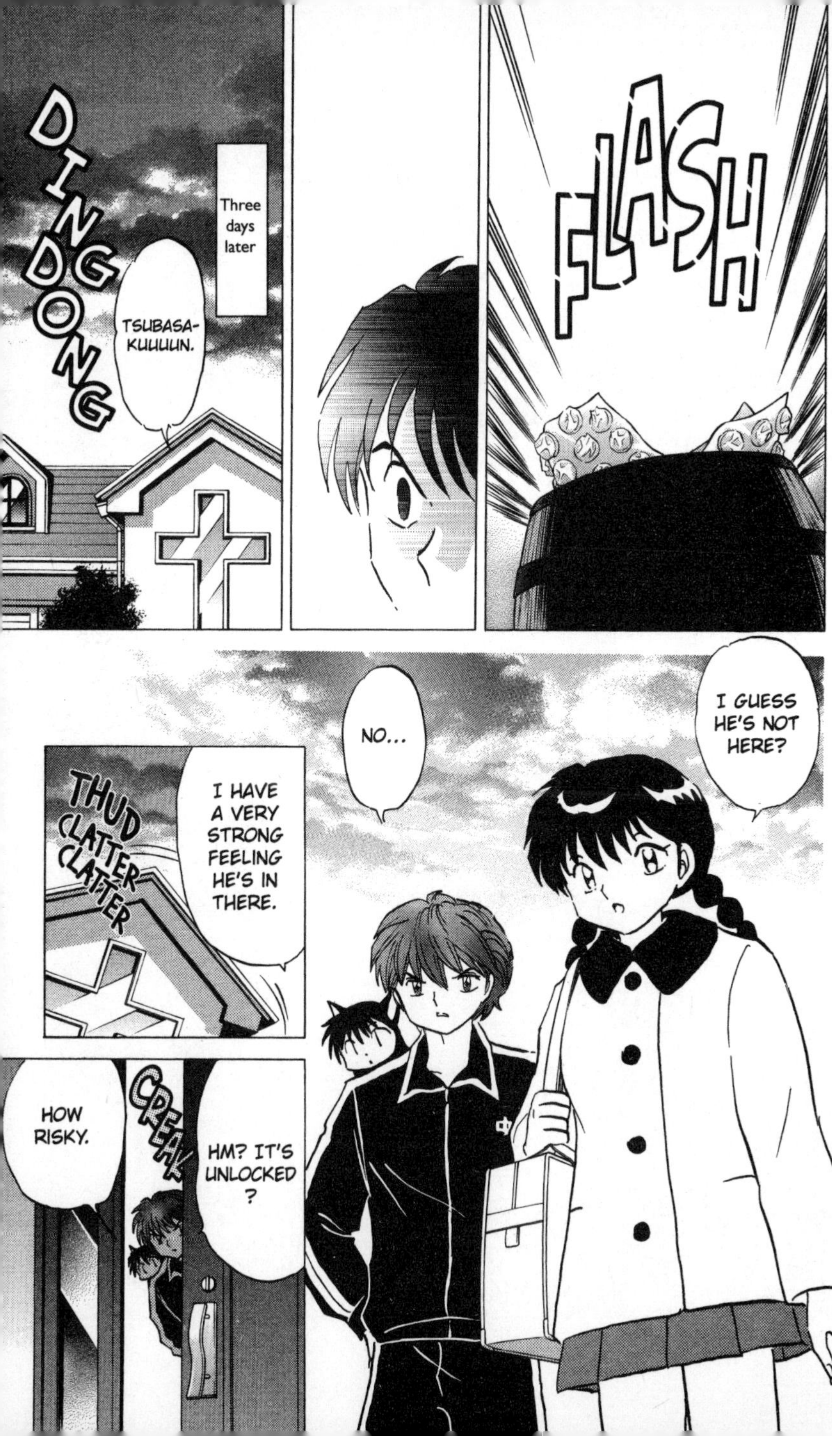
FLASH
Three days later
DING DONG
TSUBASA-KUUUUN.
I GUESS HE'S NOT HERE?
NO...
I HAVE A VERY STRONG FEELING HE'S IN THERE.
THUD
CLATTER CLATTER
CREAK
HM? IT'S UNLOCKED?
HOW RISKY.

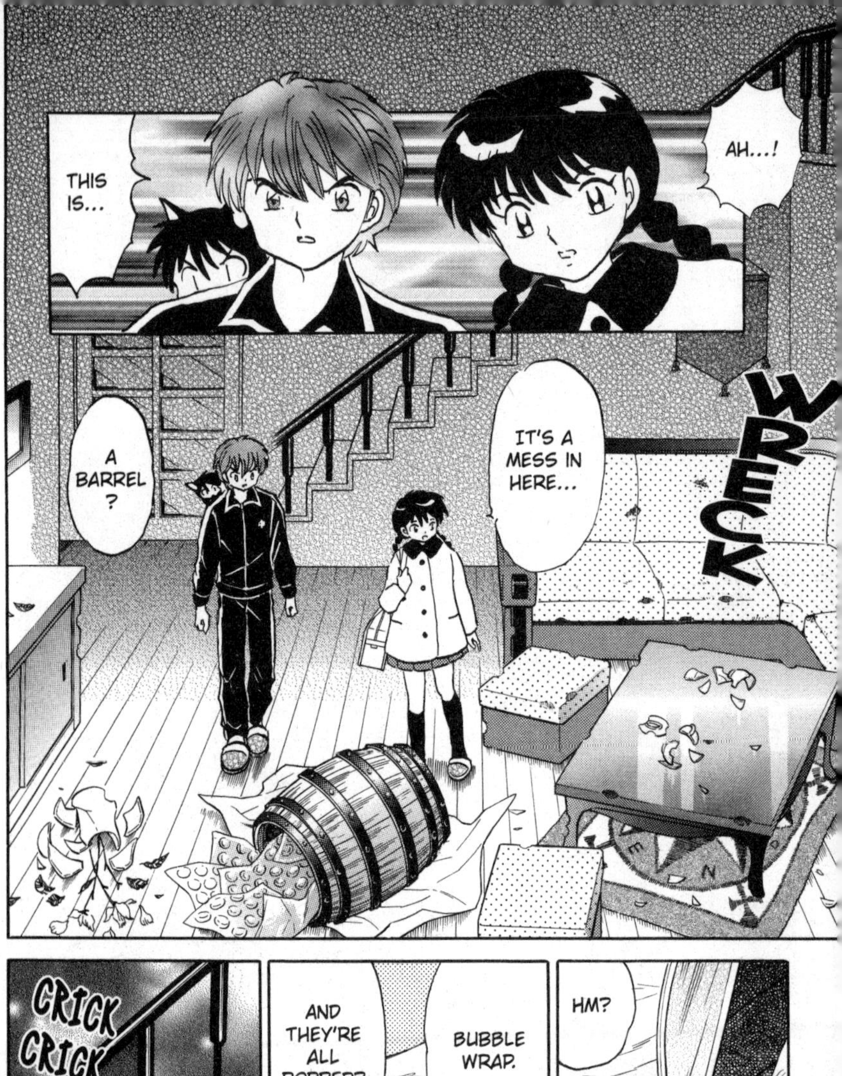
AH...!
THIS IS...
WRECK
IT'S A MESS IN HERE...
A BARREL?
HM?
BUBBLE WRAP.
AND THEY'RE ALL POPPED?
CRICK CRICK CRICK
!

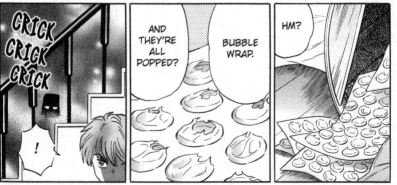

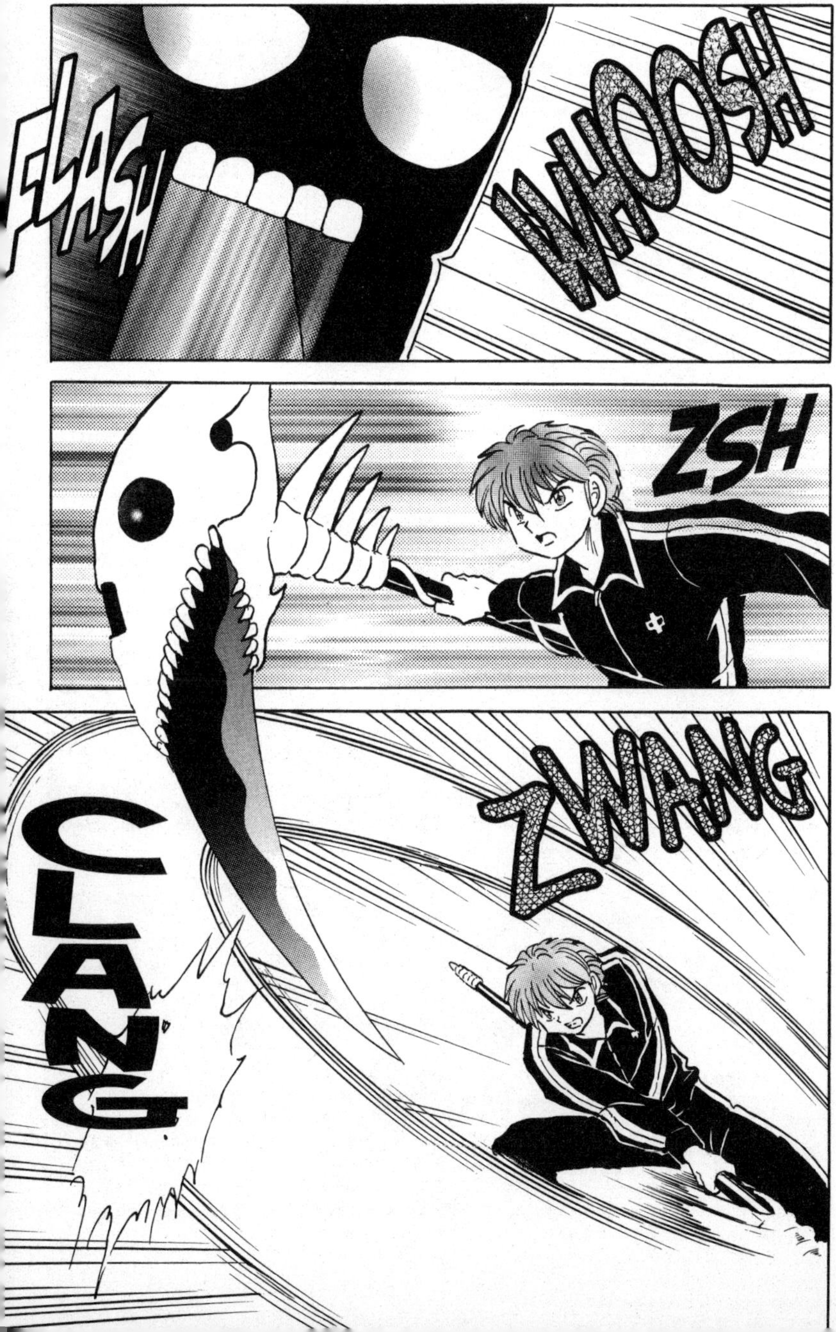
WHOOSH
FLASH
ZSH
ZWANG
CLANG

ROKUDO-KUN, YOUR SHINIGAMI SCYTHE...

!

WHAT WAS THAT?

ZSH
ZSH
ZSH

THUD

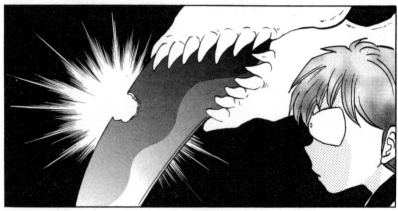

TMP
TMP TMP

MAMIYA-SAN, WHAT ARE YOU DOING IN MY HOME?

TSU-BASA-KUN.

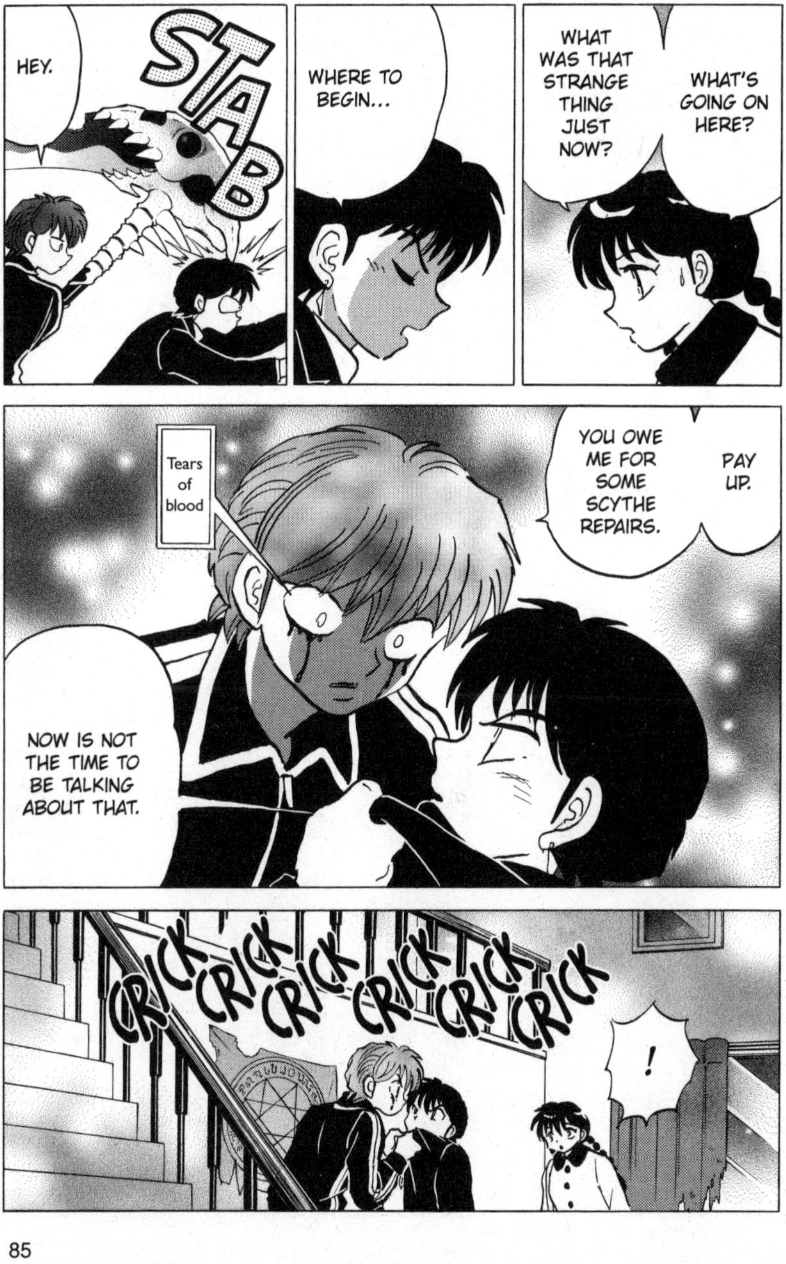
WHAT'S GOING ON HERE?
WHAT WAS THAT STRANGE THING JUST NOW?
WHERE TO BEGIN...
STAB
HEY.
PAY UP.
YOU OWE ME FOR SOME SCYTHE REPAIRS.
Tears of blood
NOW IS NOT THE TIME TO BE TALKING ABOUT THAT.
!
CRICK CRICK CRICK CRICK CRICK CRICK

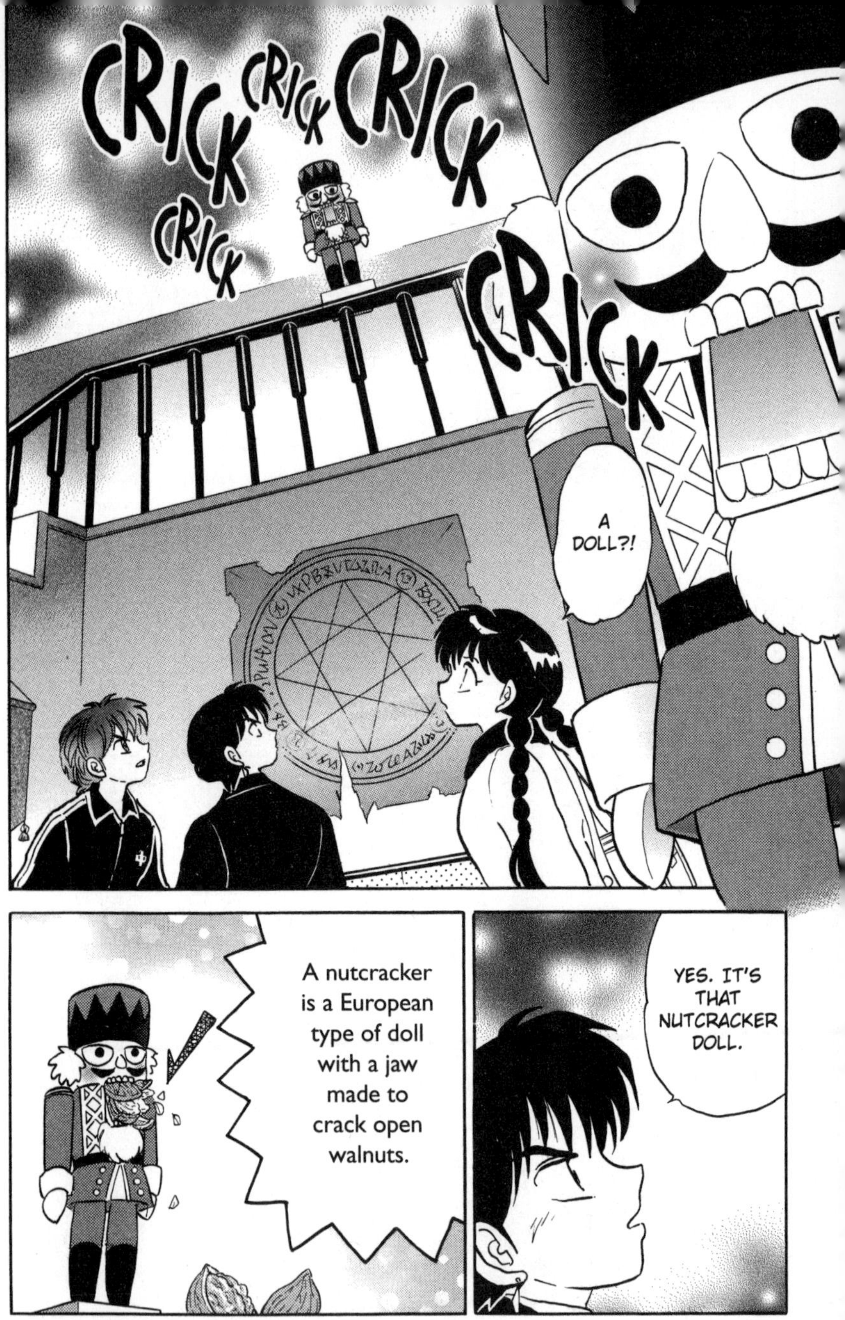
CRICK
CRICK
CRICK
CRICK
CRICK
A DOLL?!
YES. IT'S THAT NUTCRACKER DOLL.
A nutcracker is a European type of doll with a jaw made to crack open walnuts.

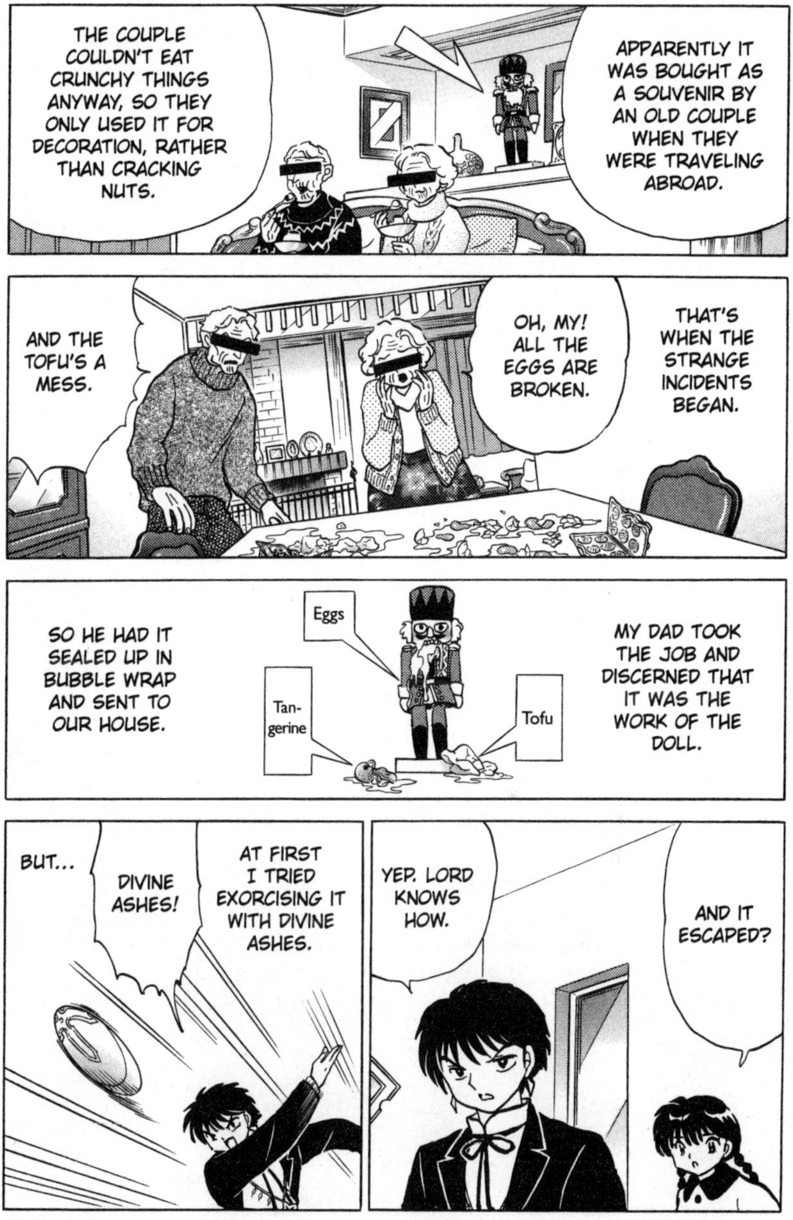
APPARENTLY IT WAS BOUGHT AS A SOUVENIR BY AN OLD COUPLE WHEN THEY WERE TRAVELING ABROAD.
THE COUPLE COULDN'T EAT CRUNCHY THINGS ANYWAY, SO THEY ONLY USED IT FOR DECORATION, RATHER THAN CRACKING NUTS.
THAT'S WHEN THE STRANGE INCIDENTS BEGAN.
OH, MY! ALL THE EGGS ARE BROKEN.
AND THE TOFU'S A MESS.
MY DAD TOOK THE JOB AND DISCERNED THAT IT WAS THE WORK OF THE DOLL.
Eggs
Tofu
Tan-gerine
SO HE HAD IT SEALED UP IN BUBBLE WRAP AND SENT TO OUR HOUSE.
AND IT ESCAPED?
YEP. LORD KNOWS HOW.
AT FIRST I TRIED EXORCISING IT WITH DIVINE ASHES.
DIVINE ASHES!
BUT...

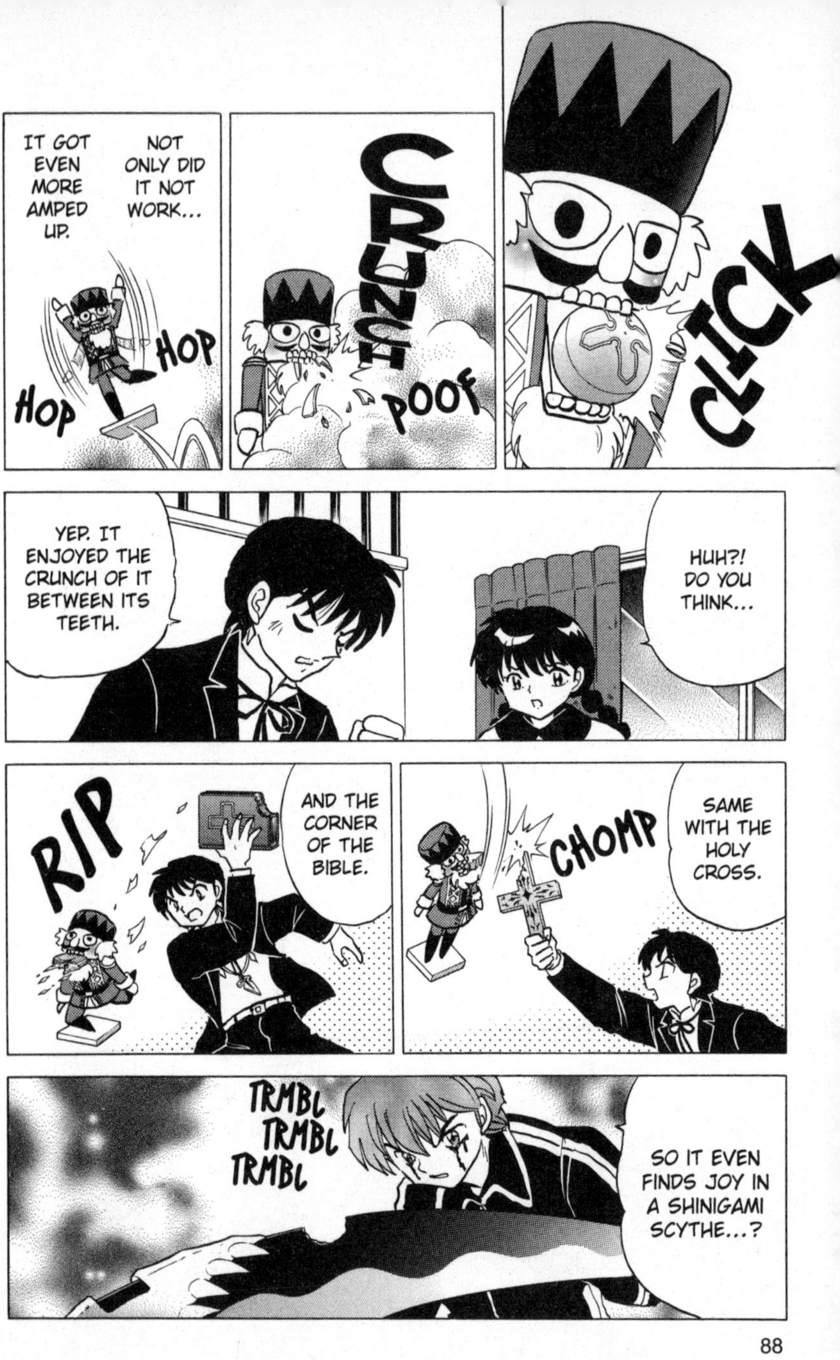
CLICK
CRUNCH
POOF
NOT ONLY DID IT NOT WORK...
IT GOT EVEN MORE AMPED UP.
HOP
HOP
HUH?! DO YOU THINK...
YEP. IT ENJOYED THE CRUNCH OF IT BETWEEN ITS TEETH.
SAME WITH THE HOLY CROSS.
CHOMP
AND THE CORNER OF THE BIBLE.
RIP
SO IT EVEN FINDS JOY IN A SHINIGAMI SCYTHE...?
TRMBL
TRMBL
TRMBL

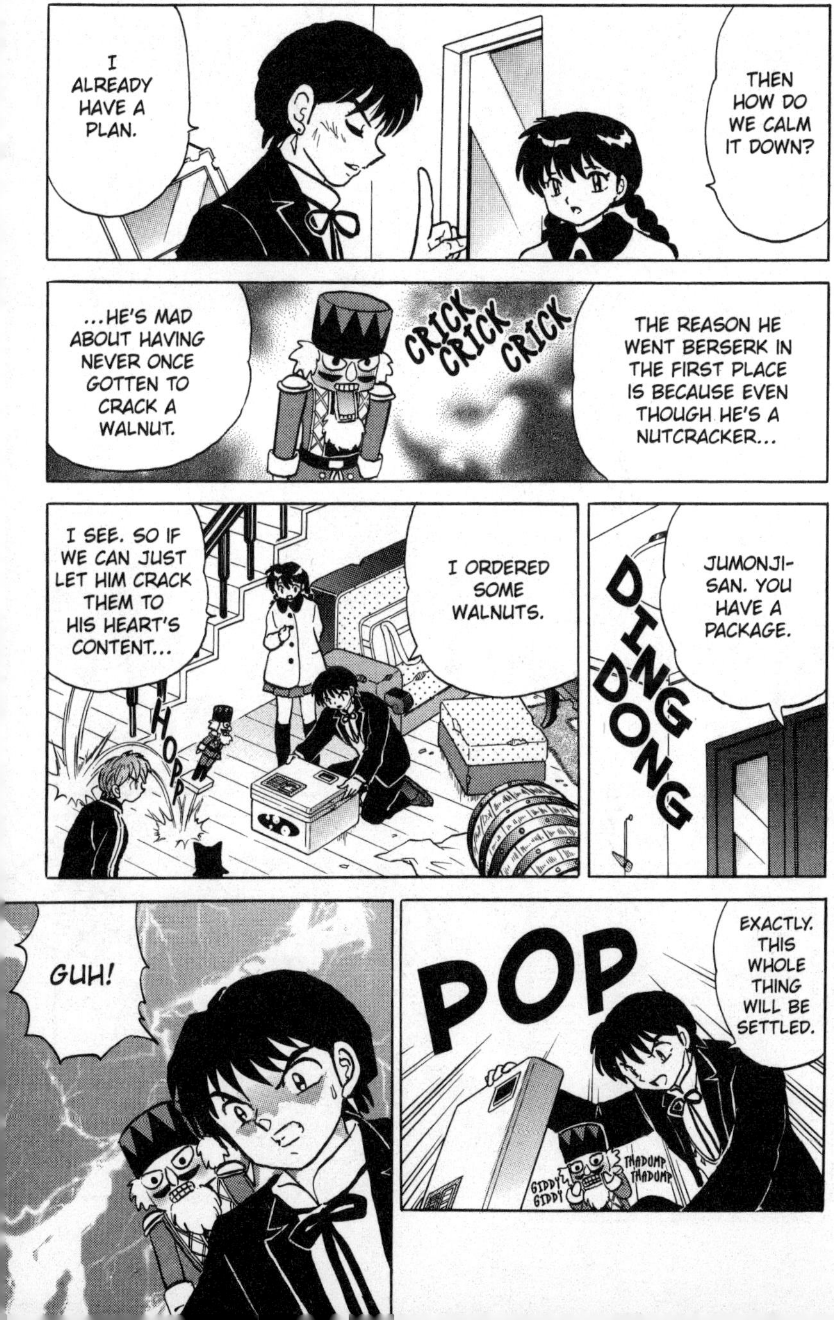
THEN HOW DO WE CALM IT DOWN?
I ALREADY HAVE A PLAN.
THE REASON HE WENT BERSERK IN THE FIRST PLACE IS BECAUSE EVEN THOUGH HE'S A NUTCRACKER...
CRICK CRICK CRICK
...HE'S MAD ABOUT HAVING NEVER ONCE GOTTEN TO CRACK A WALNUT.
DING DONG
JUMONJI-SAN. YOU HAVE A PACKAGE.
I ORDERED SOME WALNUTS.
I SEE. SO IF WE CAN JUST LET HIM CRACK THEM TO HIS HEART'S CONTENT...
HOPP
EXACTLY. THIS WHOLE THING WILL BE SETTLED.
POP
THADUMP THADUMP
GIDDY GIDDY
GUH!

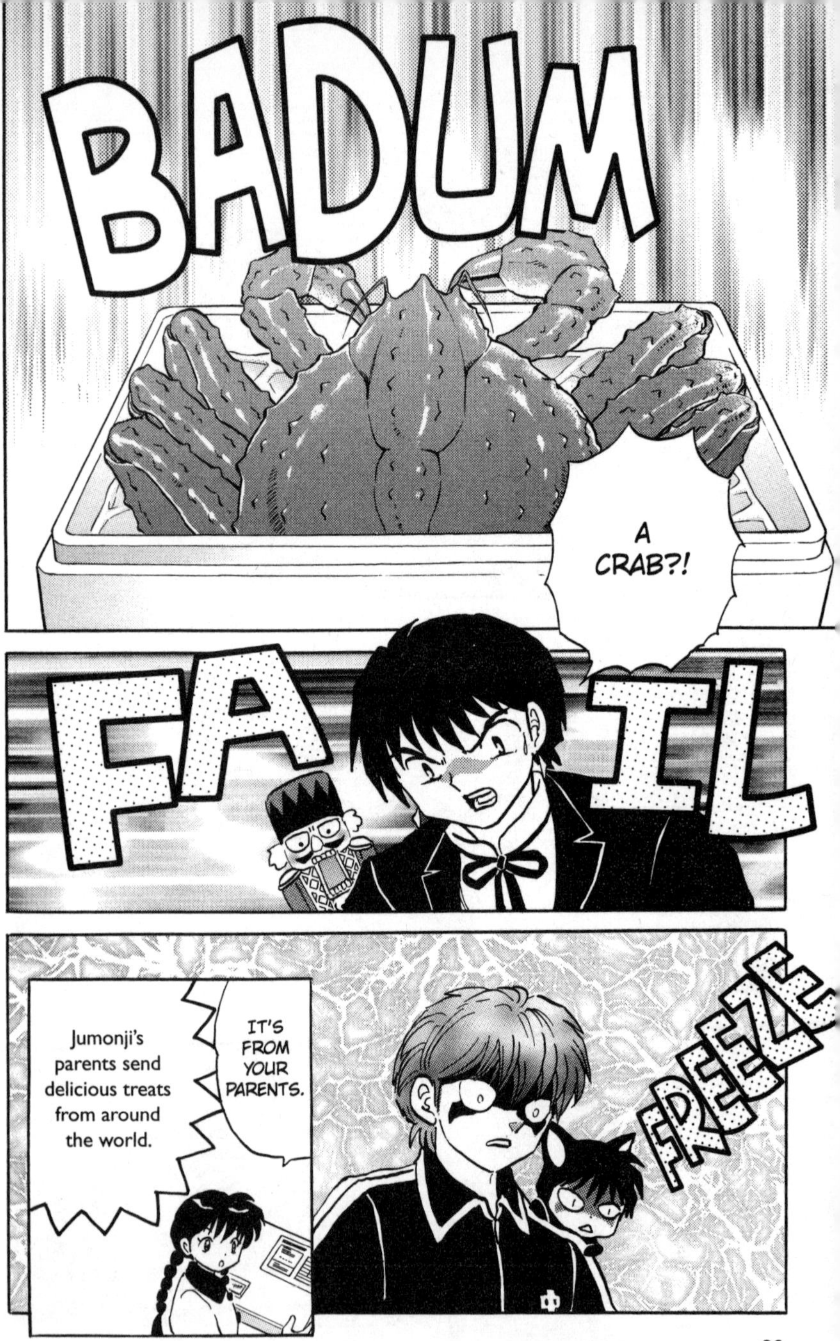
BADUM
A CRAB?!
FAIL
FREEZE
IT'S FROM YOUR PARENTS.
Jumonji's parents send delicious treats from around the world.

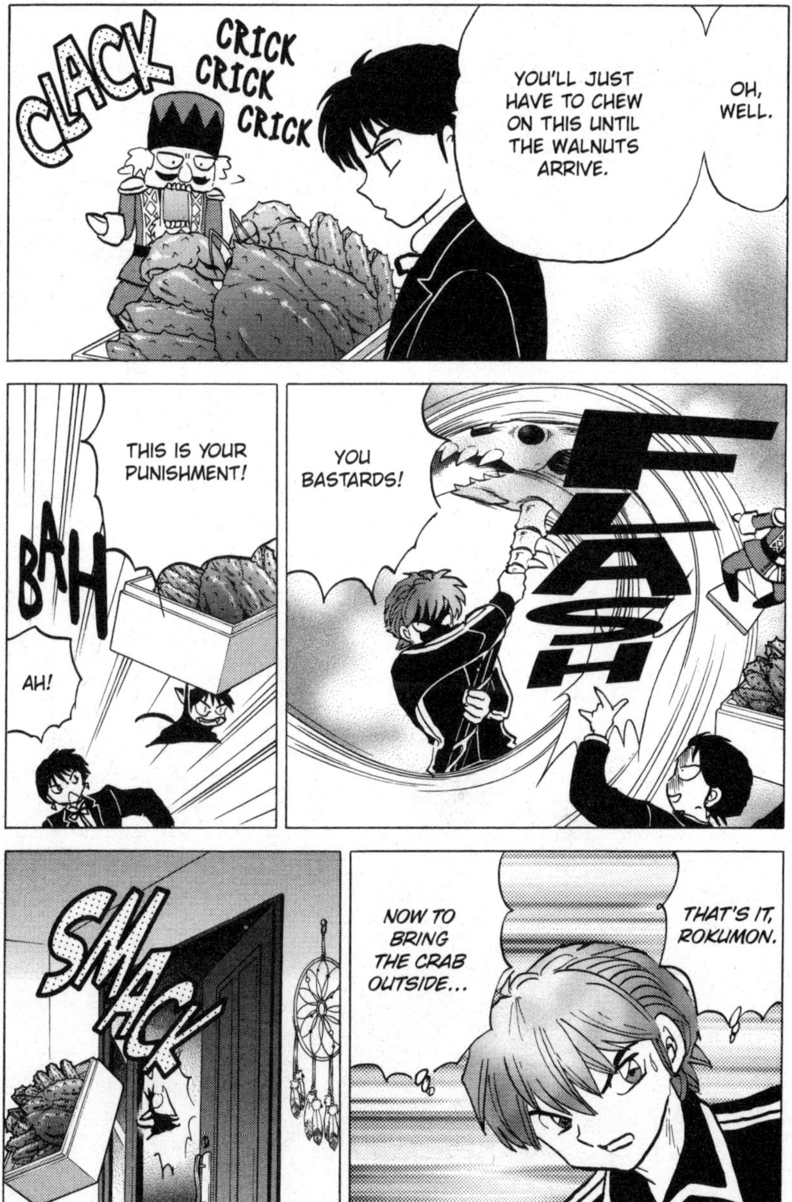
OH, WELL.
YOU'LL JUST HAVE TO CHEW ON THIS UNTIL THE WALNUTS ARRIVE.
CRICK CRICK CRICK
CLACK
FLASH
YOU BASTARDS!
THIS IS YOUR PUNISHMENT!
BAH
AH!
THAT'S IT, ROKUMON.
NOW TO BRING THE CRAB OUTSIDE...
SMACK

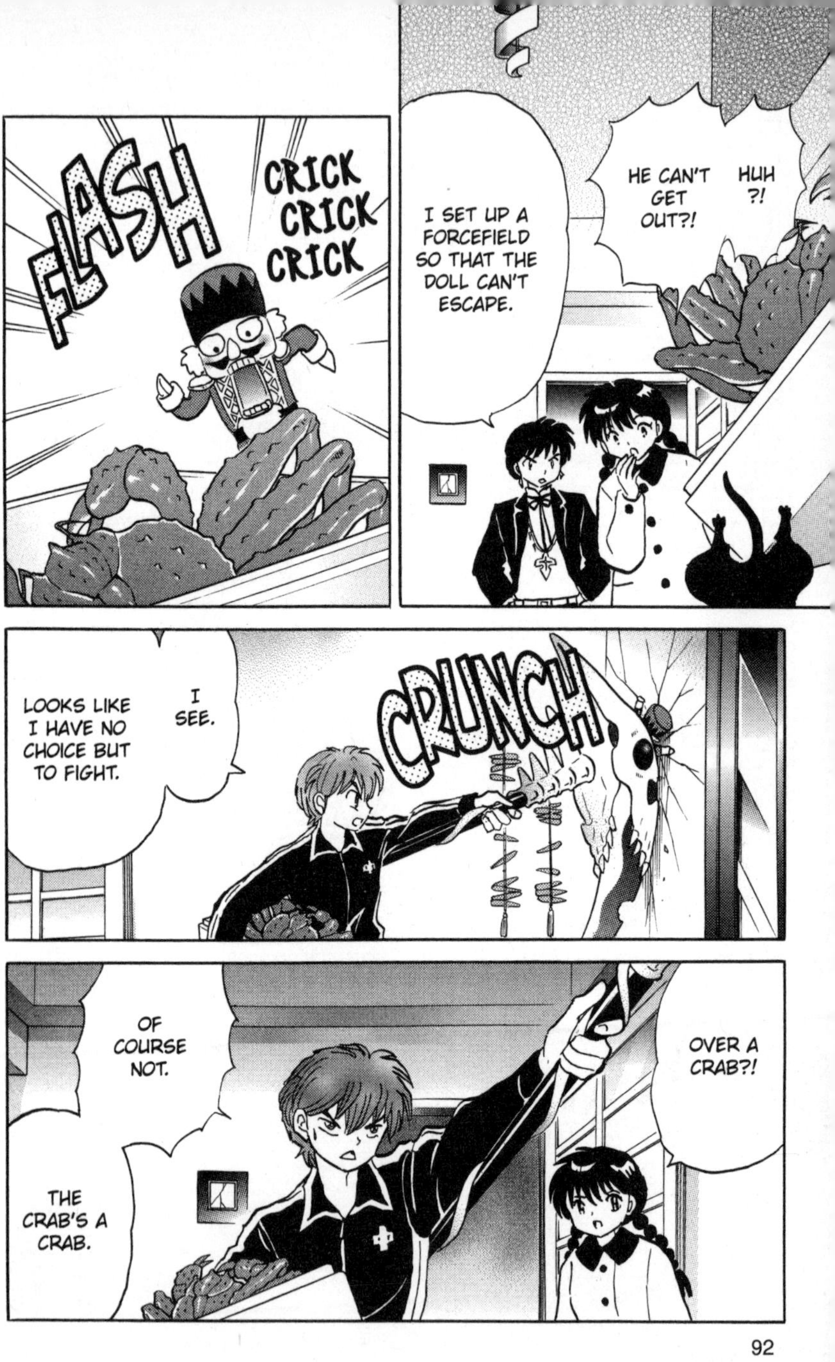
HUH ?!
HE CAN'T GET OUT?!
I SET UP A FORCEFIELD SO THAT THE DOLL CAN'T ESCAPE.
CRICK CRICK CRICK
FLASH
CRUNCH
I SEE.
LOOKS LIKE I HAVE NO CHOICE BUT TO FIGHT.
OVER A CRAB?!
OF COURSE NOT.
THE CRAB'S A CRAB.

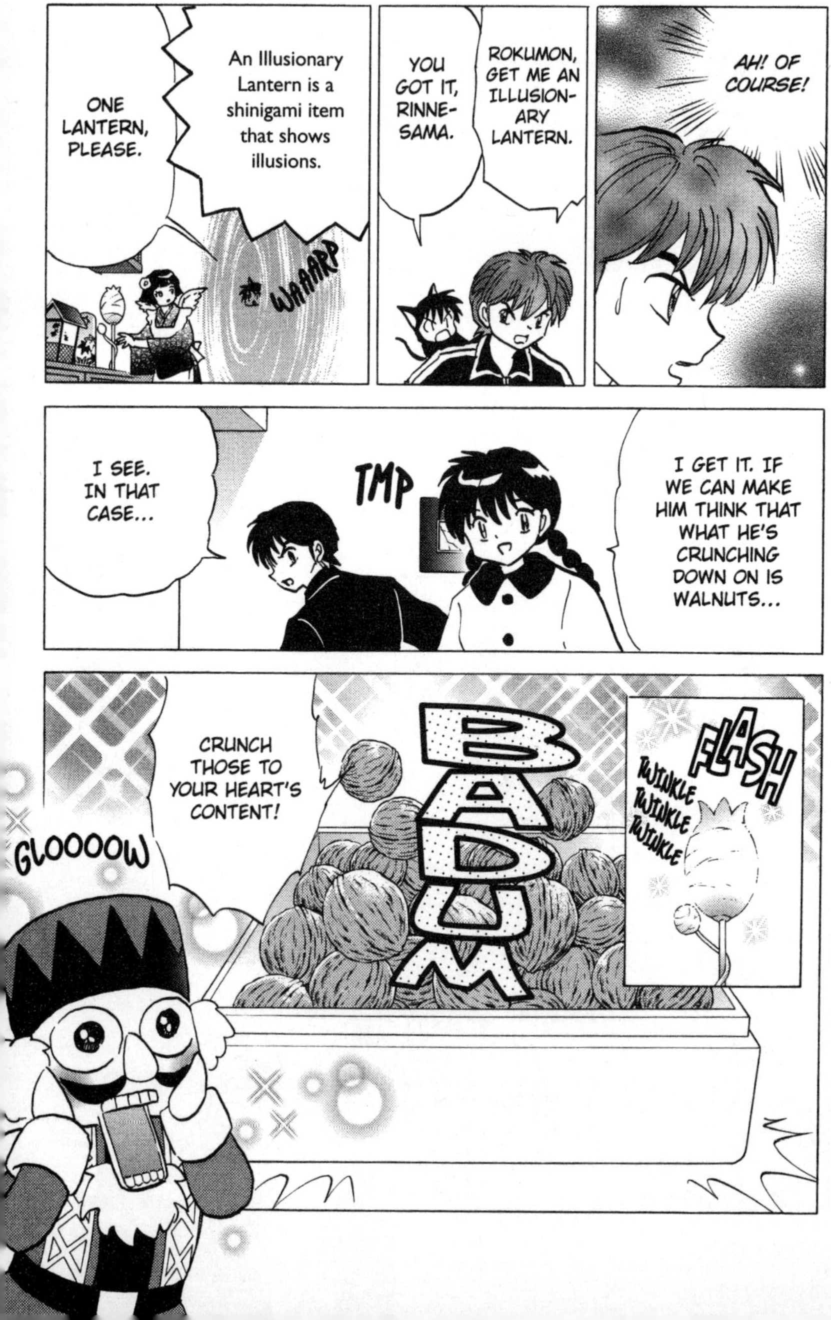
AH! OF COURSE!
ROKUMON, GET ME AN ILLUSIONARY LANTERN.
YOU GOT IT, RINNE-SAMA.
An Illusionary Lantern is a shinigami item that shows illusions.
WAAARP
ONE LANTERN, PLEASE.
I GET IT. IF WE CAN MAKE HIM THINK THAT WHAT HE'S CRUNCHING DOWN ON IS WALNUTS...
TMP
I SEE. IN THAT CASE...
FLASH
TWINKLE TWINKLE TWINKLE
BADUM
CRUNCH THOSE TO YOUR HEART'S CONTENT!
GLOOOOW

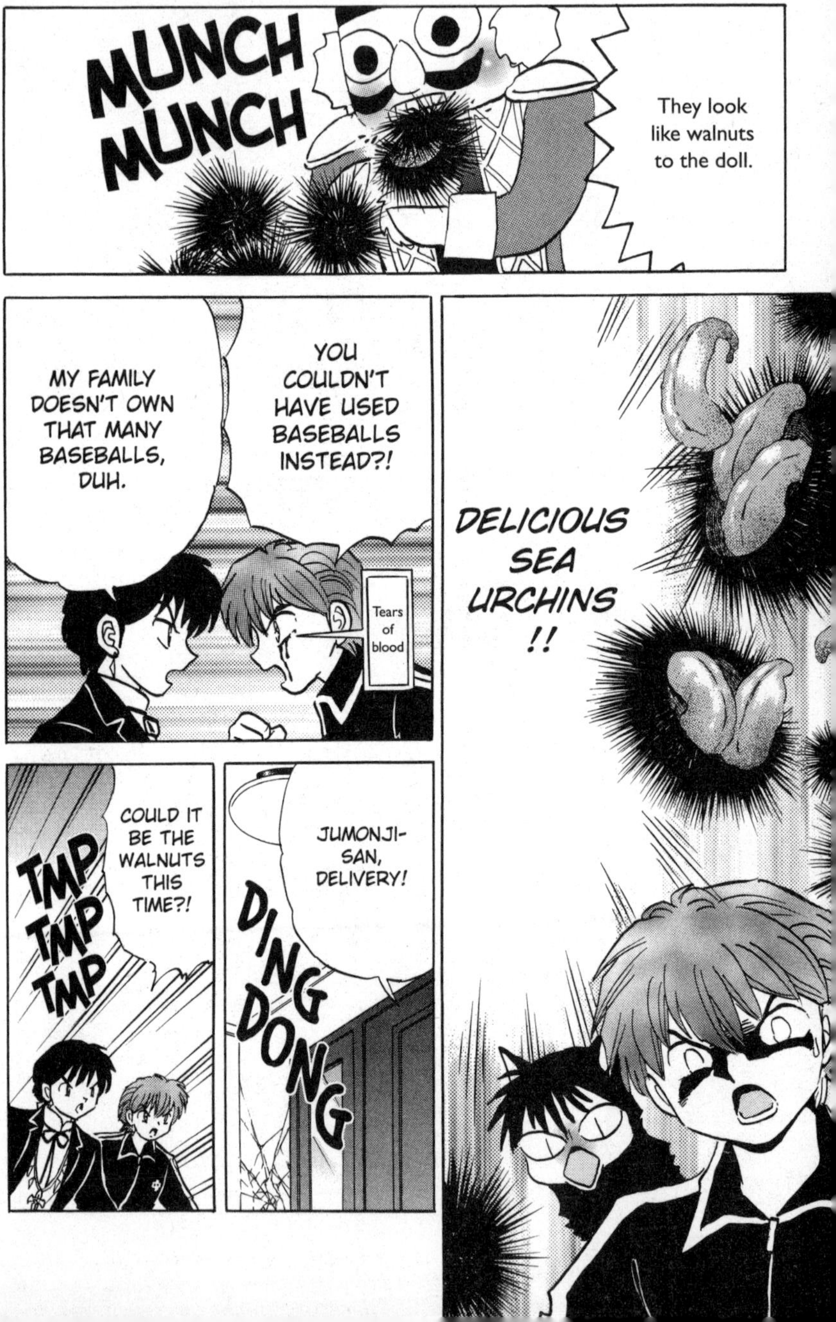
They look like walnuts to the doll.
MUNCH MUNCH
DELICIOUS SEA URCHINS !!
YOU COULDN'T HAVE USED BASEBALLS INSTEAD?!
Tears of blood
MY FAMILY DOESN'T OWN THAT MANY BASEBALLS, DUH.
JUMONJI-SAN, DELIVERY!
DING DONG
COULD IT BE THE WALNUTS THIS TIME?!
TMP TMP TMP

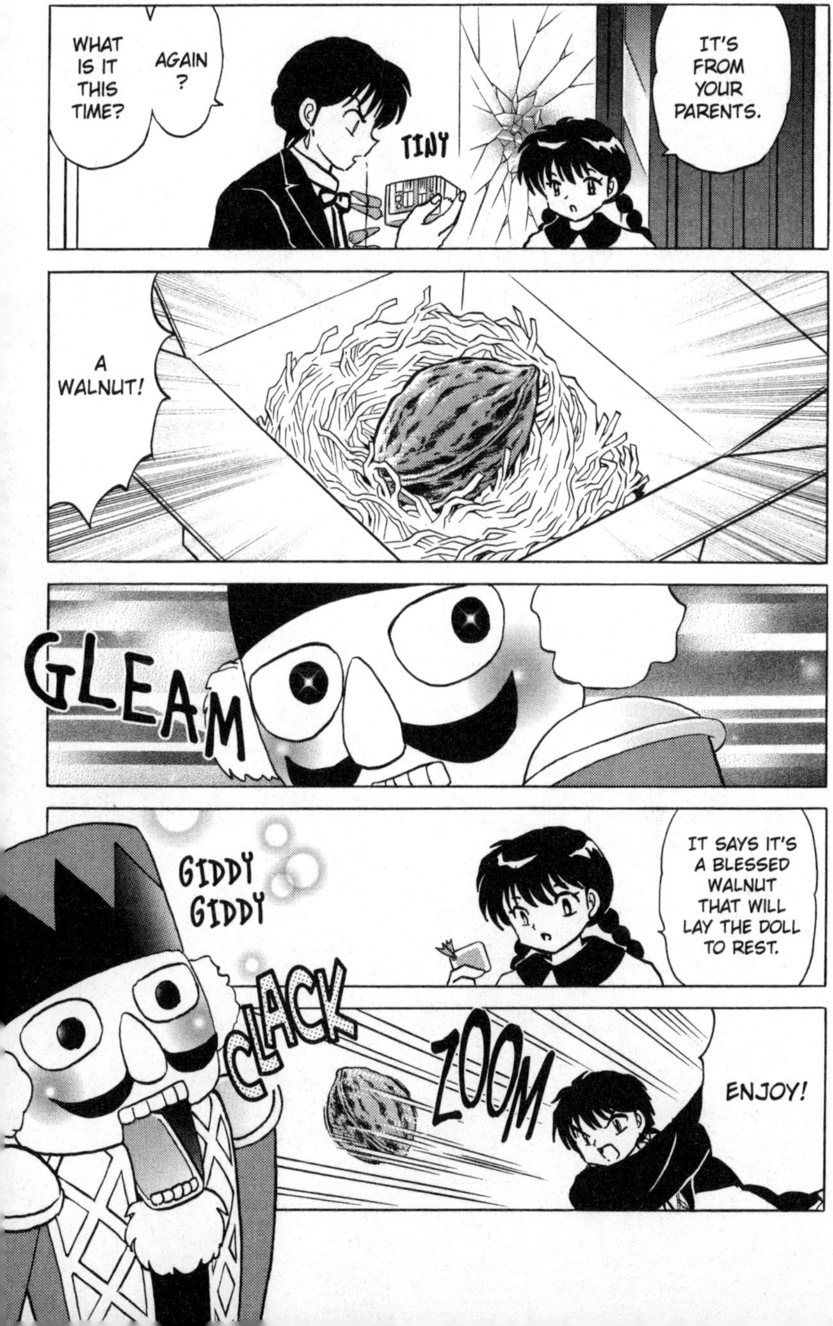
IT'S FROM YOUR PARENTS.
TINY
AGAIN?
WHAT IS IT THIS TIME?
A WALNUT!
GLEAM
IT SAYS IT'S A BLESSED WALNUT THAT WILL LAY THE DOLL TO REST.
GIDDY GIDDY
ENJOY!
ZOOM
CLACK

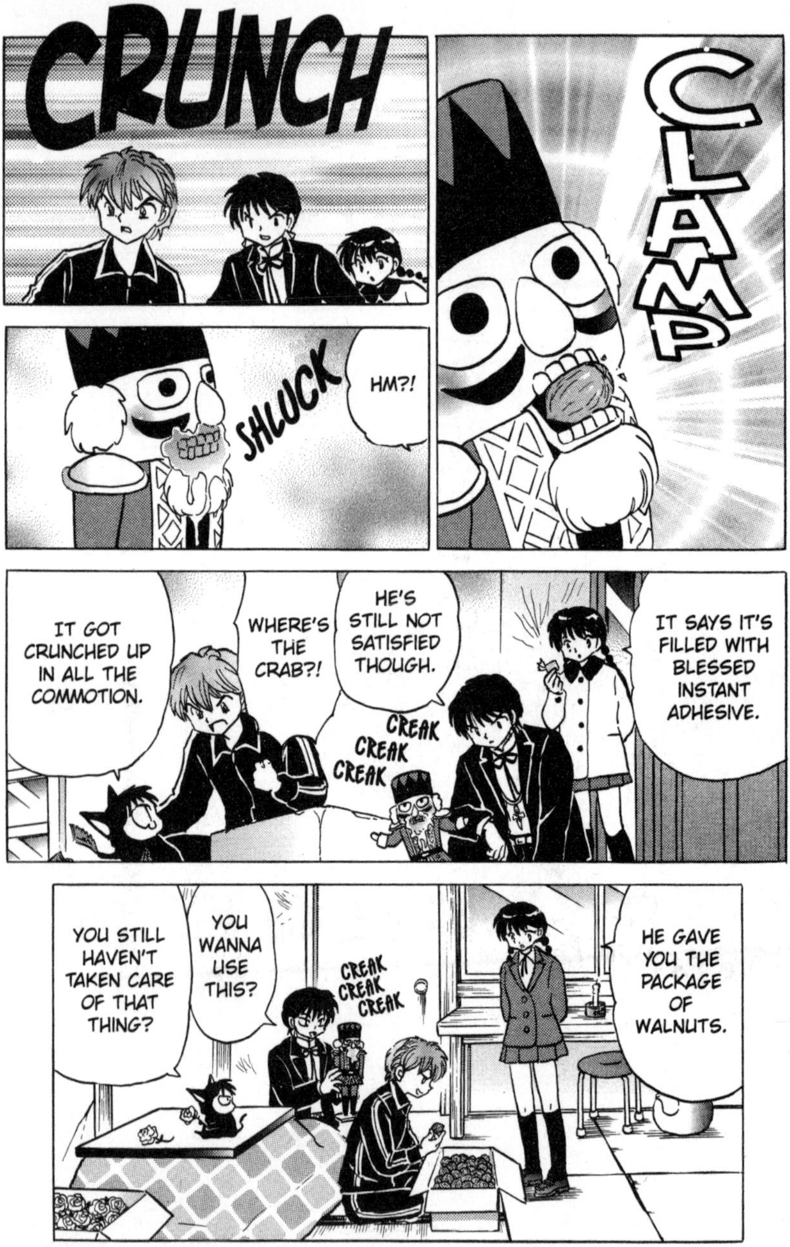
CLAMP
CRUNCH
HM?!
SHLUCK
IT SAYS IT'S FILLED WITH BLESSED INSTANT ADHESIVE.
HE'S STILL NOT SATISFIED THOUGH.
CREAK CREAK CREAK
WHERE'S THE CRAB?!
IT GOT CRUNCHED UP IN ALL THE COMMOTION.
HE GAVE YOU THE PACKAGE OF WALNUTS.
CREAK CREAK CREAK
YOU WANNA USE THIS?
YOU STILL HAVEN'T TAKEN CARE OF THAT THING?

CHAPTER 264: DECORATIONS

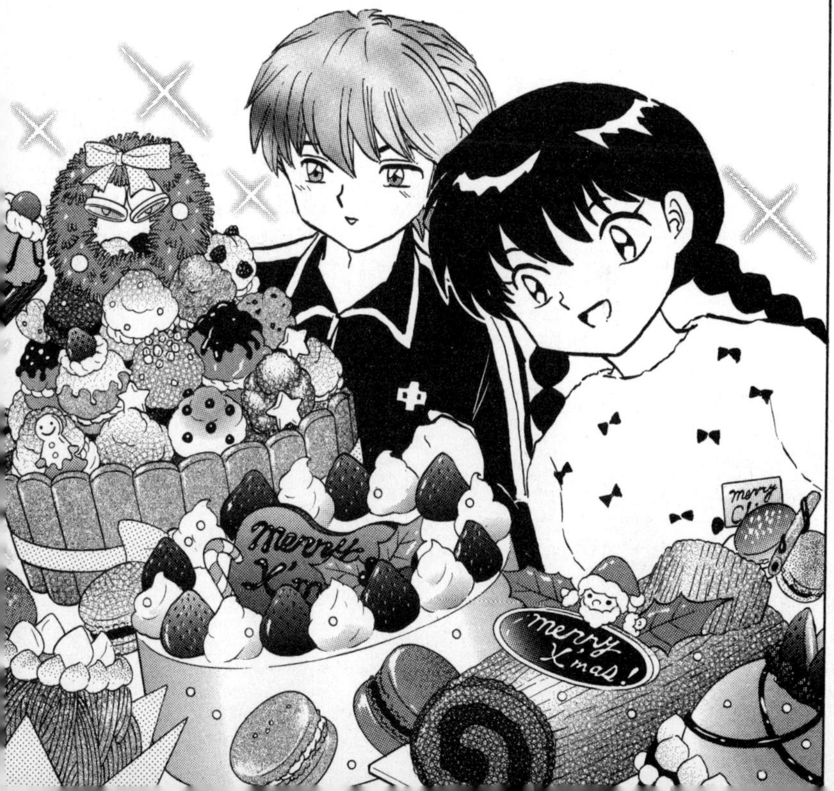
merry X'mas
merry X'mas!
merry Ch

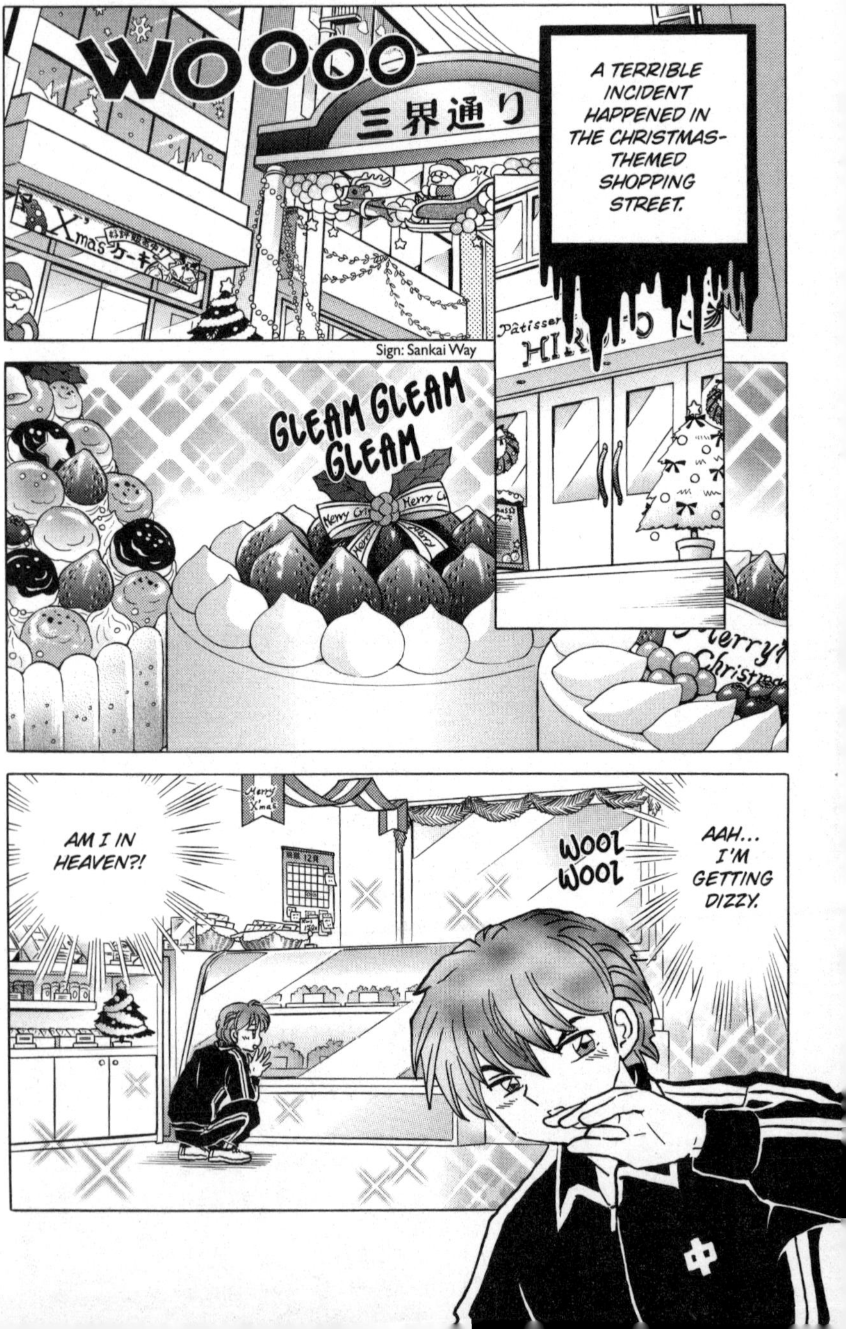
A TERRIBLE INCIDENT HAPPENED IN THE CHRISTMAS-THEMED SHOPPING STREET.
WOOOO
三界通り
Sign: Sankai Way
GLEAM GLEAM GLEAM
AAH... I'M GETTING DIZZY.
WOOZ WOOZ
AM I IN HEAVEN?!

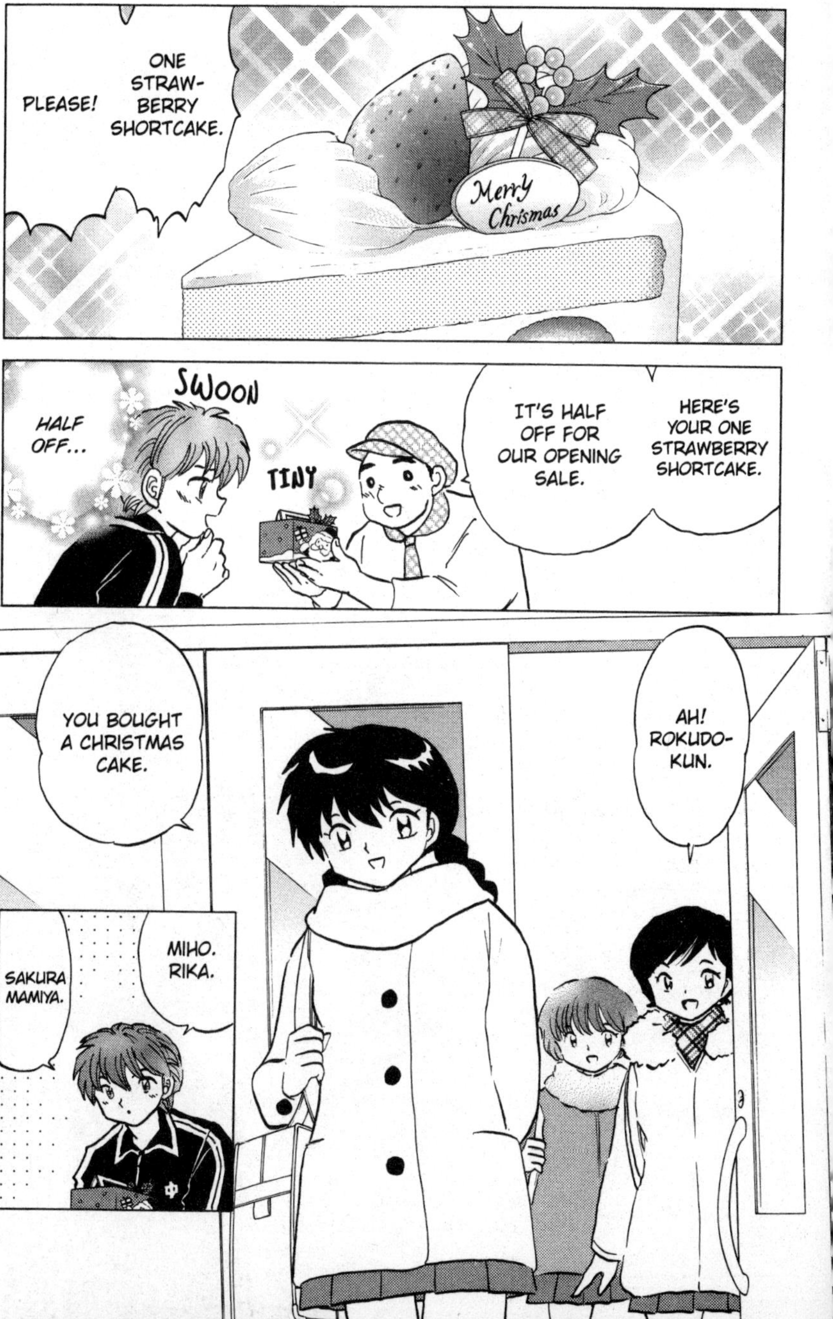
ONE STRAW-BERRY SHORTCAKE.
PLEASE!
Merry Chrismas
HERE'S YOUR ONE STRAWBERRY SHORTCAKE.
IT'S HALF OFF FOR OUR OPENING SALE.
TINY
SWOON
HALF OFF...
AH! ROKUDO-KUN.
YOU BOUGHT A CHRISTMAS CAKE.
MIHO. RIKA.
SAKURA MAMIYA.

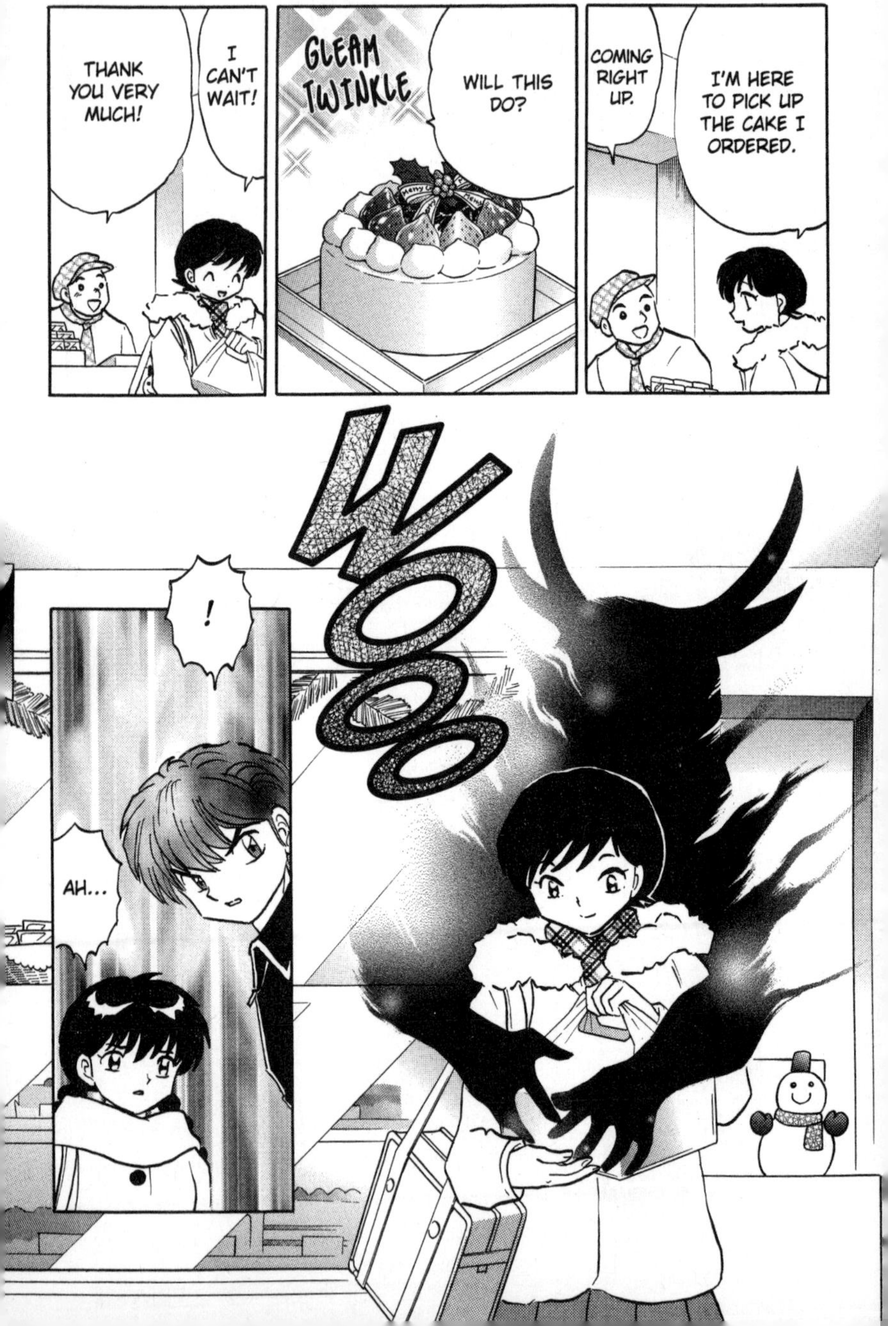
I'M HERE TO PICK UP THE CAKE I ORDERED.
COMING RIGHT UP.
WILL THIS DO?
GLEAM
TWINKLE
I CAN'T WAIT!
THANK YOU VERY MUCH!
WOOO
!
AH...

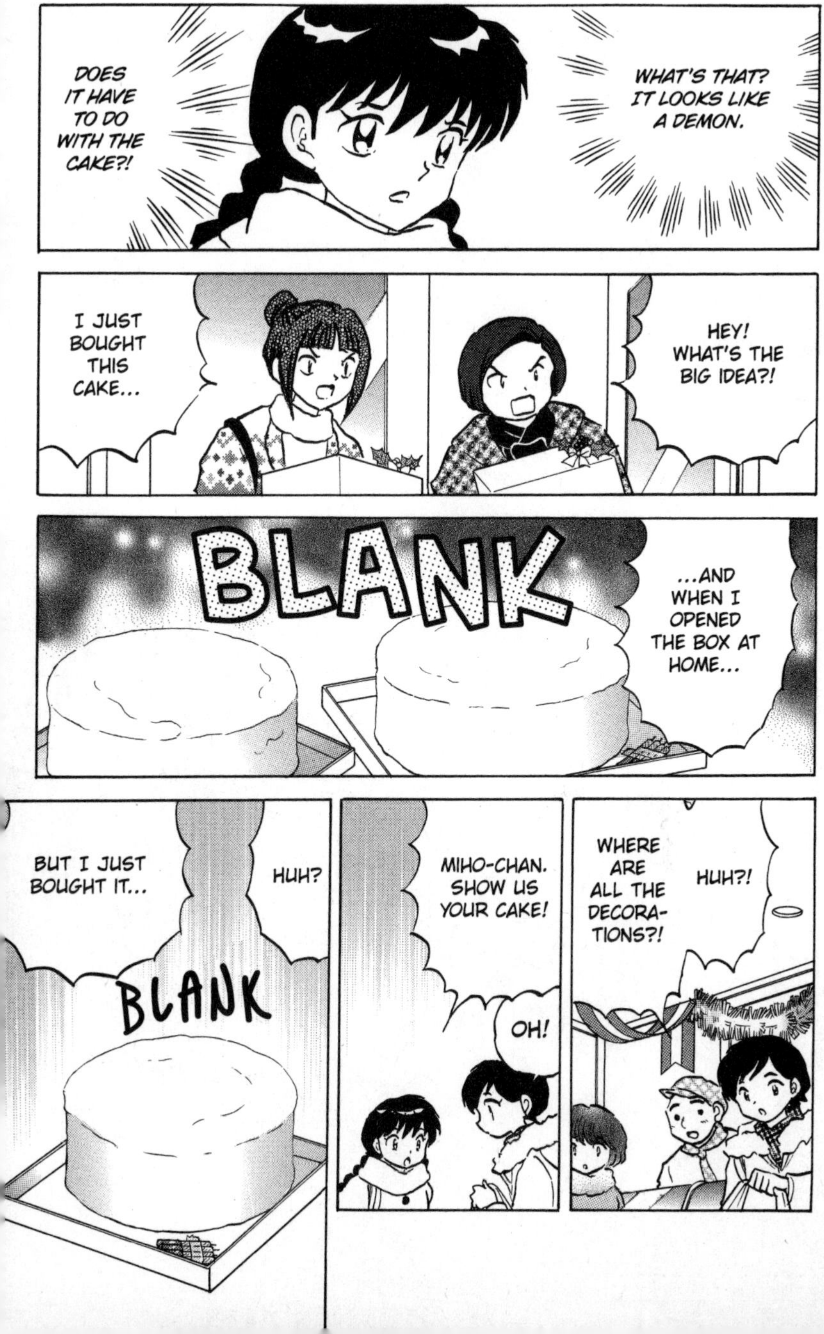
WHAT'S THAT? IT LOOKS LIKE A DEMON.
DOES IT HAVE TO DO WITH THE CAKE?!
HEY! WHAT'S THE BIG IDEA?!
I JUST BOUGHT THIS CAKE...
...AND WHEN I OPENED THE BOX AT HOME...
BLANK
HUH?!
WHERE ARE ALL THE DECORA-TIONS?!
MIHO-CHAN. SHOW US YOUR CAKE!
OH!
HUH?
BUT I JUST BOUGHT IT...
BLANK

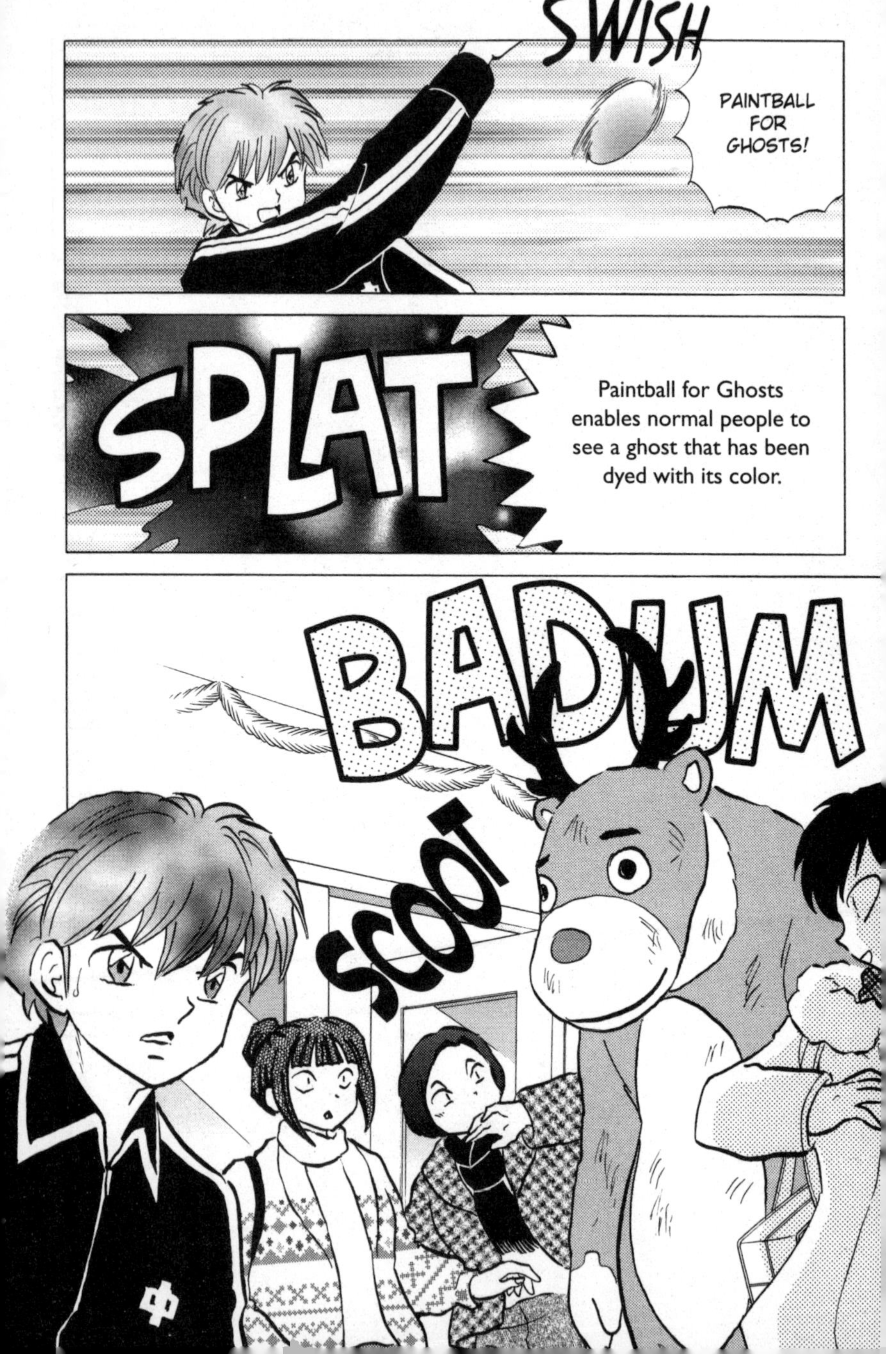
SWISH
PAINTBALL FOR GHOSTS!
SPLAT
Paintball for Ghosts enables normal people to see a ghost that has been dyed with its color.
BADUM
SCOOT

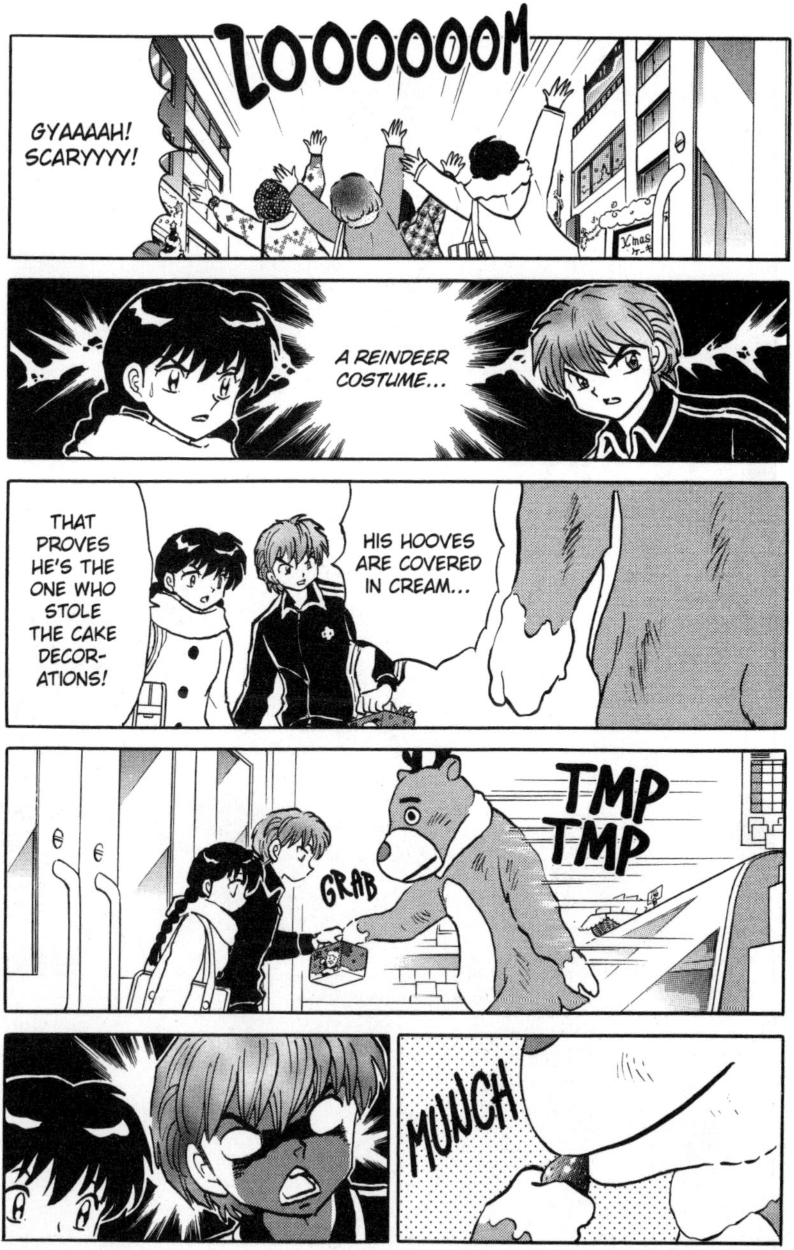
ZOOOOOOM
GYAAAAH! SCARYYYY!
A REINDEER COSTUME...
HIS HOOVES ARE COVERED IN CREAM...
THAT PROVES HE'S THE ONE WHO STOLE THE CAKE DECORATIONS!
TMP TMP
GRAB
MUNCH

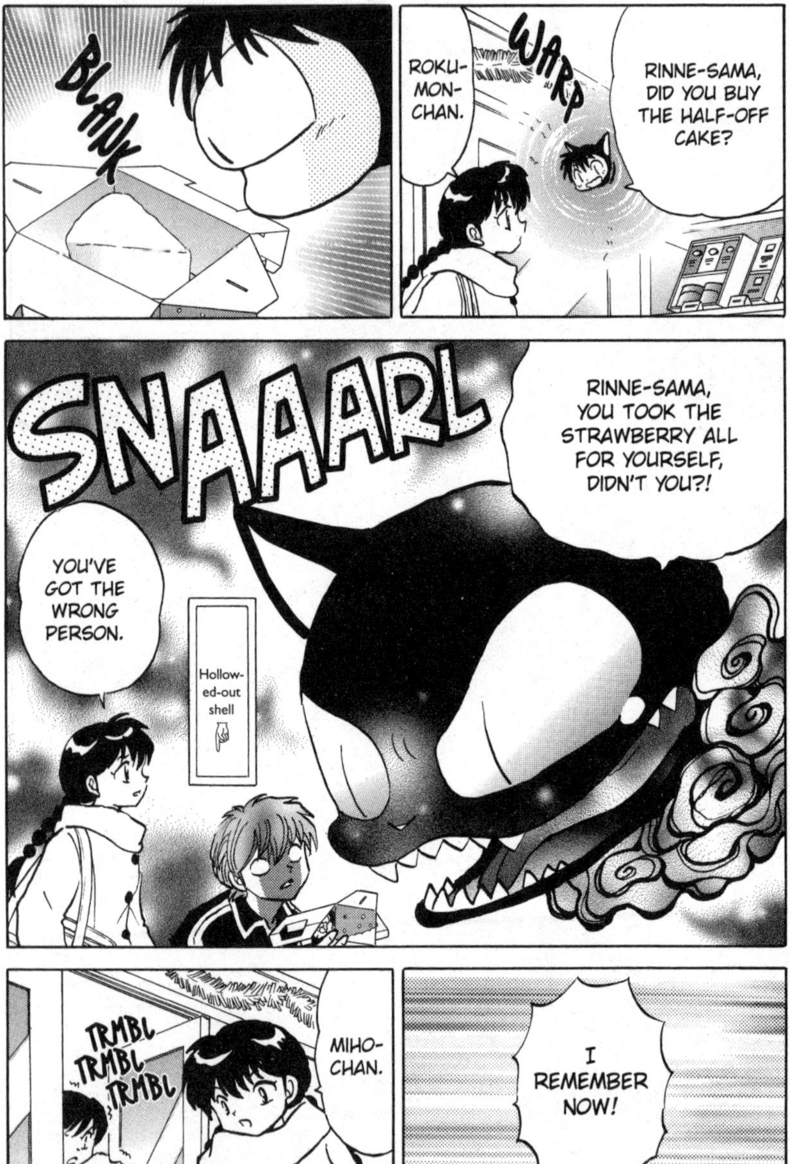
RINNE-SAMA, DID YOU BUY THE HALF-OFF CAKE?
WARP
ROKU-MON-CHAN.
BLANK
SNAAARL
RINNE-SAMA, YOU TOOK THE STRAWBERRY ALL FOR YOURSELF, DIDN'T YOU?!
YOU'VE GOT THE WRONG PERSON.
Hollowed-out shell
I REMEMBER NOW!
MIHO-CHAN.
TRMBL TRMBL TRMBL

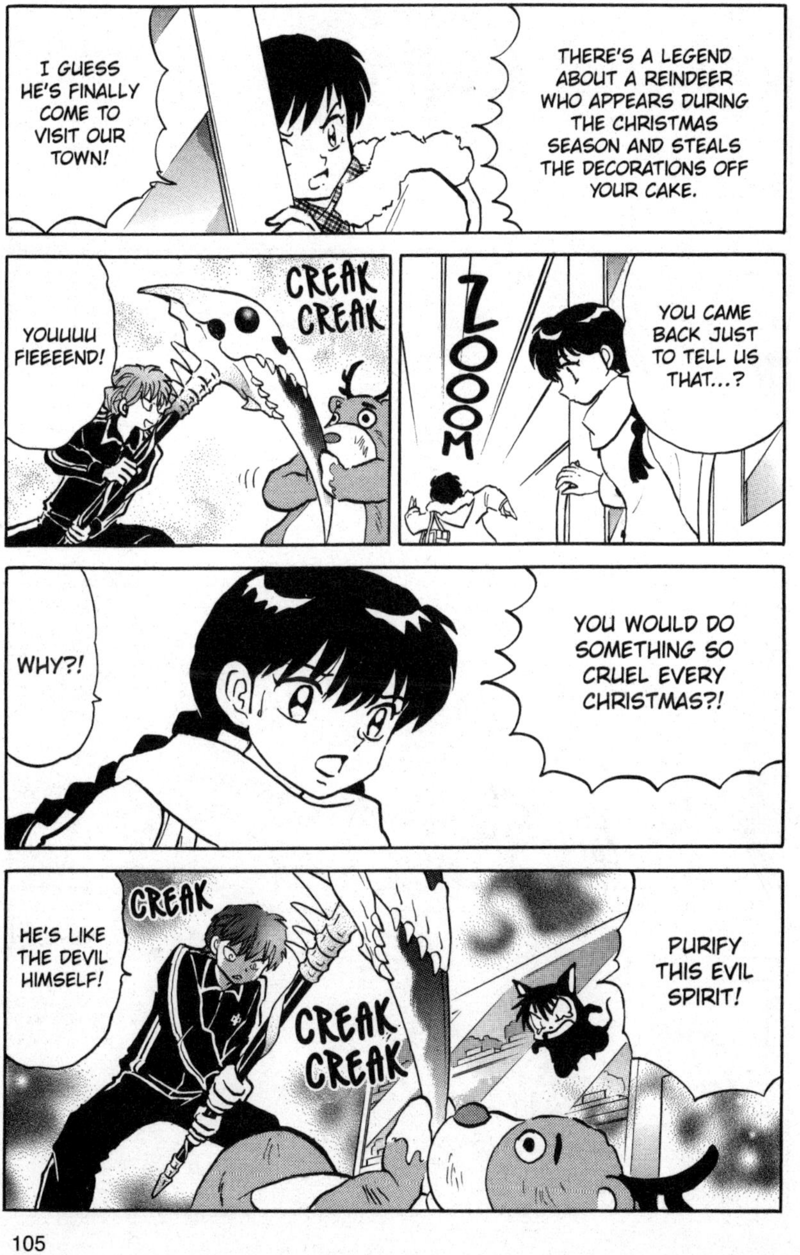
THERE'S A LEGEND ABOUT A REINDEER WHO APPEARS DURING THE CHRISTMAS SEASON AND STEALS THE DECORATIONS OFF YOUR CAKE.
I GUESS HE'S FINALLY COME TO VISIT OUR TOWN!
ZOOOM
YOU CAME BACK JUST TO TELL US THAT...?
CREAK CREAK
YOUUUU FIEEEEND!
YOU WOULD DO SOMETHING SO CRUEL EVERY CHRISTMAS?!
WHY?!
PURIFY THIS EVIL SPIRIT!
CREAK CREAK
CREAK
HE'S LIKE THE DEVIL HIMSELF!

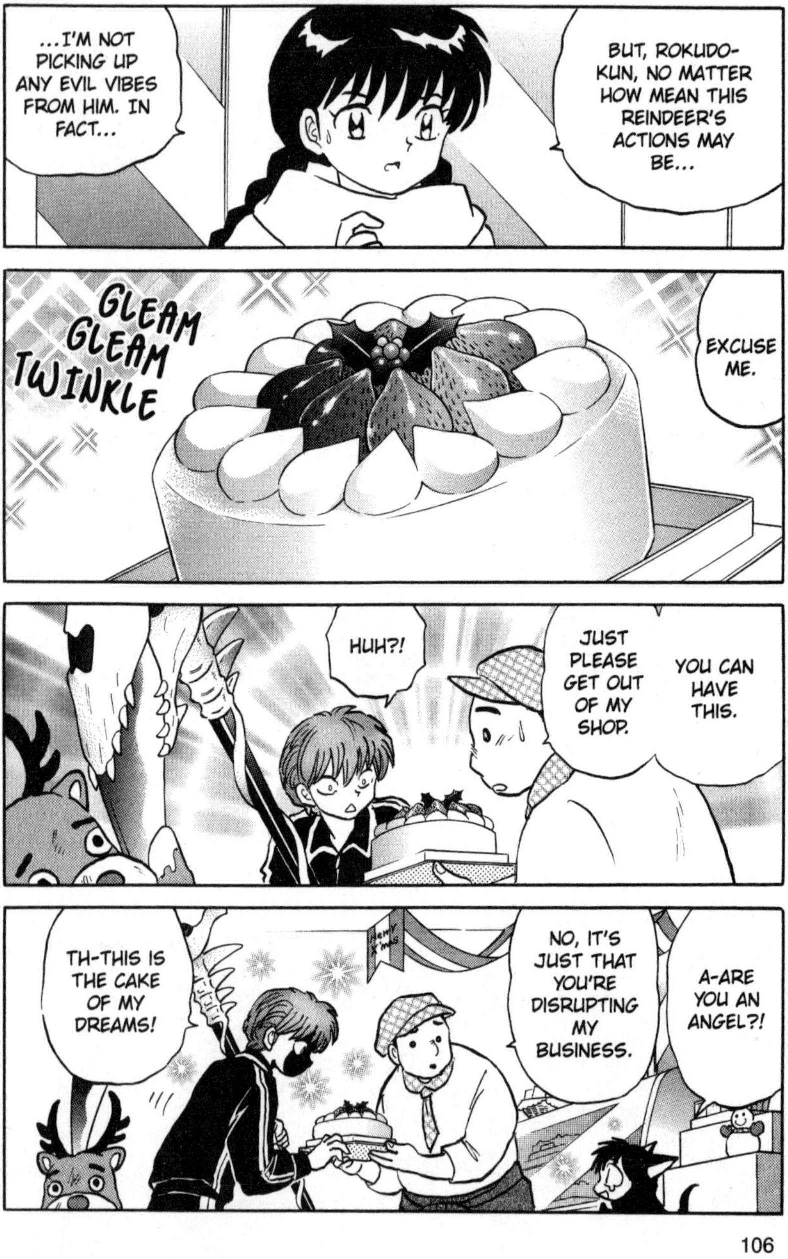
BUT, ROKUDO-KUN, NO MATTER HOW MEAN THIS REINDEER'S ACTIONS MAY BE...
...I'M NOT PICKING UP ANY EVIL VIBES FROM HIM. IN FACT...
EXCUSE ME.
GLEAM GLEAM TWINKLE
YOU CAN HAVE THIS.
JUST PLEASE GET OUT OF MY SHOP.
HUH?!
A-ARE YOU AN ANGEL?!
NO, IT'S JUST THAT YOU'RE DISRUPTING MY BUSINESS.
TH-THIS IS THE CAKE OF MY DREAMS!

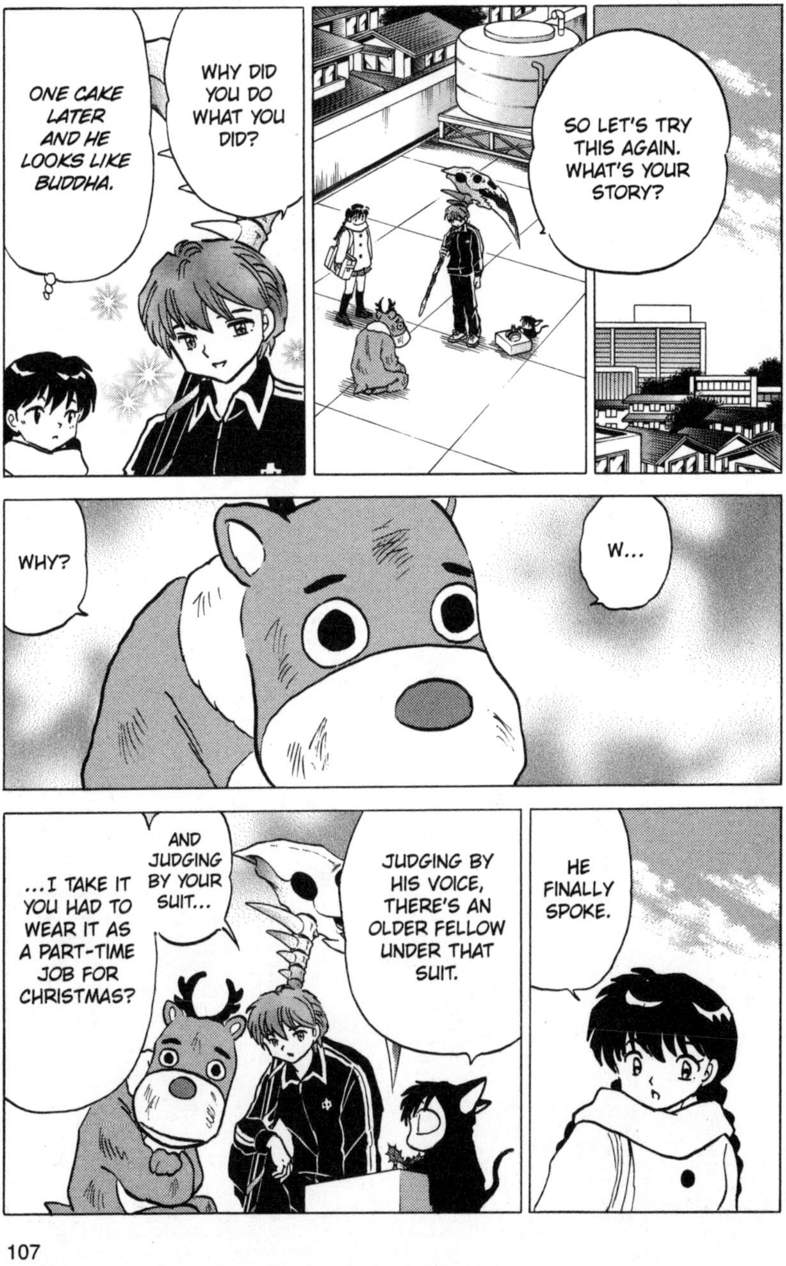
SO LET'S TRY THIS AGAIN. WHAT'S YOUR STORY?
WHY DID YOU DO WHAT YOU DID?
ONE CAKE LATER AND HE LOOKS LIKE BUDDHA.
W...
WHY?
HE FINALLY SPOKE.
JUDGING BY HIS VOICE, THERE'S AN OLDER FELLOW UNDER THAT SUIT.
AND JUDGING BY YOUR SUIT...
...I TAKE IT YOU HAD TO WEAR IT AS A PART-TIME JOB FOR CHRISTMAS?

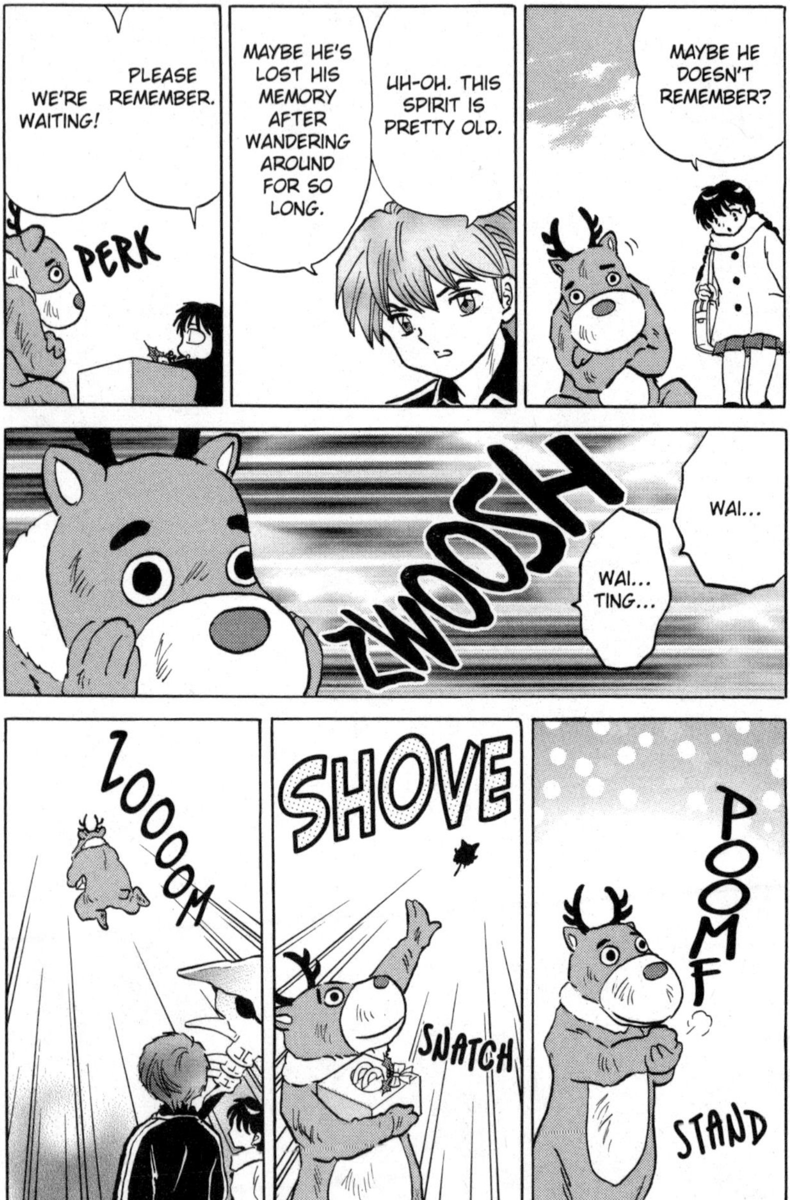
MAYBE HE DOESN'T REMEMBER?
UH-OH. THIS SPIRIT IS PRETTY OLD.
MAYBE HE'S LOST HIS MEMORY AFTER WANDERING AROUND FOR SO LONG.
PLEASE REMEMBER.
WE'RE WAITING!
PERK
WAI...
WAI... TING...
ZWOOSH
POOMF
STAND
SHOVE
SNATCH
ZOOOOOM

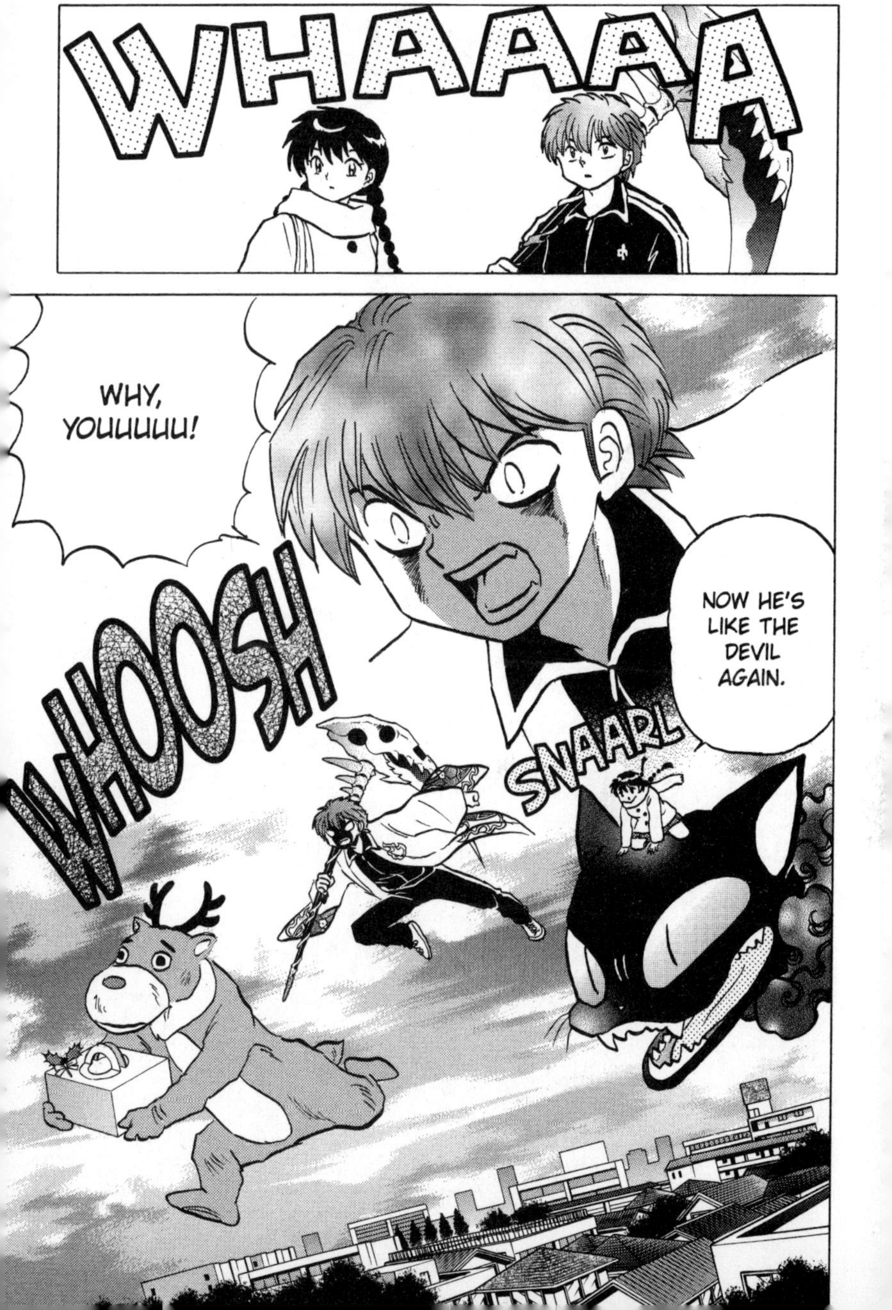
WHAAAAA
NOW HE'S LIKE THE DEVIL AGAIN.
WHY, YOUUUUU!
SNAARL
WHOOSH

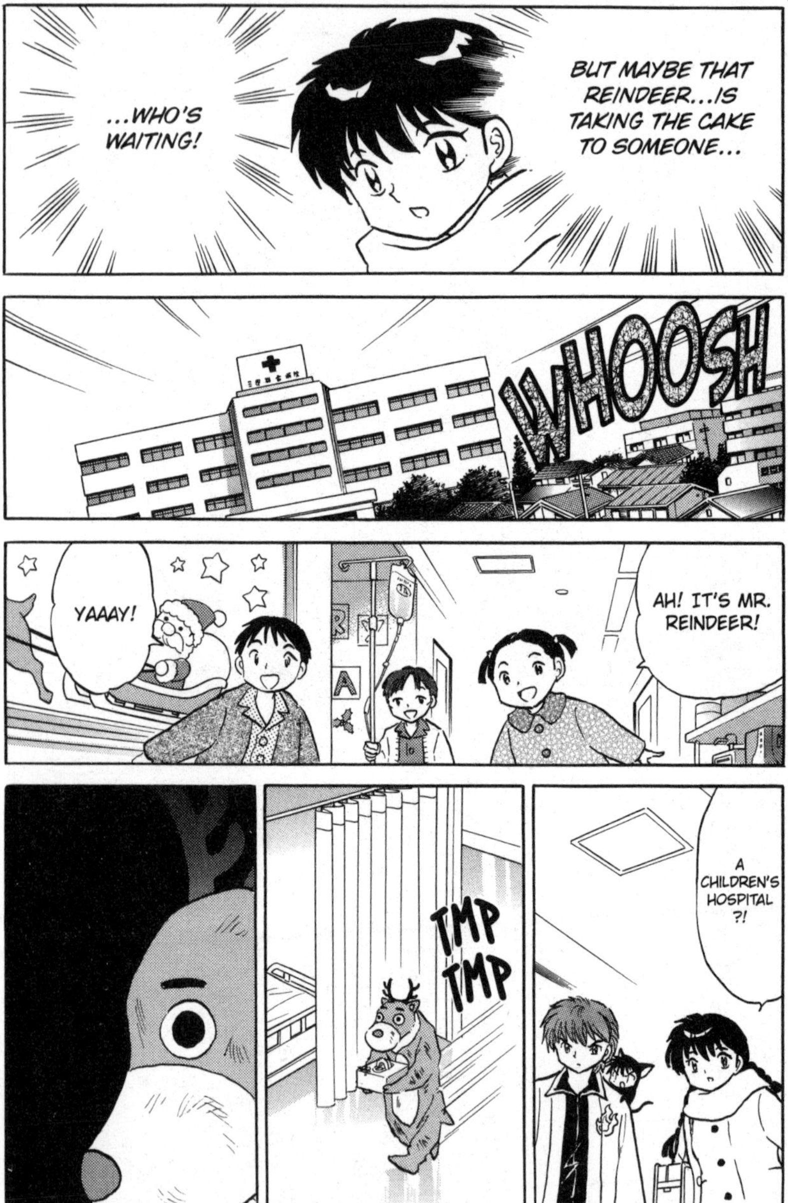
BUT MAYBE THAT REINDEER...IS TAKING THE CAKE TO SOMEONE...
...WHO'S WAITING!
WHOOSH
AH! IT'S MR. REINDEER!
YAAAY!
A CHILDREN'S HOSPITAL ?!
TMP TMP

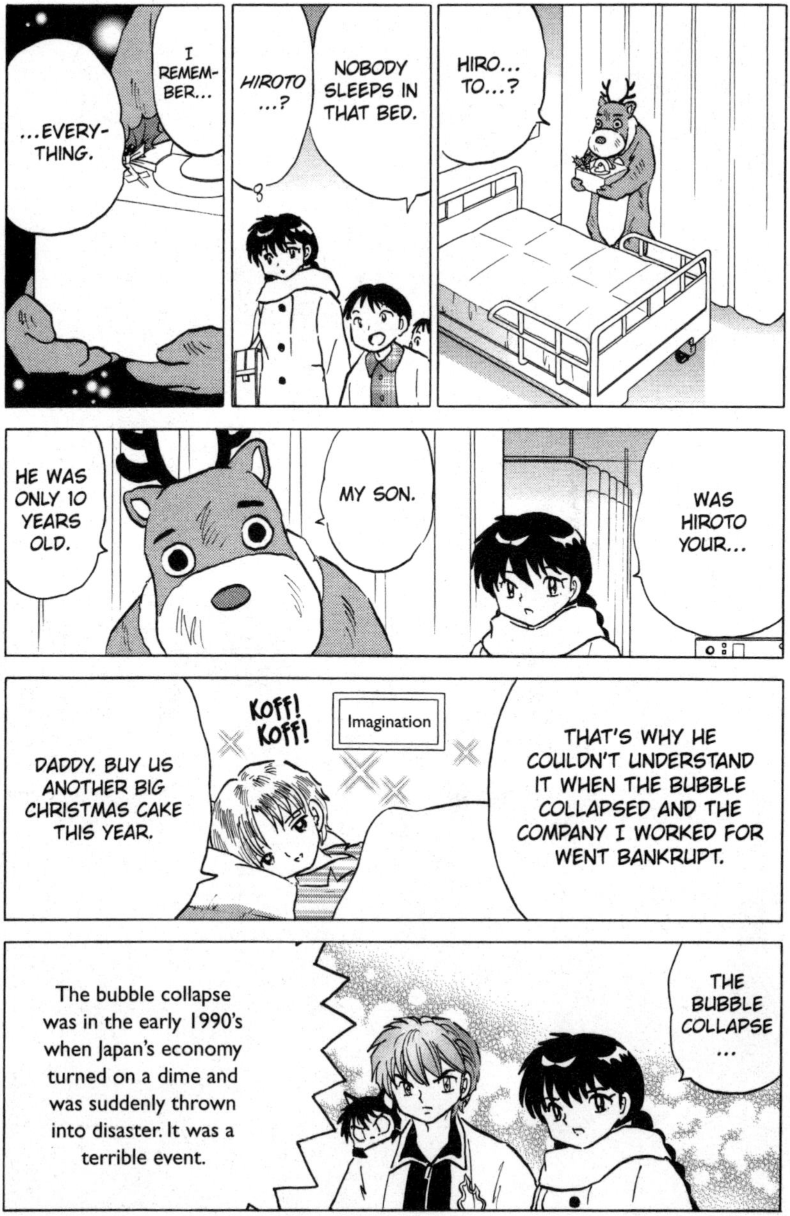
HIRO... TO...?
NOBODY SLEEPS IN THAT BED.
HIROTO ...?
I REMEMBER...
...EVERYTHING.
WAS HIROTO YOUR...
MY SON.
HE WAS ONLY 10 YEARS OLD.
THAT'S WHY HE COULDN'T UNDERSTAND IT WHEN THE BUBBLE COLLAPSED AND THE COMPANY I WORKED FOR WENT BANKRUPT.
Imagination
KOFF! KOFF!
DADDY. BUY US ANOTHER BIG CHRISTMAS CAKE THIS YEAR.
THE BUBBLE COLLAPSE ...
The bubble collapse was in the early 1990's when Japan's economy turned on a dime and was suddenly thrown into disaster. It was a terrible event.

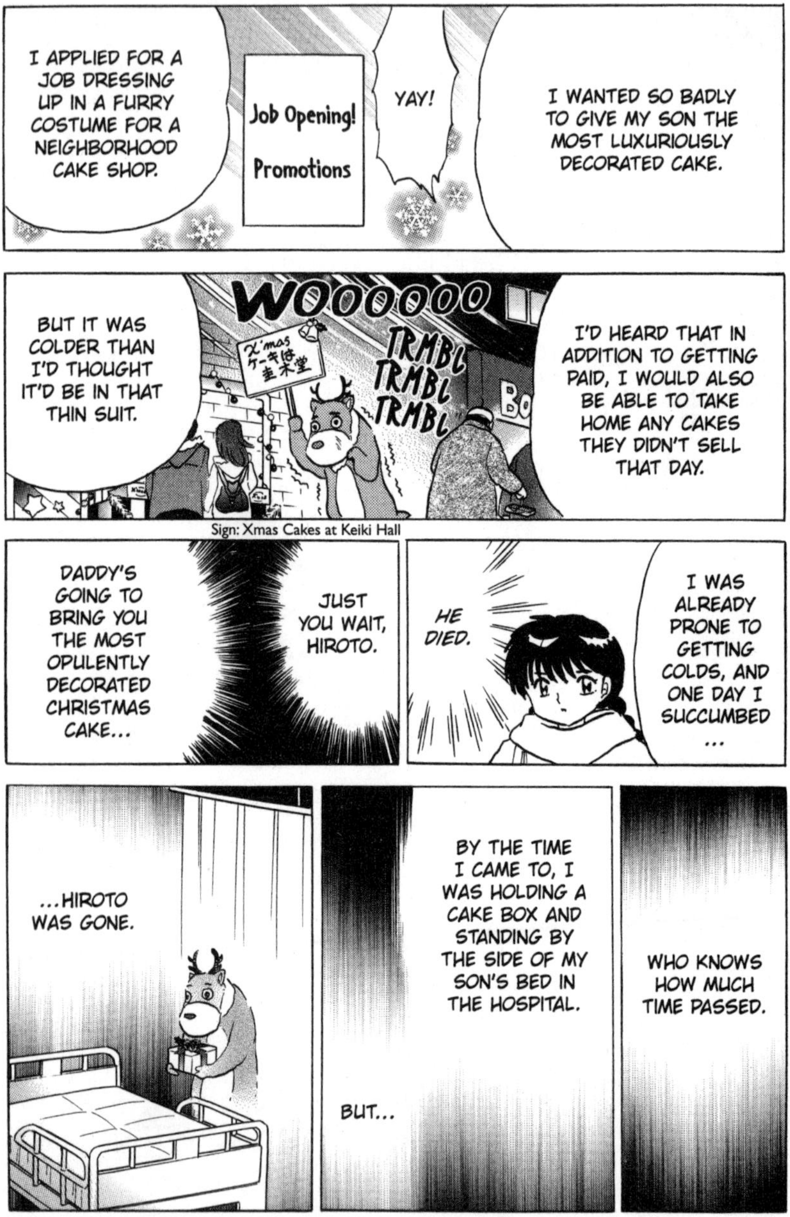
I WANTED SO BADLY TO GIVE MY SON THE MOST LUXURIOUSLY DECORATED CAKE.
YAY!
Job Opening!
Promotions
I APPLIED FOR A JOB DRESSING UP IN A FURRY COSTUME FOR A NEIGHBORHOOD CAKE SHOP.
I'D HEARD THAT IN ADDITION TO GETTING PAID, I WOULD ALSO BE ABLE TO TAKE HOME ANY CAKES THEY DIDN'T SELL THAT DAY.
WOOOOOO
TRMBL TRMBL TRMBL
X'mas ケーキは 圭木堂
BUT IT WAS COLDER THAN I'D THOUGHT IT'D BE IN THAT THIN SUIT.
I WAS ALREADY PRONE TO GETTING COLDS, AND ONE DAY I SUCCUMBED…
HE DIED.
JUST YOU WAIT, HIROTO.
DADDY'S GOING TO BRING YOU THE MOST OPULENTLY DECORATED CHRISTMAS CAKE…
WHO KNOWS HOW MUCH TIME PASSED.
BY THE TIME I CAME TO, I WAS HOLDING A CAKE BOX AND STANDING BY THE SIDE OF MY SON'S BED IN THE HOSPITAL.
BUT…
…HIROTO WAS GONE.
Sign: Xmas Cakes at Keiki Hall

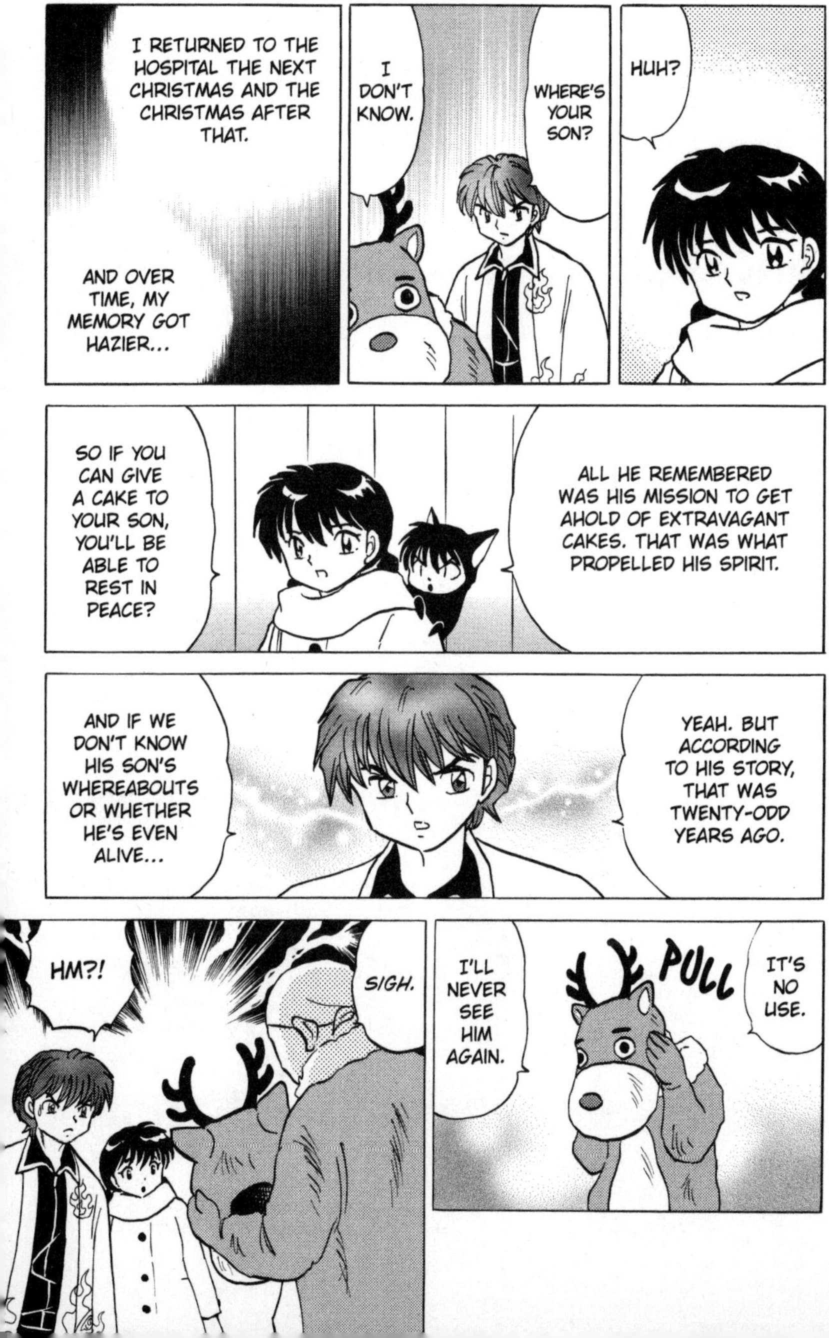
HUH?
WHERE'S YOUR SON?
I DON'T KNOW.
I RETURNED TO THE HOSPITAL THE NEXT CHRISTMAS AND THE CHRISTMAS AFTER THAT.
AND OVER TIME, MY MEMORY GOT HAZIER...
ALL HE REMEMBERED WAS HIS MISSION TO GET AHOLD OF EXTRAVAGANT CAKES. THAT WAS WHAT PROPELLED HIS SPIRIT.
SO IF YOU CAN GIVE A CAKE TO YOUR SON, YOU'LL BE ABLE TO REST IN PEACE?
YEAH. BUT ACCORDING TO HIS STORY, THAT WAS TWENTY-ODD YEARS AGO.
AND IF WE DON'T KNOW HIS SON'S WHEREABOUTS OR WHETHER HE'S EVEN ALIVE...
IT'S NO USE.
PULL
I'LL NEVER SEE HIM AGAIN.
SIGH.
HM?!

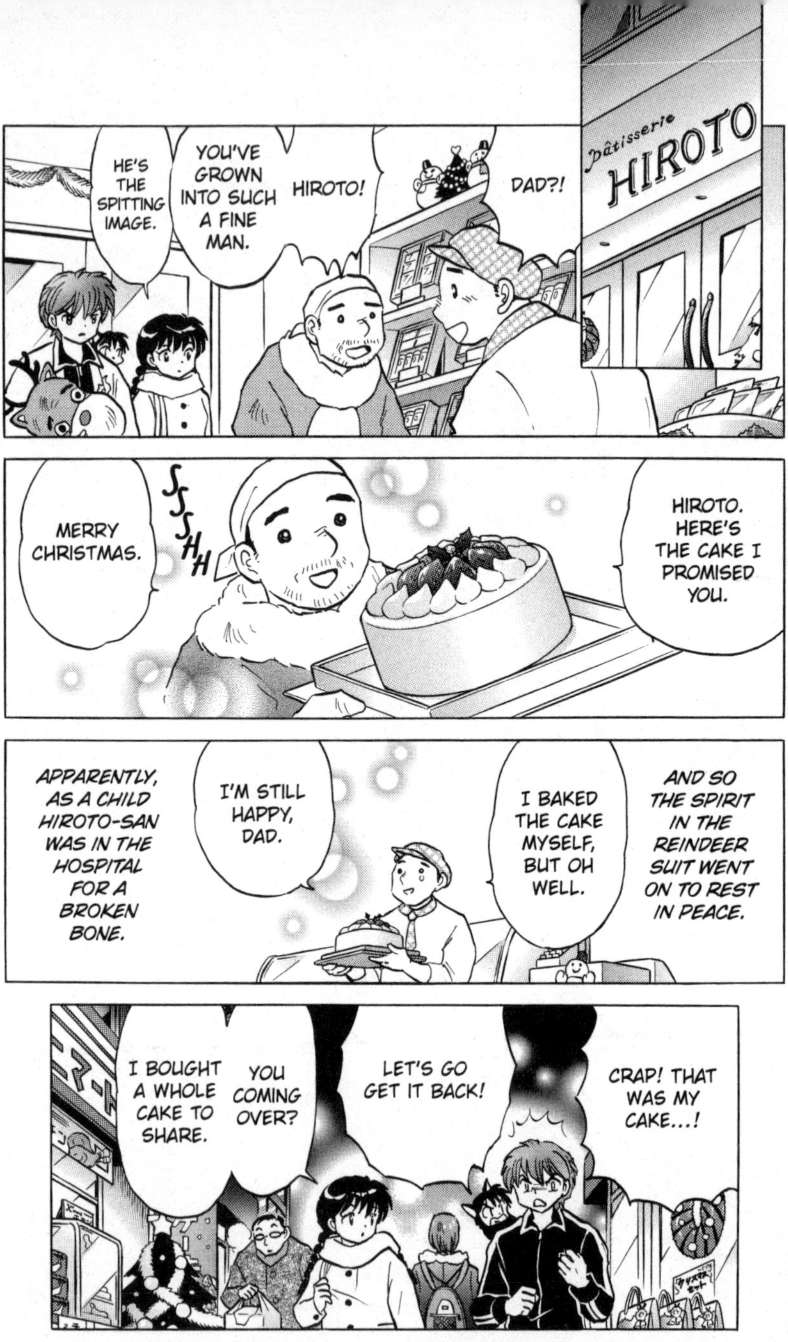
Pâtisserie HIROTO
DAD?!
HIROTO!
YOU'VE GROWN INTO SUCH A FINE MAN.
HE'S THE SPITTING IMAGE.
HIROTO. HERE'S THE CAKE I PROMISED YOU.
SSSHH
MERRY CHRISTMAS.
AND SO THE SPIRIT IN THE REINDEER SUIT WENT ON TO REST IN PEACE.
I BAKED THE CAKE MYSELF, BUT OH WELL.
I'M STILL HAPPY, DAD.
APPARENTLY, AS A CHILD HIROTO-SAN WAS IN THE HOSPITAL FOR A BROKEN BONE.
CRAP! THAT WAS MY CAKE...!
LET'S GO GET IT BACK!
YOU COMING OVER?
I BOUGHT A WHOLE CAKE TO SHARE.

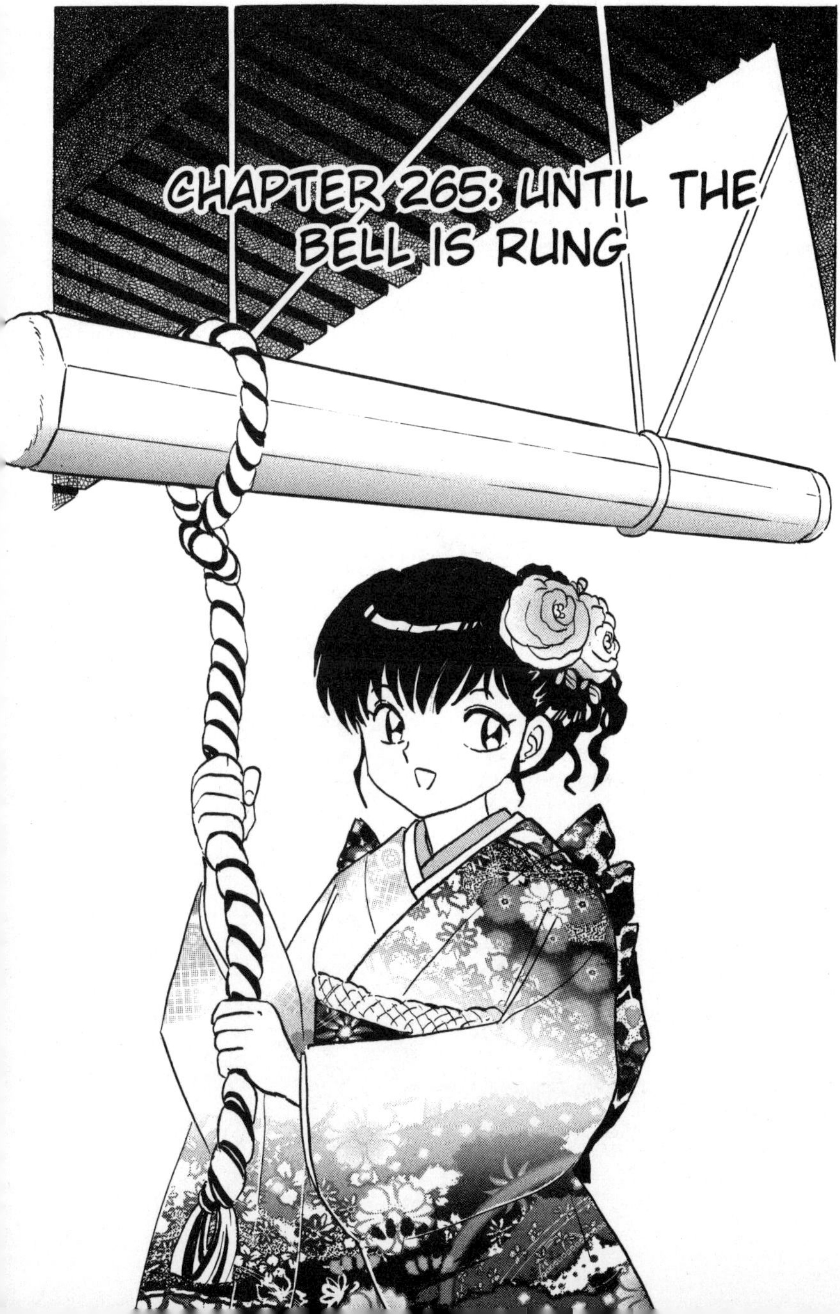
CHAPTER 265: UNTIL THE BELL IS RUNG

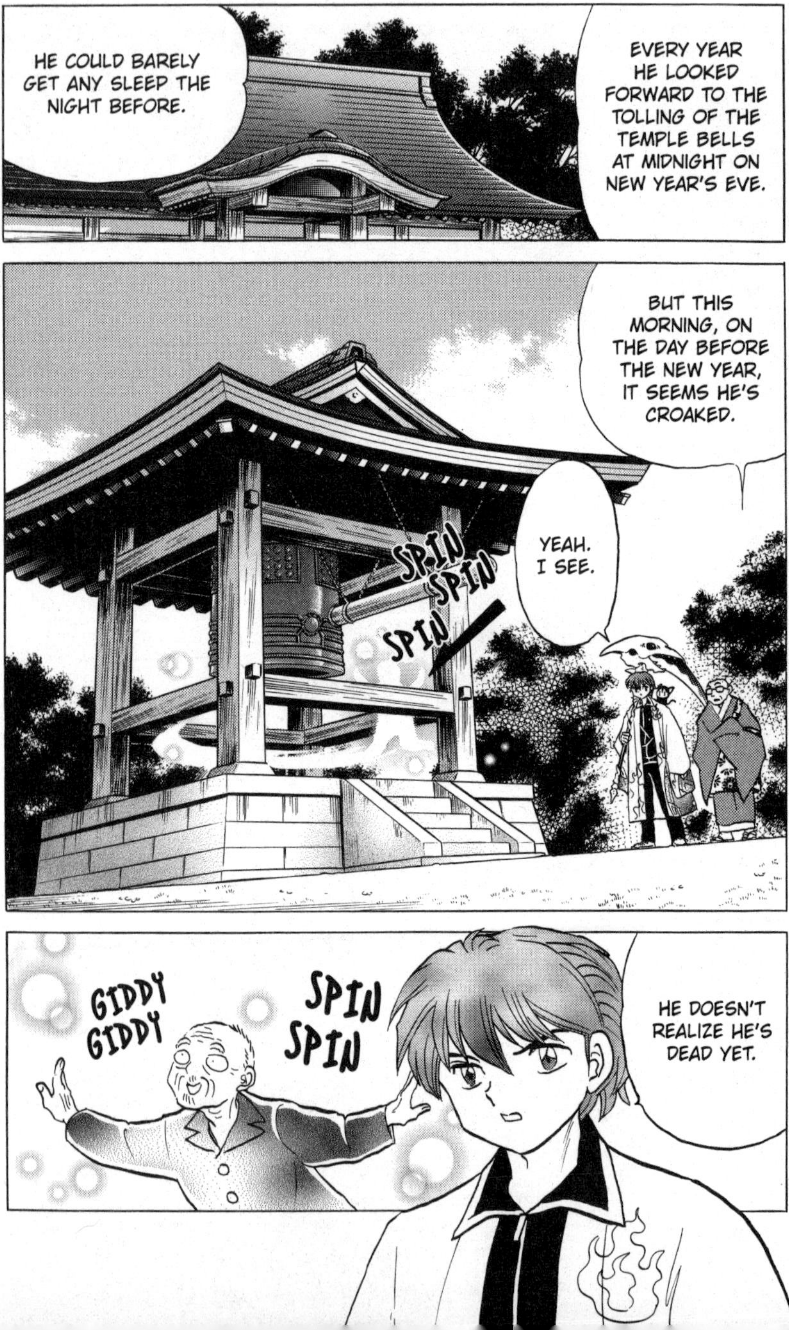
EVERY YEAR HE LOOKED FORWARD TO THE TOLLING OF THE TEMPLE BELLS AT MIDNIGHT ON NEW YEAR'S EVE.
HE COULD BARELY GET ANY SLEEP THE NIGHT BEFORE.
BUT THIS MORNING, ON THE DAY BEFORE THE NEW YEAR, IT SEEMS HE'S CROAKED.
YEAH. I SEE.
SPIN
SPIN
SPIN
HE DOESN'T REALIZE HE'S DEAD YET.
SPIN SPIN
GIDDY GIDDY

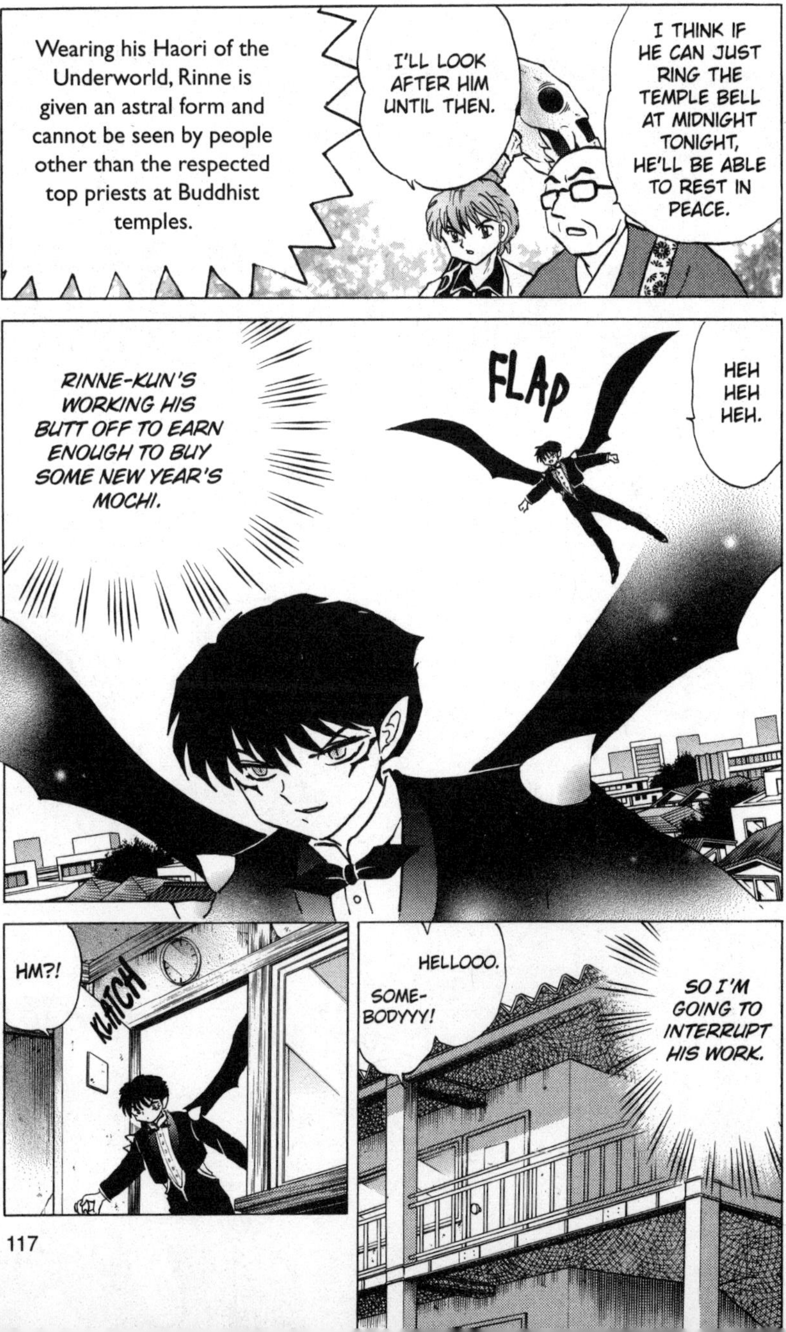
I THINK IF HE CAN JUST RING THE TEMPLE BELL AT MIDNIGHT TONIGHT, HE'LL BE ABLE TO REST IN PEACE.
I'LL LOOK AFTER HIM UNTIL THEN.
Wearing his Haori of the Underworld, Rinne is given an astral form and cannot be seen by people other than the respected top priests at Buddhist temples.
HEH HEH HEH.
FLAP
RINNE-KUN'S WORKING HIS BUTT OFF TO EARN ENOUGH TO BUY SOME NEW YEAR'S MOCHI.
SO I'M GOING TO INTERRUPT HIS WORK.
HELLOOO.
SOME-BODYYY!
KLATCH
HM?!

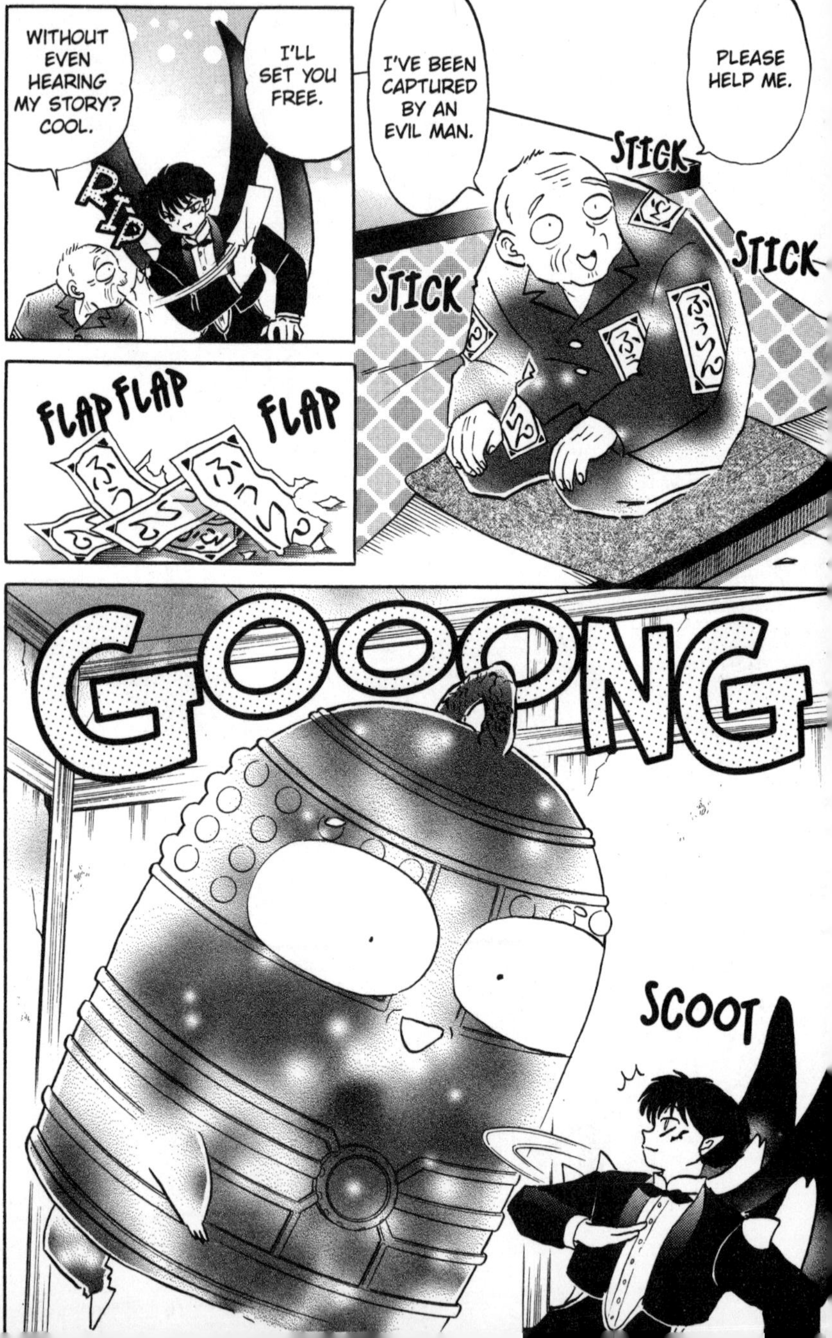
PLEASE HELP ME.
STICK
STICK
I'VE BEEN CAPTURED BY AN EVIL MAN.
STICK
I'LL SET YOU FREE.
RIP
WITHOUT EVEN HEARING MY STORY? COOL.
FLAP FLAP
FLAP
GOOONG
SCOOT

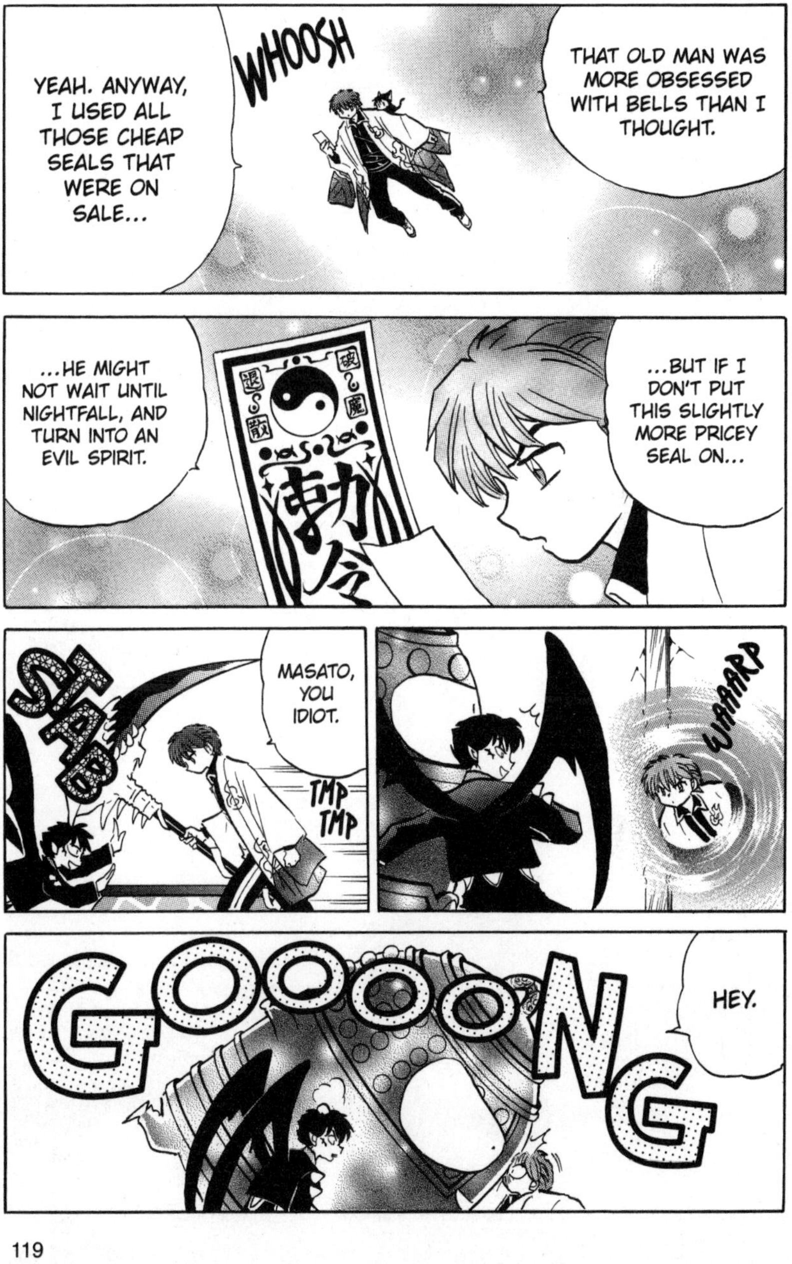
THAT OLD MAN WAS MORE OBSESSED WITH BELLS THAN I THOUGHT.
WHOOSH
YEAH. ANYWAY, I USED ALL THOSE CHEAP SEALS THAT WERE ON SALE...
...BUT IF I DON'T PUT THIS SLIGHTLY MORE PRICEY SEAL ON...
...HE MIGHT NOT WAIT UNTIL NIGHTFALL, AND TURN INTO AN EVIL SPIRIT.
WHAAARP
MASATO, YOU IDIOT.
TMP TMP
STAB
HEY.
GOOOONG

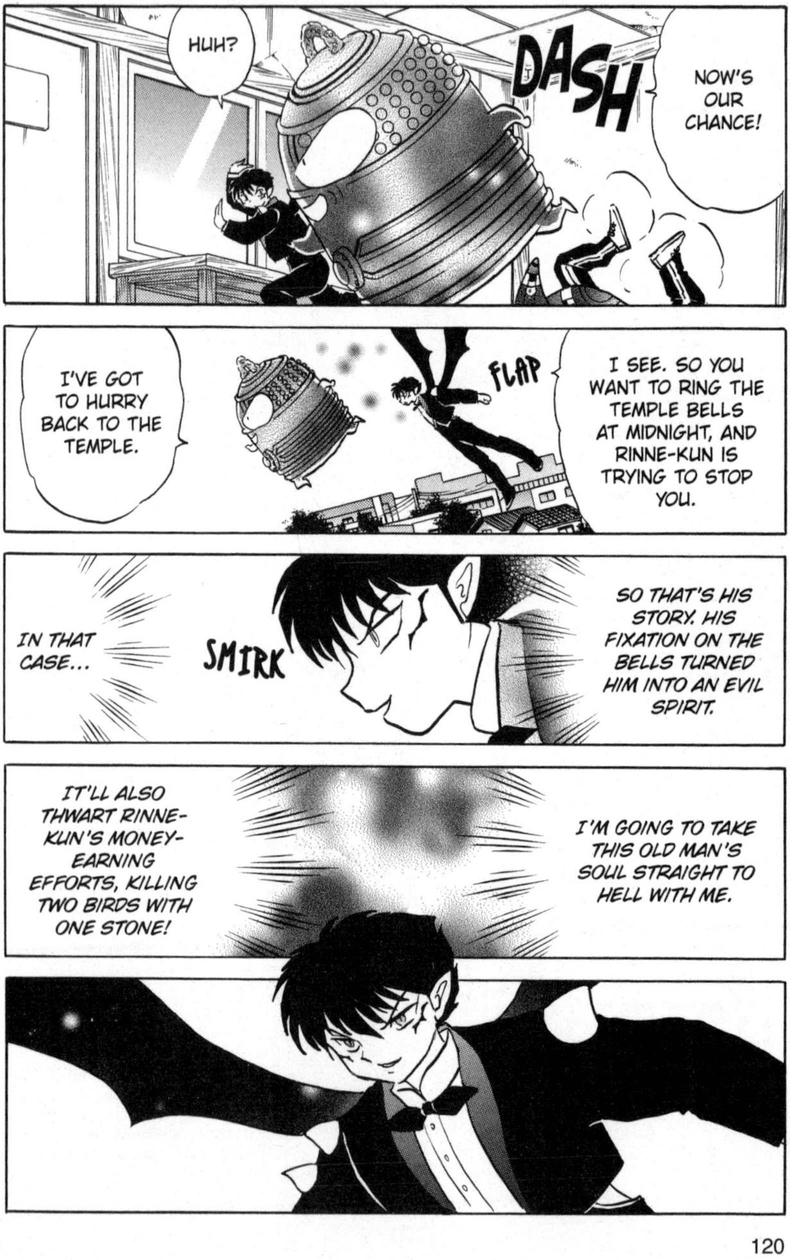
NOW'S OUR CHANCE!
DASH
HUH?
I SEE. SO YOU WANT TO RING THE TEMPLE BELLS AT MIDNIGHT, AND RINNE-KUN IS TRYING TO STOP YOU.
FLAP
I'VE GOT TO HURRY BACK TO THE TEMPLE.
SO THAT'S HIS STORY. HIS FIXATION ON THE BELLS TURNED HIM INTO AN EVIL SPIRIT.
SMIRK
IN THAT CASE...
I'M GOING TO TAKE THIS OLD MAN'S SOUL STRAIGHT TO HELL WITH ME.
IT'LL ALSO THWART RINNE-KUN'S MONEY-EARNING EFFORTS, KILLING TWO BIRDS WITH ONE STONE!

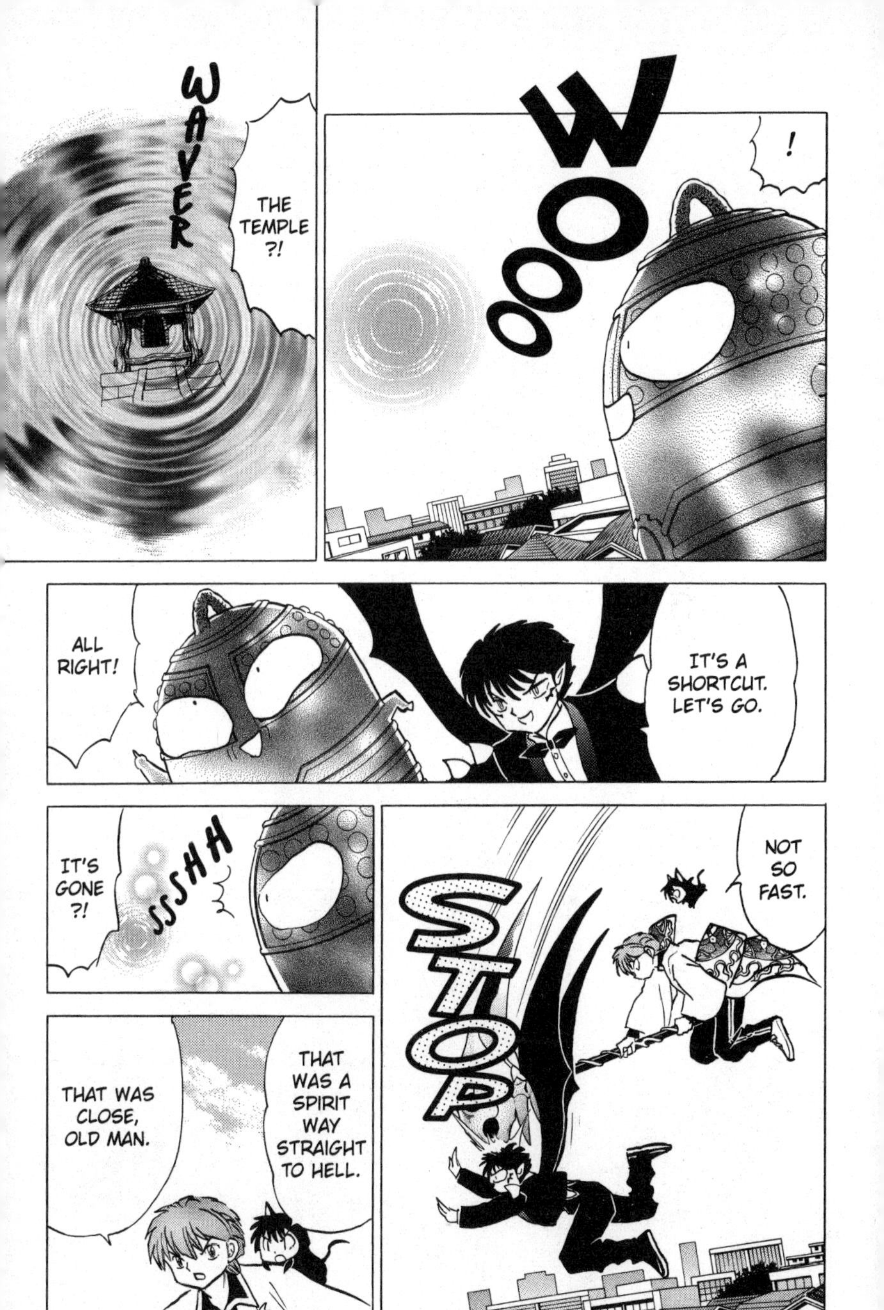
WOOO
!
WAVER
THE TEMPLE ?!
IT'S A SHORTCUT. LET'S GO.
ALL RIGHT!
NOT SO FAST.
STOP
SSSHH
IT'S GONE ?!
THAT WAS A SPIRIT WAY STRAIGHT TO HELL.
THAT WAS CLOSE, OLD MAN.

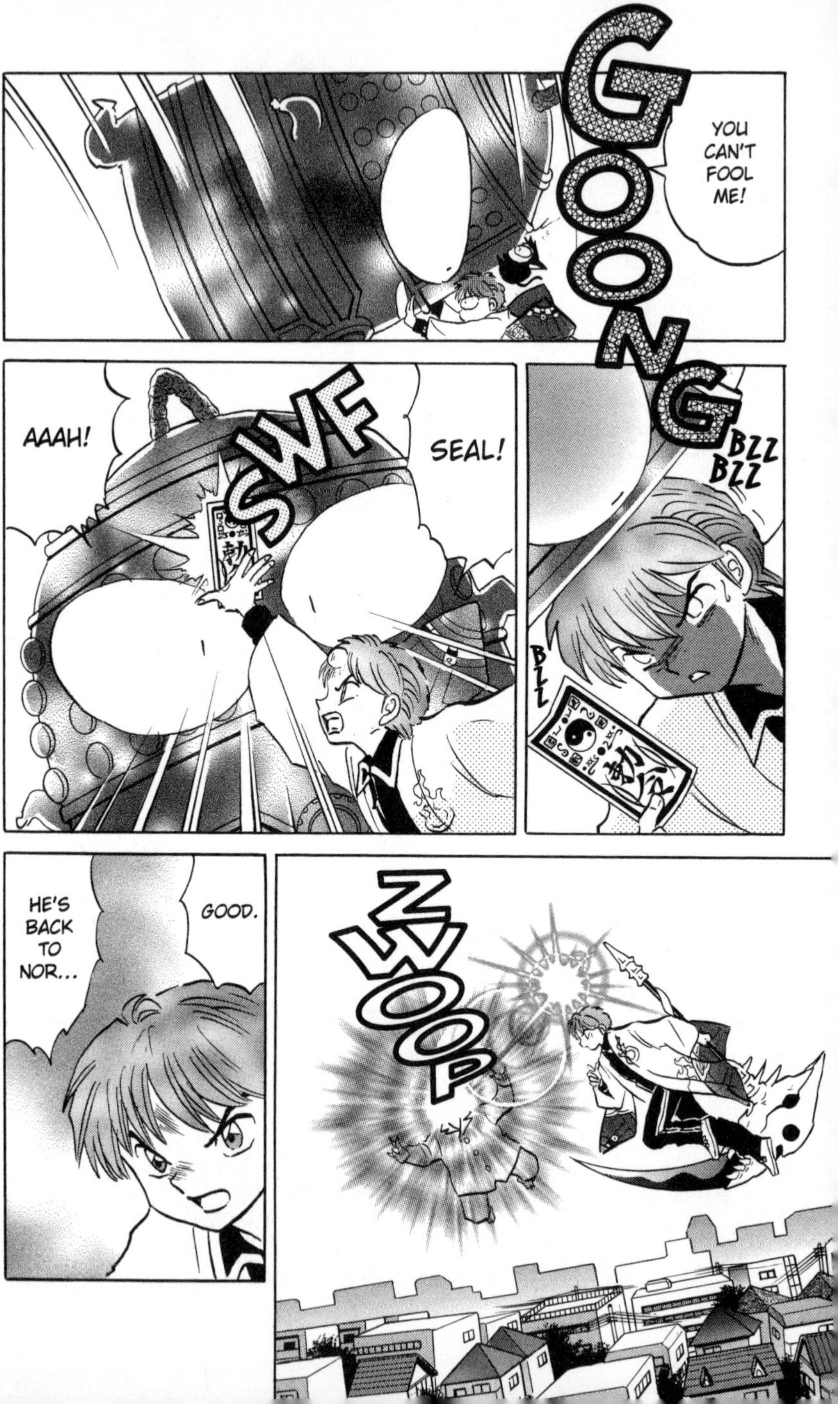
GOOONG
YOU CAN'T FOOL ME!
BZZ BZZ
BZZ
SEAL!
SWF
AAAH!
ZWOOP
GOOD.
HE'S BACK TO NOR...

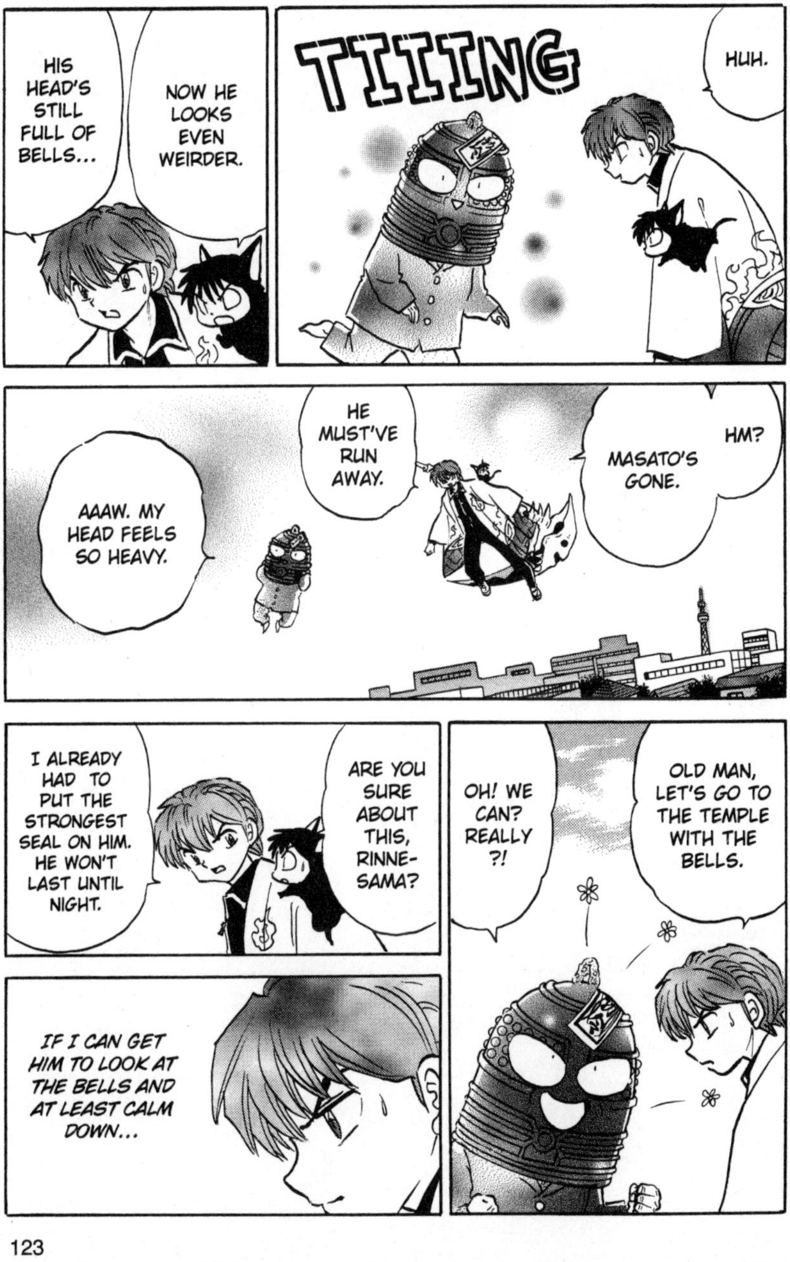
HUH.
TIIING
NOW HE LOOKS EVEN WEIRDER.
HIS HEAD'S STILL FULL OF BELLS...
HM?
MASATO'S GONE.
HE MUST'VE RUN AWAY.
AAAW. MY HEAD FEELS SO HEAVY.
OLD MAN, LET'S GO TO THE TEMPLE WITH THE BELLS.
OH! WE CAN? REALLY?!
ARE YOU SURE ABOUT THIS, RINNE-SAMA?
I ALREADY HAD TO PUT THE STRONGEST SEAL ON HIM. HE WON'T LAST UNTIL NIGHT.
IF I CAN GET HIM TO LOOK AT THE BELLS AND AT LEAST CALM DOWN...

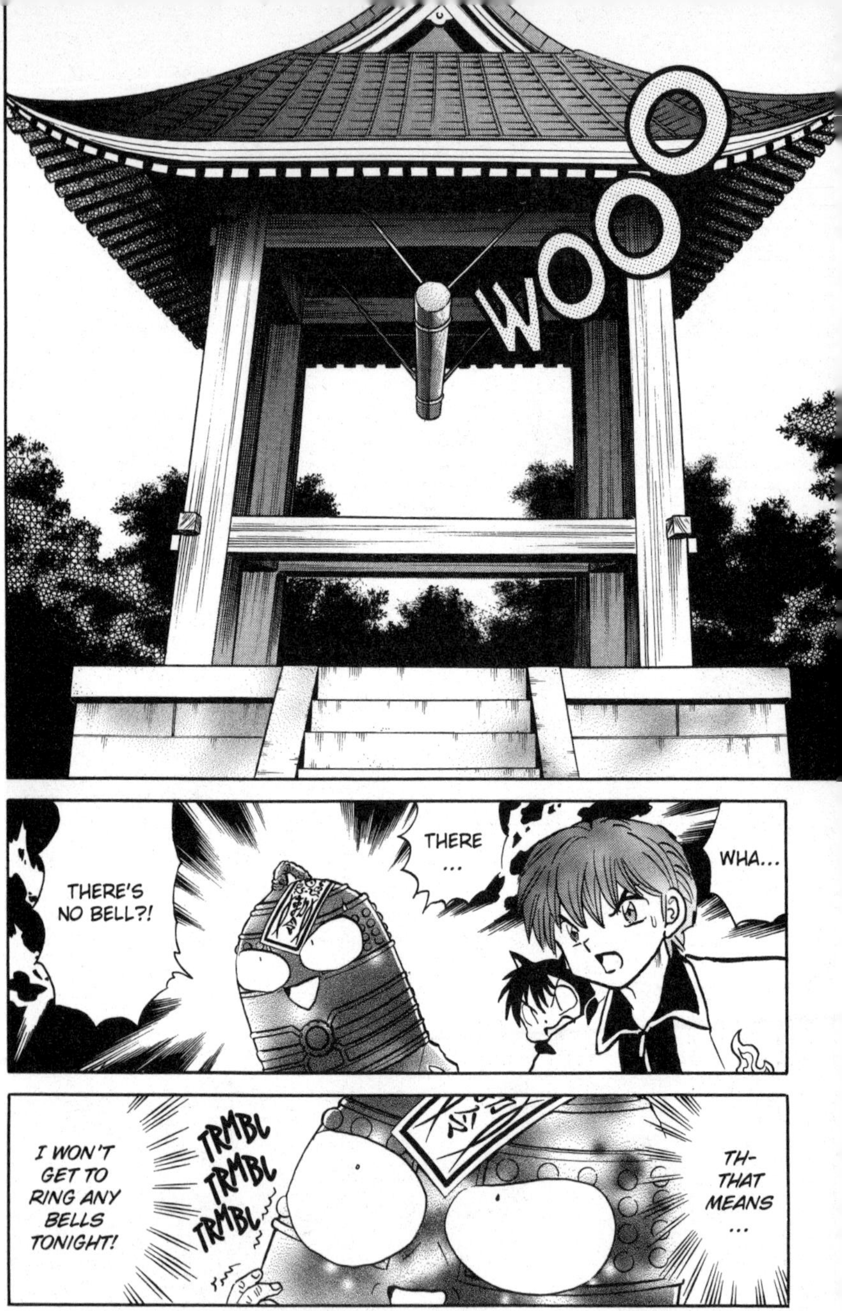
WOOOO
WHA...
THERE ...
THERE'S NO BELL?!
TH- THAT MEANS ...
TRMBL TRMBL TRMBL
I WON'T GET TO RING ANY BELLS TONIGHT!

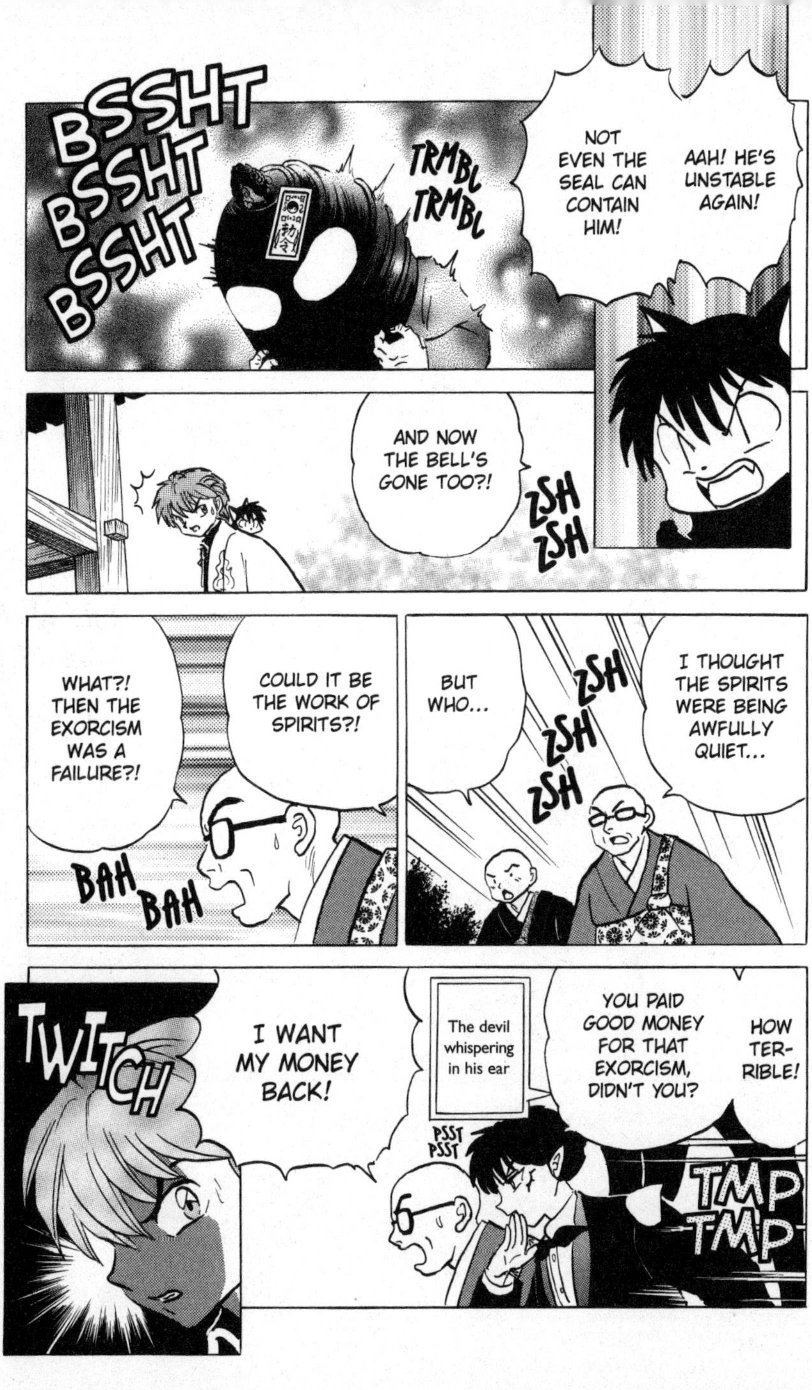
AAH! HE'S UNSTABLE AGAIN!
NOT EVEN THE SEAL CAN CONTAIN HIM!
TRMBL TRMBL
BSSHT BSSHT BSSHT
AND NOW THE BELL'S GONE TOO?!
ZSH ZSH
I THOUGHT THE SPIRITS WERE BEING AWFULLY QUIET...
ZSH ZSH ZSH
BUT WHO...
COULD IT BE THE WORK OF SPIRITS?!
WHAT?! THEN THE EXORCISM WAS A FAILURE?!
BAH BAH
HOW TER-RIBLE!
YOU PAID GOOD MONEY FOR THAT EXORCISM, DIDN'T YOU?
The devil whispering in his ear
TMP TMP
PSST PSST
I WANT MY MONEY BACK!
TWITCH

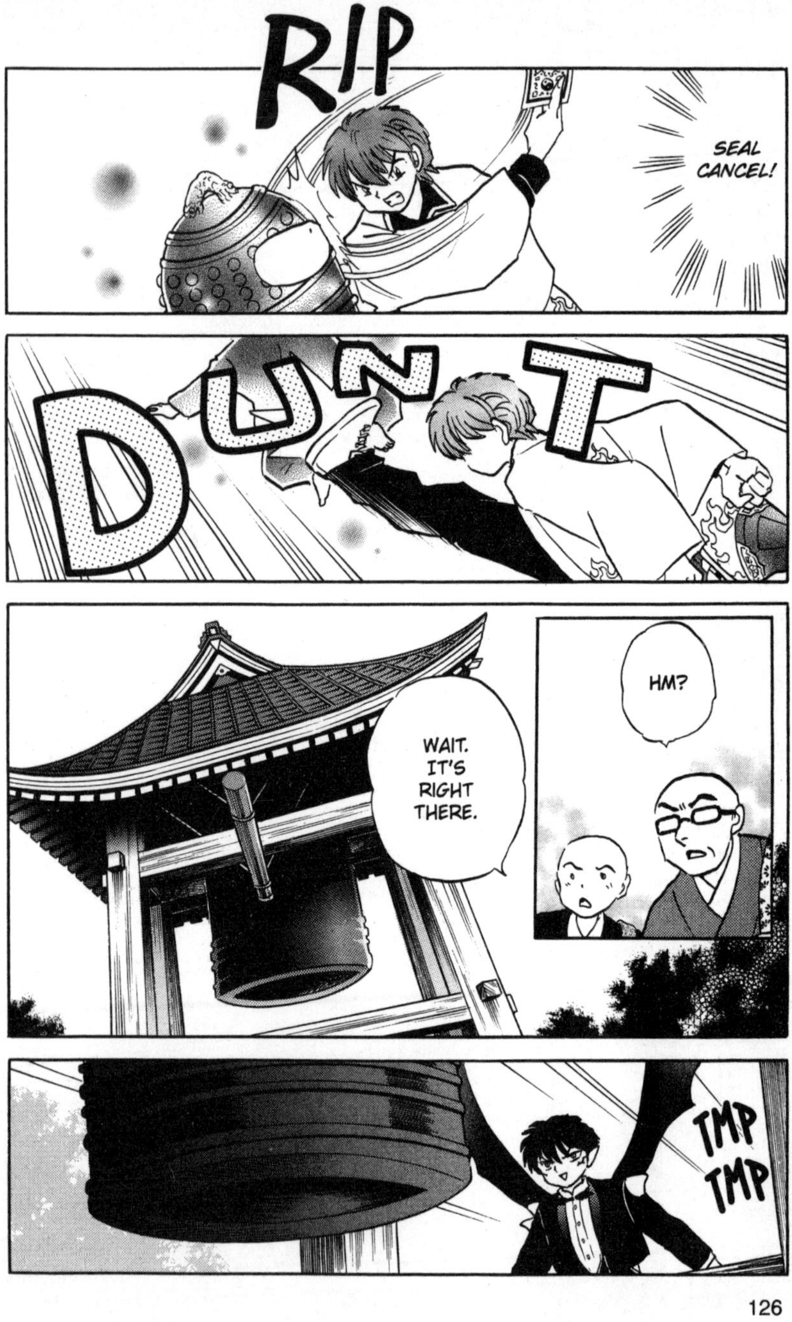
SEAL CANCEL!
RIP
DUNT
HM?
WAIT. IT'S RIGHT THERE.
TMP TMP

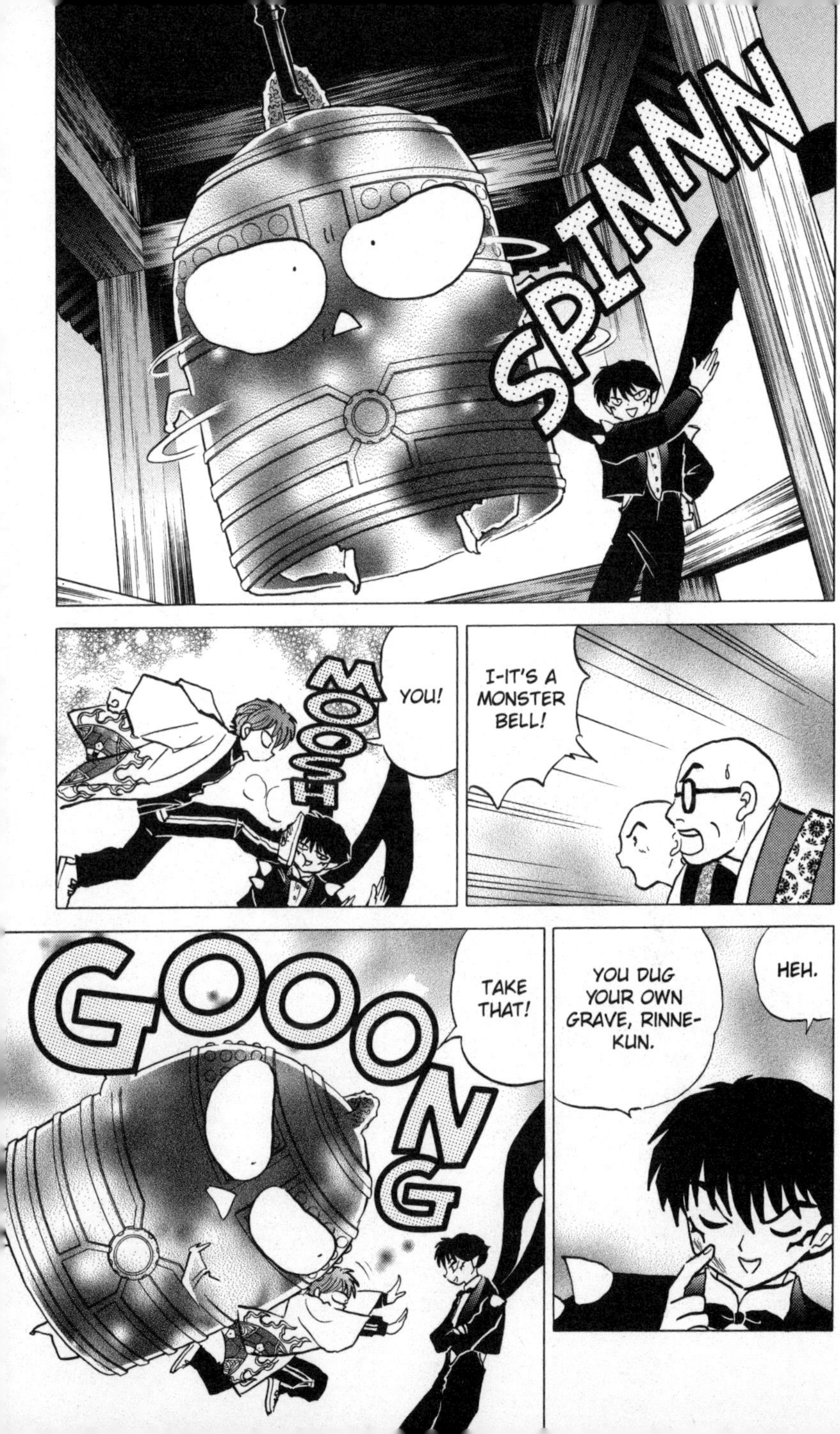
SPINNNN
I-IT'S A MONSTER BELL!
YOU!
WOOOSH
HEH.
YOU DUG YOUR OWN GRAVE, RINNE-KUN.
TAKE THAT!
GOOOONG

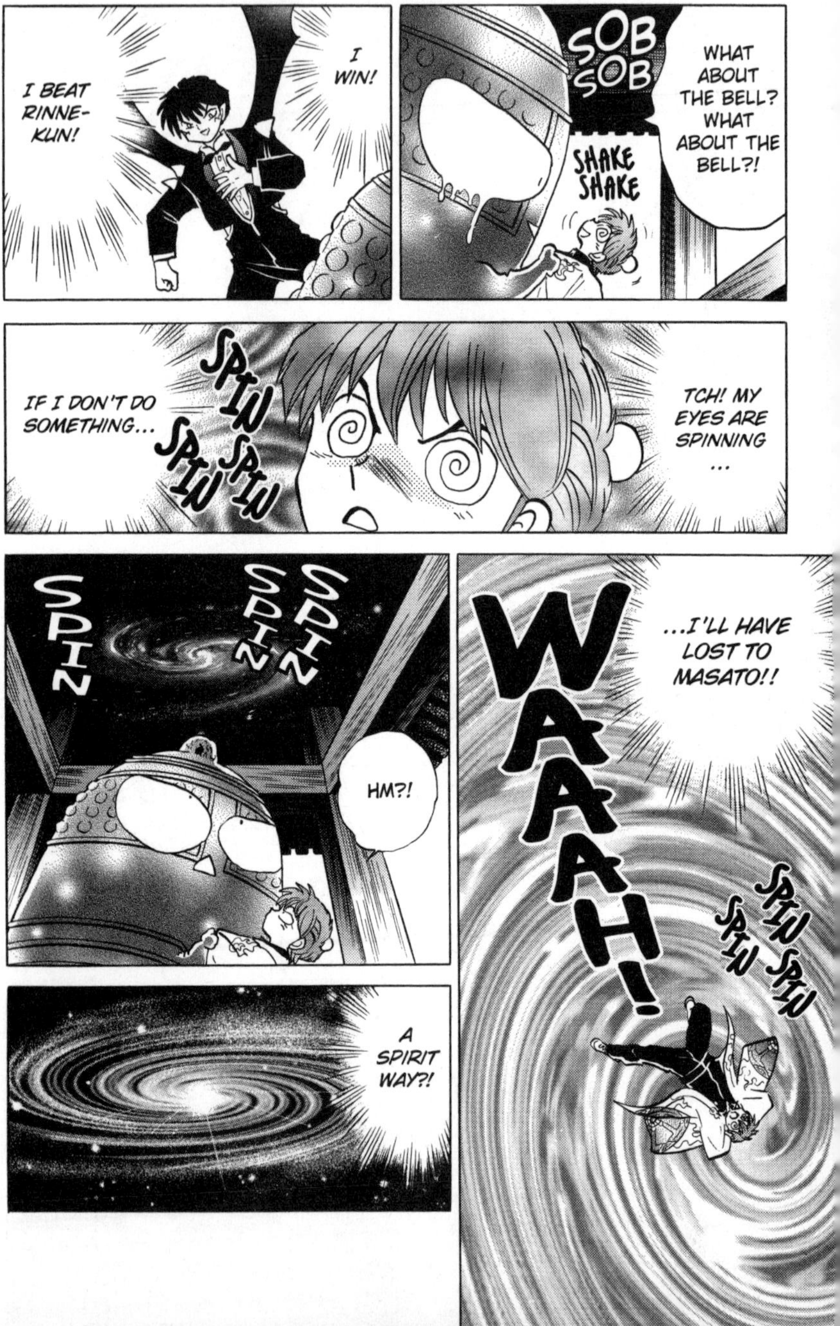
SOB SOB
WHAT ABOUT THE BELL? WHAT ABOUT THE BELL?!
SHAKE SHAKE
I WIN!
I BEAT RINNE-KUN!
TCH! MY EYES ARE SPINNING ...
SPIN SPIN SPIN SPIN
IF I DON'T DO SOMETHING...
...I'LL HAVE LOST TO MASATO!!
WAAAH!
SPIN SPIN SPIN SPIN
SPIN SPIN SPIN
HM?!
A SPIRIT WAY?!

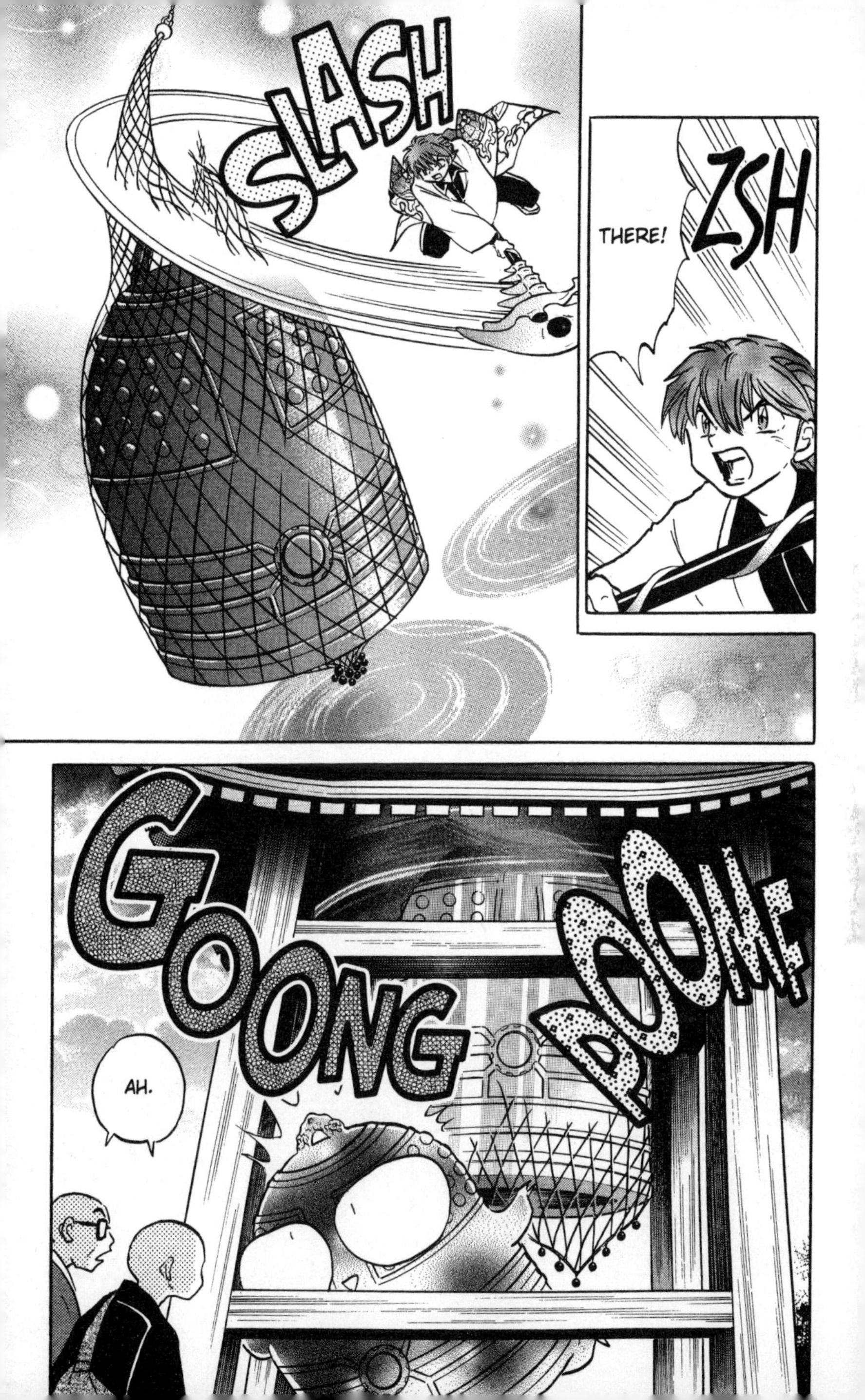
THERE!
ZSH
SLASH
BOOM!
GOOONG
AH.

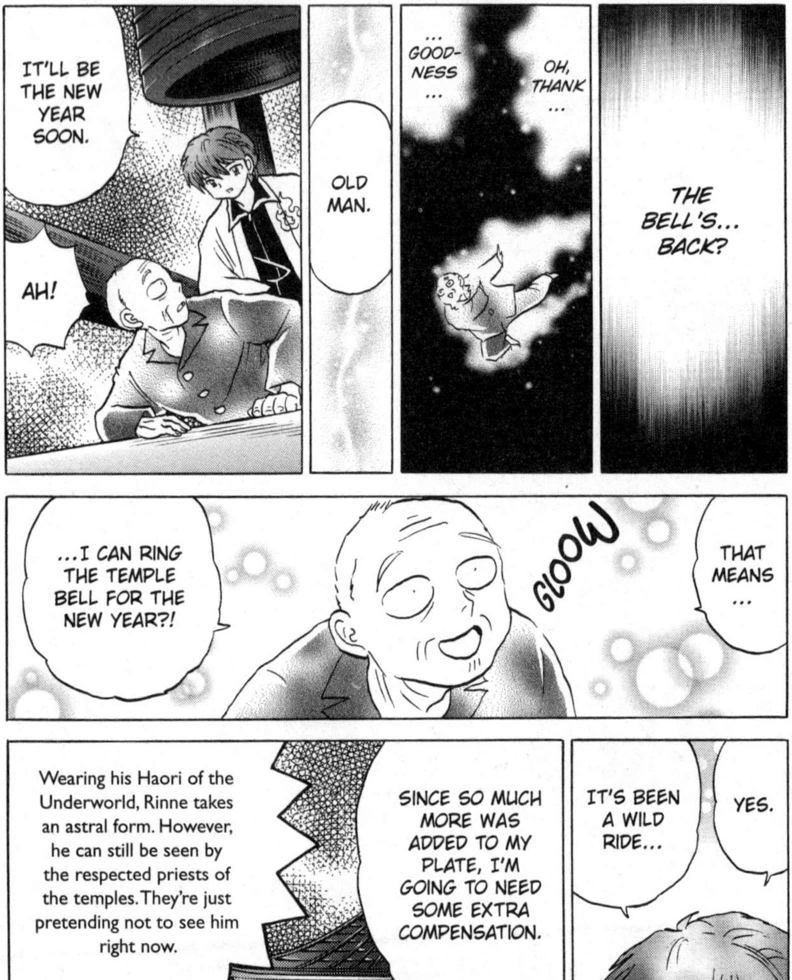
THE BELL'S... BACK?
OH, THANK ...
... GOODNESS ...
OLD MAN.
IT'LL BE THE NEW YEAR SOON.
AH!
THAT MEANS ...
GLOOW
...I CAN RING THE TEMPLE BELL FOR THE NEW YEAR?!
YES.
IT'S BEEN A WILD RIDE...
SINCE SO MUCH MORE WAS ADDED TO MY PLATE, I'M GOING TO NEED SOME EXTRA COMPENSATION.
Wearing his Haori of the Underworld, Rinne takes an astral form. However, he can still be seen by the respected priests of the temples. They're just pretending not to see him right now.

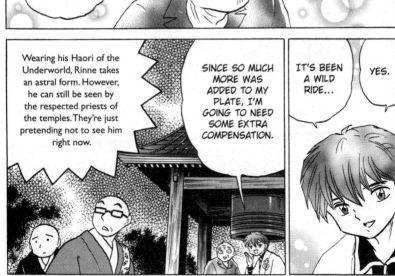

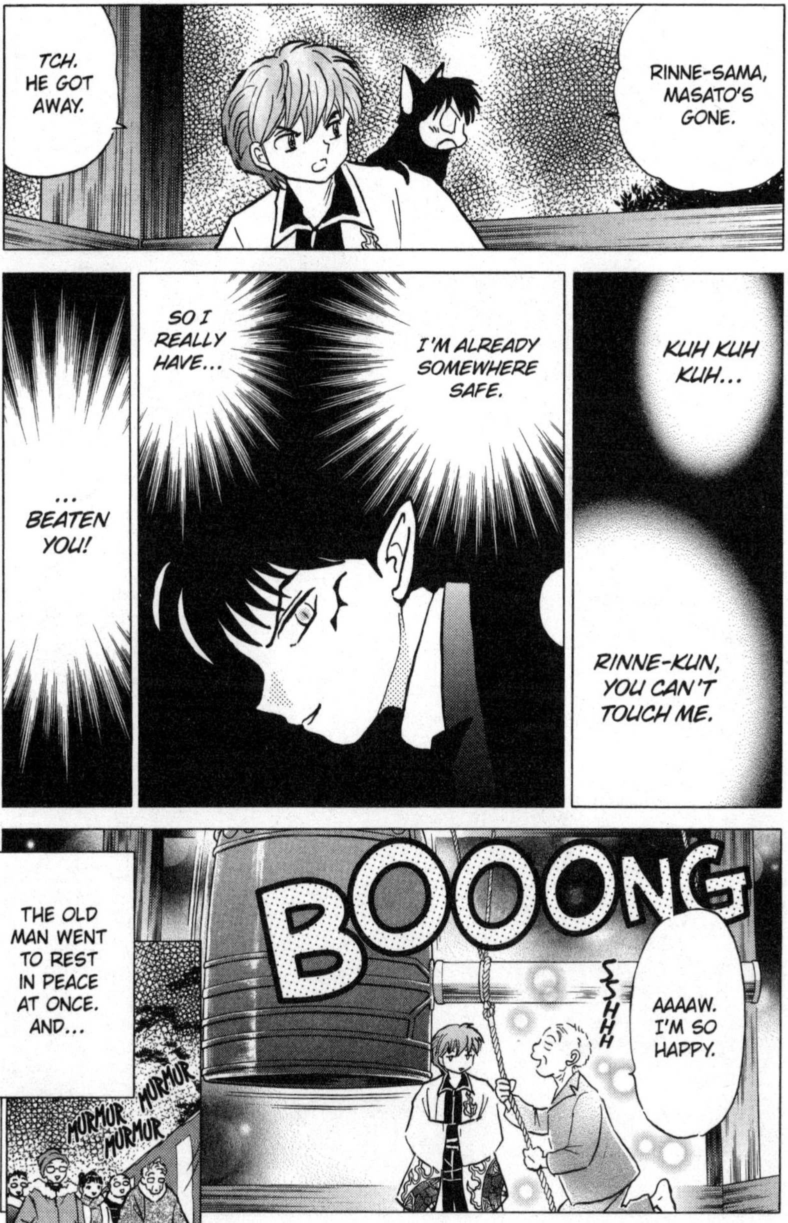
RINNE-SAMA, MASATO'S GONE.
TCH. HE GOT AWAY.
KUH KUH KUH...
RINNE-KUN, YOU CAN'T TOUCH ME.
I'M ALREADY SOMEWHERE SAFE.
SO I REALLY HAVE...
... BEATEN YOU!
BOOOONG
AAAAW. I'M SO HAPPY.
SHHH
THE OLD MAN WENT TO REST IN PEACE AT ONCE. AND...
MURMUR MURMUR MURMUR

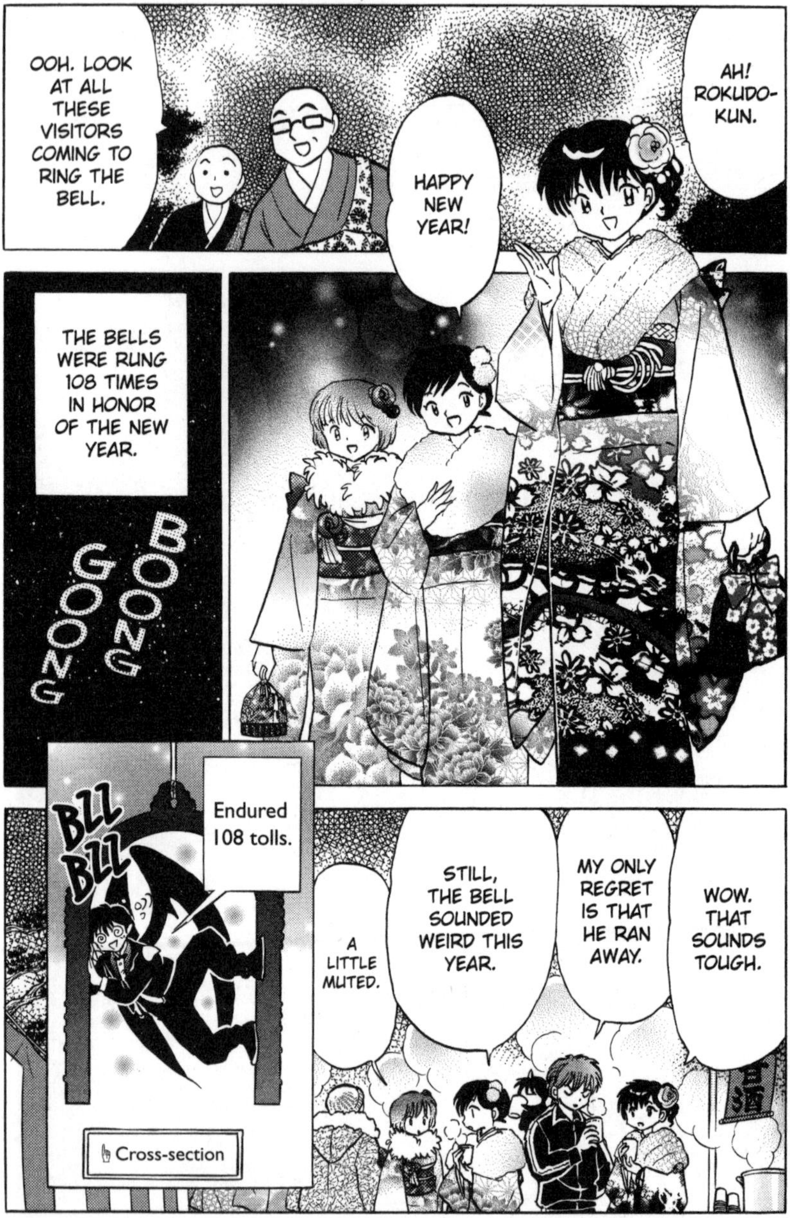
AH! ROKUDO-KUN.
HAPPY NEW YEAR!
OOH. LOOK AT ALL THESE VISITORS COMING TO RING THE BELL.
THE BELLS WERE RUNG 108 TIMES IN HONOR OF THE NEW YEAR.
BOOONG
GOOONG
WOW. THAT SOUNDS TOUGH.
MY ONLY REGRET IS THAT HE RAN AWAY.
STILL, THE BELL SOUNDED WEIRD THIS YEAR.
A LITTLE MUTED.
Endured 108 tolls.
BZZ BZZ
Cross-section

CHAPTER 266: THE EVIL SPIRIT'S LEGACY

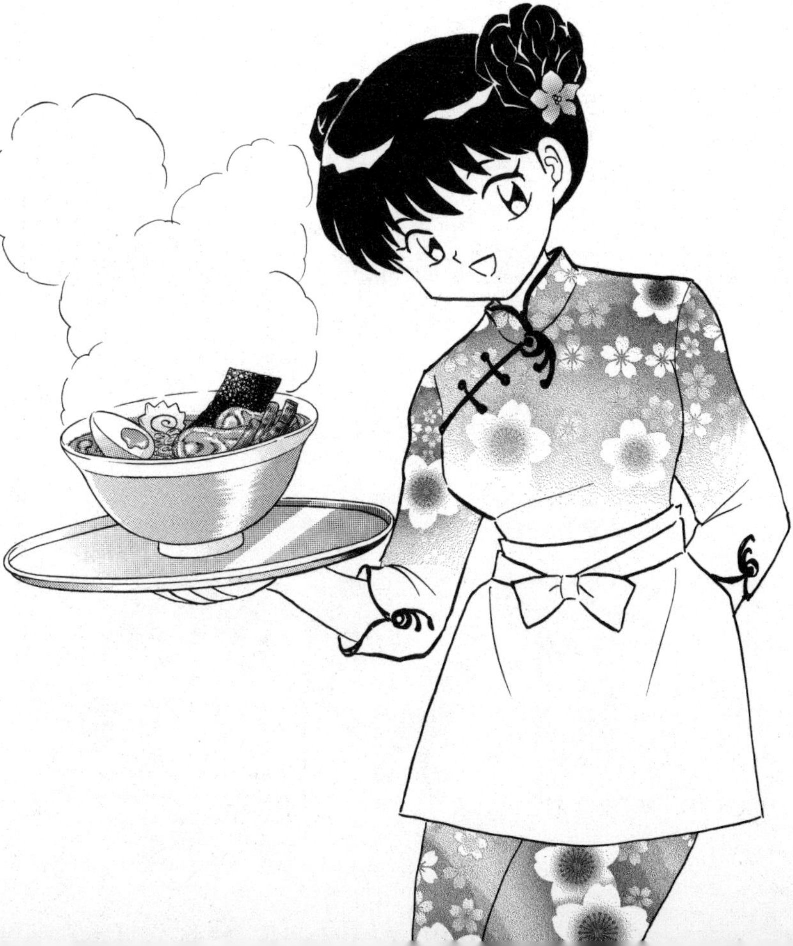

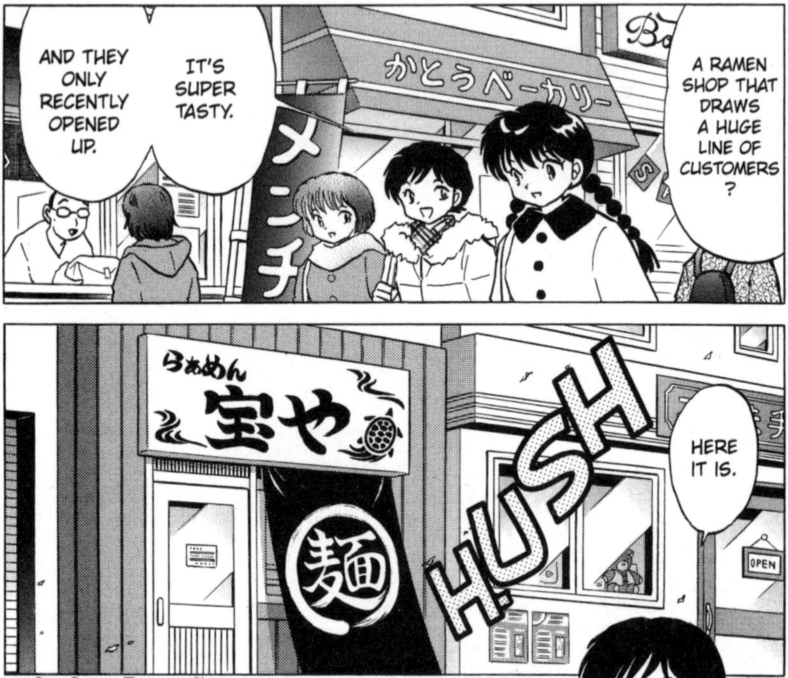
A RAMEN SHOP THAT DRAWS A HUGE LINE OF CUSTOMERS?
IT'S SUPER TASTY.
AND THEY ONLY RECENTLY OPENED UP.
HERE IT IS.
HUSH
OPEN

Sign: Ramen Treasure Shop Curtain: Noodles

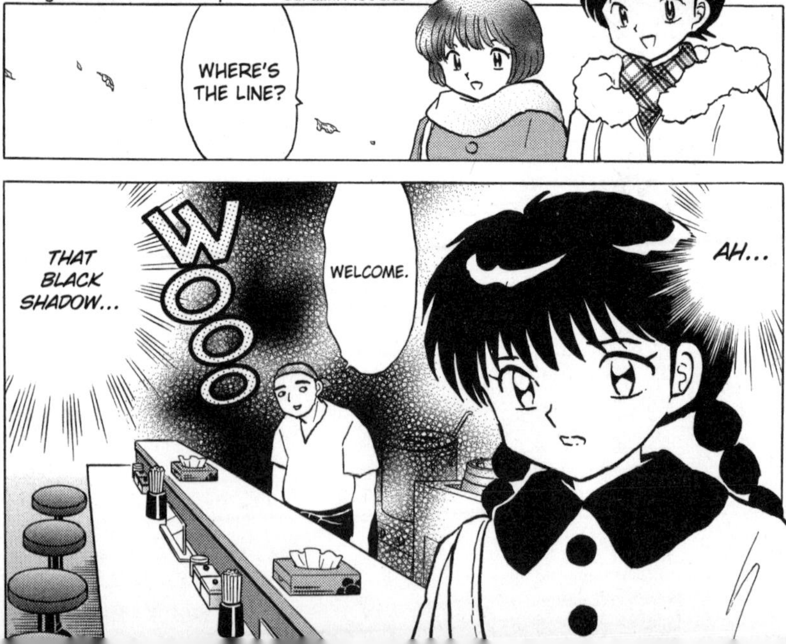
WHERE'S THE LINE?
AH...
WELCOME.
WOOOO
THAT BLACK SHADOW...

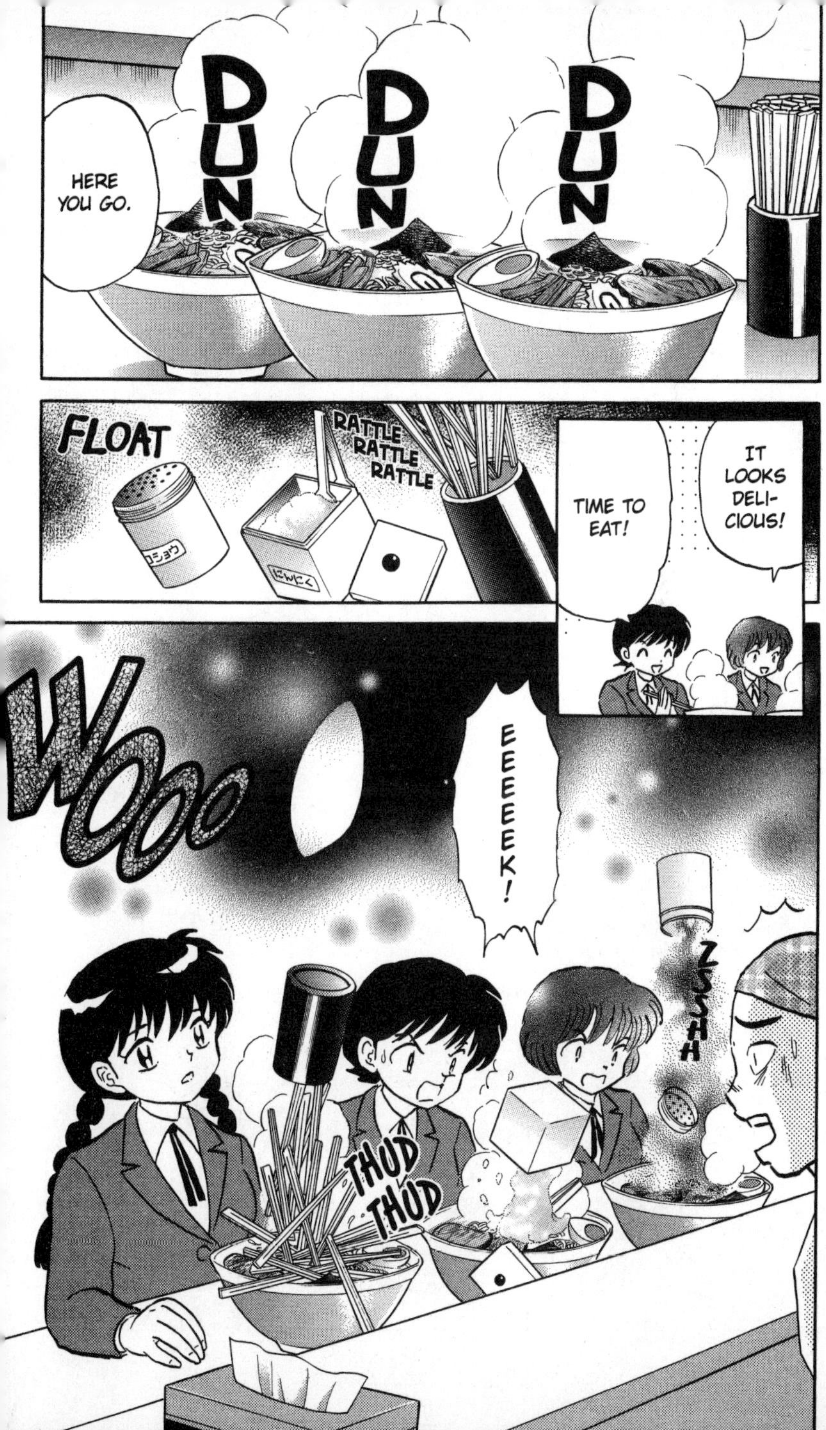
DUN
DUN
DUN
HERE YOU GO.
IT LOOKS DELI- CIOUS!
TIME TO EAT!
RATTLE RATTLE RATTLE
FLOAT
にんにく
コショウ
EEEEEEK!
WOOOO
ZSSHH
THUD THUD

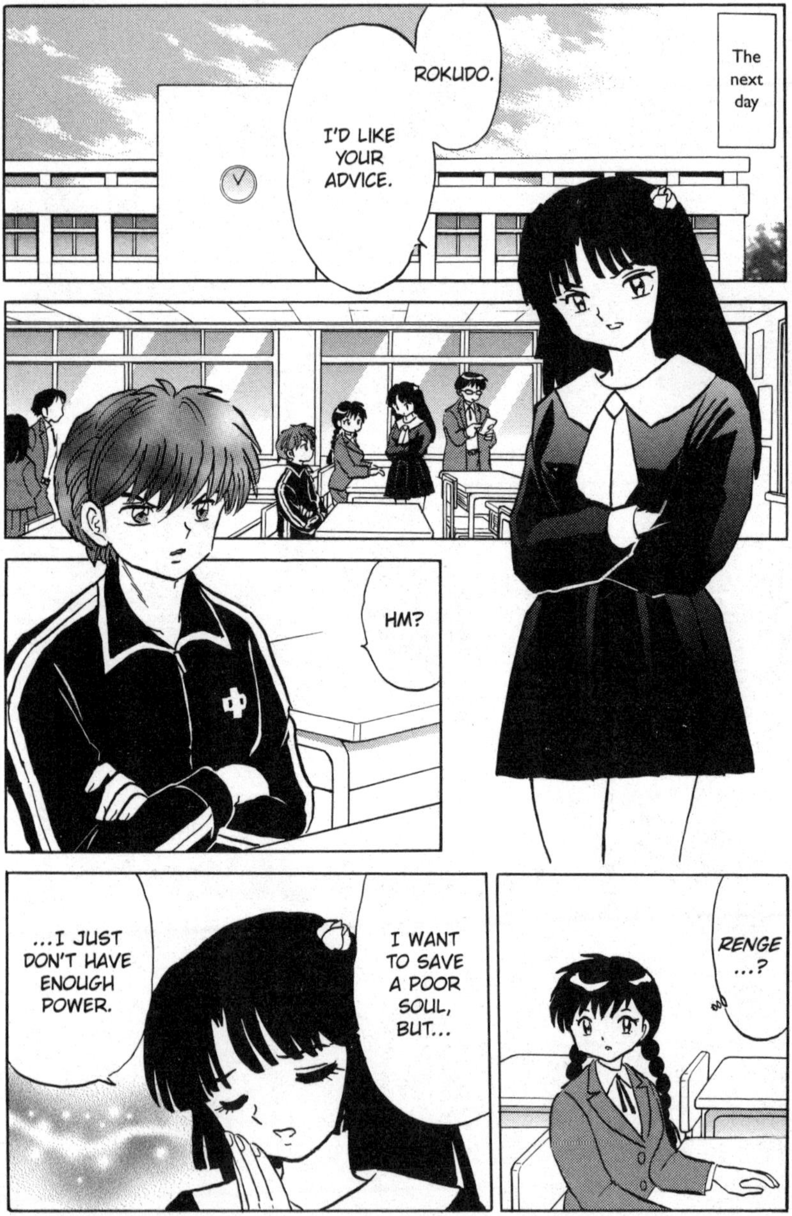
The next day
ROKUDO.
I'D LIKE YOUR ADVICE.
HM?
RENGE ...?
I WANT TO SAVE A POOR SOUL, BUT...
...I JUST DON'T HAVE ENOUGH POWER.

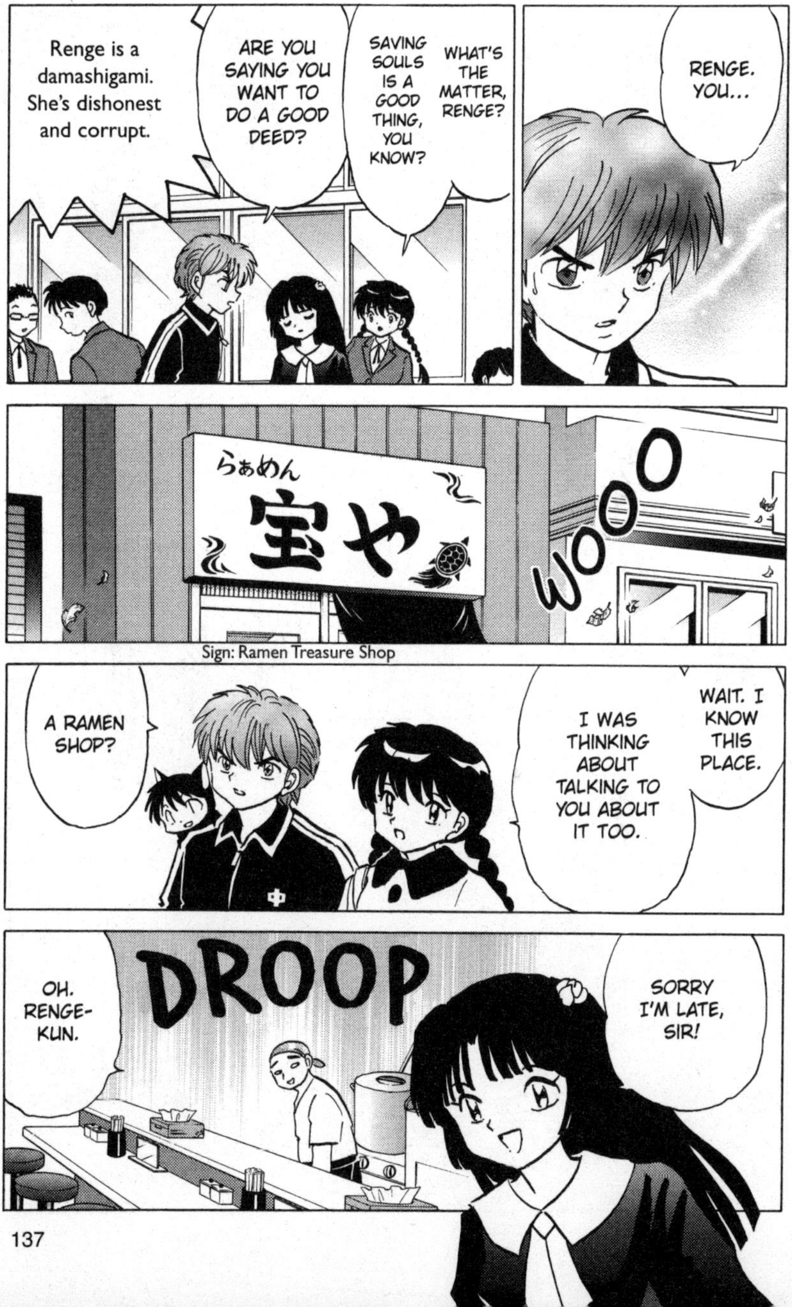
RENGE. YOU...
WHAT'S THE MATTER, RENGE?
SAVING SOULS IS A GOOD THING, YOU KNOW?
ARE YOU SAYING YOU WANT TO DO A GOOD DEED?
Renge is a damashigami. She's dishonest and corrupt.
らぁめん
宝や
WOOOO
Sign: Ramen Treasure Shop
WAIT. I KNOW THIS PLACE.
I WAS THINKING ABOUT TALKING TO YOU ABOUT IT TOO.
A RAMEN SHOP?
SORRY I'M LATE, SIR!
DROOP
OH. RENGE-KUN.

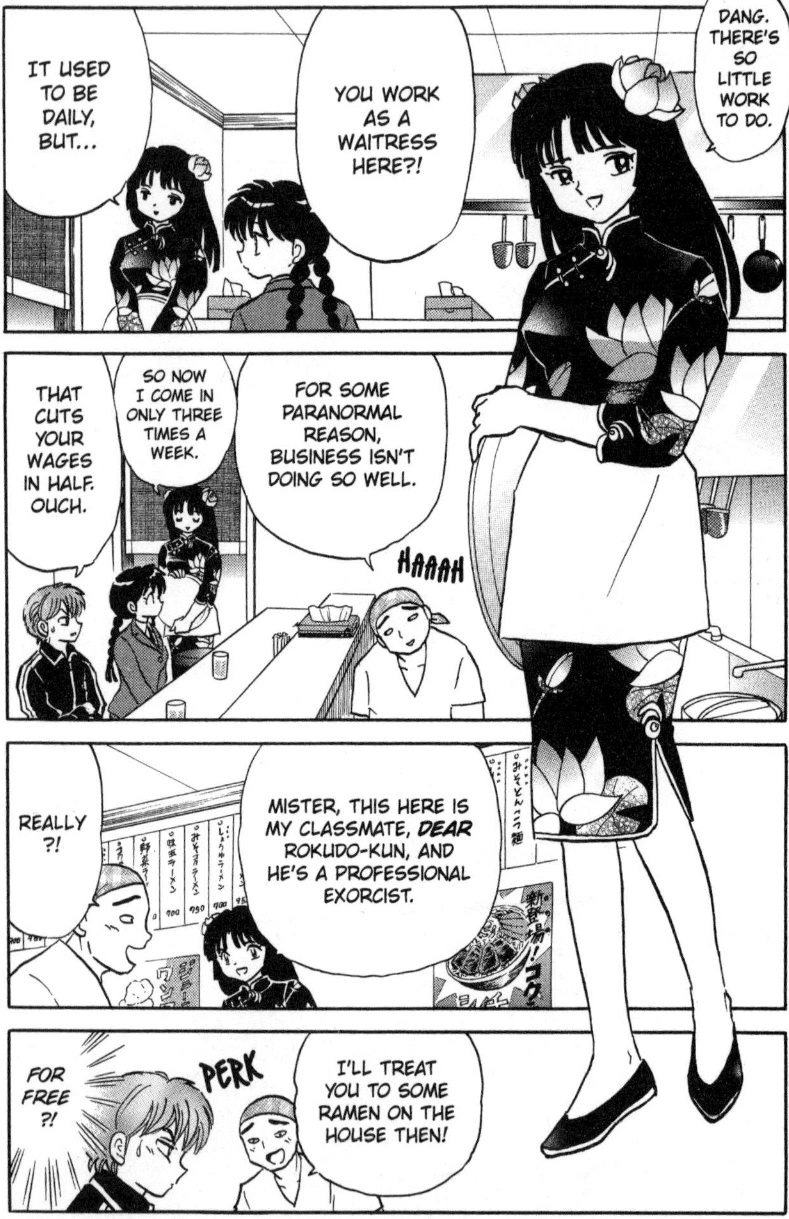
DANG. THERE'S SO LITTLE WORK TO DO.
YOU WORK AS A WAITRESS HERE?!
IT USED TO BE DAILY, BUT...
FOR SOME PARANORMAL REASON, BUSINESS ISN'T DOING SO WELL.
HAAAH
SO NOW I COME IN ONLY THREE TIMES A WEEK.
THAT CUTS YOUR WAGES IN HALF. OUCH.
MISTER, THIS HERE IS MY CLASSMATE, ***DEAR*** ROKUDO-KUN, AND HE'S A PROFESSIONAL EXORCIST.
REALLY ?!
I'LL TREAT YOU TO SOME RAMEN ON THE HOUSE THEN!
PERK
FOR FREE ?!

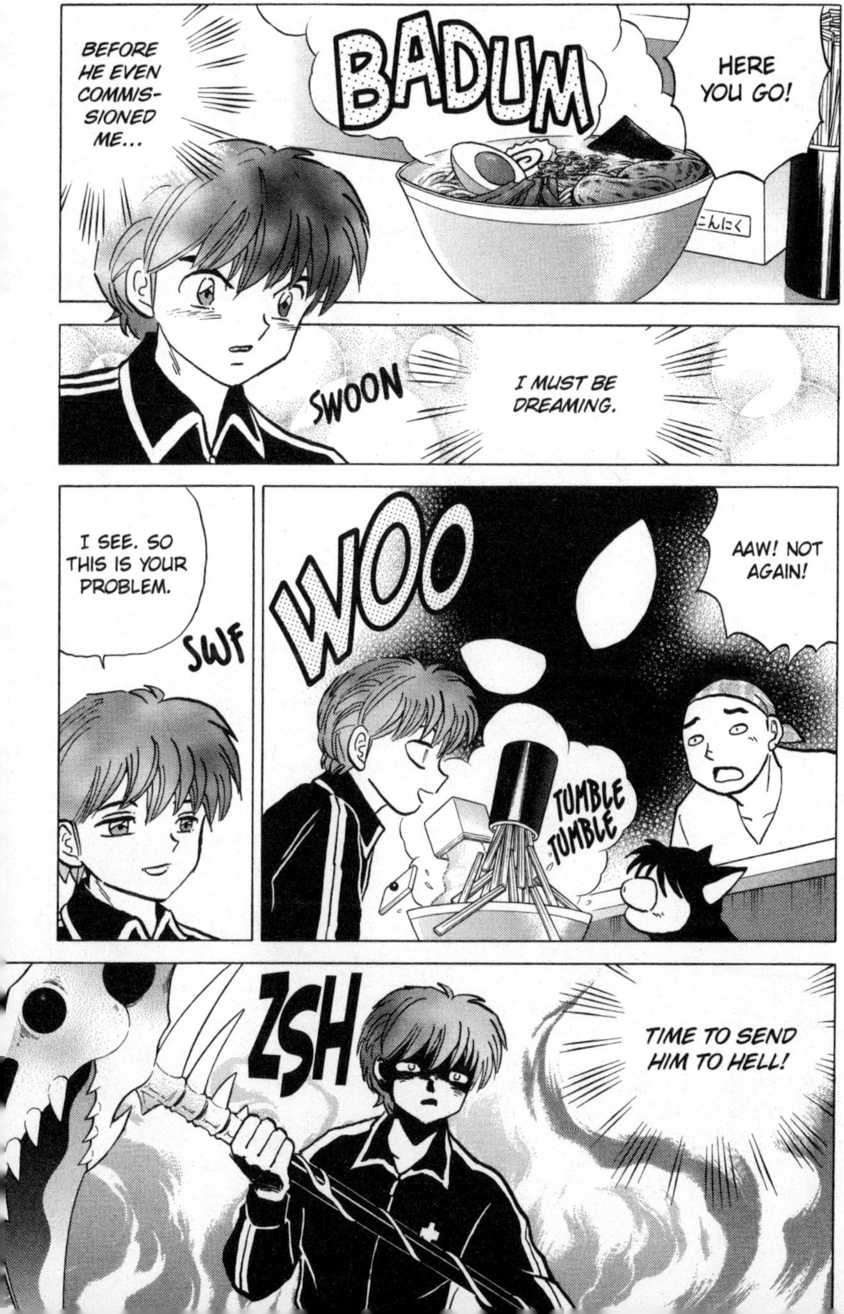
HERE YOU GO!
BADUM
BEFORE HE EVEN COMMIS- SIONED ME...
にんにく
I MUST BE DREAMING.
SWOON
AAW! NOT AGAIN!
WOO
TUMBLE TUMBLE
SWF
I SEE. SO THIS IS YOUR PROBLEM.
TIME TO SEND HIM TO HELL!
ZSH

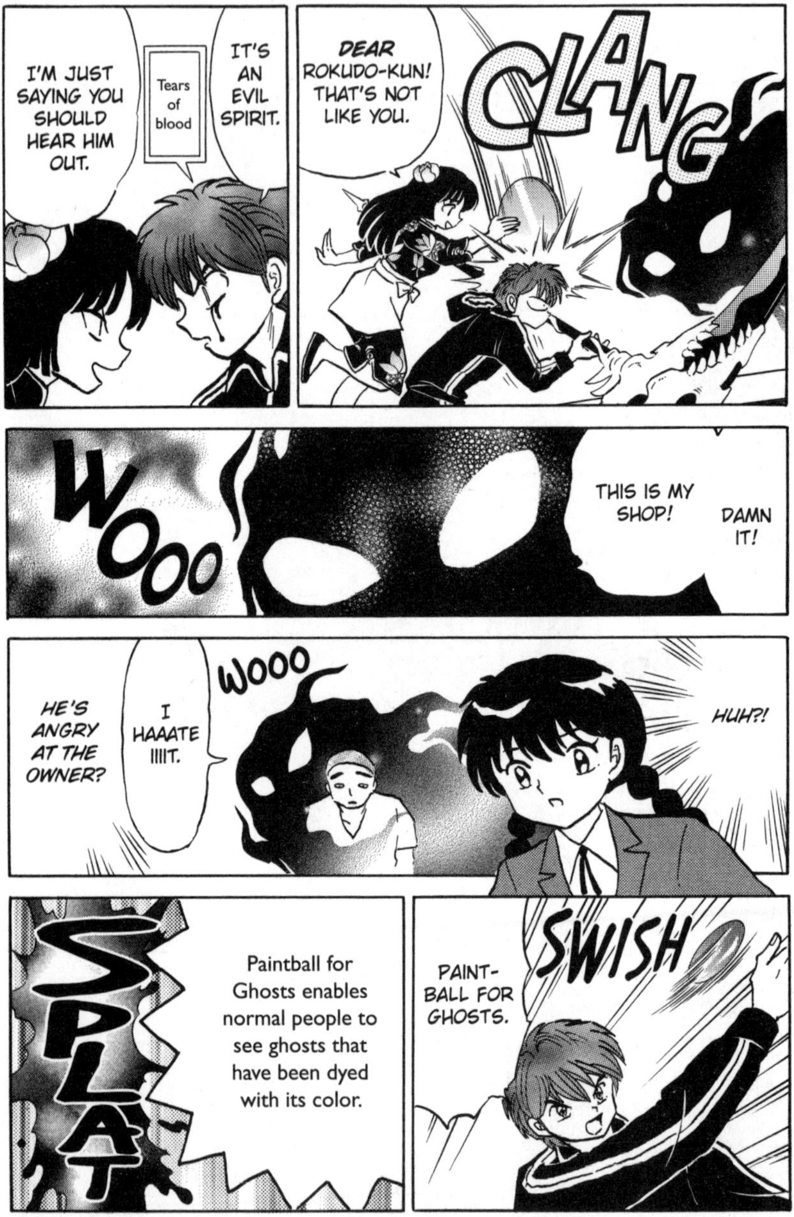
CLANG
DEAR ROKUDO-KUN! THAT'S NOT LIKE YOU.
IT'S AN EVIL SPIRIT.
Tears of blood
I'M JUST SAYING YOU SHOULD HEAR HIM OUT.
DAMN IT!
THIS IS MY SHOP!
WOOO
HUH?!
WOOO
I HAAATE IIIIT.
HE'S ANGRY AT THE OWNER?
SWISH
PAINT-BALL FOR GHOSTS.
Paintball for Ghosts enables normal people to see ghosts that have been dyed with its color.
SPLAT

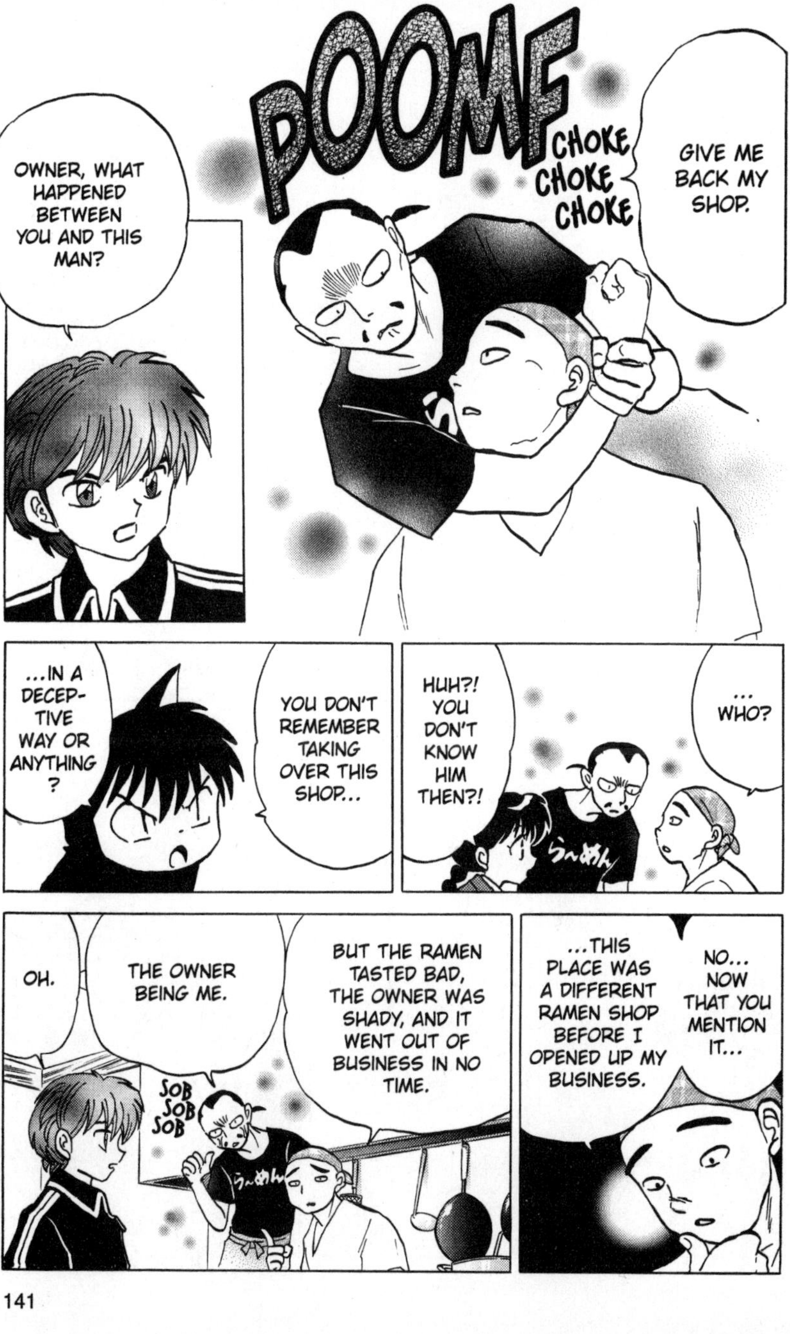
GIVE ME BACK MY SHOP.
POOMF
CHOKE CHOKE CHOKE
OWNER, WHAT HAPPENED BETWEEN YOU AND THIS MAN?
...WHO?
HUH?! YOU DON'T KNOW HIM THEN?!
YOU DON'T REMEMBER TAKING OVER THIS SHOP...
...IN A DECEPTIVE WAY OR ANYTHING?
NO... NOW THAT YOU MENTION IT...
...THIS PLACE WAS A DIFFERENT RAMEN SHOP BEFORE I OPENED UP MY BUSINESS.
BUT THE RAMEN TASTED BAD, THE OWNER WAS SHADY, AND IT WENT OUT OF BUSINESS IN NO TIME.
THE OWNER BEING ME.
SOB SOB SOB
OH.

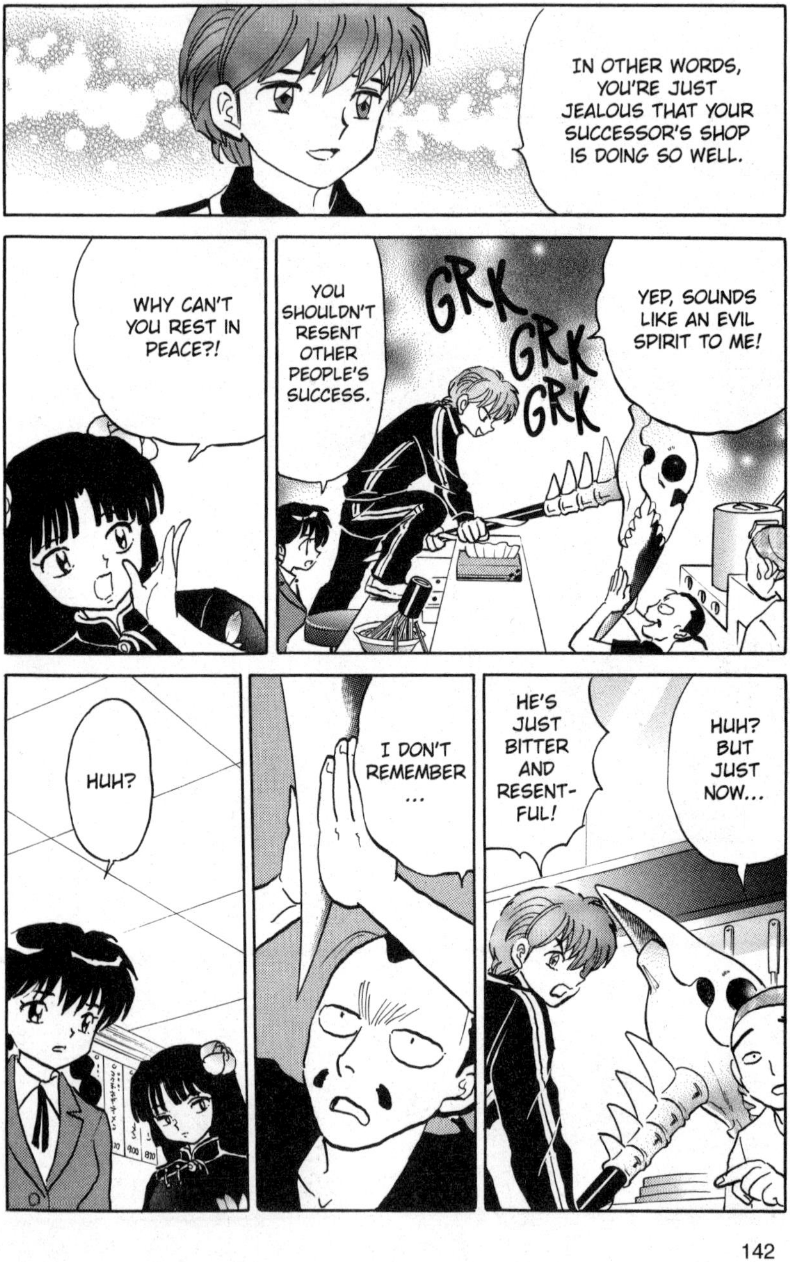
IN OTHER WORDS, YOU'RE JUST JEALOUS THAT YOUR SUCCESSOR'S SHOP IS DOING SO WELL.
YEP, SOUNDS LIKE AN EVIL SPIRIT TO ME!
GRK GRK GRK
YOU SHOULDN'T RESENT OTHER PEOPLE'S SUCCESS.
WHY CAN'T YOU REST IN PEACE?!
HUH? BUT JUST NOW...
HE'S JUST BITTER AND RESENT-FUL!
I DON'T REMEMBER ...
HUH?

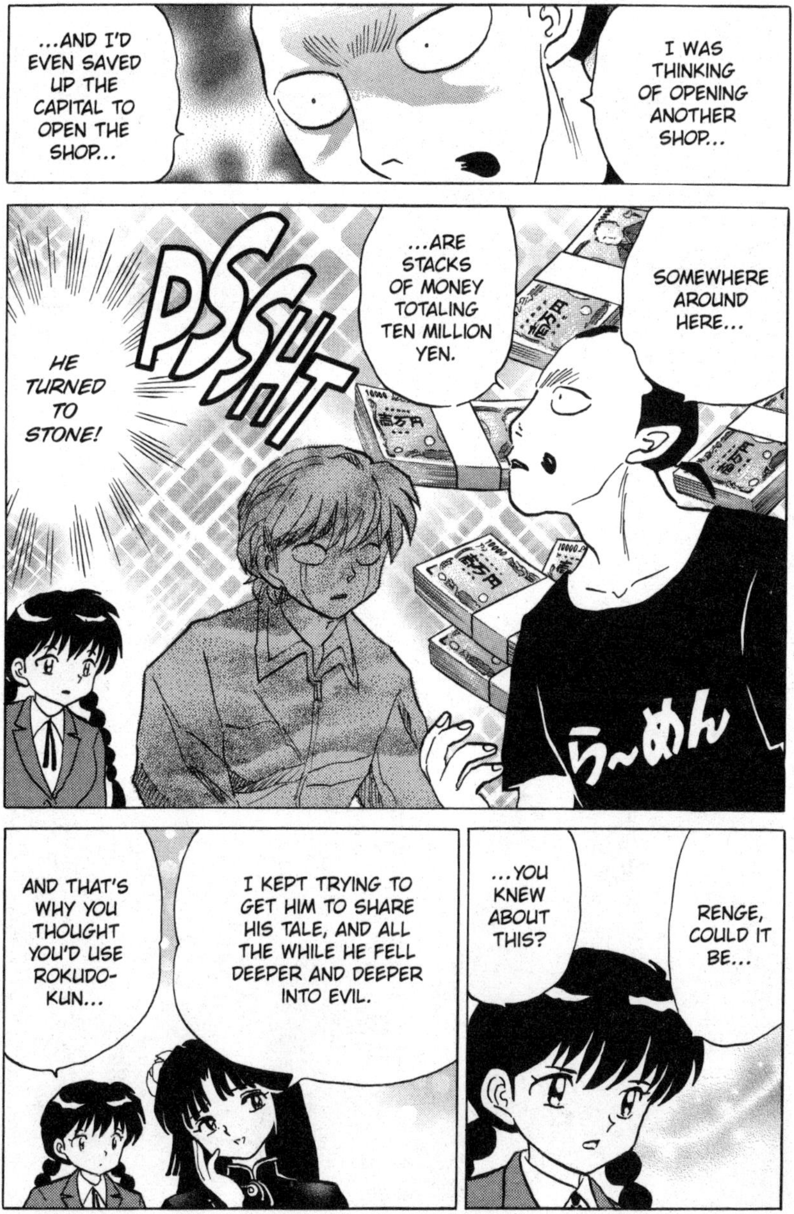
I WAS THINKING OF OPENING ANOTHER SHOP...
...AND I'D EVEN SAVED UP THE CAPITAL TO OPEN THE SHOP...
SOMEWHERE AROUND HERE...
...ARE STACKS OF MONEY TOTALING TEN MILLION YEN.
PSSHT
HE TURNED TO STONE!
ら〜めん
RENGE, COULD IT BE...
...YOU KNEW ABOUT THIS?
I KEPT TRYING TO GET HIM TO SHARE HIS TALE, AND ALL THE WHILE HE FELL DEEPER AND DEEPER INTO EVIL.
AND THAT'S WHY YOU THOUGHT YOU'D USE ROKUDO-KUN...

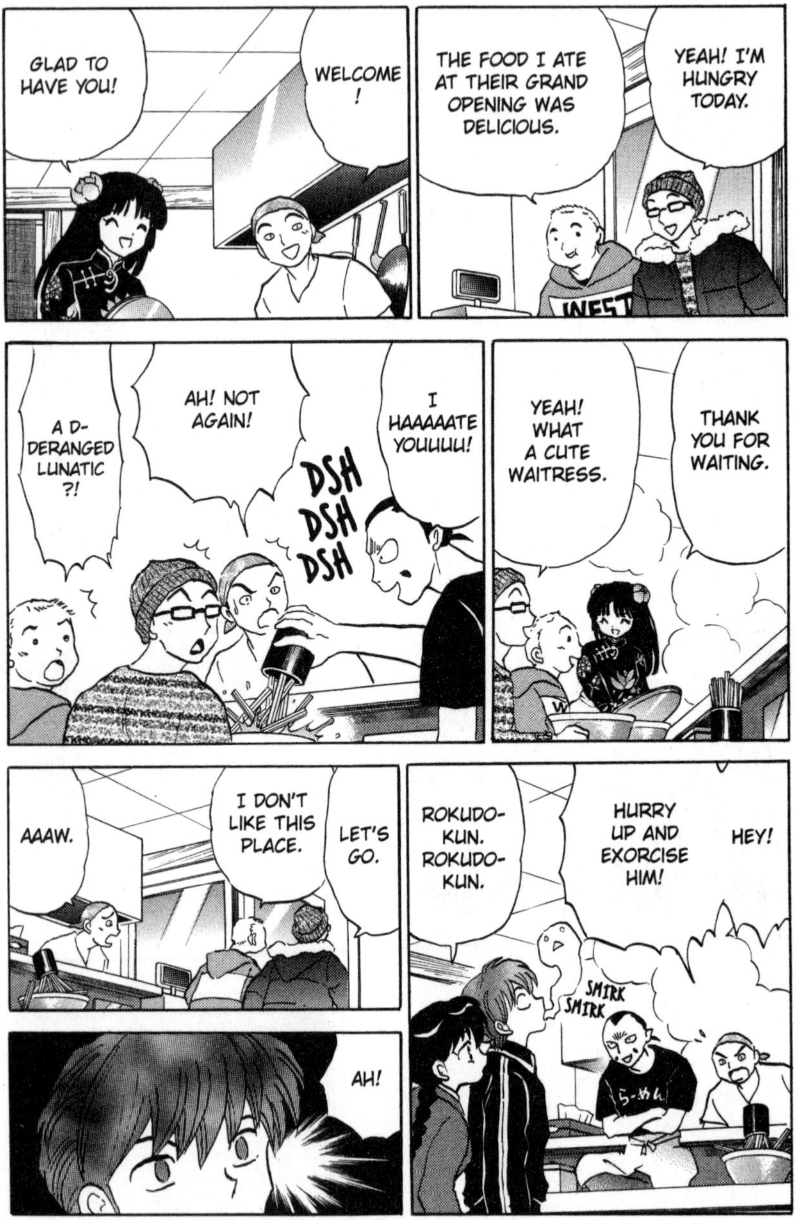

YEAH! I'M HUNGRY TODAY.
THE FOOD I ATE AT THEIR GRAND OPENING WAS DELICIOUS.
WELCOME!
GLAD TO HAVE YOU!
THANK YOU FOR WAITING.
YEAH! WHAT A CUTE WAITRESS.
I HAAAAATE YOUUUU!
DSH DSH DSH
AH! NOT AGAIN!
A D-DERANGED LUNATIC?!
HEY!
HURRY UP AND EXORCISE HIM!
ROKUDO-KUN. ROKUDO-KUN.
SMIRK SMIRK
LET'S GO.
I DON'T LIKE THIS PLACE.
AAAW.
AH!

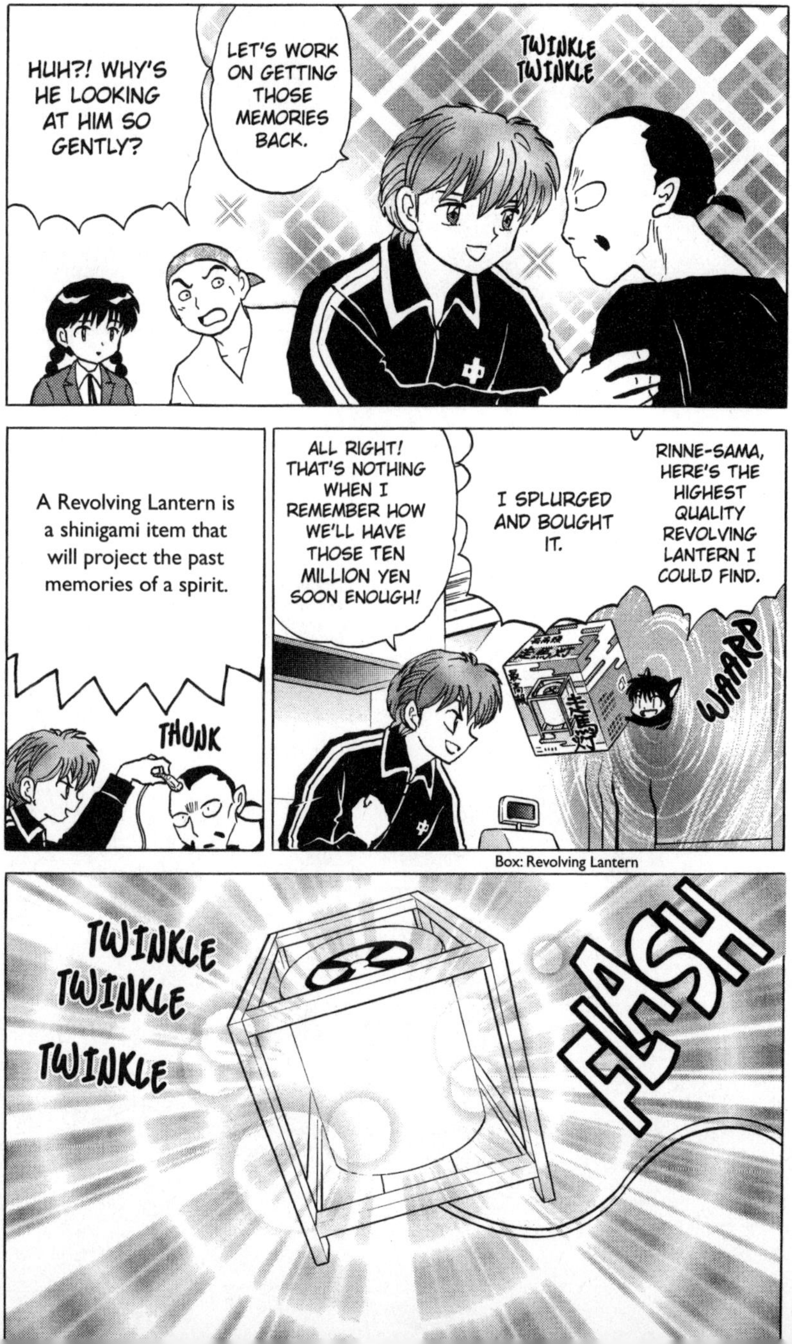
TWINKLE TWINKLE
LET'S WORK ON GETTING THOSE MEMORIES BACK.
HUH?! WHY'S HE LOOKING AT HIM SO GENTLY?
RINNE-SAMA, HERE'S THE HIGHEST QUALITY REVOLVING LANTERN I COULD FIND.
I SPLURGED AND BOUGHT IT.
WARP
ALL RIGHT! THAT'S NOTHING WHEN I REMEMBER HOW WE'LL HAVE THOSE TEN MILLION YEN SOON ENOUGH!
Box: Revolving Lantern
A Revolving Lantern is a shinigami item that will project the past memories of a spirit.
THUNK
FLASH
TWINKLE TWINKLE TWINKLE

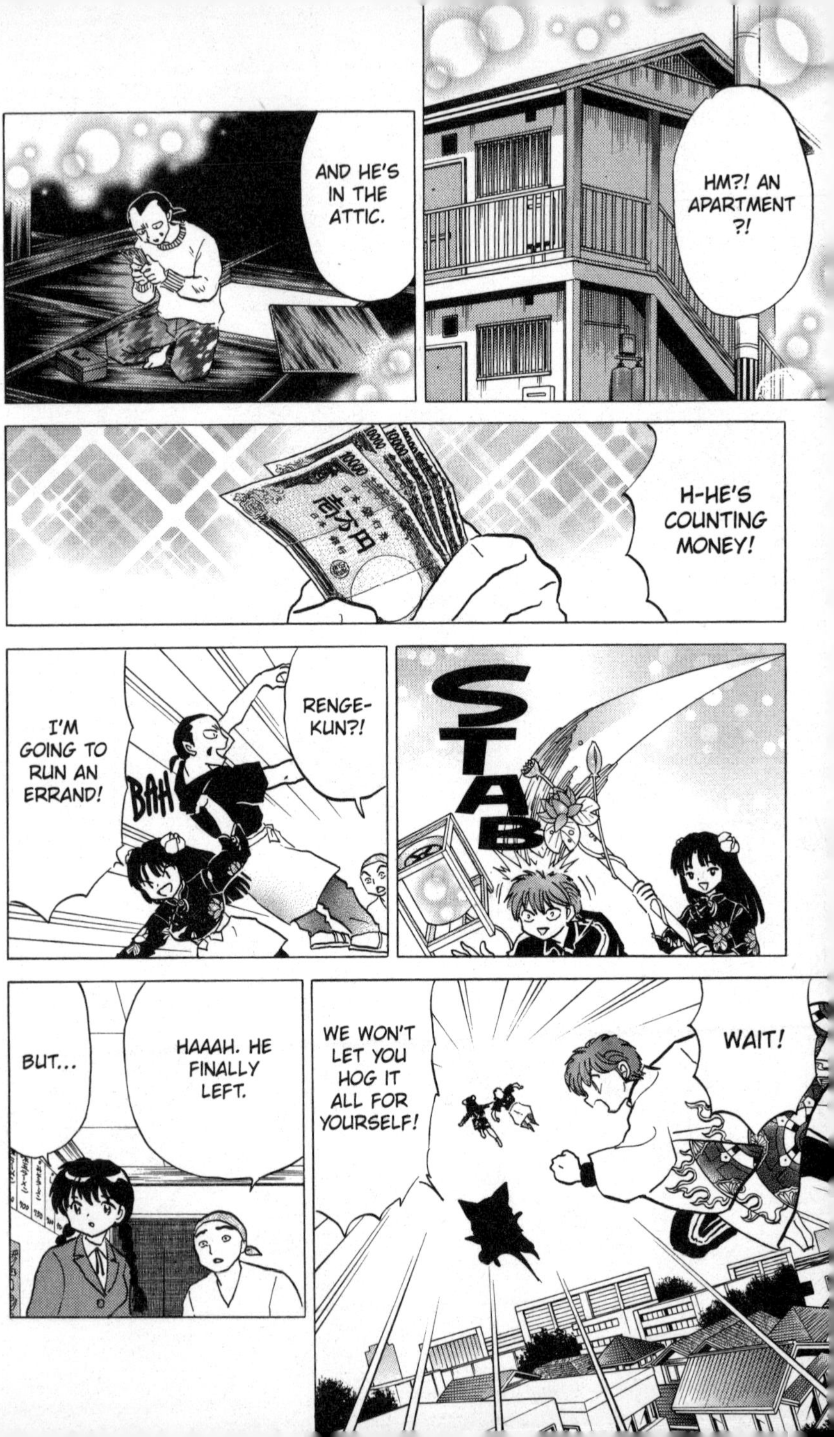
HM?! AN APARTMENT ?!
AND HE'S IN THE ATTIC.
H-HE'S COUNTING MONEY!
STAB
RENGE-KUN?!
I'M GOING TO RUN AN ERRAND!
BAH
WAIT!
WE WON'T LET YOU HOG IT ALL FOR YOURSELF!
HAAAH. HE FINALLY LEFT.
BUT...

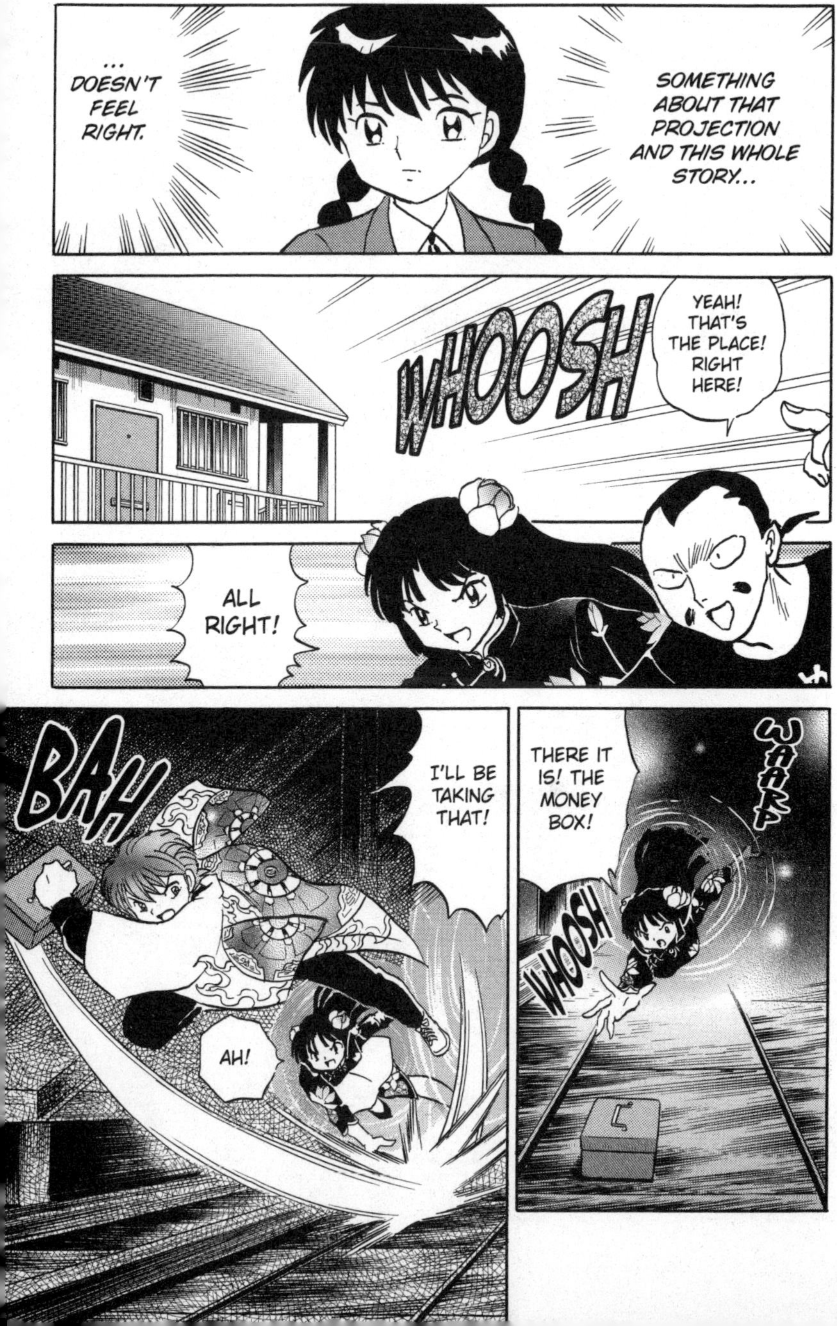
SOMETHING ABOUT THAT PROJECTION AND THIS WHOLE STORY...
... DOESN'T FEEL RIGHT.
YEAH! THAT'S THE PLACE! RIGHT HERE!
WHOOSH
ALL RIGHT!
WAARP
THERE IT IS! THE MONEY BOX!
WHOOSH
BAH
I'LL BE TAKING THAT!
AH!

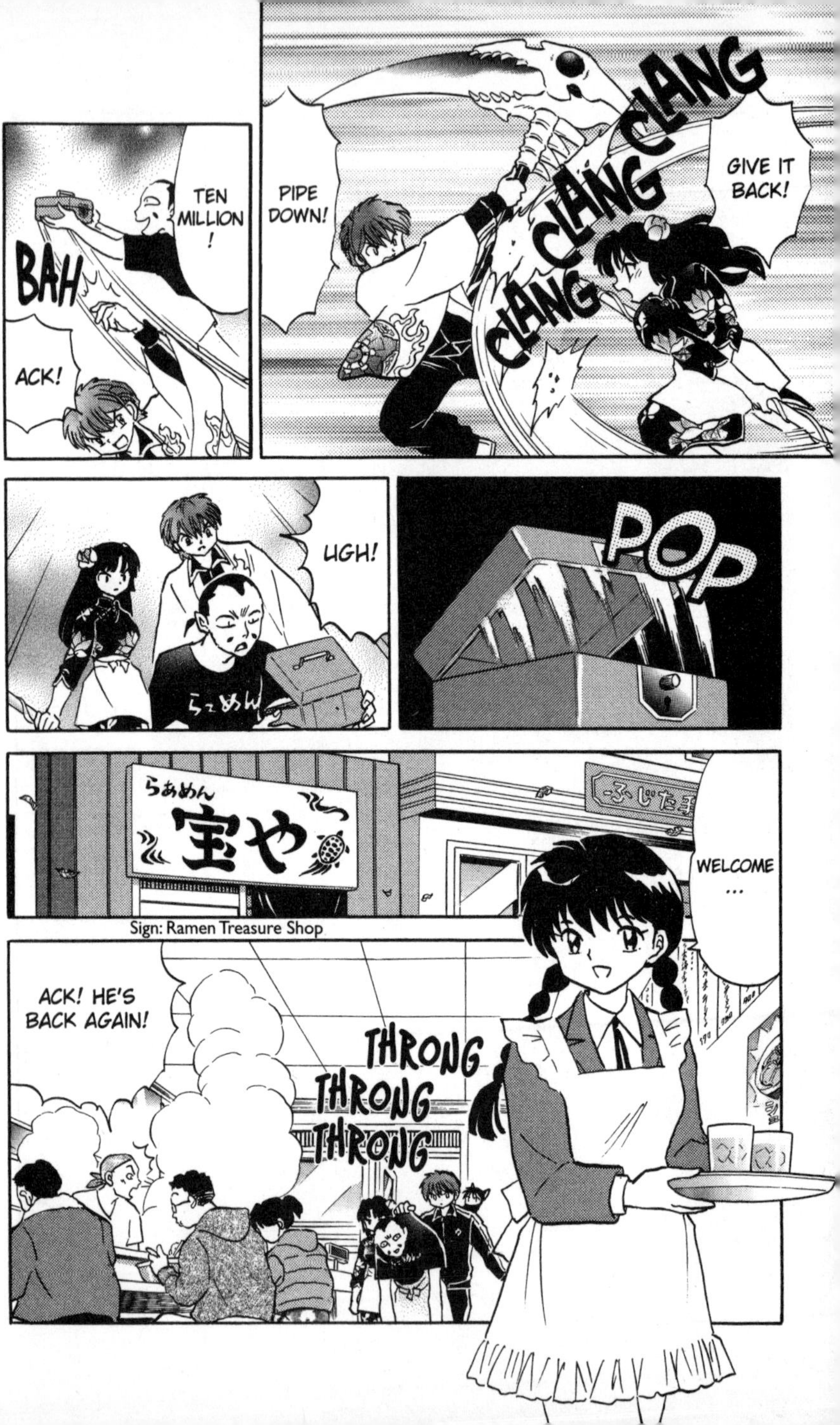
GIVE IT BACK!
PIPE DOWN!
CLANG CLANG CLANG CLANG
TEN MILLION!
BAH
ACK!
POP
UGH!
らぁめん
WELCOME...
らあめん 宝や
ACK! HE'S BACK AGAIN!
THRONG THRONG THRONG
Sign: Ramen Treasure Shop

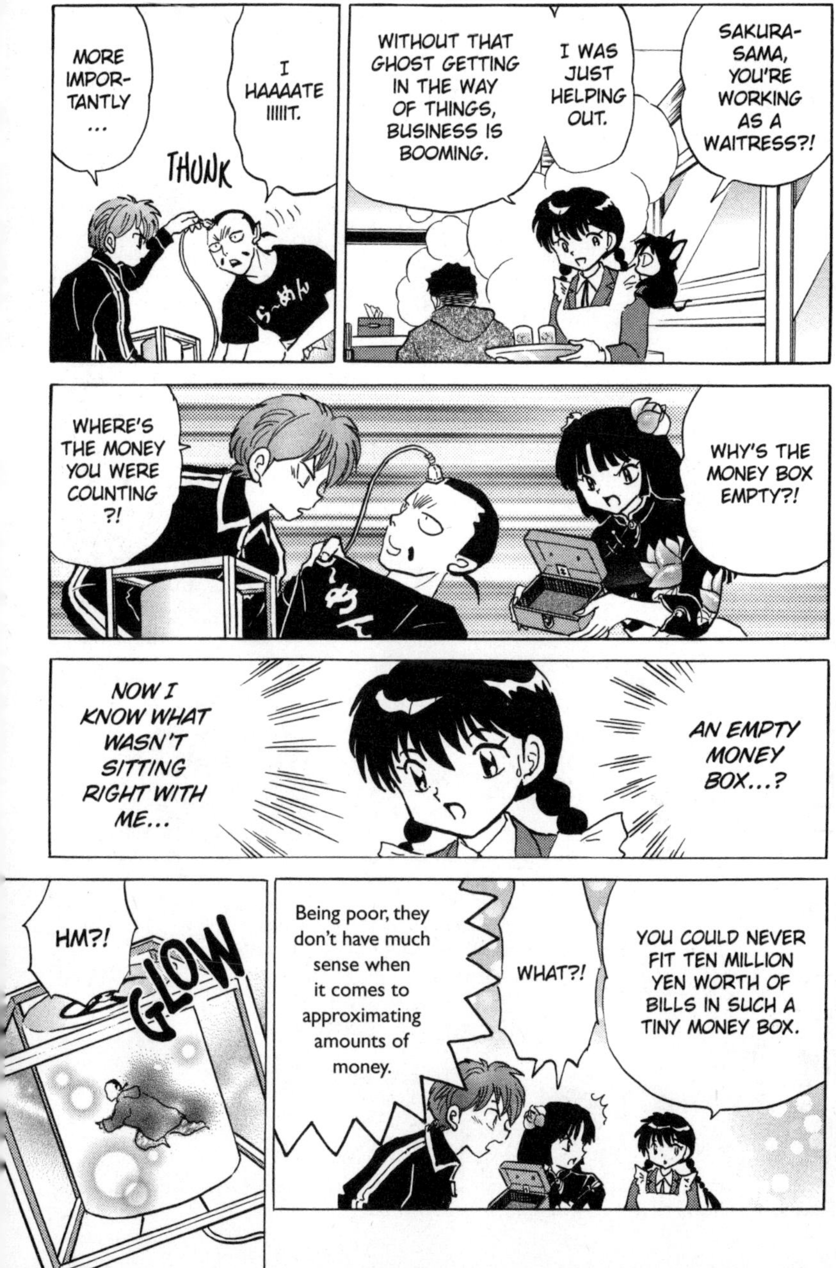
SAKURA-SAMA, YOU'RE WORKING AS A WAITRESS?!
I WAS JUST HELPING OUT.
WITHOUT THAT GHOST GETTING IN THE WAY OF THINGS, BUSINESS IS BOOMING.
I HAAAATE IIIIIT.
THUNK
MORE IMPOR-TANTLY...
WHY'S THE MONEY BOX EMPTY?!
WHERE'S THE MONEY YOU WERE COUNTING?!
AN EMPTY MONEY BOX...?
NOW I KNOW WHAT WASN'T SITTING RIGHT WITH ME...
YOU COULD NEVER FIT TEN MILLION YEN WORTH OF BILLS IN SUCH A TINY MONEY BOX.
WHAT?!
Being poor, they don't have much sense when it comes to approximating amounts of money.
HM?!
GLOW

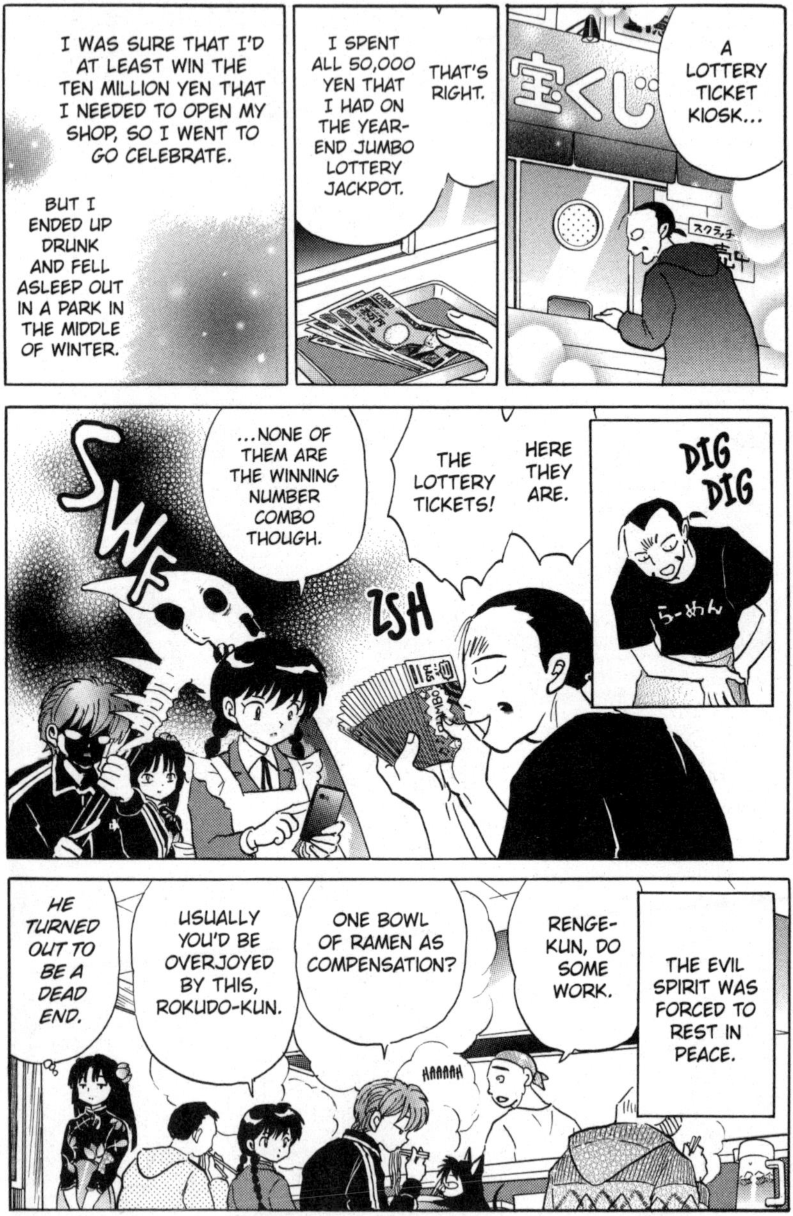
宝くじ
A LOTTERY TICKET KIOSK...
THAT'S RIGHT.
I SPENT ALL 50,000 YEN THAT I HAD ON THE YEAR-END JUMBO LOTTERY JACKPOT.
I WAS SURE THAT I'D AT LEAST WIN THE TEN MILLION YEN THAT I NEEDED TO OPEN MY SHOP, SO I WENT TO GO CELEBRATE.
BUT I ENDED UP DRUNK AND FELL ASLEEP OUT IN A PARK IN THE MIDDLE OF WINTER.
DIG DIG
らーめん
HERE THEY ARE.
THE LOTTERY TICKETS!
ZSH
JUMBO
...NONE OF THEM ARE THE WINNING NUMBER COMBO THOUGH.
SWF
THE EVIL SPIRIT WAS FORCED TO REST IN PEACE.
RENGE-KUN, DO SOME WORK.
HAAAAH
ONE BOWL OF RAMEN AS COMPENSATION?
USUALLY YOU'D BE OVERJOYED BY THIS, ROKUDO-KUN.
HE TURNED OUT TO BE A DEAD END.

CHAPTER 267: MONSTROUS HINT

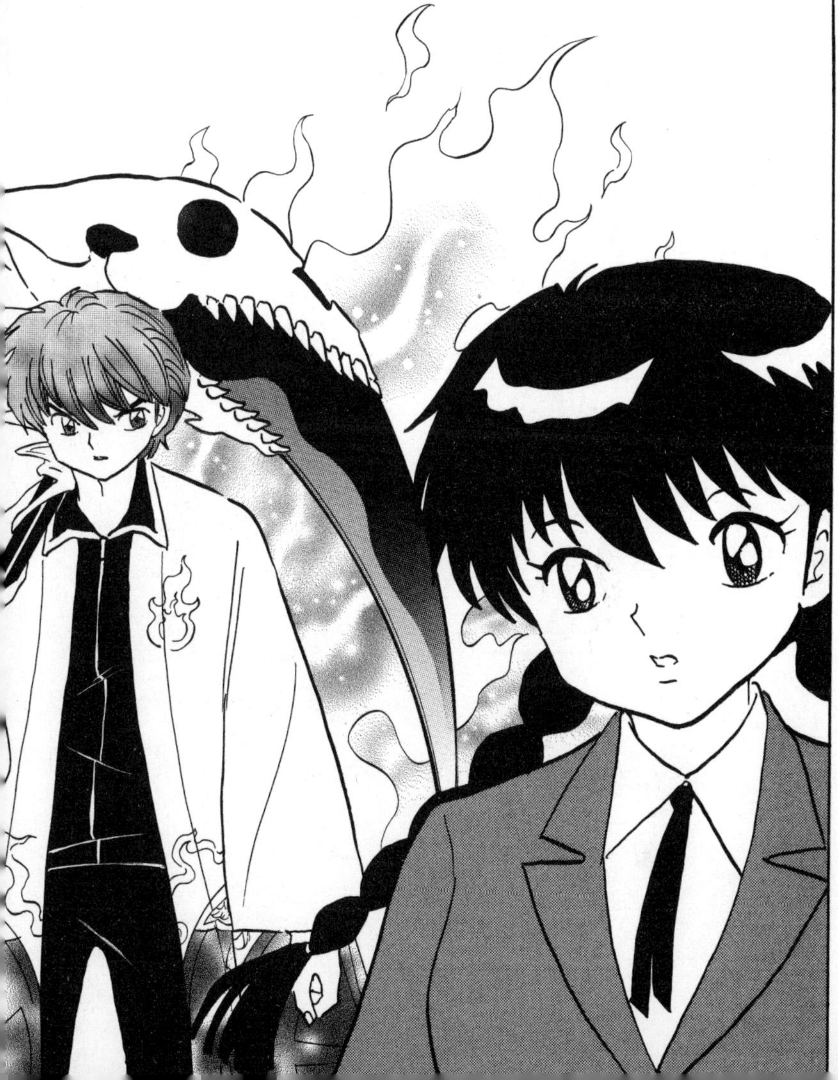

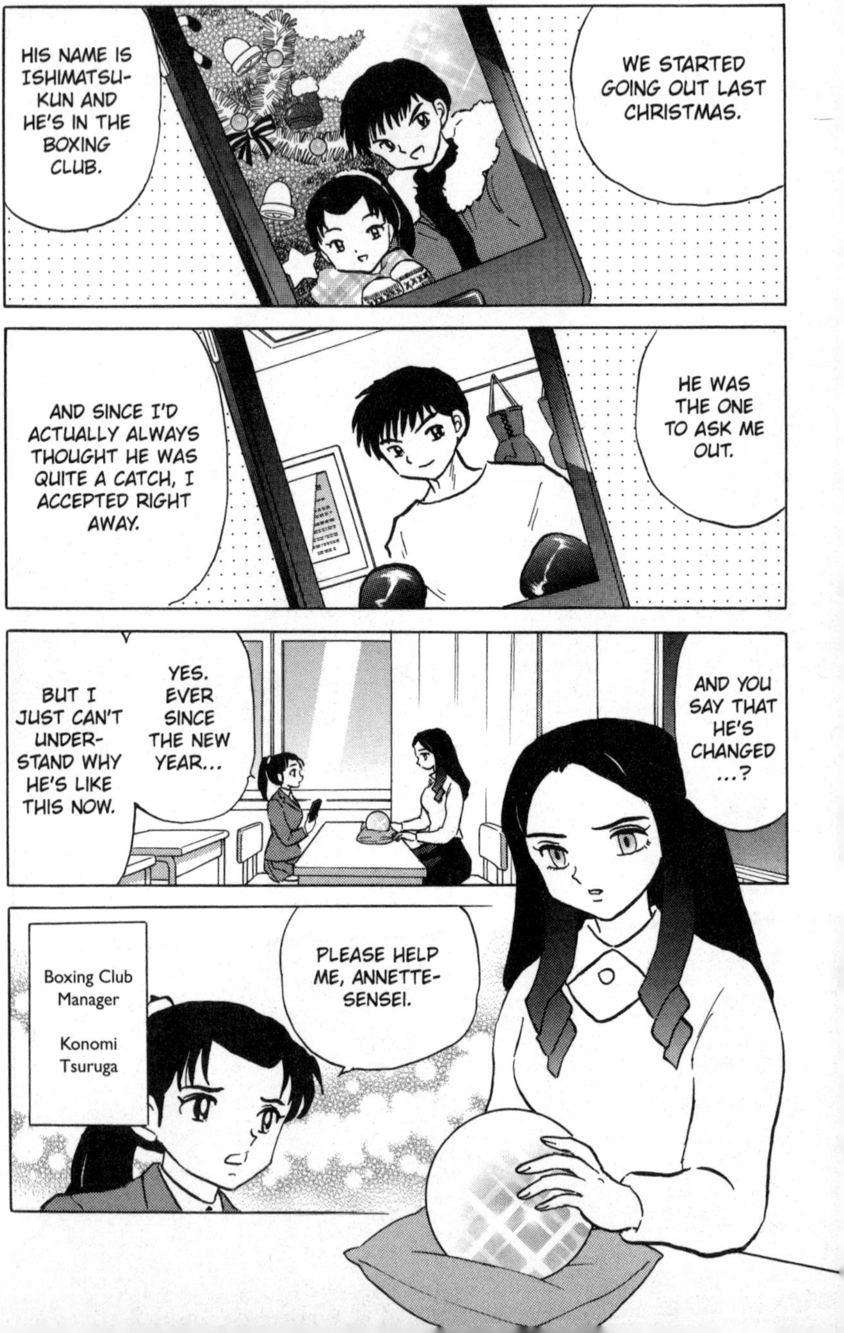
WE STARTED GOING OUT LAST CHRISTMAS.
HIS NAME IS ISHIMATSU-KUN AND HE'S IN THE BOXING CLUB.
HE WAS THE ONE TO ASK ME OUT.
AND SINCE I'D ACTUALLY ALWAYS THOUGHT HE WAS QUITE A CATCH, I ACCEPTED RIGHT AWAY.
AND YOU SAY THAT HE'S CHANGED ...?
YES. EVER SINCE THE NEW YEAR...
BUT I JUST CAN'T UNDER-STAND WHY HE'S LIKE THIS NOW.
PLEASE HELP ME, ANNETTE-SENSEI.
Boxing Club Manager
Konomi Tsuruga

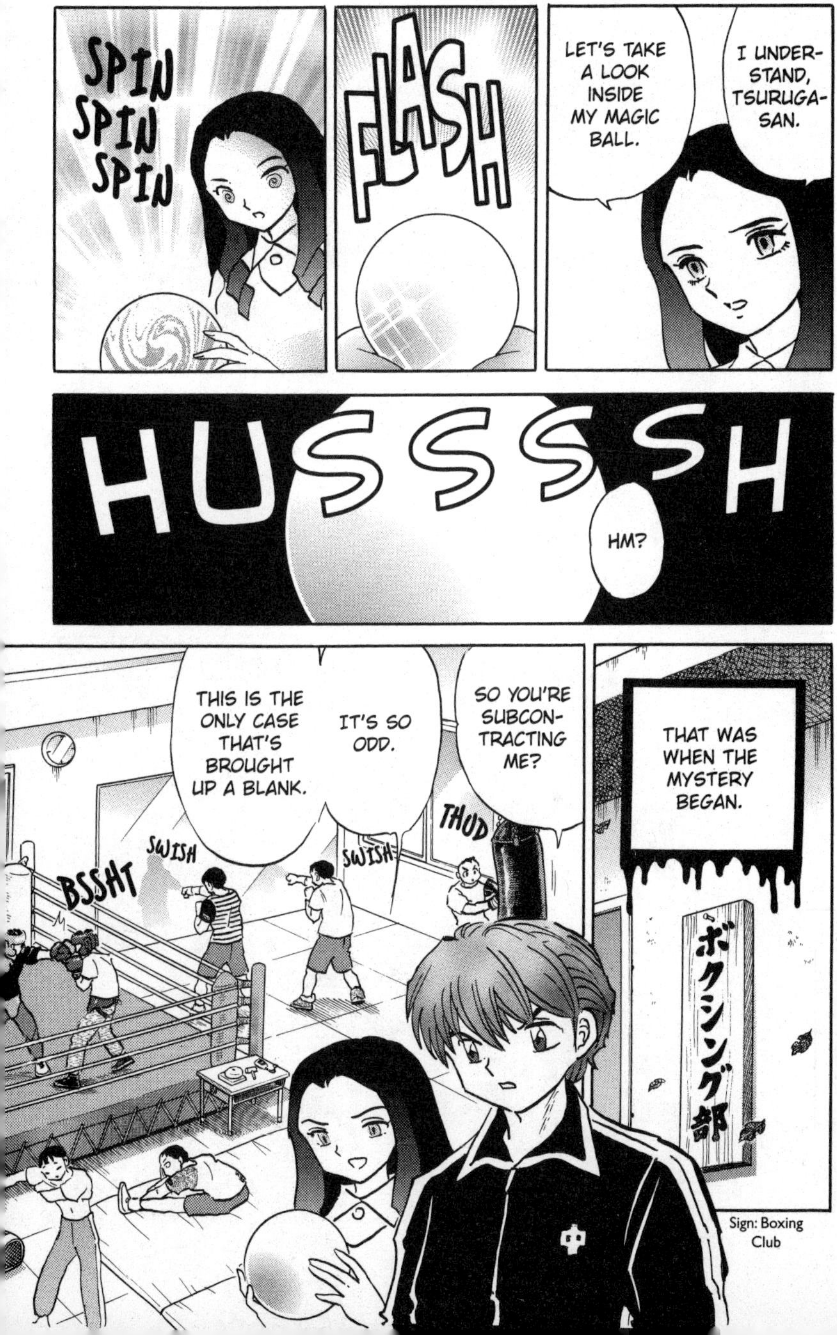
I UNDER-STAND, TSURUGA-SAN.
LET'S TAKE A LOOK INSIDE MY MAGIC BALL.
FLASH
SPIN SPIN SPIN
HUSSSSH
HM?
THAT WAS WHEN THE MYSTERY BEGAN.
ボクシング部
SO YOU'RE SUBCON-TRACTING ME?
IT'S SO ODD.
THIS IS THE ONLY CASE THAT'S BROUGHT UP A BLANK.
THUD
SWISH
SWISH
BSSHT
Sign: Boxing Club

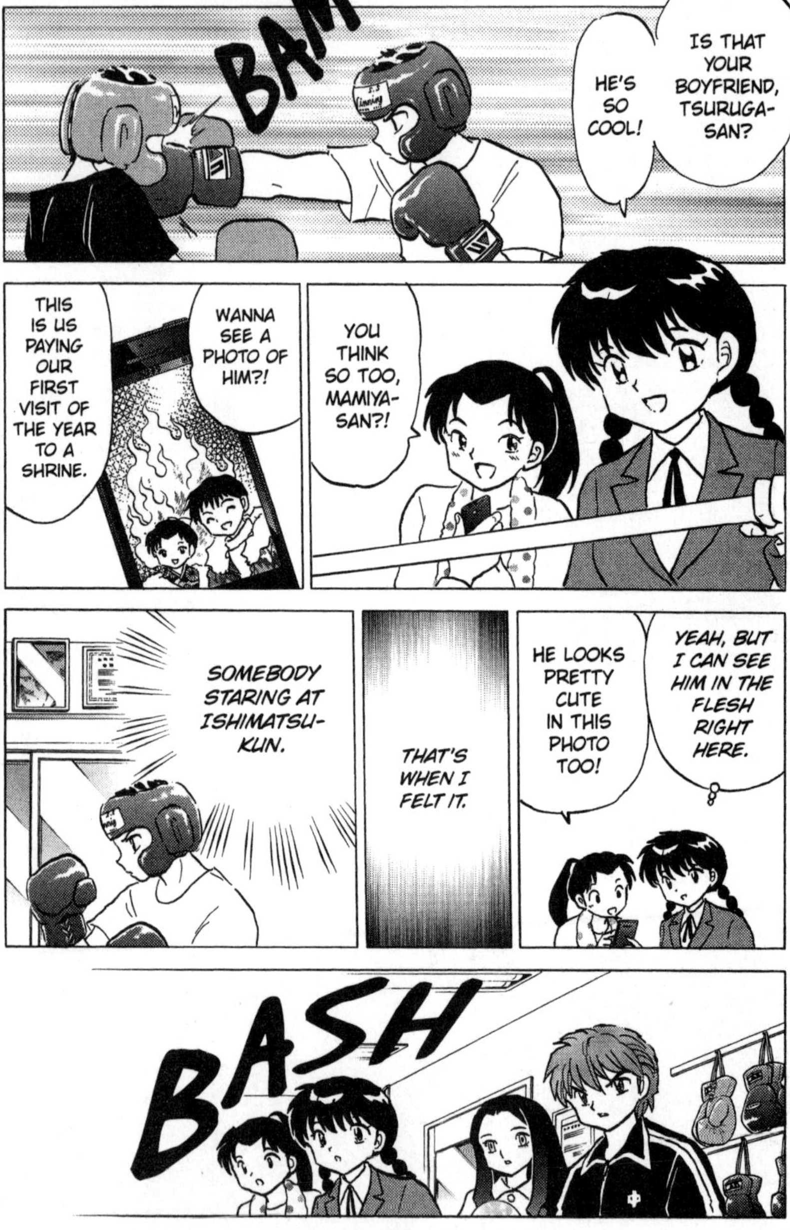
IS THAT YOUR BOYFRIEND, TSURUGA-SAN?
HE'S SO COOL!
BAM
YOU THINK SO TOO, MAMIYA-SAN?!
WANNA SEE A PHOTO OF HIM?!
THIS IS US PAYING OUR FIRST VISIT OF THE YEAR TO A SHRINE.
YEAH, BUT I CAN SEE HIM IN THE FLESH RIGHT HERE.
HE LOOKS PRETTY CUTE IN THIS PHOTO TOO!
THAT'S WHEN I FELT IT.
SOMEBODY STARING AT ISHIMATSU-KUN.
BASH

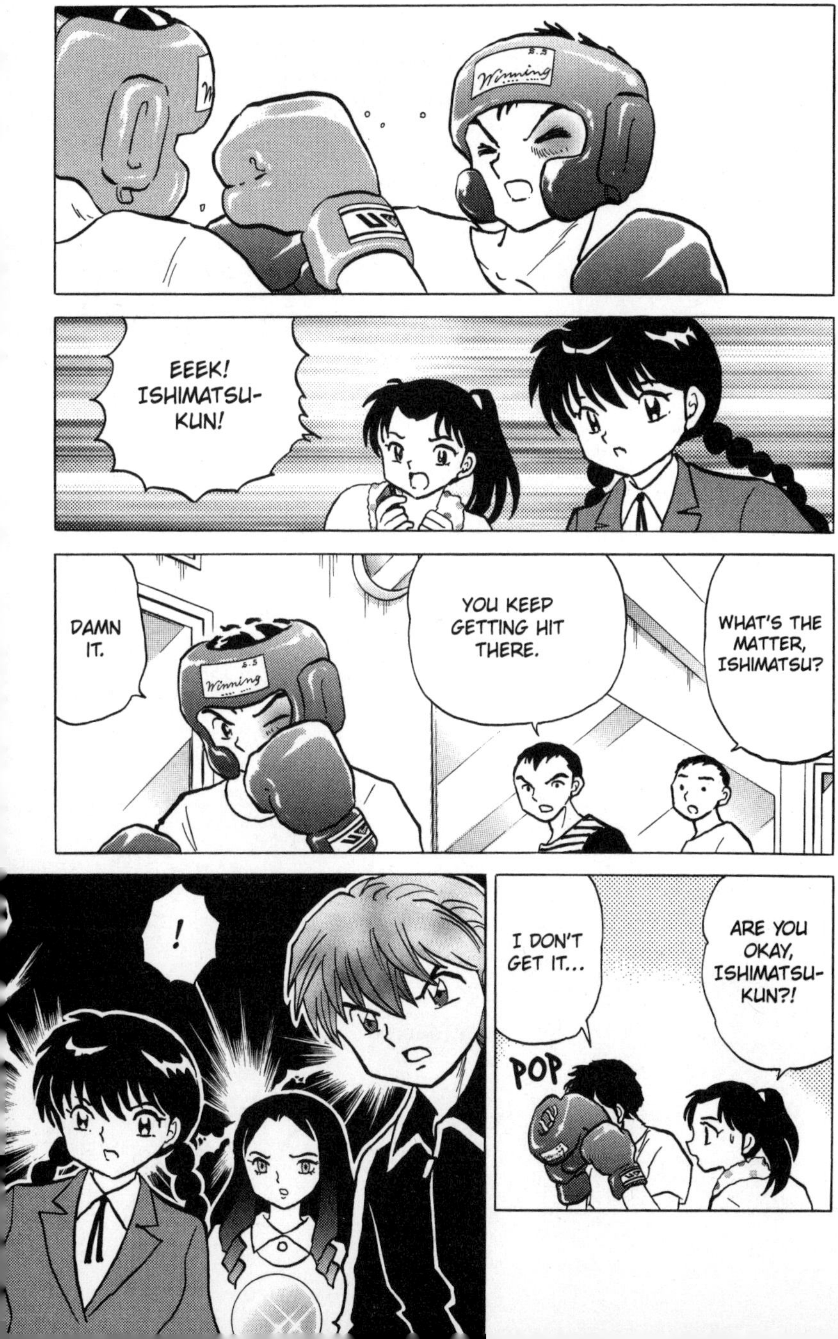
EEEK! ISHIMATSU-KUN!
WHAT'S THE MATTER, ISHIMATSU?
YOU KEEP GETTING HIT THERE.
DAMN IT.
ARE YOU OKAY, ISHIMATSU-KUN?!
I DON'T GET IT...
POP
!

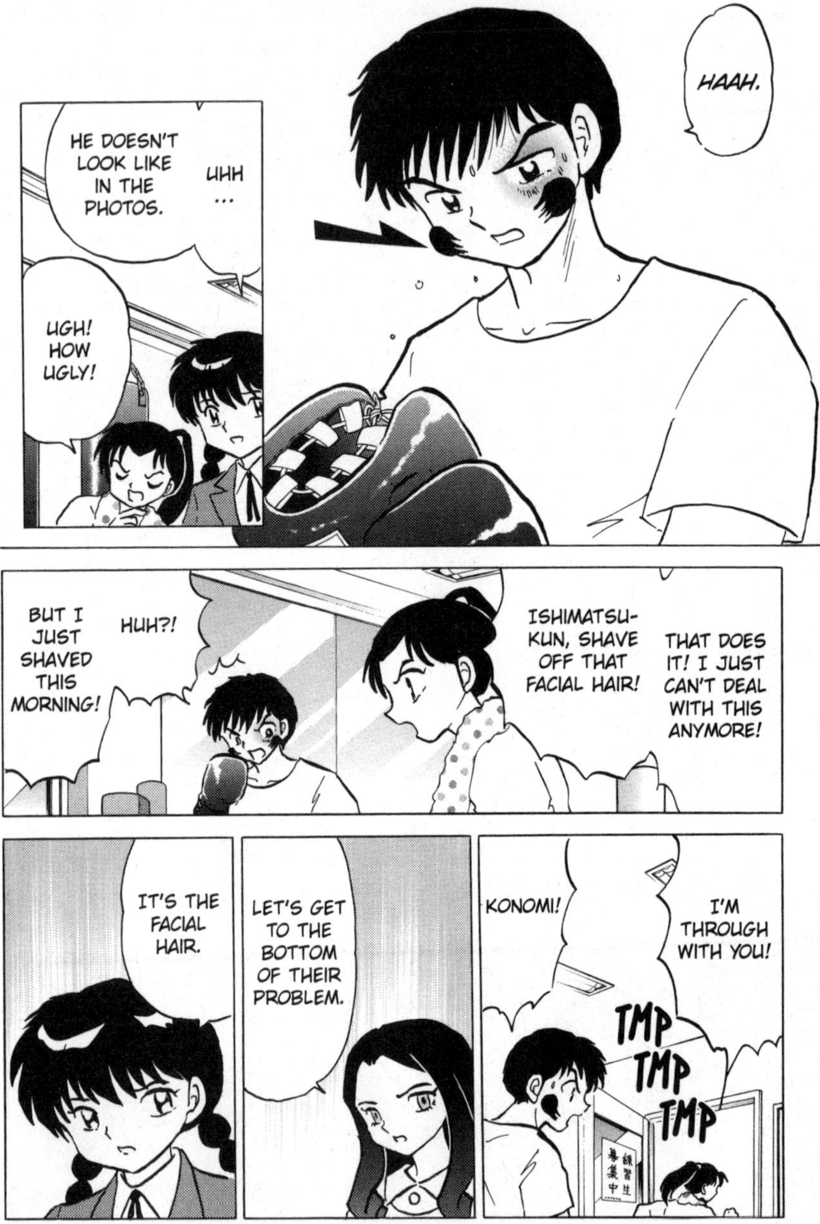
HAAH.
HE DOESN'T LOOK LIKE IN THE PHOTOS.
UHH ...
UGH! HOW UGLY!
THAT DOES IT! I JUST CAN'T DEAL WITH THIS ANYMORE!
ISHIMATSU-KUN, SHAVE OFF THAT FACIAL HAIR!
HUH?!
BUT I JUST SHAVED THIS MORNING!
I'M THROUGH WITH YOU!
KONOMI!
TMP
TMP
TMP
LET'S GET TO THE BOTTOM OF THEIR PROBLEM.
IT'S THE FACIAL HAIR.

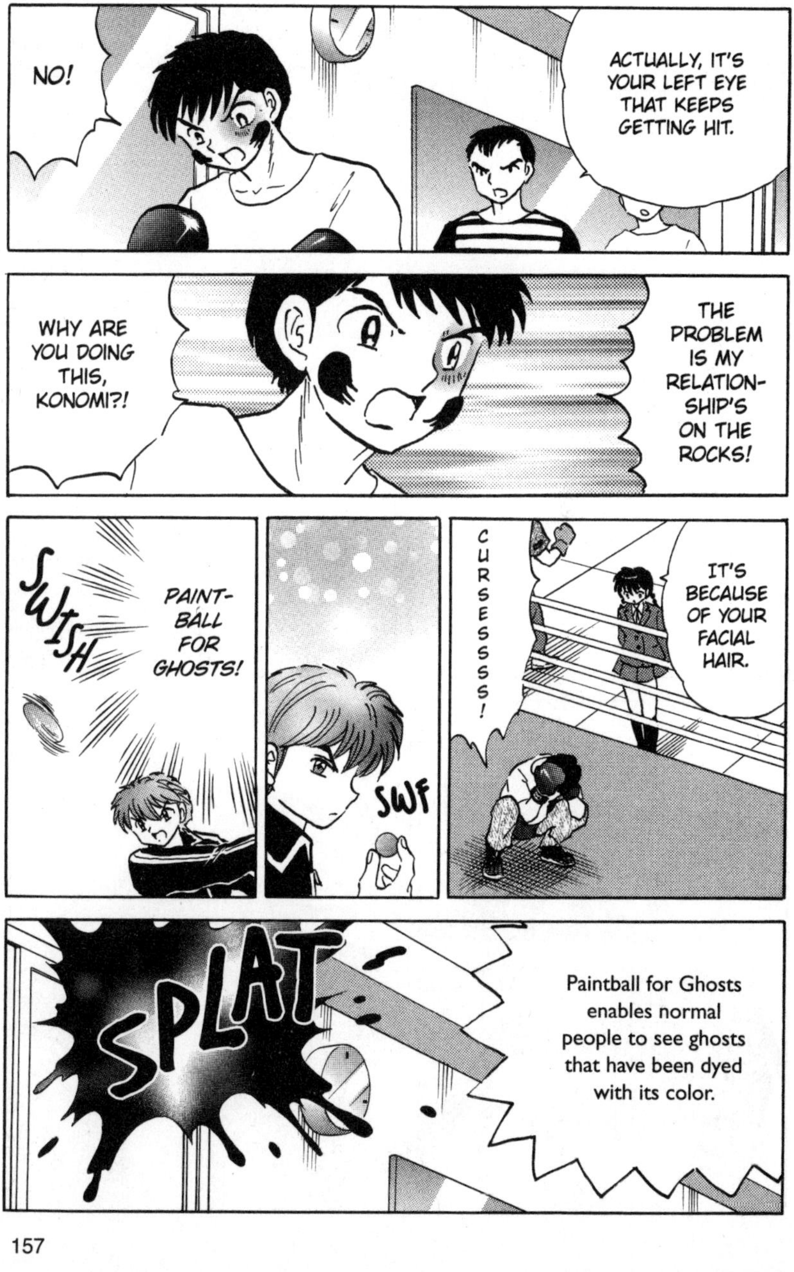
ACTUALLY, IT'S YOUR LEFT EYE THAT KEEPS GETTING HIT.
NO!
THE PROBLEM IS MY RELATIONSHIP'S ON THE ROCKS!
WHY ARE YOU DOING THIS, KONOMI?!
IT'S BECAUSE OF YOUR FACIAL HAIR.
CURSESSSS!
SWF
PAINT-BALL FOR GHOSTS!
SWISH
SPLAT
Paintball for Ghosts enables normal people to see ghosts that have been dyed with its color.

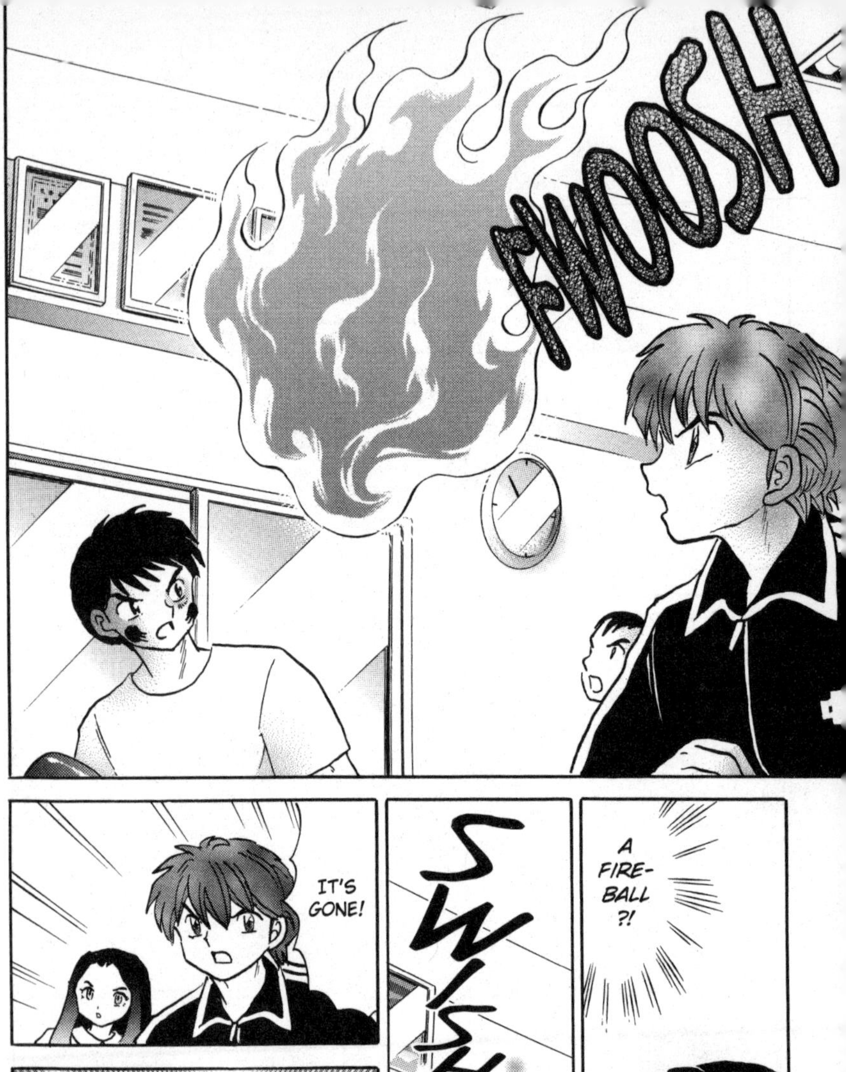
FWOOSH
A FIRE-BALL ?!
SWISH
IT'S GONE!
FLASH

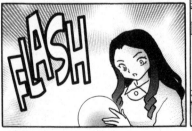

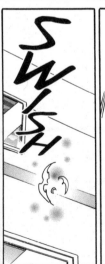

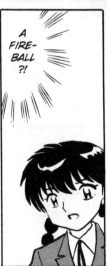

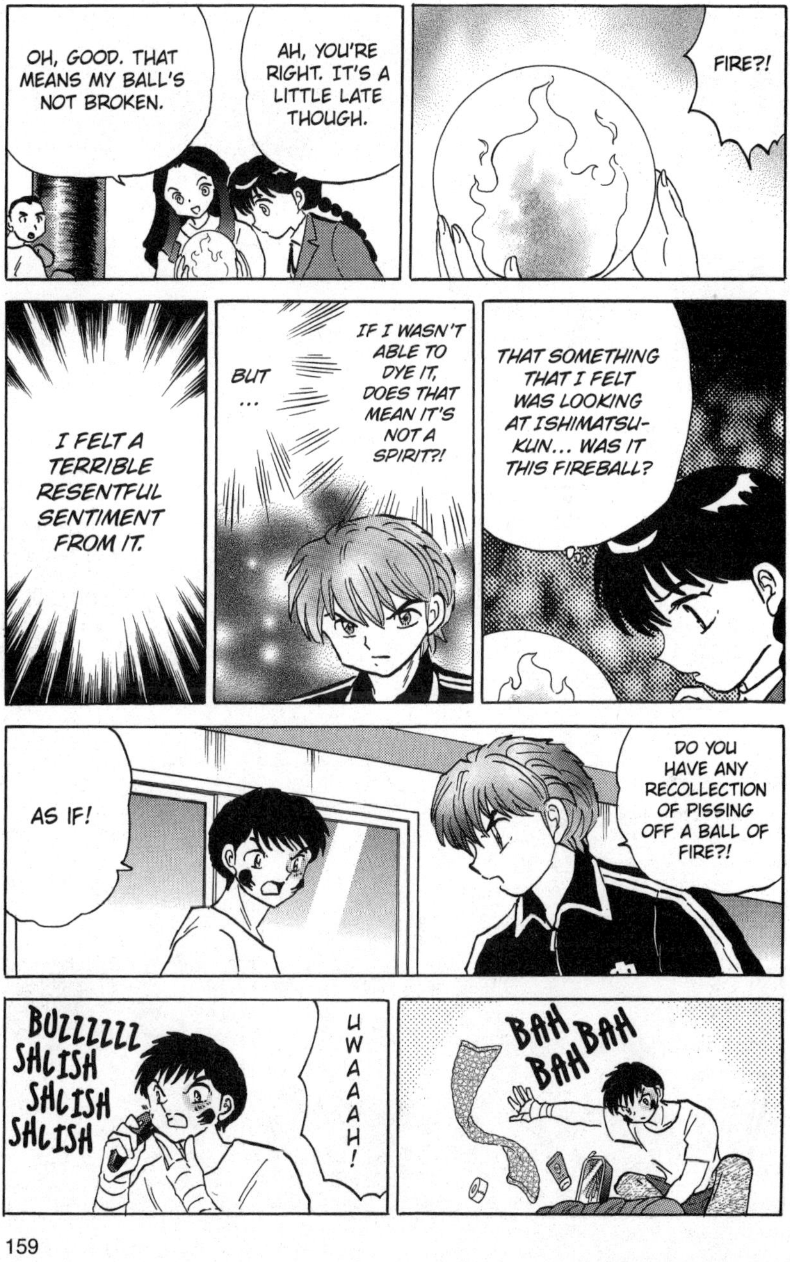
FIRE?!
AH, YOU'RE RIGHT. IT'S A LITTLE LATE THOUGH.
OH, GOOD. THAT MEANS MY BALL'S NOT BROKEN.
THAT SOMETHING THAT I FELT WAS LOOKING AT ISHIMATSU-KUN... WAS IT THIS FIREBALL?
IF I WASN'T ABLE TO DYE IT, DOES THAT MEAN IT'S NOT A SPIRIT?!
BUT ...
I FELT A TERRIBLE RESENTFUL SENTIMENT FROM IT.
DO YOU HAVE ANY RECOLLECTION OF PISSING OFF A BALL OF FIRE?!
AS IF!
BAH BAH BAH
UWAAAAH!
BUZZZZZZZ
SHLISH SHLISH SHLISH

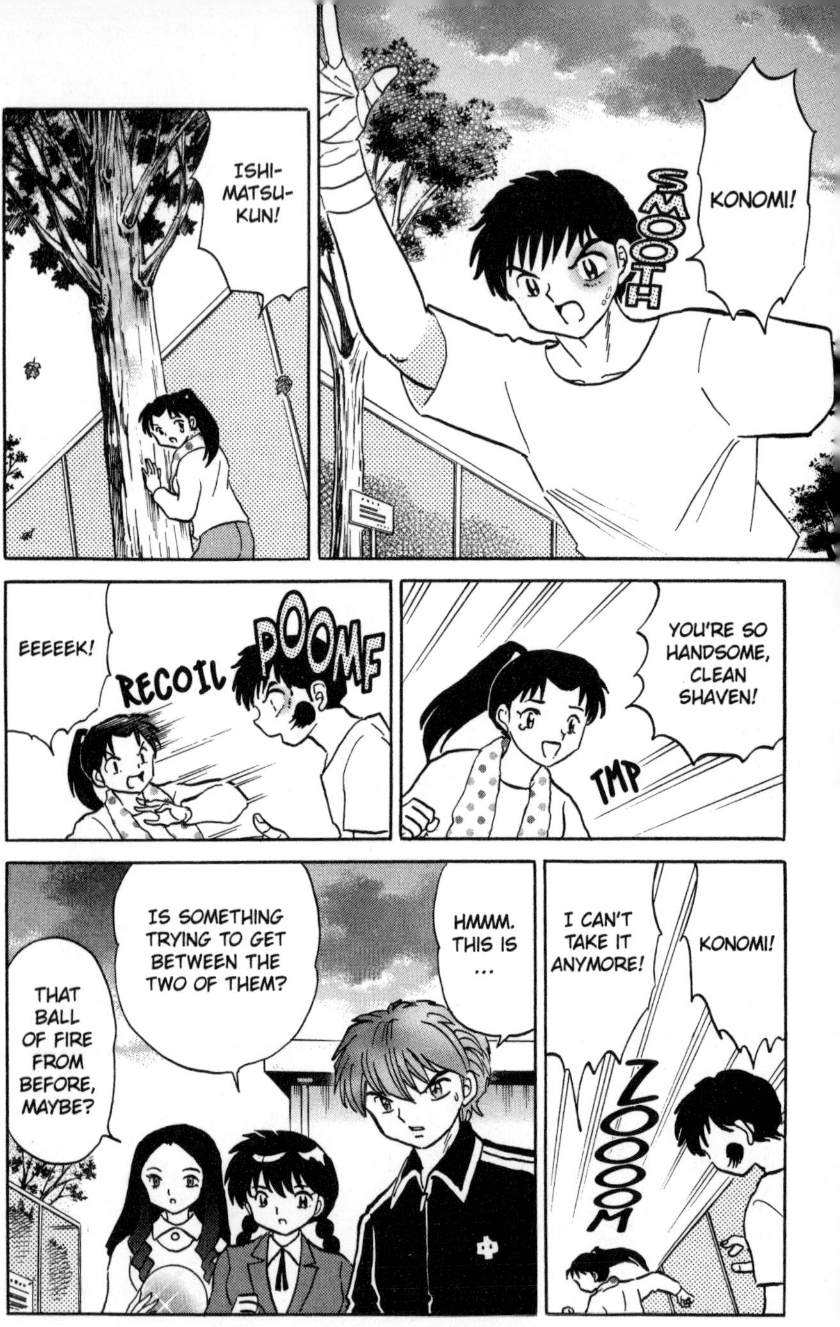
KONOMI!
SMOOTH
ISHI-MATSU-KUN!
YOU'RE SO HANDSOME, CLEAN SHAVEN!
TMP
POOMF
RECOIL
EEEEEK!
KONOMI!
I CAN'T TAKE IT ANYMORE!
ZOOOOOM
HMMM. THIS IS ...
IS SOMETHING TRYING TO GET BETWEEN THE TWO OF THEM?
THAT BALL OF FIRE FROM BEFORE, MAYBE?

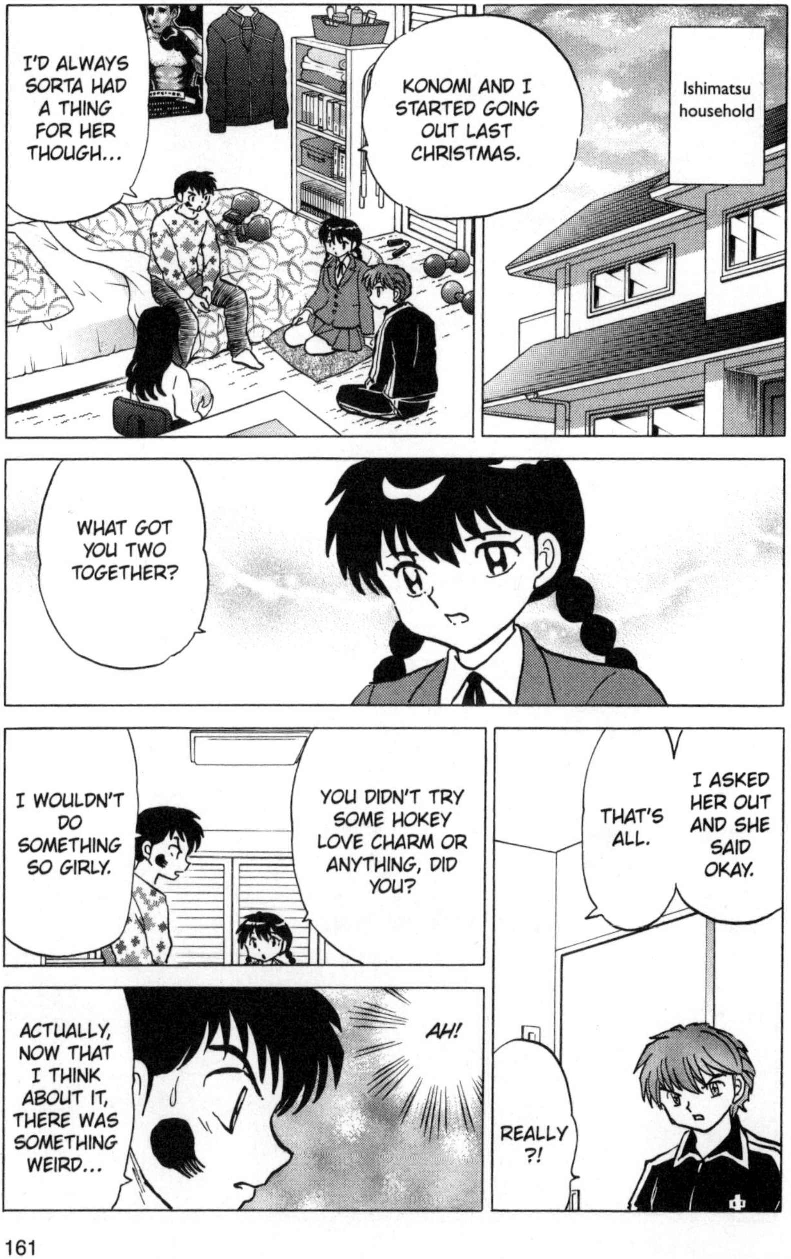
Ishimatsu household
KONOMI AND I STARTED GOING OUT LAST CHRISTMAS.
I'D ALWAYS SORTA HAD A THING FOR HER THOUGH...
WHAT GOT YOU TWO TOGETHER?
I ASKED HER OUT AND SHE SAID OKAY.
THAT'S ALL.
REALLY ?!
YOU DIDN'T TRY SOME HOKEY LOVE CHARM OR ANYTHING, DID YOU?
I WOULDN'T DO SOMETHING SO GIRLY.
AH!
ACTUALLY, NOW THAT I THINK ABOUT IT, THERE WAS SOMETHING WEIRD...

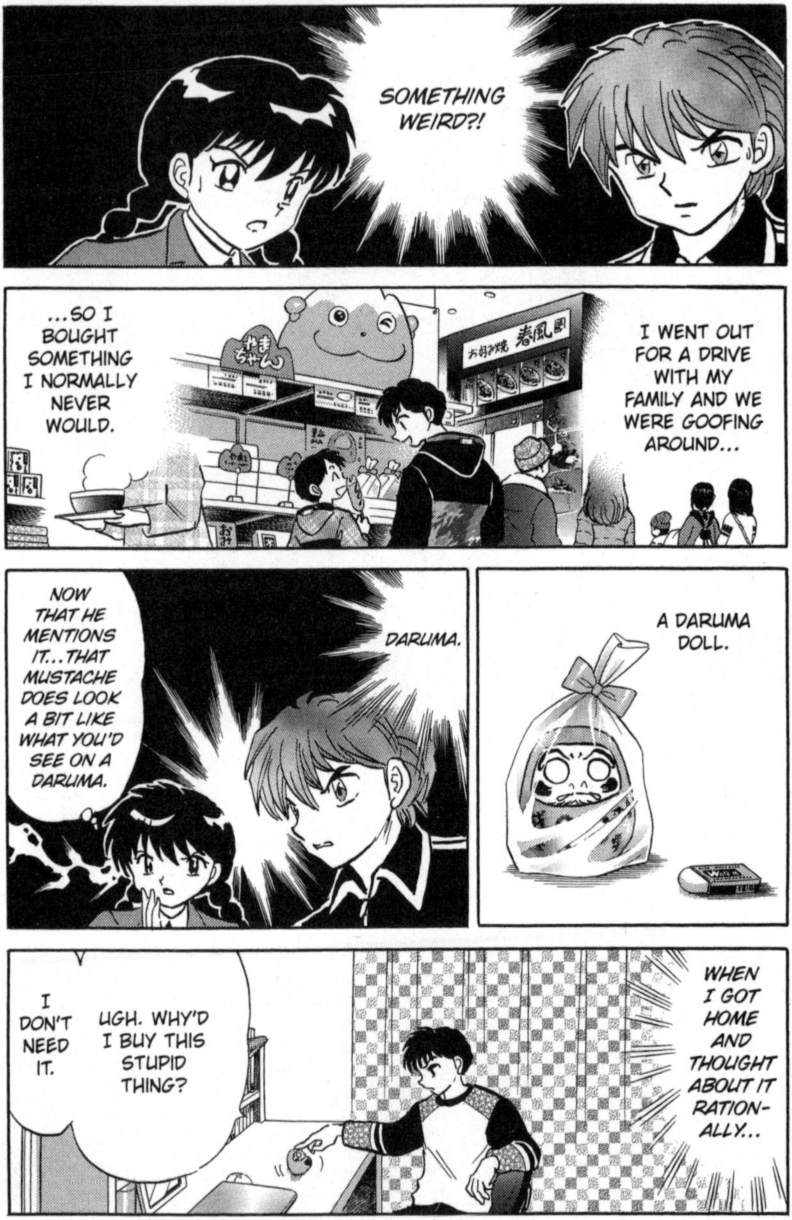
SOMETHING WEIRD?!
I WENT OUT FOR A DRIVE WITH MY FAMILY AND WE WERE GOOFING AROUND...
...SO I BOUGHT SOMETHING I NORMALLY NEVER WOULD.
A DARUMA DOLL.
DARUMA.
NOW THAT HE MENTIONS IT...THAT MUSTACHE DOES LOOK A BIT LIKE WHAT YOU'D SEE ON A DARUMA.
WHEN I GOT HOME AND THOUGHT ABOUT IT RATIONALLY...
UGH. WHY'D I BUY THIS STUPID THING?
I DON'T NEED IT.

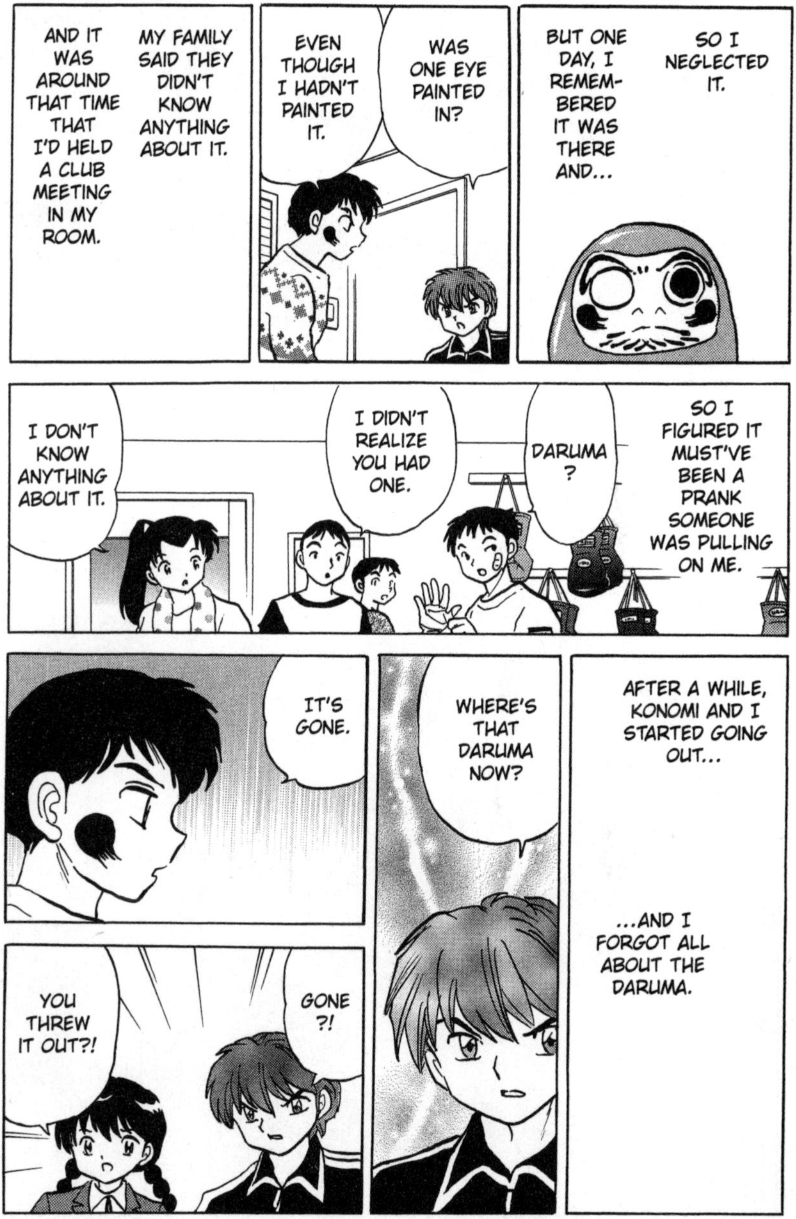
SO I NEGLECTED IT.
BUT ONE DAY, I REMEMBERED IT WAS THERE AND...
WAS ONE EYE PAINTED IN?
EVEN THOUGH I HADN'T PAINTED IT.
MY FAMILY SAID THEY DIDN'T KNOW ANYTHING ABOUT IT.
AND IT WAS AROUND THAT TIME THAT I'D HELD A CLUB MEETING IN MY ROOM.
SO I FIGURED IT MUST'VE BEEN A PRANK SOMEONE WAS PULLING ON ME.
DARUMA?
I DIDN'T REALIZE YOU HAD ONE.
I DON'T KNOW ANYTHING ABOUT IT.
AFTER A WHILE, KONOMI AND I STARTED GOING OUT...
...AND I FORGOT ALL ABOUT THE DARUMA.
WHERE'S THAT DARUMA NOW?
IT'S GONE.
GONE?!
YOU THREW IT OUT?!

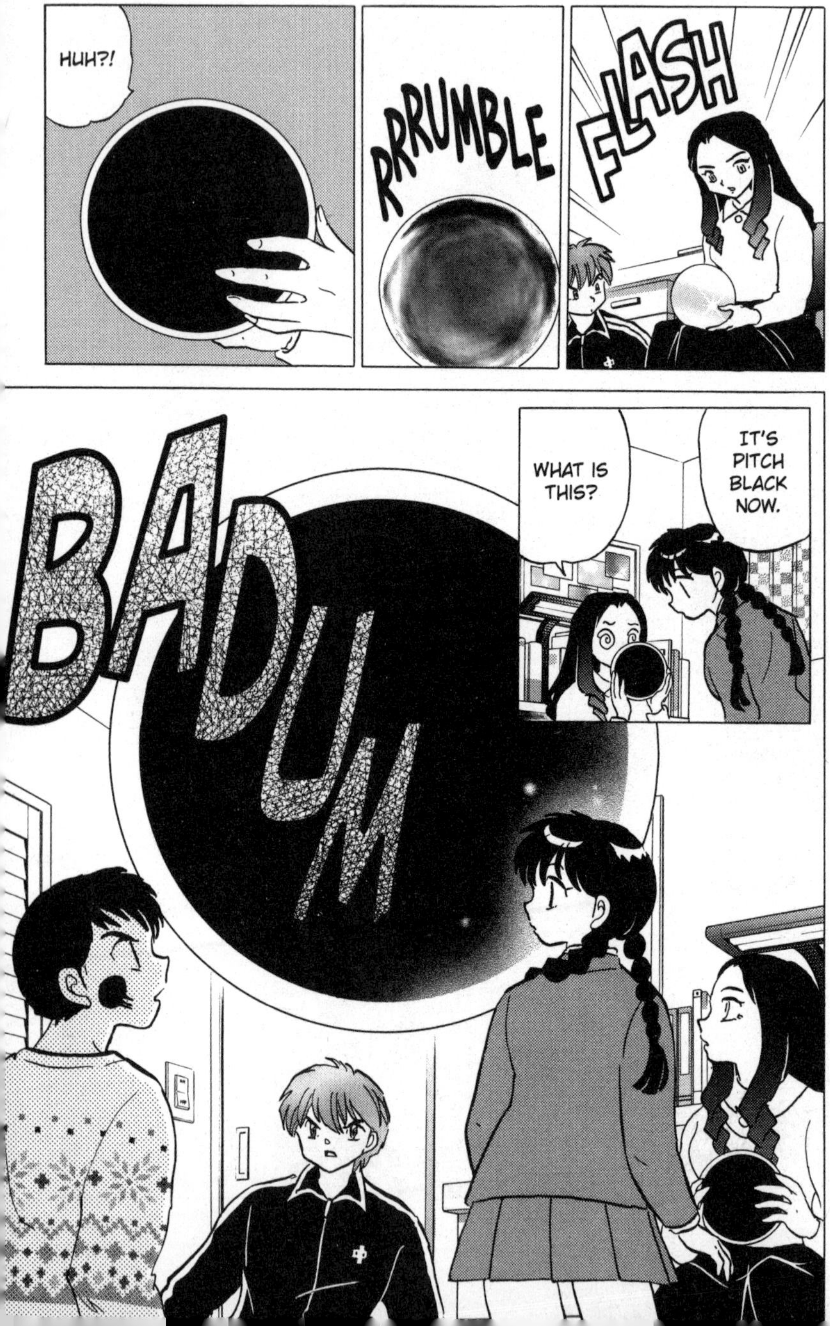
FLASH
RRRUMBLE
HUH?!
IT'S PITCH BLACK NOW.
WHAT IS THIS?
BADUM

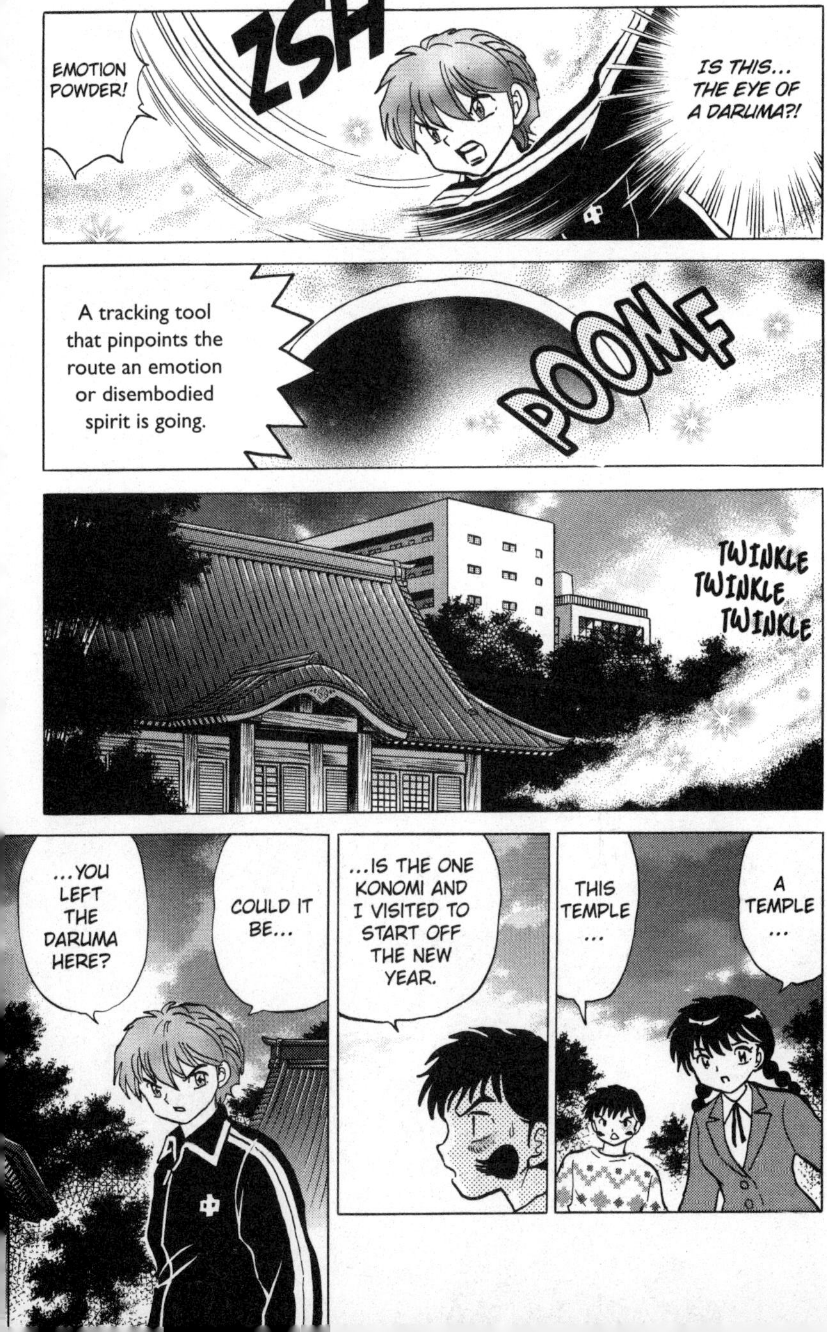
IS THIS... THE EYE OF A DARUMA?!
ZSH
EMOTION POWDER!
POOMF
A tracking tool that pinpoints the route an emotion or disembodied spirit is going.
TWINKLE TWINKLE TWINKLE
A TEMPLE ...
THIS TEMPLE ...
...IS THE ONE KONOMI AND I VISITED TO START OFF THE NEW YEAR.
COULD IT BE...
...YOU LEFT THE DARUMA HERE?

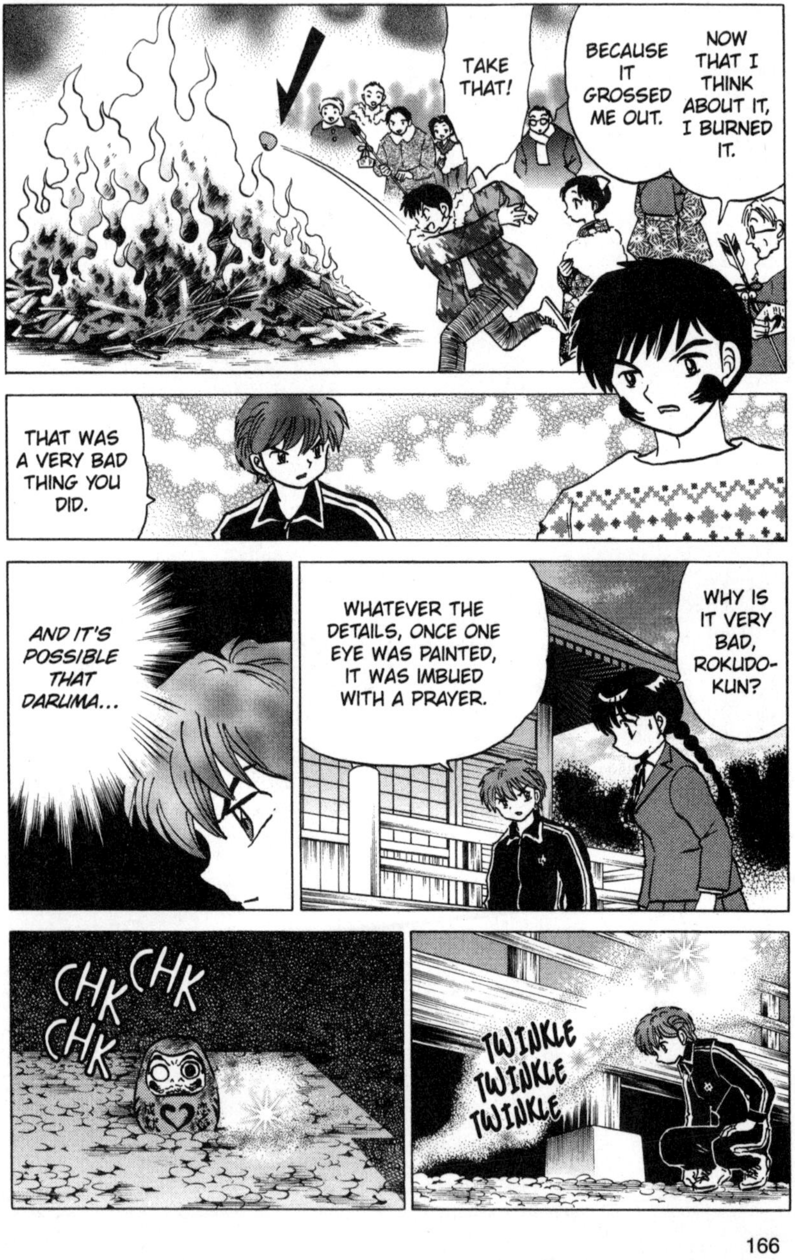
NOW THAT I THINK ABOUT IT, I BURNED IT.
BECAUSE IT GROSSED ME OUT.
TAKE THAT!
THAT WAS A VERY BAD THING YOU DID.
WHY IS IT VERY BAD, ROKUDO-KUN?
WHATEVER THE DETAILS, ONCE ONE EYE WAS PAINTED, IT WAS IMBUED WITH A PRAYER.
AND IT'S POSSIBLE THAT DARUMA...
TWINKLE TWINKLE TWINKLE
CHK CHK CHK

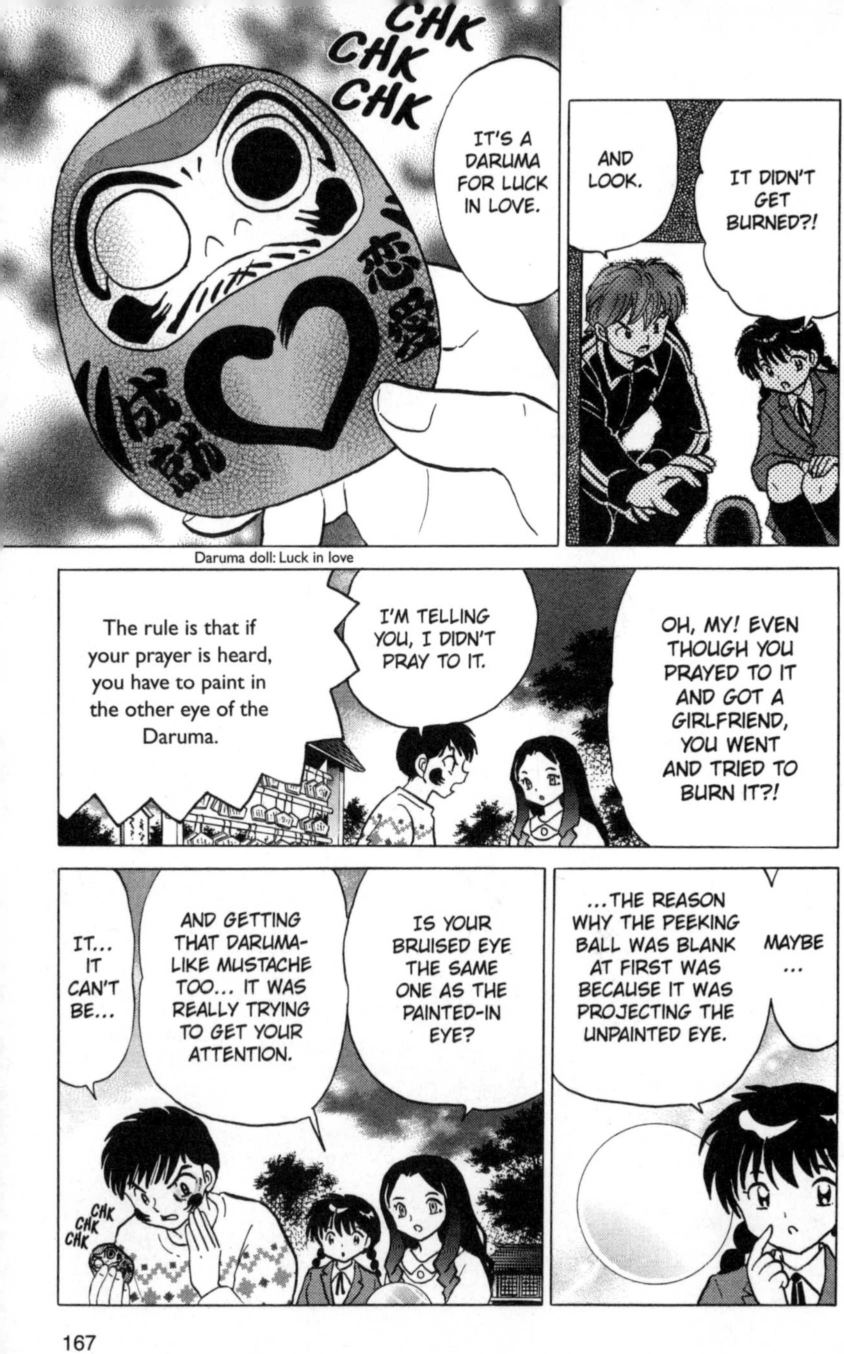
AND LOOK.
IT DIDN'T GET BURNED?!
CHK CHK CHK
IT'S A DARUMA FOR LUCK IN LOVE.
Daruma doll: Luck in love
OH, MY! EVEN THOUGH YOU PRAYED TO IT AND GOT A GIRLFRIEND, YOU WENT AND TRIED TO BURN IT?!
I'M TELLING YOU, I DIDN'T PRAY TO IT.
The rule is that if your prayer is heard, you have to paint in the other eye of the Daruma.
MAYBE...
...THE REASON WHY THE PEEKING BALL WAS BLANK AT FIRST WAS BECAUSE IT WAS PROJECTING THE UNPAINTED EYE.
IS YOUR BRUISED EYE THE SAME ONE AS THE PAINTED-IN EYE?
AND GETTING THAT DARUMA-LIKE MUSTACHE TOO... IT WAS REALLY TRYING TO GET YOUR ATTENTION.
IT... IT CAN'T BE...
CHK CHK CHK

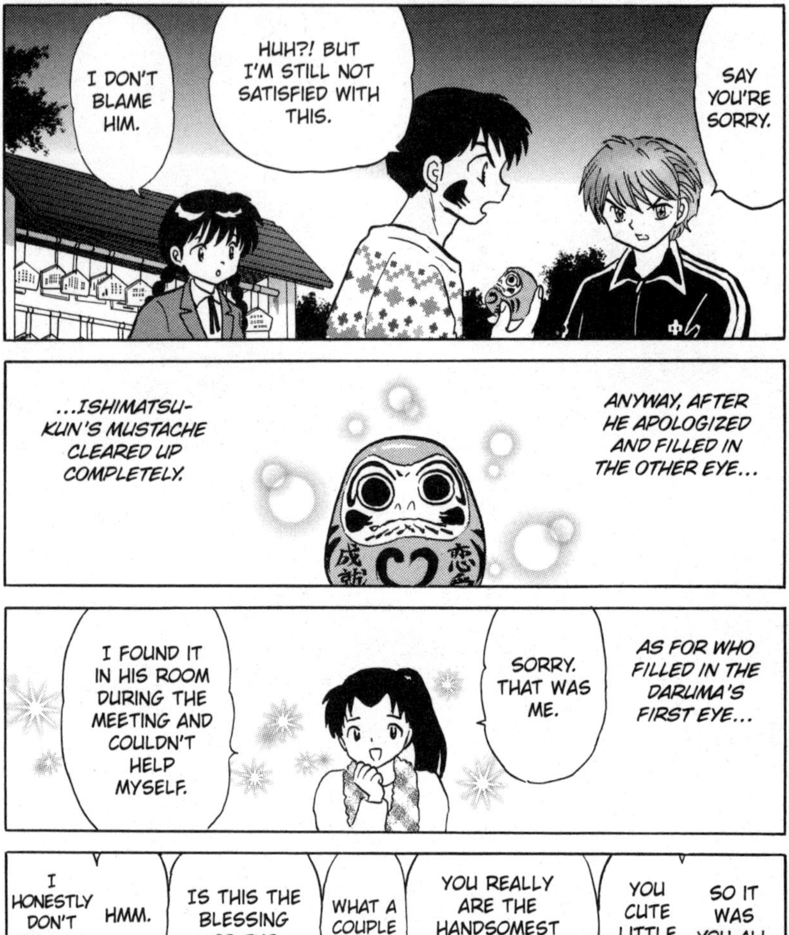
SAY YOU'RE SORRY.
HUH?! BUT I'M STILL NOT SATISFIED WITH THIS.
I DON'T BLAME HIM.
ANYWAY, AFTER HE APOLOGIZED AND FILLED IN THE OTHER EYE...
...ISHIMATSU-KUN'S MUSTACHE CLEARED UP COMPLETELY.
AS FOR WHO FILLED IN THE DARUMA'S FIRST EYE...
SORRY. THAT WAS ME.
I FOUND IT IN HIS ROOM DURING THE MEETING AND COULDN'T HELP MYSELF.
SO IT WAS YOU ALL ALONG, KONOMI.
YOU CUTE LITTLE THING.
YOU REALLY ARE THE HANDSOMEST WITHOUT THAT MUSTACHE.
WHAT A COUPLE OF LOVE-BIRDS.
IS THIS THE BLESSING OF THE DARUMA?
HMM.
I HONESTLY DON'T REALLY CARE.

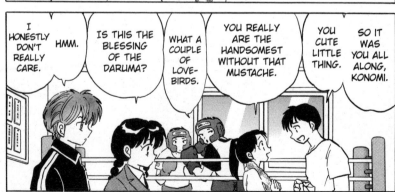

CHAPTER 268: RUMOR

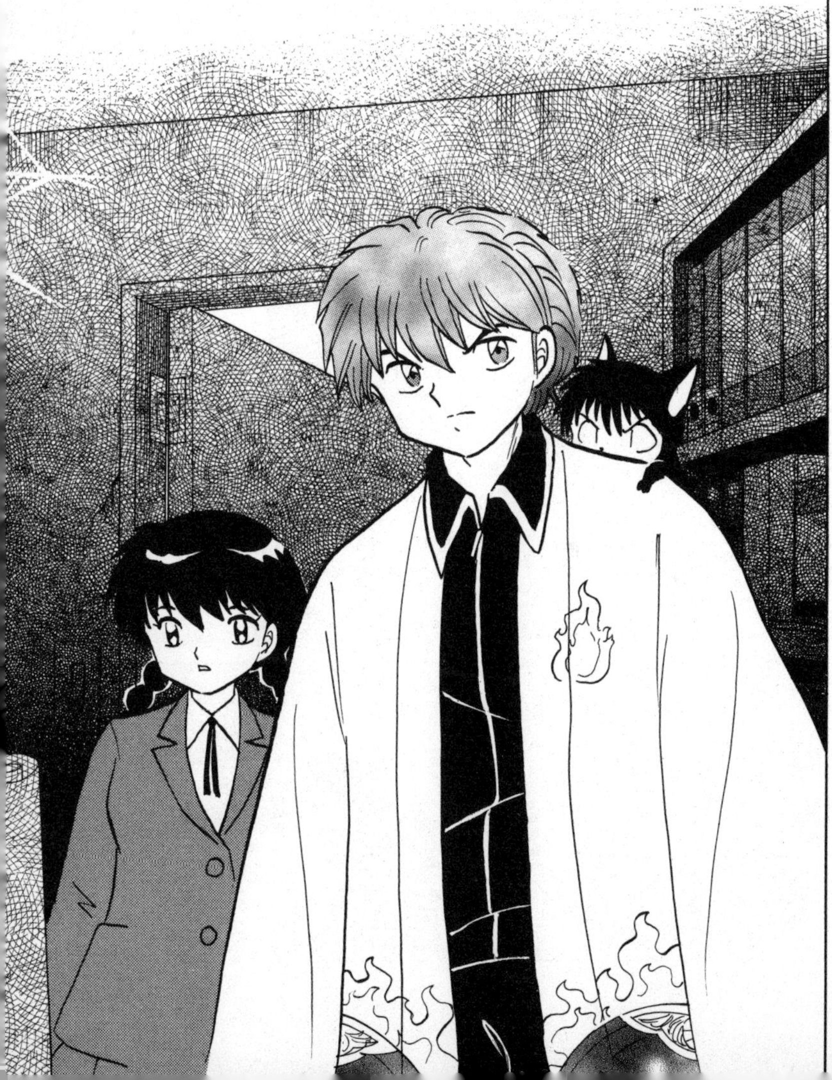

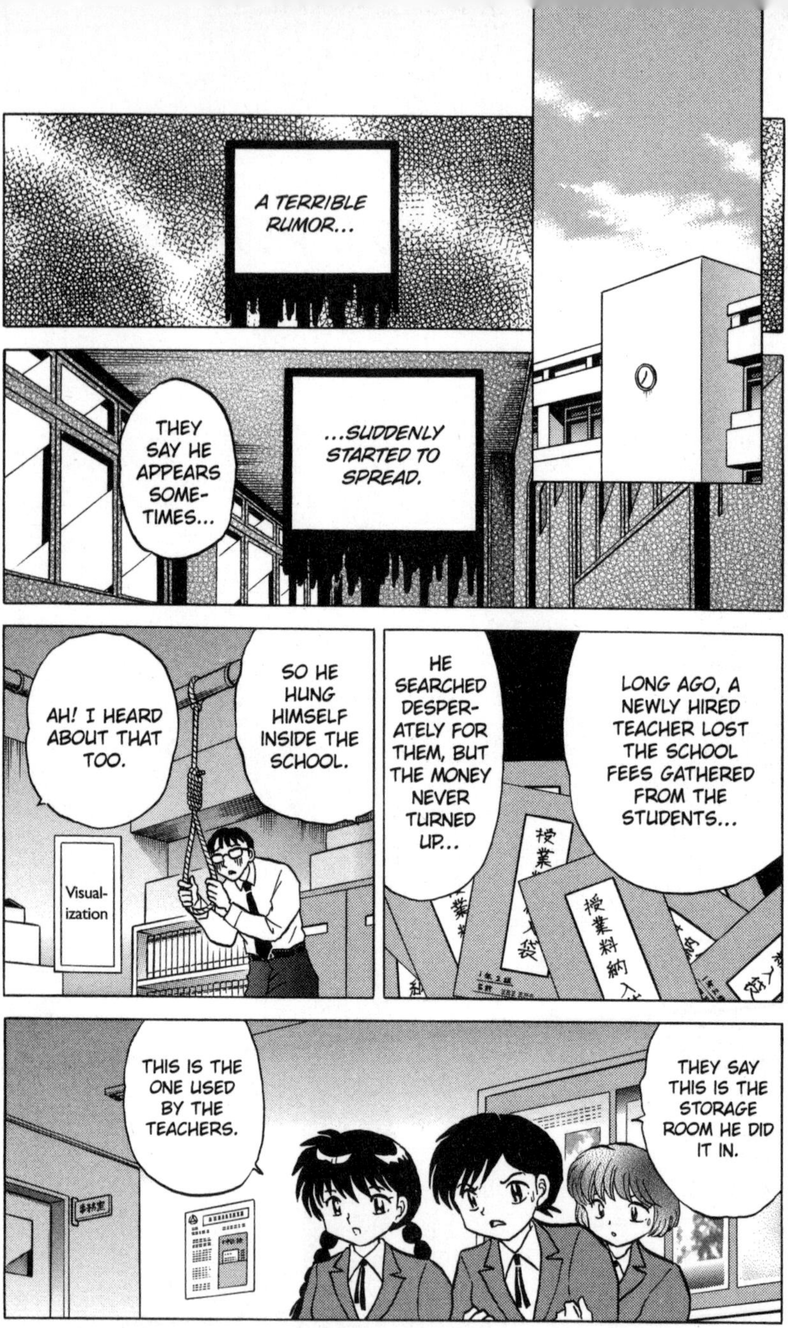
A TERRIBLE RUMOR...
...SUDDENLY STARTED TO SPREAD.
THEY SAY HE APPEARS SOMETIMES...
LONG AGO, A NEWLY HIRED TEACHER LOST THE SCHOOL FEES GATHERED FROM THE STUDENTS...
HE SEARCHED DESPERATELY FOR THEM, BUT THE MONEY NEVER TURNED UP...
SO HE HUNG HIMSELF INSIDE THE SCHOOL.
AH! I HEARD ABOUT THAT TOO.
Visualization
THEY SAY THIS IS THE STORAGE ROOM HE DID IT IN.
THIS IS THE ONE USED BY THE TEACHERS.

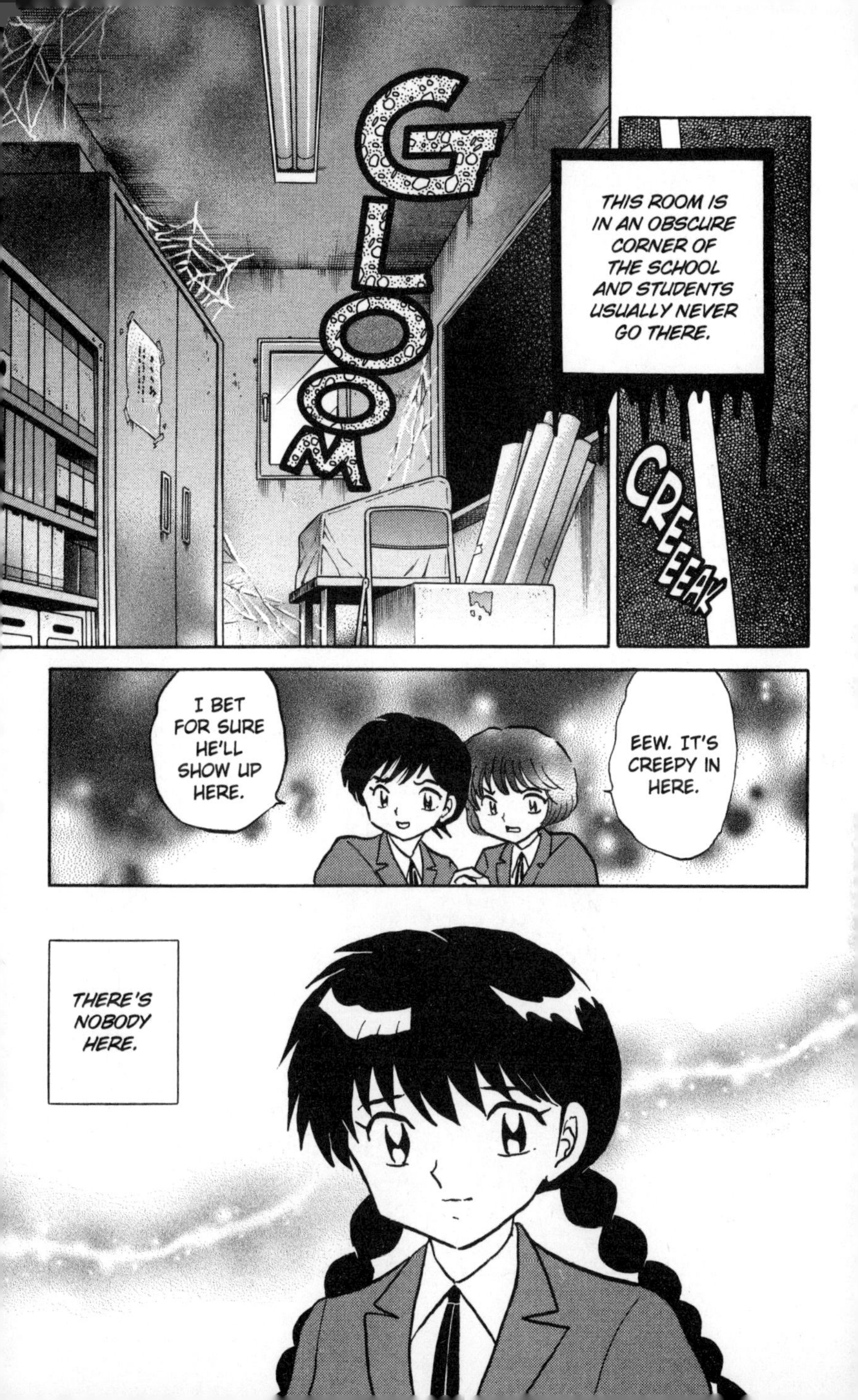
THIS ROOM IS IN AN OBSCURE CORNER OF THE SCHOOL AND STUDENTS USUALLY NEVER GO THERE.
CREEEEAK
GLOOM
EEW. IT'S CREEPY IN HERE.
I BET FOR SURE HE'LL SHOW UP HERE.
THERE'S NOBODY HERE.

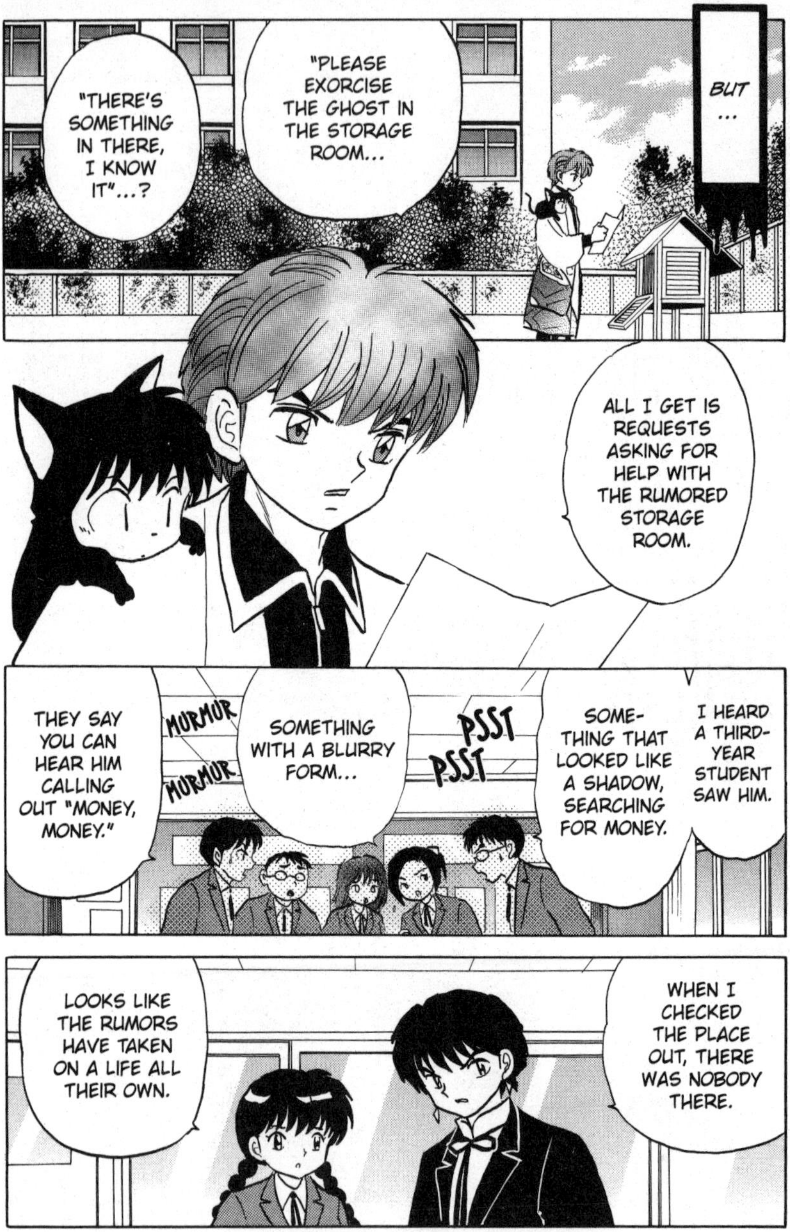
BUT...
"PLEASE EXORCISE THE GHOST IN THE STORAGE ROOM...
"THERE'S SOMETHING IN THERE, I KNOW IT"...?
ALL I GET IS REQUESTS ASKING FOR HELP WITH THE RUMORED STORAGE ROOM.
I HEARD A THIRD-YEAR STUDENT SAW HIM.
SOME-THING THAT LOOKED LIKE A SHADOW, SEARCHING FOR MONEY.
PSST PSST
SOMETHING WITH A BLURRY FORM...
MURMUR MURMUR
THEY SAY YOU CAN HEAR HIM CALLING OUT "MONEY, MONEY."
WHEN I CHECKED THE PLACE OUT, THERE WAS NOBODY THERE.
LOOKS LIKE THE RUMORS HAVE TAKEN ON A LIFE ALL THEIR OWN.

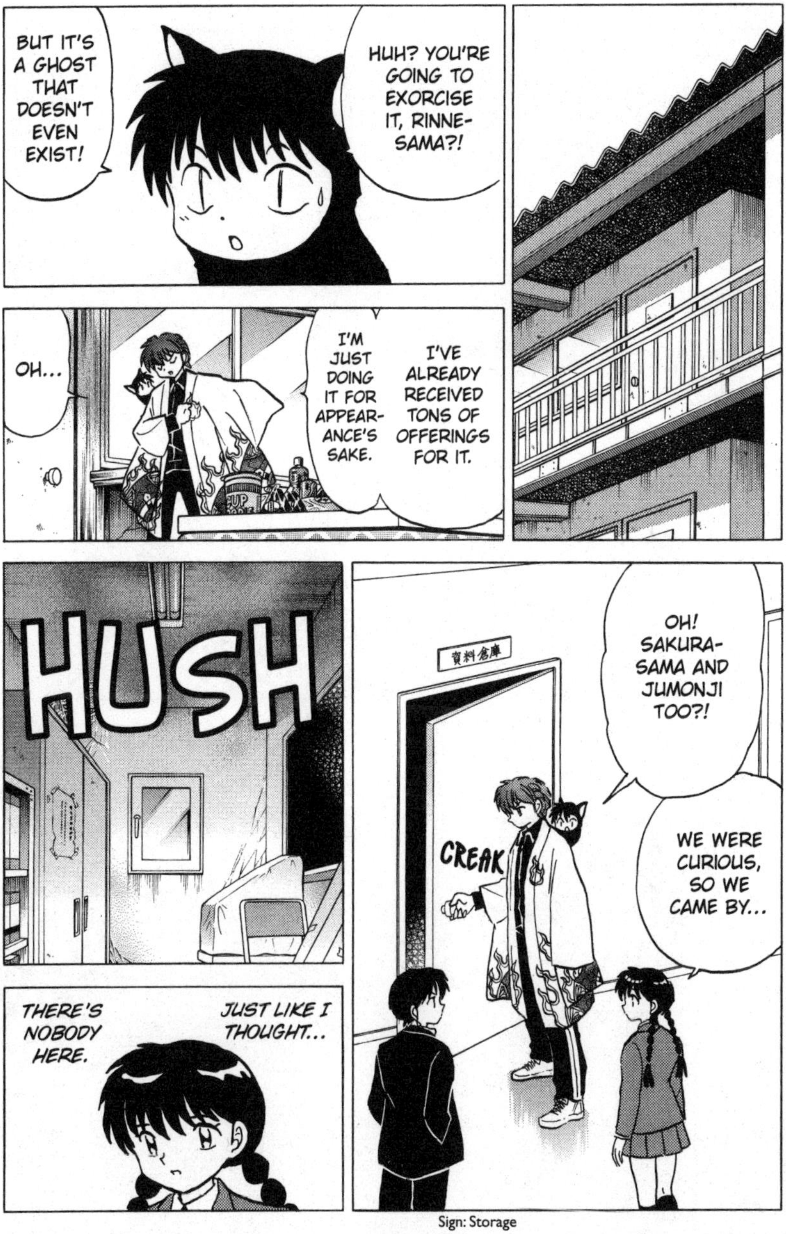
HUH? YOU'RE GOING TO EXORCISE IT, RINNE-SAMA?!
BUT IT'S A GHOST THAT DOESN'T EVEN EXIST!
I'VE ALREADY RECEIVED TONS OF OFFERINGS FOR IT.
I'M JUST DOING IT FOR APPEARANCE'S SAKE.
OH...
OH! SAKURA-SAMA AND JUMONJI TOO?!
資料倉庫
CREAK
WE WERE CURIOUS, SO WE CAME BY...
HUSH
JUST LIKE I THOUGHT...
THERE'S NOBODY HERE.

Sign: Storage

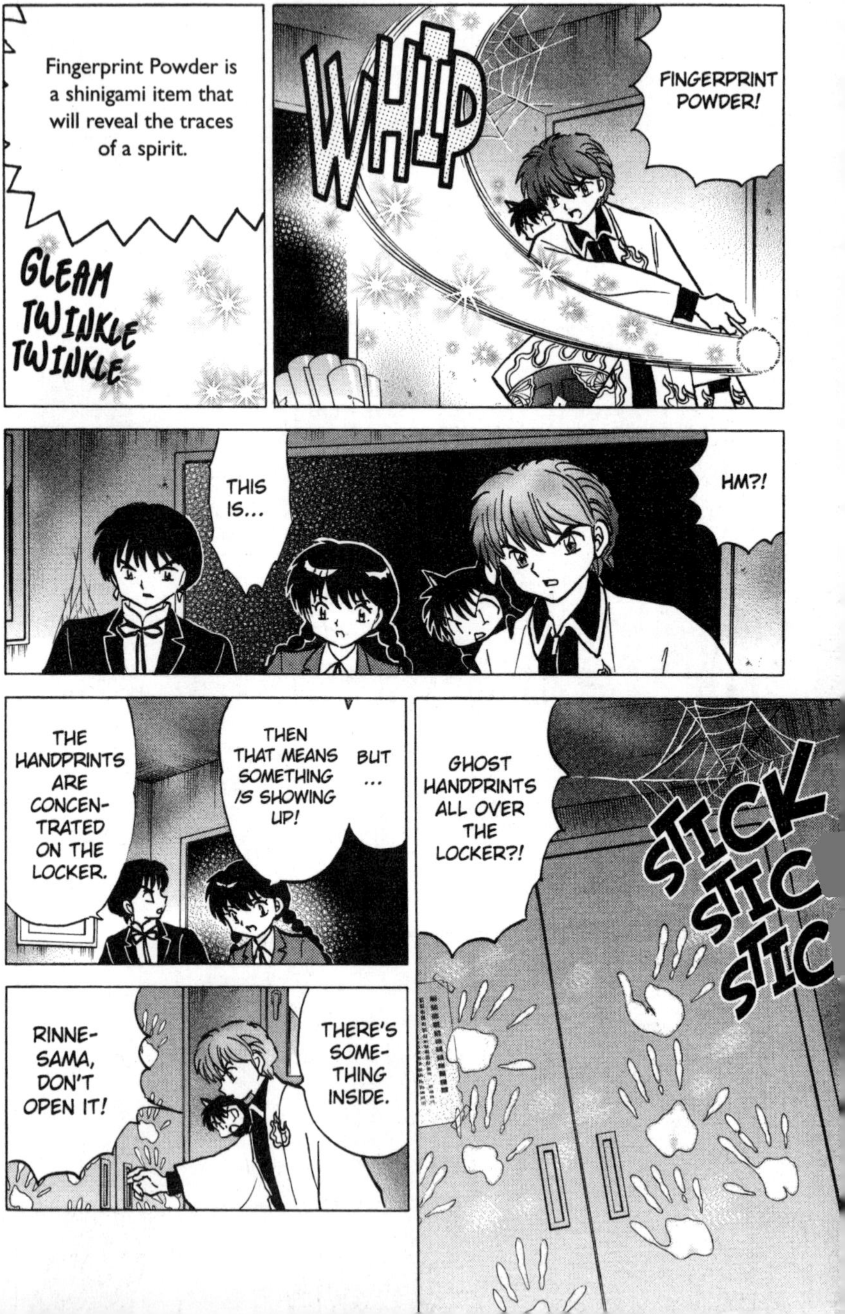
WHIP
FINGERPRINT POWDER!
Fingerprint Powder is a shinigami item that will reveal the traces of a spirit.
GLEAM TWINKLE TWINKLE
HM?!
THIS IS...
GHOST HANDPRINTS ALL OVER THE LOCKER?!
STICK STIC STIC
BUT ...
THEN THAT MEANS SOMETHING IS SHOWING UP!
THE HANDPRINTS ARE CONCEN-TRATED ON THE LOCKER.
THERE'S SOME-THING INSIDE.
RINNE-SAMA, DON'T OPEN IT!

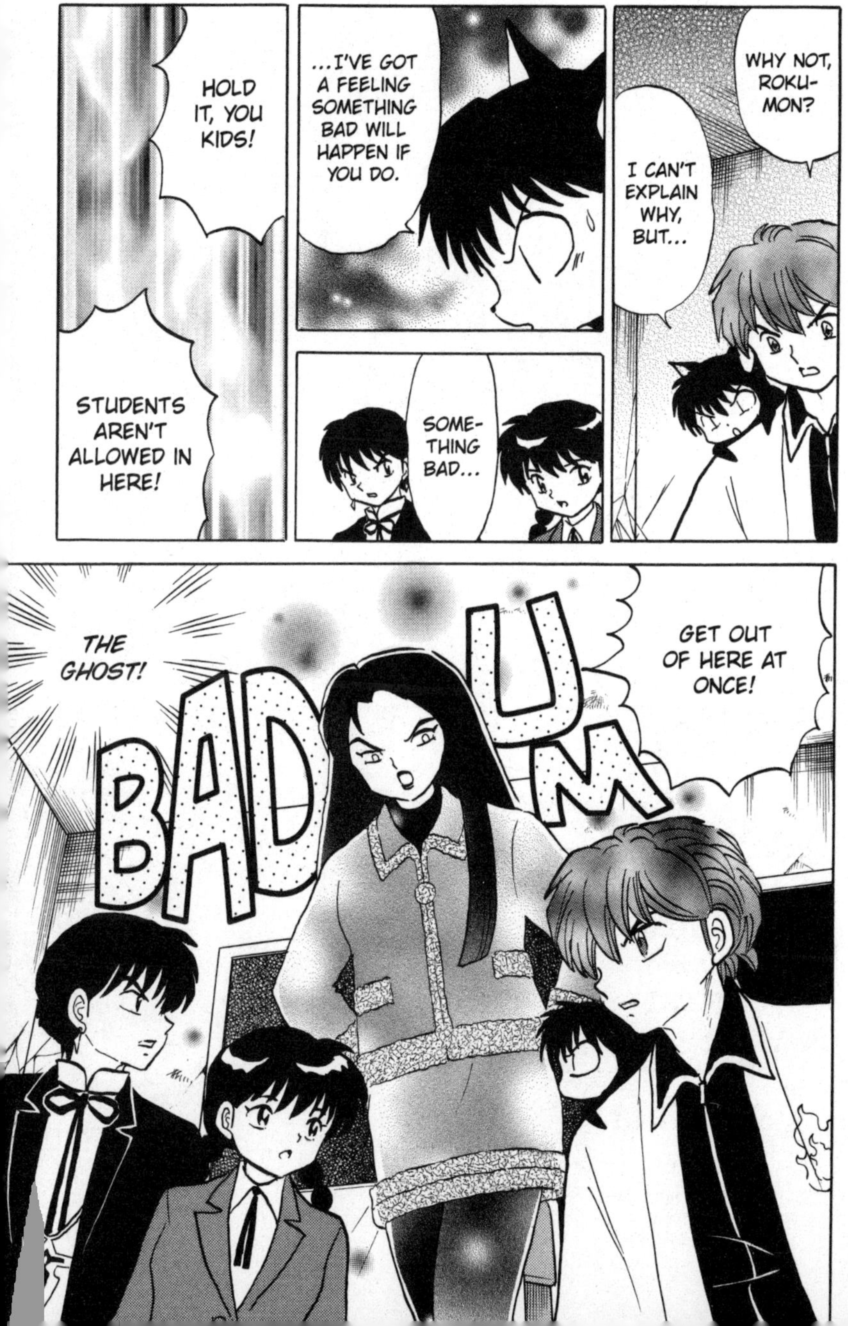
WHY NOT, ROKU-MON?
I CAN'T EXPLAIN WHY, BUT...
...I'VE GOT A FEELING SOMETHING BAD WILL HAPPEN IF YOU DO.
SOME-THING BAD...
HOLD IT, YOU KIDS!
STUDENTS AREN'T ALLOWED IN HERE!
GET OUT OF HERE AT ONCE!
BADUM
THE GHOST!

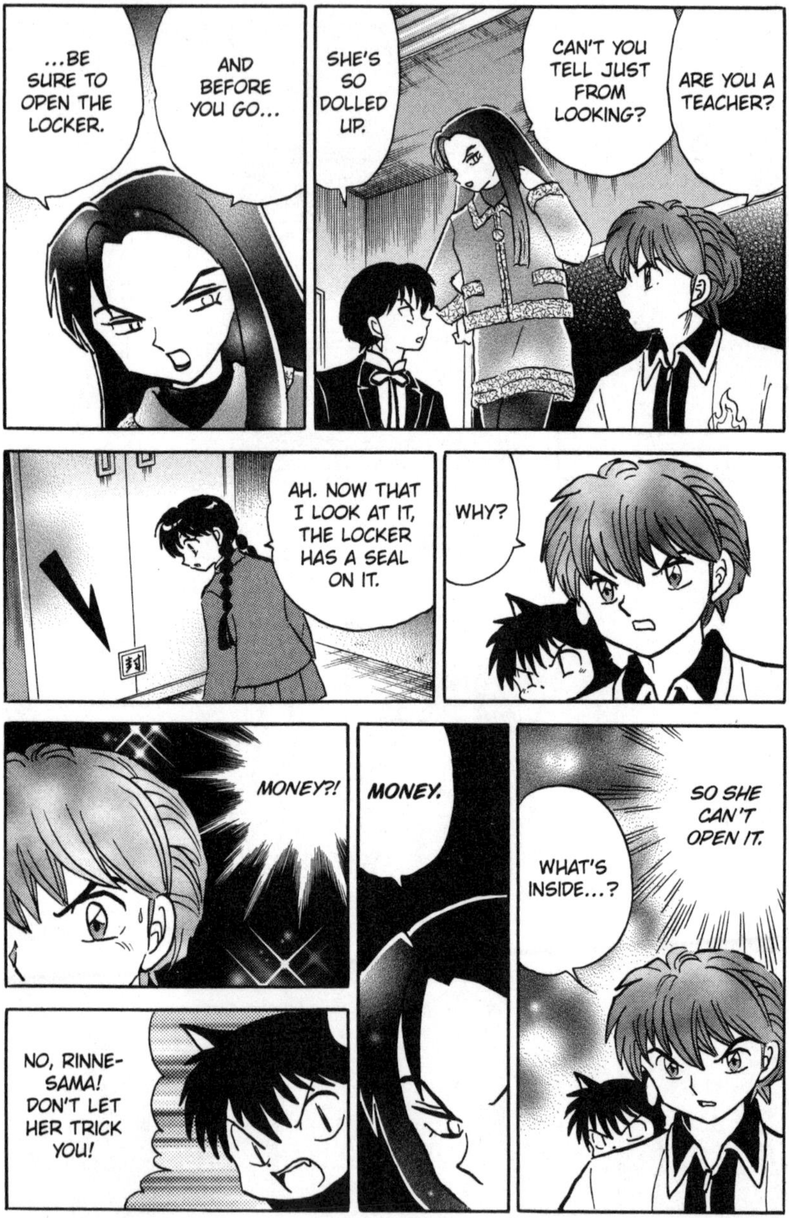
ARE YOU A TEACHER?
CAN'T YOU TELL JUST FROM LOOKING?
SHE'S SO DOLLED UP.
AND BEFORE YOU GO...
...BE SURE TO OPEN THE LOCKER.
WHY?
AH. NOW THAT I LOOK AT IT, THE LOCKER HAS A SEAL ON IT.
SO SHE CAN'T OPEN IT.
WHAT'S INSIDE...?
MONEY.
MONEY?!
NO, RINNE-SAMA! DON'T LET HER TRICK YOU!

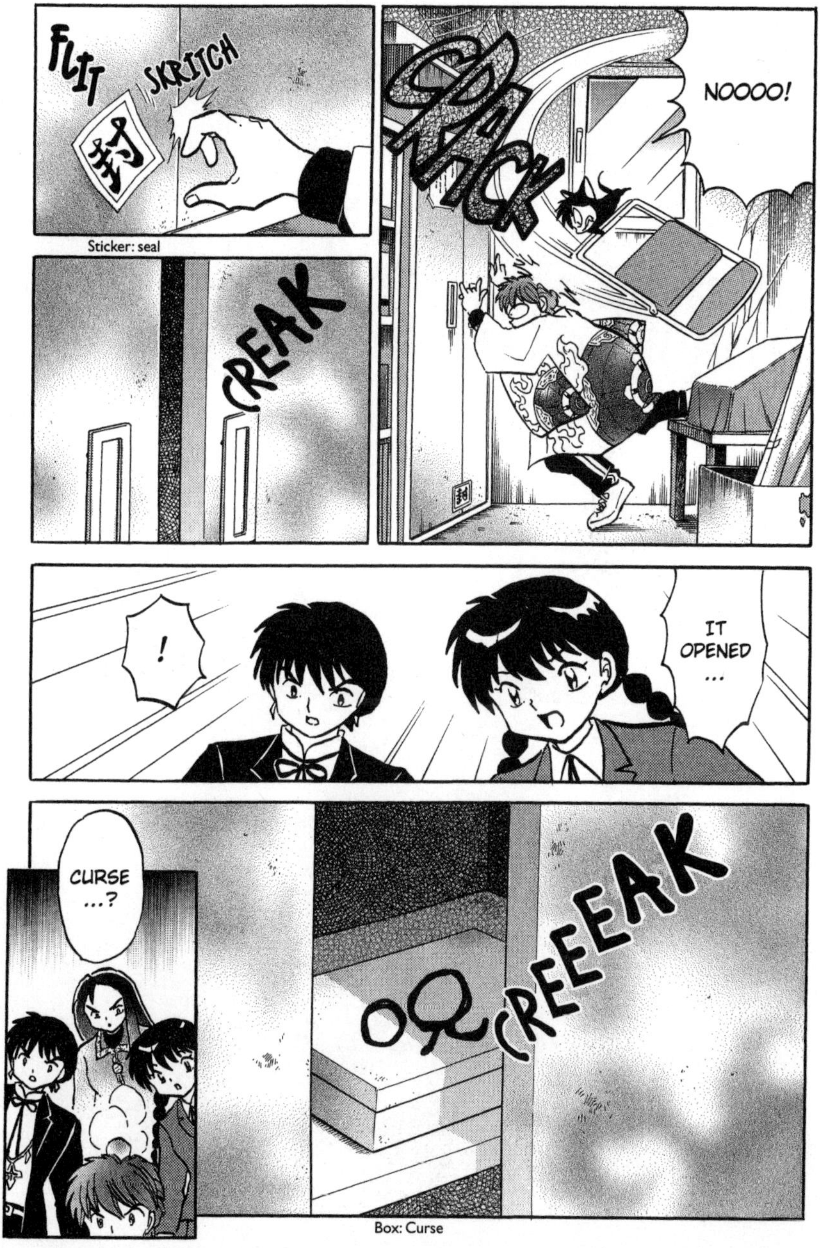
CRACK
NOOOO!
FLIT
SKRITCH
CREAK
IT OPENED ...
!
CREEEAK
CURSE ...?
Sticker: seal

Box: Curse

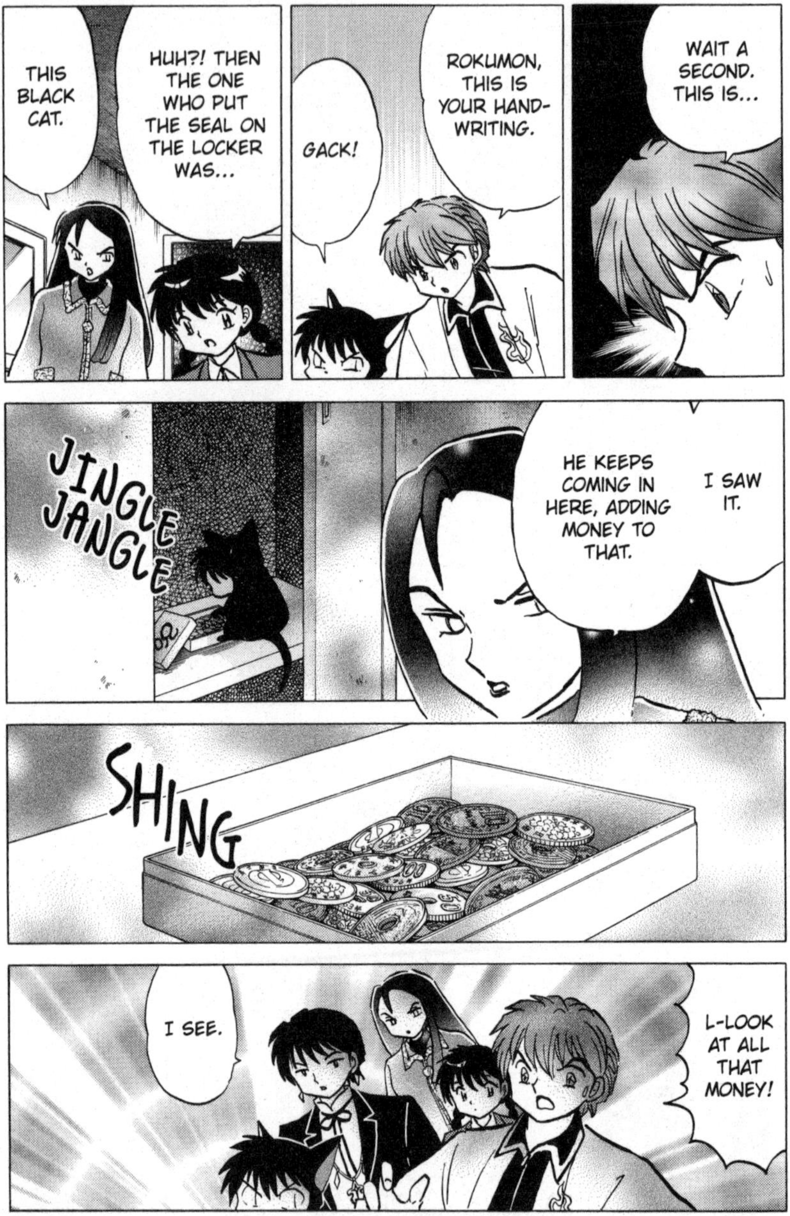
WAIT A SECOND. THIS IS...
ROKUMON, THIS IS YOUR HAND-WRITING.
GACK!
HUH?! THEN THE ONE WHO PUT THE SEAL ON THE LOCKER WAS...
THIS BLACK CAT.
I SAW IT.
HE KEEPS COMING IN HERE, ADDING MONEY TO THAT.
JINGLE JANGLE
SHING
L-LOOK AT ALL THAT MONEY!
I SEE.

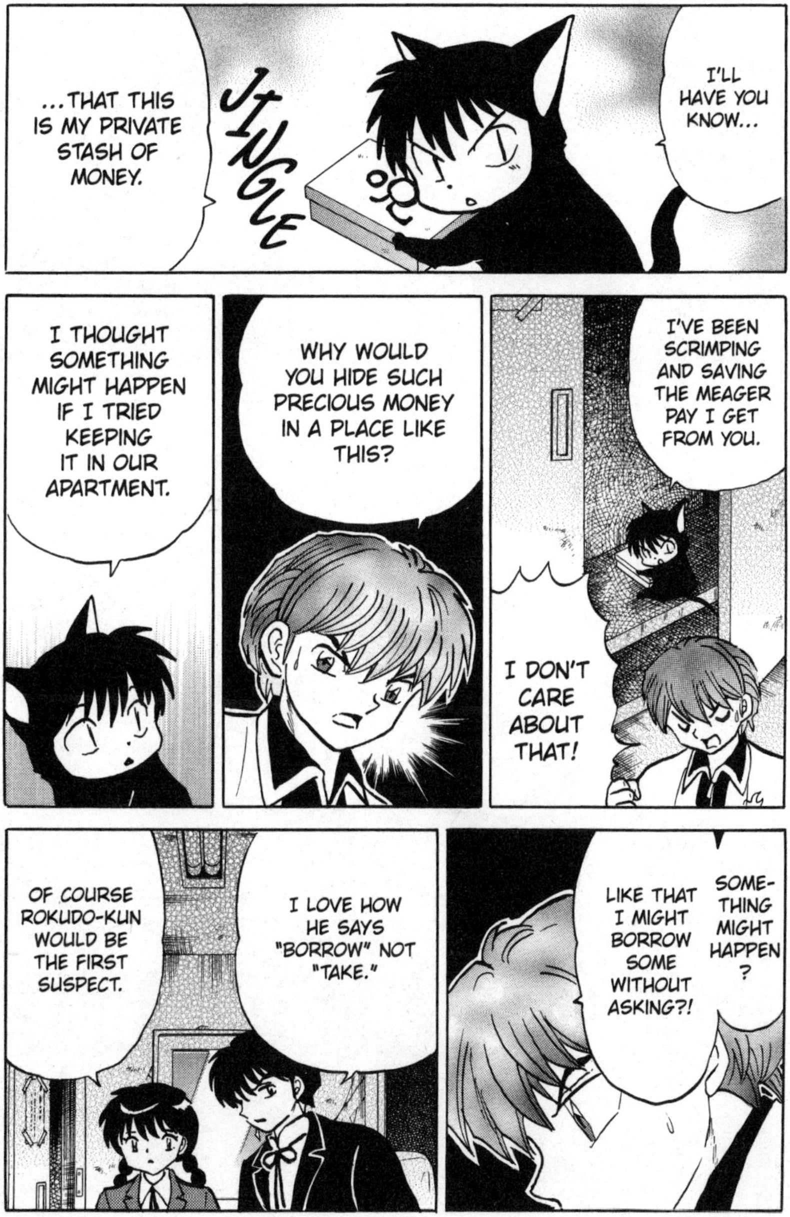
I'LL HAVE YOU KNOW...
JINGLE
...THAT THIS IS MY PRIVATE STASH OF MONEY.
I'VE BEEN SCRIMPING AND SAVING THE MEAGER PAY I GET FROM YOU.
I DON'T CARE ABOUT THAT!
WHY WOULD YOU HIDE SUCH PRECIOUS MONEY IN A PLACE LIKE THIS?
I THOUGHT SOMETHING MIGHT HAPPEN IF I TRIED KEEPING IT IN OUR APARTMENT.
SOME-THING MIGHT HAPPEN?
LIKE THAT I MIGHT BORROW SOME WITHOUT ASKING?!
I LOVE HOW HE SAYS "BORROW" NOT "TAKE."
OF COURSE ROKUDO-KUN WOULD BE THE FIRST SUSPECT.

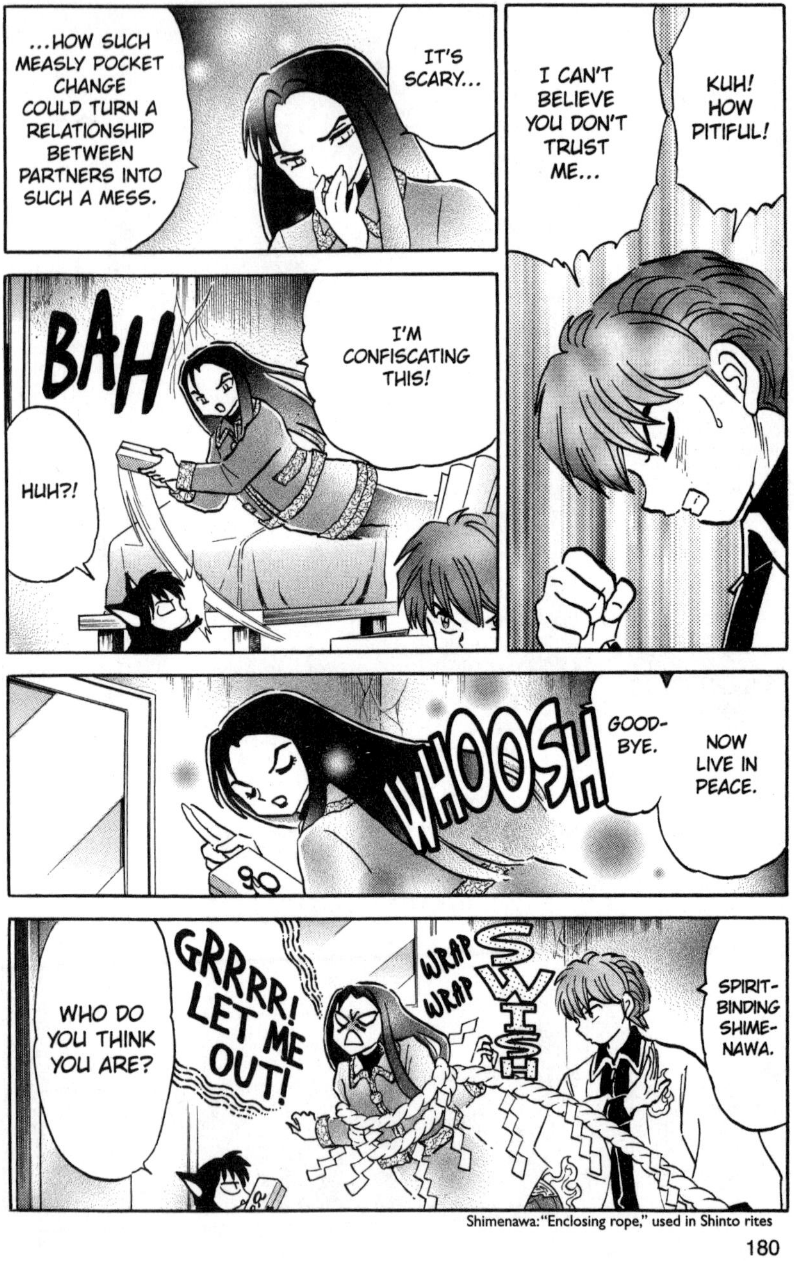
KUH! HOW PITIFUL!
I CAN'T BELIEVE YOU DON'T TRUST ME...
IT'S SCARY...
...HOW SUCH MEASLY POCKET CHANGE COULD TURN A RELATIONSHIP BETWEEN PARTNERS INTO SUCH A MESS.
I'M CONFISCATING THIS!
BAH
HUH?!
GOOD-BYE.
NOW LIVE IN PEACE.
WHOOSH
SPIRIT-BINDING SHIME-NAWA.
SWISH
WRAP WRAP
GRRRR! LET ME OUT!
WHO DO YOU THINK YOU ARE?

Shimenawa: "Enclosing rope," used in Shinto rites

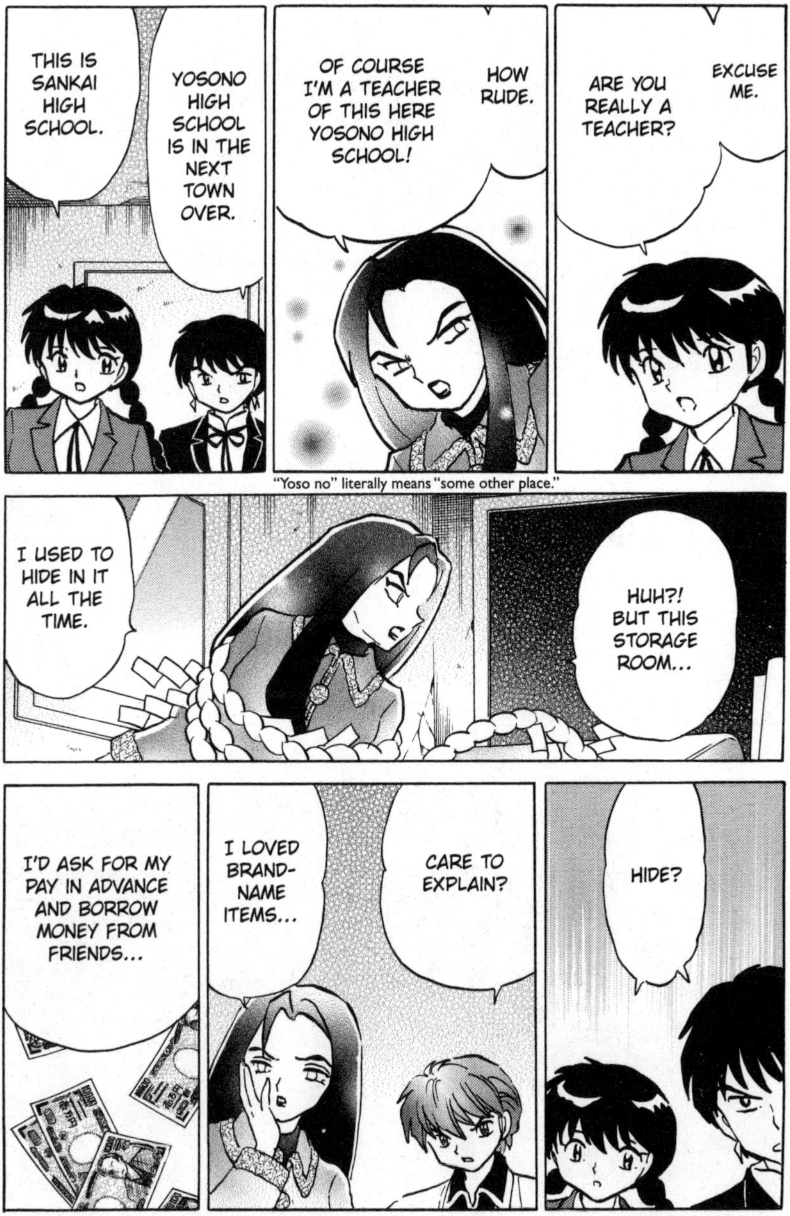
EXCUSE ME.
ARE YOU REALLY A TEACHER?
HOW RUDE.
OF COURSE I'M A TEACHER OF THIS HERE YOSONO HIGH SCHOOL!
YOSONO HIGH SCHOOL IS IN THE NEXT TOWN OVER.
THIS IS SANKAI HIGH SCHOOL.
HUH?! BUT THIS STORAGE ROOM...
I USED TO HIDE IN IT ALL THE TIME.
HIDE?
CARE TO EXPLAIN?
I LOVED BRAND-NAME ITEMS...
I'D ASK FOR MY PAY IN ADVANCE AND BORROW MONEY FROM FRIENDS...

"Yoso no" literally means "some other place."

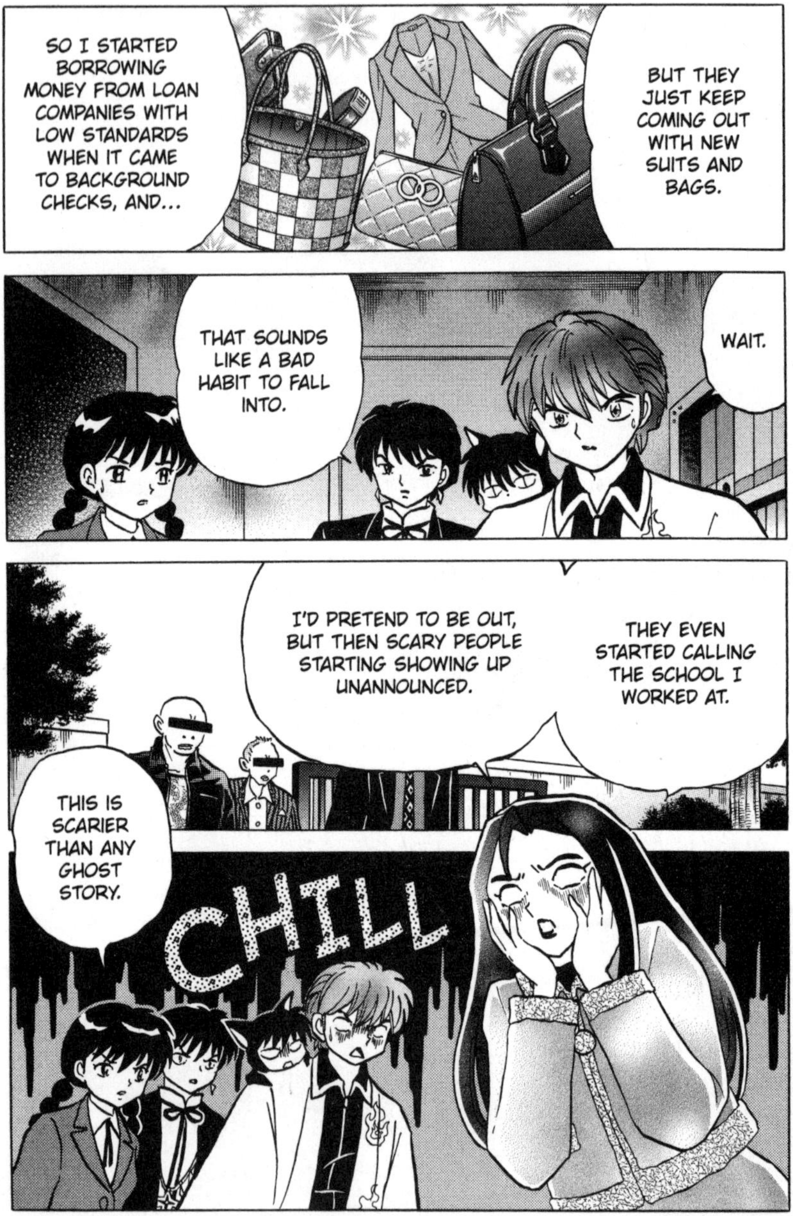
BUT THEY JUST KEEP COMING OUT WITH NEW SUITS AND BAGS.
SO I STARTED BORROWING MONEY FROM LOAN COMPANIES WITH LOW STANDARDS WHEN IT CAME TO BACKGROUND CHECKS, AND...
WAIT.
THAT SOUNDS LIKE A BAD HABIT TO FALL INTO.
THEY EVEN STARTED CALLING THE SCHOOL I WORKED AT.
I'D PRETEND TO BE OUT, BUT THEN SCARY PEOPLE STARTING SHOWING UP UNANNOUNCED.
CHILL
THIS IS SCARIER THAN ANY GHOST STORY.

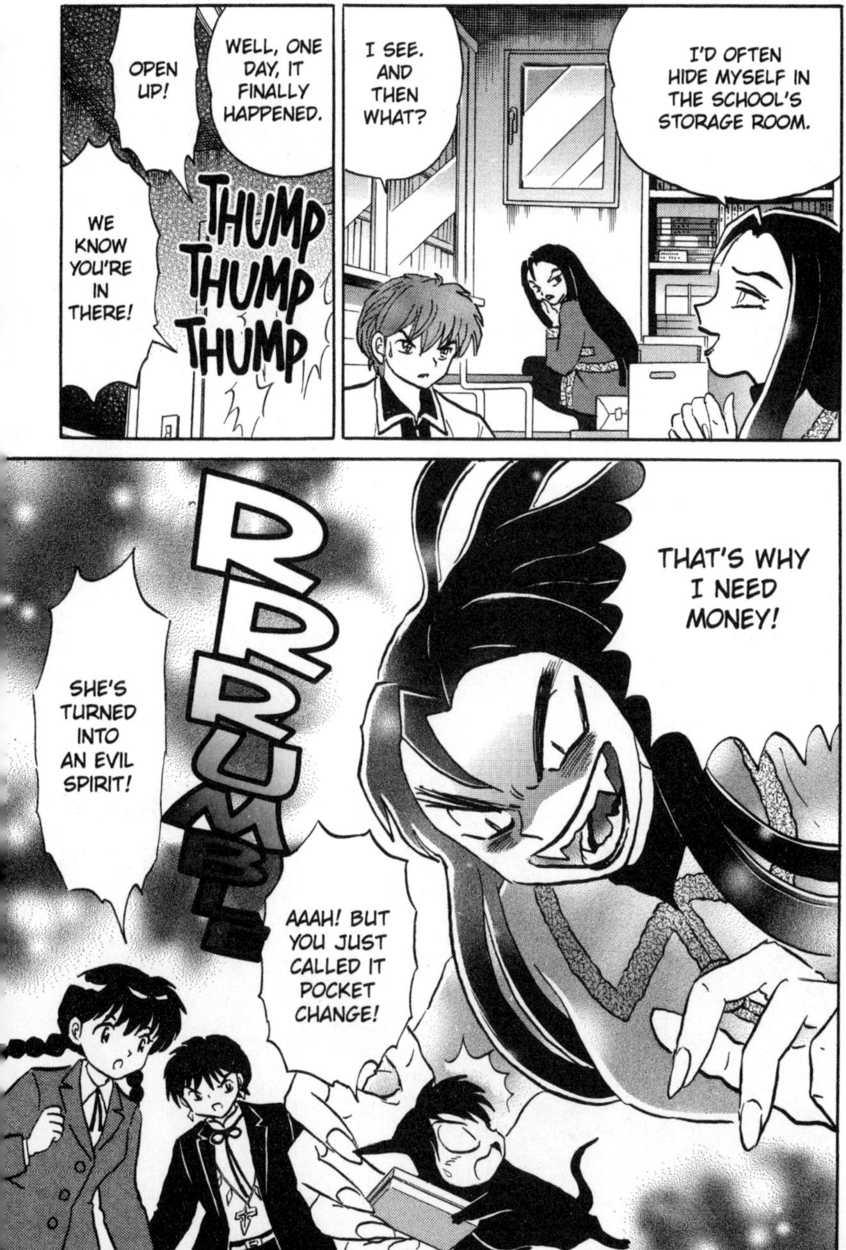
I'D OFTEN HIDE MYSELF IN THE SCHOOL'S STORAGE ROOM.
I SEE. AND THEN WHAT?
WELL, ONE DAY, IT FINALLY HAPPENED.
OPEN UP!
THUMP THUMP THUMP
WE KNOW YOU'RE IN THERE!
THAT'S WHY I NEED MONEY!
RRRUMBLE
SHE'S TURNED INTO AN EVIL SPIRIT!
AAAH! BUT YOU JUST CALLED IT POCKET CHANGE!

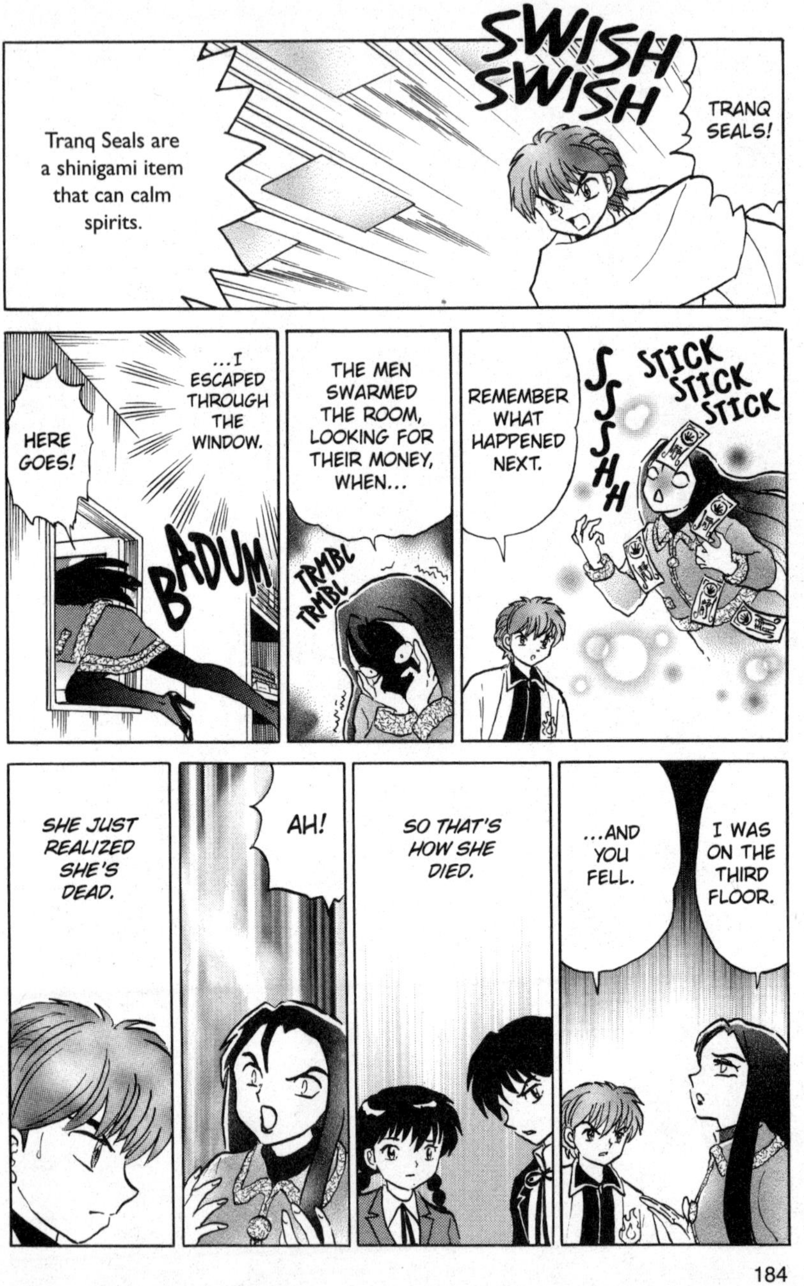
SWISH SWISH
TRANQ SEALS!
Tranq Seals are a shinigami item that can calm spirits.
STICK STICK STICK
SSSHH
REMEMBER WHAT HAPPENED NEXT.
THE MEN SWARMED THE ROOM, LOOKING FOR THEIR MONEY, WHEN...
TRMBL TRMBL
...I ESCAPED THROUGH THE WINDOW.
HERE GOES!
BADUM
I WAS ON THE THIRD FLOOR.
...AND YOU FELL.
SO THAT'S HOW SHE DIED.
AH!
SHE JUST REALIZED SHE'S DEAD.

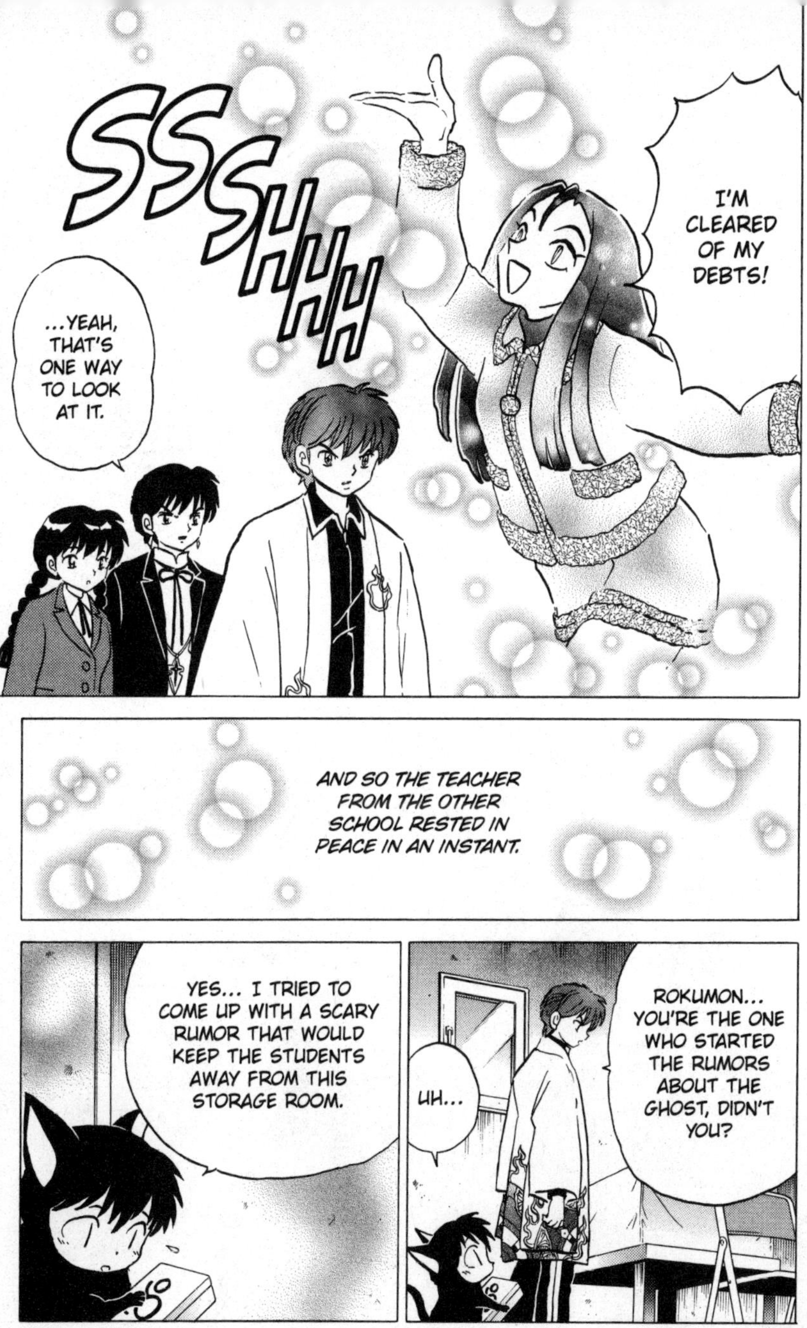
I'M CLEARED OF MY DEBTS!
SSSHHHH
...YEAH, THAT'S ONE WAY TO LOOK AT IT.
AND SO THE TEACHER FROM THE OTHER SCHOOL RESTED IN PEACE IN AN INSTANT.
ROKUMON... YOU'RE THE ONE WHO STARTED THE RUMORS ABOUT THE GHOST, DIDN'T YOU?
UH...
YES... I TRIED TO COME UP WITH A SCARY RUMOR THAT WOULD KEEP THE STUDENTS AWAY FROM THIS STORAGE ROOM.

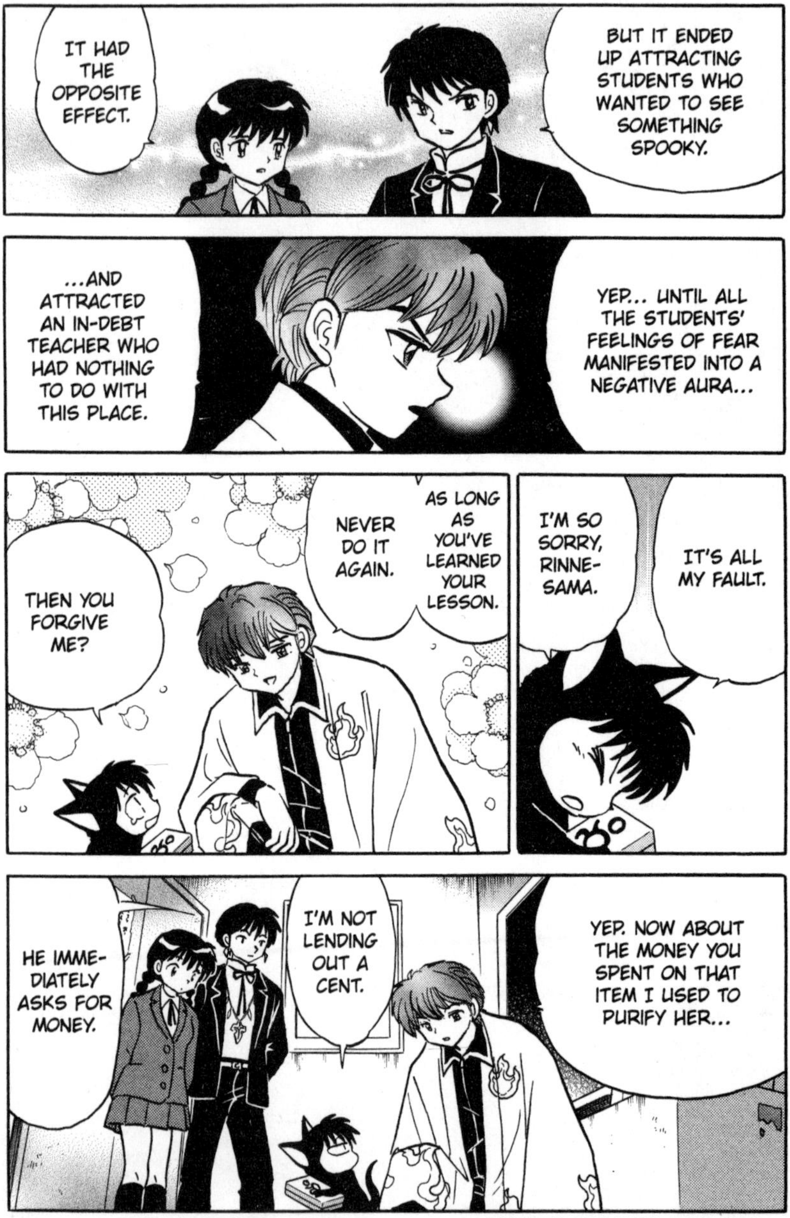
BUT IT ENDED UP ATTRACTING STUDENTS WHO WANTED TO SEE SOMETHING SPOOKY.
IT HAD THE OPPOSITE EFFECT.
YEP... UNTIL ALL THE STUDENTS' FEELINGS OF FEAR MANIFESTED INTO A NEGATIVE AURA...
...AND ATTRACTED AN IN-DEBT TEACHER WHO HAD NOTHING TO DO WITH THIS PLACE.
IT'S ALL MY FAULT.
I'M SO SORRY, RINNE-SAMA.
AS LONG AS YOU'VE LEARNED YOUR LESSON.
NEVER DO IT AGAIN.
THEN YOU FORGIVE ME?
YEP. NOW ABOUT THE MONEY YOU SPENT ON THAT ITEM I USED TO PURIFY HER...
I'M NOT LENDING OUT A CENT.
HE IMME-DIATELY ASKS FOR MONEY.

RIN-NE VOLUME 27 - END -

Rumiko Takahashi

The spotlight on Rumiko Takahashi's career began in 1978 when she won an honorable mention in Shogakukan's annual New Comic Artist Contest for *Those Selfish Aliens*. Later that same year, her boy-meets-alien comedy series, *Urusei Yatsura*, was serialized in *Weekly Shonen Sunday*. This phenomenally successful manga series was adapted into anime format and spawned a TV series and half a dozen theatrical-release movies, all incredibly popular in their own right. Takahashi followed up the success of her debut series with one blockbuster hit after another—*Maison Ikkoku* ran from 1980 to 1987, *Ranma ½* from 1987 to 1996, and *Inuyasha* from 1996 to 2008. Other notable works include *Mermaid Saga*, *Rumic Theater*, and *One-Pound Gospel*.

Takahashi won the prestigious Shogakukan Manga Award twice in her career, once for *Urusei Yatsura* in 1981 and the second time for *Inuyasha* in 2002. A majority of the Takahashi canon has been adapted into other media such as anime, live-action TV series, and film. Takahashi's manga, as well as the other formats her work has been adapted into, have continued to delight generations of fans around the world. Distinguished by her wonderfully endearing characters, Takahashi's work adeptly incorporates a wide variety of elements such as comedy, romance, fantasy, and martial arts. While her series are difficult to pin down into one simple genre, the signature style she has created has come to be known as the "Rumic World." Rumiko Takahashi is an artist who truly represents the very best from the world of manga.

RIN-NE

VOLUME 27
Shonen Sunday Edition

STORY AND ART BY
RUMIKO TAKAHASHI

KYOKAI NO RINNE Vol. 27
by Rumiko TAKAHASHI

Original Japanese edition published by SHOGAKUKAN.
English translation rights in the United States of America, Canada, the United Kingdom and Ireland arranged with SHOGAKUKAN.

Translation/Christine Dashiell
Touch-up Art & Lettering/Evan Waldinger
Design/Yukiko Whitley
Editor/Megan Bates

Printed in the U.S.A.

Published by VIZ Media, LLC
P.O. Box 77010
San Francisco, CA 94107

10 9 8 7 6 5 4 3 2 1
First printing, July 2018

ratings.viz.com RATED T+ OLDER TEEN

PARENTAL ADVISORY
RIN-NE is rated T+ for Older Teen and is recommended for ages 16 and up. This volume contains adult language and supernatural themes.

VIZ MEDIA
viz.com

SHONEN SUNDAY
shonensunday.com

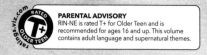

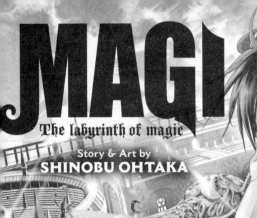

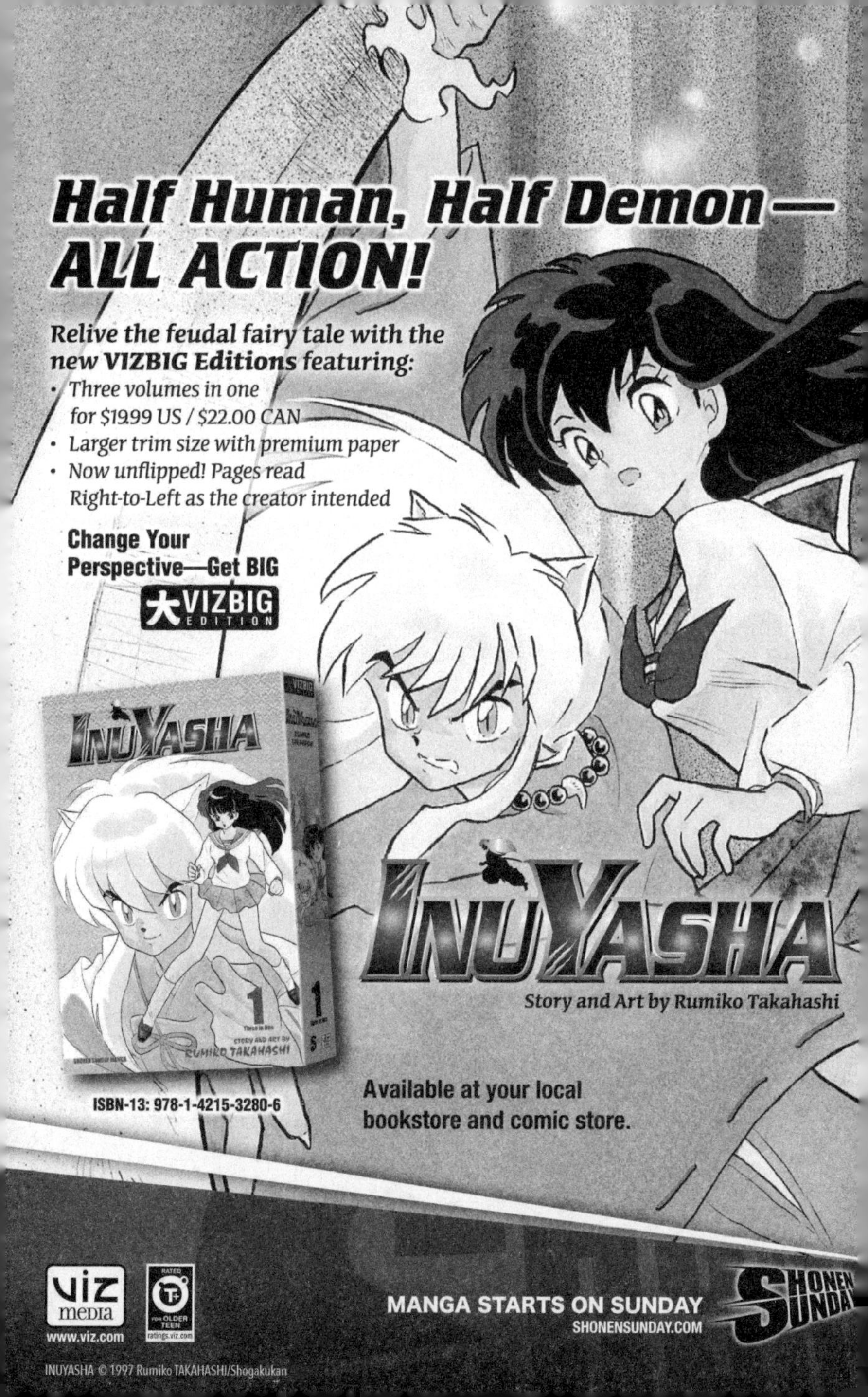
Half Human, Half Demon—
ALL ACTION!
Relive the feudal fairy tale with the new VIZBIG Editions featuring:
• Three volumes in one for $19.99 US / $22.00 CAN
• Larger trim size with premium paper
• Now unflipped! Pages read Right-to-Left as the creator intended
Change Your Perspective—Get BIG
大 VIZBIG EDITION
INUYASHA
ISBN-13: 978-1-4215-3280-6
INUYASHA
Story and Art by Rumiko Takahashi
Available at your local bookstore and comic store.
viz media
www.viz.com
RATED T+ FOR OLDER TEEN
ratings.viz.com
MANGA STARTS ON SUNDAY
SHONENSUNDAY.COM
SHONEN SUNDAY
INUYASHA © 1997 Rumiko TAKAHASHI/Shogakukan

Hey! You're Reading in the Wrong Direction!

This is the end of this graphic novel!

To properly enjoy this VIZ graphic novel, please turn it around and begin reading from right to left. Unlike English, Japanese is read right to left, so Japanese comics are read in reverse order from the way English comics are typically read.

This book has been printed in the original Japanese format in order to preserve the orientation of the original artwork. Have fun with it!

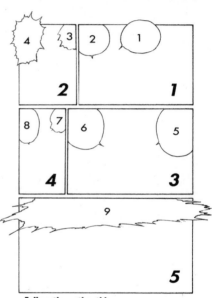

Follow the action this way